MANAGEMENT CONCEPT AND ORGANISATIONAL BEHAVIOUR

Management Concept and Organisational Behaviour

[For B.Com./M.Com., and other Management Courses of All Universities]

By
VED PRAKASH

ANMOL PUBLICATIONS PVT. LTD.
NEW DELHI - 110 002 (INDIA)

ANMOL PUBLICATIONS PVT. LTD.
4374/4B, Ansari Road, Daryaganj
New Delhi - 110 002
Ph.: 23261597, 23278000
Visit us at: www.anmolpublications.com

Management Concept and Organisational Behaviour

First Published, 2005

ISBN 81-261-2160-2

PRINTED IN INDIA

Published by J.L. Kumar for Anmol Publications Pvt. Ltd., New Delhi - 110 002 and Printed at Mehra Offset Press, Delhi.

Contents

Preface

Management Concept and Organisational Behaviour as a paper is being taught at the graduate and post graduate level in M.Com. and Management courses syllabus in almost all the Indian Universities and Institutions. The various courses conducted by management institutions at the Central and State level too have been considered in respect of their syllabus, course contents and requirements. Thus the material presented here would be of interest as well as great use to the students of M.Com. and other Management Courses. This book will provide complete knowledge of process, planning, controlling, behaviour of management and organisation.

The major topics dealt in this book are—Management Process and Thought; Aspects of Planning and Controlling; Group Dynamics; Motivational Process; Leadership Theories and Behaviour; Organisation and Effectiveness; Organisational Behaviour; Organisational Conflict; Organisational Communication; Organisational Change and Development; Decision Making; Formal and Informal Organisations; Organisation Culture.

Ved Prakash

1

Management Process and Thought

PROCESS OF MANAGEMENT

Management is defined as a process. Process means a series of operations or actions necessary to achieve certain results. A process has a beginning and a termination. It consists of some distinct stages or steps which take place in a sequential manner. The process of management is characterised by the following features:

1. **Circular.** The managerial functions are interactive in nature. This means they are contained within each other. For example, planning, organising, directing and controlling all may occur with the planning process.

   In a way, all functions may be considered as sub-functions of each other. A preceding element of the management process influences all the succeeding elements and is in turn influenced by them. Therefore, management is a circular and not a linear process.

2. **Continuity.** Management is a continuous process. This process is analysed into serveral elements like planning, organising, staffing, directing and controlling. But this does not mean that the process always begins with planning and comes to an end with controlling. The elements or functions are interrelated and interdependent. The functions may be used and the sequence may begin with any function and the entire process cycle may be completed. It is, therefore, undersirable to insist that a manager must perform the functions always in a definite chronological sequence.

3. **Social.** Management is a human and social process and not a mehanical one. It influences significantly the people inside and outside an organisation and the society as a whole. Management has far-reaching social consequences. Therefore, a manager while taking decision must remember the likely impact of his decision on society. Moreover, the management process is carried out by people, through people and for people.

4. **Composite.** All the managerial functions must be considered in their totality because management process is an organic and integrated whole. Each function makes a distinct contribution to this process but cannot be considered in isolation. All the functions contribute to the whole and derive strength from each other. The final outcome is greater than the aggregate of their individual contributions.

Management is a distinct process consisting of planning, organising, staffing, directing and controlling. The job of a manager is to coordinate and utilise human and other resources (inputs) to achieve certain objectives (outputs) like profits, growth, stability, etc. The process of management involves the determination of goals and converting these goals into results. It is that process by which managers create, maintain and operate purposive organisations through systematic, coordinated and co-operative human effort. It is a never-ending and dynamic process.

The work a manager performs is of special nature. It involves certain activities or functions by which inputs are converted into outputs. A manager combines and integrates men, money, materials, machinery and method to achieve serveral results like goods and services, productivity, growth etc.

The work of a manager can be compared with the job of an orchestra coductor. The conductor of an orchestra harmonises and blends together the efforts of different members of the orchestra team so that the team produces goods music and entertainment.

MAIN FUNCTIONS OF MANAGEMENT

The elements of management process are known as functions of management. There is, however, no single list of functions acceptable to all. Various authors have classified these functions differently. Henry Fayol has classified them into planning. organising, commanding, coordinating and controlling. Luther Gullick has given keyword 'POSDCORB' which stands for Planning (P), Organising (O), Staffing (S), Directing (D), Controlling (Co), Reporting (R) and Budgeting (B). Koontz and O'Donnell have suggested planning, organising, staffing, directing and controlling. Ernest Dale has in addition mentioned innovation and representation.

Almost all authorities agree on the basic functions of planning, organising and controlling. Modern writers treat staffing as a separate function whereas the classical writers consdiered staffing as a part of organising. In view of the growing signficance of human resource management staffing should be considered a separate function. In order to get things done, a manager has to guide, motivate, lead and communicate with his subordinates. Therefore, directing names, *e.g.* executing, commanding, actuating, etc. Thus, the function of management may be classified in the following table :—

Table : Managerial Functions and Sub-functions

Functions	*Sub-functions*
Planning	Forecasting, decision-making, strategy farmulation, policy-making, programming, scheduling, budgeting, problem-solving, innovation, investigation and research.
Organising	Functionalistion, divisionalisation, departmentalisation, delegation, decnetralisation, activity analysis, task allocation.
Staffing	Manpower planning, recruitment, selection, training, placement, compensation, promotion, appraisal, etc.
Directing	Supervision, motivation, communication, leadership, activating, etc.
Controlling	Fixation of standards, recording, measurement, reporting, corrective action.

Managerial functions should be differentiated from operative functions of business. Operative functions include production, making, financing, personnel, etc. Operative functions are also known as the functional areas of business. Operative functions differ according to the nature and size of business. For instance, there is no prodcution function in a retail store. On the other hand, managerial functions are essential in all organisations irrespective of their nature and size. Every operative function of business requires planning, organising, staffing, directing and controlling.

Managerial Functions	*Operative Functions*
1. Planning	1. Production
2. Organising	2. Marketing
3. Staffing	4. Purchasing
4. Directing	4. Financing
5. Controlling	5. Personnel

Thus, after studying the opinions of different authors on the functions of management, it may be concluded that there are five main functions of Management: *(1)* Planning *(2)* Organisation *(3)* Staffing *(4)* Directing *(5)* Controlling. Explanation of these functions is as under:

1. Planning. Planning is the process of decision making. What to do? Where to do? When to do? How to do? etc., are the questions which are decided by the process of planning. Planning is to decide at present about future so that pre-determined objects of the business or industrial enterprise may be accomplished with certainty and economy. Planning also includes the selection of best available alternative out of different alternatives available. Therefore, the planning may be defined as the determination of what is to be done in future. In every business, whether large or small, planning is an important function of management because it is necessary to decide in advance what we want to do in future. Urwick was of the opinion that effective planning must be based upon some certain and specified objects and must be simple, flexible and balanced.

Thus, the planning process involves seven sub-activities. These are as under:

(i) Forecasting;

(ii) Objects—economic and social objects;

(ii) Policies regarding all the activities;

(iv) Programmes;

(v) Schedules;

(vi) Procedures;

(vii) Objectives.

2. Organisation. An efficient organisation is necessary for the accomplishment of pre-determined objects of a business or industrial enterprise. All the employees of an enterprise must work on the basis of mutual co-operation and trust. The term 'Organisation' has been defined a follows:

According to **Louis A. Allen,** "Organisation is the process of identifying and grouping work to be performed, defining and delegating the reponsibility and authority, and establishing the relationship for the purpose of enabling people to work most effectively together in accomplishing objective."

According to **L.F. Urwick,** "Organisation is determining the activities what are necessary to any purpose or plan and arrange them in groups which may be assigned to individuals."

Thus, organisation may be defined as the organisation of all the resources of production into a well defined and determined activity. Organisation is as important in an enterprise as the brain in human body. As the brain directs, regulates and controls all the parts and activities of human body, an efficient organisation directs, regulates and controls the activities of different departments of an enterprise.

Five steps are inovlved in the process of Organisation. These steps may be summarized as under:

(i) To determine the activities of enterprise of the accomplishment of pre-determined objects.

(ii) To classify these activities into different parts and groups.

(iii) To assign the activities of each to different persons according to their abilities.

(iv) To define the rights and duties of all the employees of enterprise.

(v) To delegate adequate power for the discharge of duties.

(vi) To establish sweet relations between officers and employees of all the departments.

3. Staffing. The success of an enterprise depends to a large extent upon the qualification, experiene and efficiency of its employees. Therefore, the selection of right persons for the jobs and their placement at the right jobs is very important function of management. While performing this function, the management estimates the number of employees required, determines their qualifications and selects the required employees on this basis. This process is called staffing. It has been defined by various authors as follows:

According to **Theo Haimann,** "Staffing is concerned with placement, growth and development of all those members of the organisation whose function is to get things done through the efforts of other individuals."

According to **Koontz O' Donnell,** "Staffing involves manning the organisation structure through proper and effective selection, appraisal and development of personnel to file the roles designed intc the structure."

Thus, staffing means the selection, training, development and appraisal of personnel required for the accomplishment of objectives of an enterprise. It includes the following steps: *(i)* To forecast the needs of employees; *(ii)* To determine their qualification; *(iii)* To recruit; *(iv)* To train them; *(v)* To assign them the particular jobs; *(vi)* To evaluate their performance; *(vii)* To arrange for their promotion and transfers; *(viii)* Determination of personnel policies; *(ix)* To maintain proper records about employees.

4. Direction. Management is an art of getting things done through and with others. To get the things done through others, it becomes necessary that the activities of others are directed properly in the right direction. Direction is that function of Management which initiates organisational efforts, converts the managerial decisions into reality and helps the business enterprise in achieving its objects. The term direction has been defined as under:

According to **Theo Haimann,** "Direction consists of the process and techniques utilised in issuing the instructions and making certain that operations are carried as originally planned. Directing is the process around which all the performance revolves."

According to **Koontz & O' Donnell,** "Direction is the executive function of guiding and observing subordinates."

Thus, direction means to direct, regulate and supervise the activities of all the employees so that pre-determined objects of an enterprise may be accomplished. Three functions are performed in the process of direction:

(i) To issue the instructions and to give the orders.

(ii) To train the subordinates and to direct them to do their work in the best manner.

(iii) To supervise the works of subordinates and to check it at times whether they are doing their works as directed.

5. Control. Control is a process in which certain methods and techniques are adopted for the accomplishment of pre-determined objects of the enterprise. It ensures that all the activities of enterprise are being carried out as originally planned. In the process of control, data of actual, results are collected and compared with the plans and targets, the points of variations are determined and attempts are made to remove these variations. Thus, control means an activity to check whether the activities of enterprise are in accordance with the plan. If there is any difference, to take the remedial steps so that all the activities may go in accordance with the pre-determined plans. The term 'control' has been defined as under:

According to **E.F.L. Brech,** "Control is the process of checking actual performance against the agreed standards or plans, with a view to ensuring its adequate progress or satisfactory performance, and also recording the such experience as gained as a contribution to possible future needs.

According to **George R. Terry,** "Controlling is determining what is being accomplished, that is, evaluating the performance and if necessary, applying corrective measures so that the performance takes place according to plans."

According to **Henry Fayol,** "Control consits in verifying whether every thing occurs in conformity with the plans adopted, instructions, issued and the principles established. It has the objects to point out the weaknesses and errors in order to rectify them and to prevent recurrence. It operates on everything, people and activities."

Above discussion makes it clear that the process of control has the following four elements:

(i) To determine the objectives and targets which are to be accomplished.

(ii) To determine the process—how, by whom, and when the plan is to be executed.

(iii) To decide the process to do the things in the best possible manner.

(iv) Evaluation of the actual performance.

FEATURES OF MANAGEMENT

Perhaps systems approach has attracted the maximum attention of thinkers in management particularly in the present era. Though this approach is of compartively recent origin, starting late 1950, it has assumed considerable importance in analysing the phenomena of management. It is an integrating approach which considers management in its totality based on empirical data. The basic idea of systems approach is that any object must rely on a method of analysis involving simultaneous variations of mutually dependent variables. This happens when systems approach is applied in management.

A system is an assemblage of thing connected or interrelated so as to form a complex unity; a whole composed of parts and sub-parts in orderly arrangement according to some scheme or plan. This has been defined as "an organised or complex whole; and assemblage or combination of things or parts forming a complex unitary whole." On the basis of this definition, various features of system can be indetified:

1. A system is bsically a combination of parts, sub-systems. Each part may have various sub-parts. When a sub-system is considered as a system without a reference to the system of which it is a part, it has the same feature of a system. Thus a hierarchy of systems and sub-systems can be arranged. For example, the universe is a system of heavenly bodies which includes many sub-systems of stars called galaxies. Within a galaxy, there is solar system. When we consider galaxy as a system, solar system may become a sub-systems but we can also consider solar system consisting of so many planets.
2. A system is not merely the totality of parts and sub-parts but their arrangement is more important. The whole becomes greater than the total of individual parts because of the type of arrangement made in these parts and subparts. Thus a system is an interdependent framework in which various parts are arranged.
3. Parts and sub-parts of a system are mutually related to each other, some more, some less; some directly, some indirectly. This relationship is not natural, given, or unalterable in a social system. The relationship is in the context of the whole. Any change in one part may affect other parts also. Therefore, how various parts are given relationship is important for the functioning of the system.
4. A system can be identified because it has a boundary. In the case of physical system, this boundary is quite visible and, therefore, the system can be identified easily. However, in the case of a social system, the boundary is not visible because it is not like a line or wall that functions to preserve or to define what is inside. Instead, the boundary

maintains proper relationship between the system and its environement—objects lying outside the system. Identification of this boundary in the case of human organisation facilitates the management of a system by differentiating those which can be controlled because they are the parts of the system and those which cannot be controlled because they are outside the system.

5. The boundary of a system classified it into two parts: closed system and open system. All living organisms are open systems while all non-living systems are closed systems. The major differences between the two are as follows:

   (i) Closed systems are those that have no interaction with environment, that is, no outside systems impinge on them or for which no outside systems are to be considered. Open systems are those that interact with their environment, that is, they have systems with which they relate, exchange, and communicate.

   (ii) Closed systems are generally mechanical, for example, an automatic watch. Therefore, once they are set, they work. However, open systems are affected by environmental factors and they have to be adjusted according to environment.

   (iii) Closed systems are self-contained and self-maintaining as they do not interact with the environment. Open systems interact with the environment and in this interaction, they import energy and export output. Because of this interaction, closed systems are rigid and static but open systems are dynamic and flexible as they are subject to change by enviromental forces.

   (iv) Closed systems are like closed loop while open systems are characterised by negative entropy. They import more energy than is expended or consumed. Thus, they can grow over the period of time. When this relationship is reversed, the open systems decline.

(v) Open systems have feedback mechanism that helps them to maintain homoeostatic, a kind of equilibrium. Homoeostatic is a process through which a system regulates itself around a stable state. For example, human body works on the principle of homoeostatic. It maintains its temperature relatively at a constant level despite variations in the environmental temperature. Similarly thermostat maintains this equilibrium. However, organisational equilibrium is not static. It being a dynamic system, gets feedback to maintain dynamic equilibrium.

The distinction between closed and open systems is there but really no system is a closed one but has some properties of open systems. The classification of various systems into closed and open is not very proper. Therefore, it is more appropriate to think of systesm in terms of the degree to which they are open or closed rather than using a dichotomy of open-close.

6. System transforms inputs into outputs. This transformation process is essential for the survival of the system. There are three aspects involved in this transformation process: inputs, mediator, outputs. Inputs are taken form the environment, transformed into outputs, and given back to the environment. Various inputs may be in the form of information, money, materials, human resources, etc. Outputs may be in the form of goods and services. The total relationship may be called as input-output process and system works as mediator in this process. However, in this proess, system restores some of the inputs taken from the environment. Restoring the inputs taken from the environment helps the system maintain its structure and avoid decay and death. Thus the system can grow over the period of time.

FEATURES OF MANAGEMENT AS SYSTEM

Under the systems appraoch, management is regarded as a system. It draws heavily from systems concepts. When systems concept are applied to management, it is taken in the following ways:

1. Management as a Social System. Management can be considered as a system. Therefore, management has all the characteristics of a system as discussed above. However, management is a social system and unlike biological or mechanical systems, it has the characteristics of social systems. This concept of social system is quite different from cooperative social system as discussed earlier. Management as a system consists of many sub-systems which are integrated to constitute an entity.

2. Management as Open System. Management, like any other social system, is an open system. In interacts with its environment. Out of this interaction, it takes various resources, allocates and combines these resources to produce desirable outputs which are exported to the environment. Thus management works as input-output mediator. These features of management suggests that it is not free to decide the things on its own but due weightage has to be given to the environmental factors affecting the management of an organisation.

3. Dynamic. Management as a system is dynamic. It suggests that management attempts at achieving equilibrium in the organisation. However, this equilibrium is not static as happens in mechanical systems. Management moves towards growth and expansion by preserving some of the energy. Managerial effectiveness depends on this energy exchange. Therefore, it is not only the internal process that determines the effectiveness of management but also how it interacts with the changing environment in terms of taking inputs and giving outputs also determines its effectivenss.

4. Adaptive. Organisation being an open system, its survival and growth in a dynamic environment demands an adaptive system which can continuously adjust to changing environment. Management tends to achieve environmental constancy by bringing the external world under control, or bringing internal modification of organisation functioning to meet the needs of the changing world. Since there is a provision of feedback mechanism, management can evaluate its performance and take corrective actions.

5. Multivariable. Management is multivariable and involves taking into account many variables simultaneously. This feature of management suggests that there is no simple cause-effect phenomenon, rather an event may be the result of so many variables which themselves are interrelated and interdependent. This interrelatedness and interedependence makes managing a quite complex process.

6. Probabilistic. Management is probabilistic and not deterministic. A deterministic model always specified the use of model in a condition with predetermined results. Therefore, the outcome of an action can be predicted accurately. For example, if one wants to get the total of 250 and 500, he can press the button of a calculator and gets 750. This is possible because the outcome is certain. In the case of probabilistic model, the outcome can be assigned only probability and not certainty. For example, if a coin is tossed, the probability of getting a head is 0.5. But one cannot say with certainty that there will be 50 heads out of tossing of a coin 100 times. Management being probabilistic points out only the probability and never the certainty of the performance and consequent results. Management has to function in the face of many dynamic variables and there cannot be absolute predictability of these variables.

7. Multi-level and Multidimensional. Systems approach of management points out the multilevel and multidimensional features of management. It has both macro and micro approaches. At macro level, it can be applied to suprasystem, say, a business system as a whole. At micro level, it can be applied to an organisation. Even it can be applied to a subsystem of an organisation. However, it has the same characteristics at all these levels: suprasystem level, system level, and subsystem level.

8. Multi-disciplinary. Management is basically multidiscipliary. It draws and integrates knowledge from various disciplines and schools of thought. It draws heavily from economics, psychology, sociology, anthropology, matehmatics, statistics, operations, research, systems analysis, and so on. It takes only the relevant aspects from these disciplines. Thus management is not only of the disciplines mentioned above but it includes it itself the above disciplines. The integration of relevant knowledge from these disciplines is the major contribution of systems approach of management.

9. An Integrated Approach. System approach of management takes an integrated view of managing. It identifies the reason for a phenomenon in its wider context taking into the total factors affecting the phenomenon. In other approaches, a particular phenomenon has been explained in terms of a single factor or cluster of factors. Management tries to integrate the various factors to find out the reasons behind a phenomenon. It emphasises on how the management of one subsystem of the organisation should be taken in relation with others because other subsystems become environment for the given system. Thus the problem in one subsystem should not be traced into the subsystem only but in a much wider context.

Implications of Systems Approach

Systems approach of management provides an integrated approach of managing. This considers management in its totality. The integrative approach of managing can be best understood by quoting Churchman on the systems approach of management. He writes as follows:

> "There is a story often told in logic text about a group of blind men who were assigned the task of discovering an elephant. Each blind man was located at a different part of the body. A horrendous argument arose in which each claimed to have a complete understanding of the total elephantine system. What is interesting about this story is not so much the fate of the blind men but the magnificent role that the teller had given himself, namely, the ability to see the whole elephant and consequently the ridiculous behaviour of the blind system describers. The story is in fact a piece of arrogance. It assumes that a very logically astute man always gets on the top of a situation so to speak, and look at the foolishness of the poeple who are incapable of seeing the whole."

The quotation aptly describes how management problems should be seen in an organisation, that is, by taking the totality of the organisation and not a part of it. This implies that there should be integration of various forces affecting management. We have entered in a period that forces us to find out more accurate answers to the questions involving the wholeness of an operation. This age of synthesis forces management to think out in new and different ways, as suggested by the systems approach. In this view, the whole is not merely a combination of its different parts but more than that.

Systems approach possesses the conceptual level of managerial analysis much higher than any other approach. It discards the simplistic approach of managerial analysis and suggests that management of an organisation must be consistent with the demands of organisational enviornment and the needs of its members. It provides a framework through which organisation-environment interaction can be analysed and facilitaties decsion-making, since the system within which mangers make decisions can be provided as a more explict framework, decision-making is easier to handle.

LIMITATIONS OF SYSTEM APPROCH

Though system approach possesses conceptual framework of much higher order as compared to other approaches, it may be emphasised that this in no way is the unified theory of management. Systems approach came in a big way in managerial analysis and raised the hope of becoming a general and unified theory of management. A general and unified theory can be applied to all types of organisations, presenting their comprehensive analysis so that those who want to study organisations from different angles can derive knowledge. However, this promise could not be fulfilled because systesm appraoch suffers from two reasons.

1. **Abstract Approach.** It is often suggested that systems approach is too abstract to be of much use to practising managers. It merely indicates that various parts of the organisation are interrelated. Similarly, an organisation is a social system and, therefore, is related with other organisations in the society. This is true and significant for

managing. But it fails to spell out precisely relationships among these. Therefore, its contribution to managing is limited. For example, it is one thing to say that economic forces trigger social, technical and pychological changes in the organisation. But this is not enough for managing an organisation.

2. **Lack of Universality.** System approach of management lacks universality and its precepts cannot be applied to all organisations. For example, systems approach provide modern structural forms, cybernetic system for control and communication. These systems are suitable for large and complex organisations but are not suitable for small organisations. Since the most modern organisations are large and complex, it is argued that systems approach is applicable in general. This may be true but the role of a theory is not to prescribe actions for a particular category of organisations, rather, the theory should specify the relationships among different variables which can be applied to all organisations.

   If systems approach is seen in this perspective, some people believe that the approach is as incomplete as other. In fact, they argue that this approach does not offer anything new. The managers have been doing their jobs seeing the problems as a network of interrelated elements with interaction between environments inside and outside of their organisations. Looking into these shortcomings of systems approach, researchers have tried to modify the systems approach. This attempt has led to the emergence of a separate, though related, approach, situational or contingency approach.

REASONS AND PROBLEMS DUE TO VARIOUS SCHOOLS

The management literature is full of repetition and apparent contradictions quite often causing confusion due to multiplicity of schools of thought. There are various reasons for the emergence of management thought and all of them try to provide the answer to the question: how can organisation be made effective? Therefore confusion arises in understanding the exact nature of management. Some of the major reasons for the situation are as follows:

1. Semantic Problems. The most important reason for management theory jungle is the semantic problems in the management literature. This is because of the non-standardised use of various terms. Even terms like management and organisation have not been defined precisely. For example, management can be defined as a process, as a science, as an art, as group of people, or as profession. Thus people are not quite sure about the exact nature of management. When they use the term management, they attach a particular meaning which may be different from the meaning attached by others. This may create problem in understanding the true nature of management. Besides, there are several other terms where semantic problems arise, such as decision-making leadership, human relations, and so on.

2. Contributions from Different Disciplines. Organisations have been the central focus of study by various disciplines and each of these disciplines analyses the organisational functioning from a different angle. For example, sociologists have viewed the central problem in an organisation as the cooperative social system, psychologists see the same problem as interpersonal, while anthropologists look at the problem from value and judgment point of view. Naturally their orientations differ not only in terms of identifying the organisational problems but also in suggesting the solutions of the problems.

3. Misunderstanding of Management Principles. There is often misunderstanding of management principles because of their inexact nature. Principles are fundamental truths, or what are believed to be truth at a given point of time, explaining the relationship between two or more variables. There are two types of problems in management principles. First, these have been evolved out of limited researches or experiences. Therefore, they do not meet the requirements of rigorous scientific methods. When a person puts any of these principles at test, they have to evoke positive response and, thus, cannot be termed as principles. In fact, it is not clear whether many management principles are just action recommendations or definitions, and ambiguity prevails leading to emergence of divergent thoughts over a single phenomenon. Second, some of the approaches have been disapproved because of lack of emperical testability of some of the principles in a particular approach. For example, whole classical theory have been discarded because some of the classical principles have been found inapplicable. Similar thing has happened in other theories also.

The various factors discussed above are the major sources of management theory jungle which still persists. The existence of various approaches makes the situation confusing in perceiving correctly the basic nature of management for *(i)* analysing and understanding its functioning; and *(ii)* identifying and providing the solution of the problems involved therein. There are so much confusion and contradictions in various schools of management that many people suggest that a single approach in studying the management is not sufficient. A particular approach or combination of approaches would be sufficient for studying management which meets the following criteria:

1. The approach should deal with an area of knowledge and inquiry, that is management.
2. The approach should be useful in improving practice and task of management.
3. The approach should not be lost in sematics, specially when unstandardised one is not understandable to practitioners.
4. The approach should give direction and efficiency to reasearch and dissemination of knowledge.
5. The approach must recognise that it is a part of a larger universe of knowledge.

Below is given the discussion of important approaches of management bringing out the major features, uses, and limitations of each.

Empirical Approach

The empirial school of management bases its methods on a close study of past managerial experience and management cases. As such, it is also known as case approach or management experience approach. The major contributors in the field are Earnest Dale, Mooney and Reiley, Urwick and other management practitioners. According to this approach, management is considered a study of managers in practice. The intention of studying experience is to draw generalisations and to develop means of teaching experiences to other practioners and students. Attempts are made to duplicate successful experiences while avoiding unsuccessful ones. The major features of this approach are as follows:

1. Management is basically a study of managerial experiences and can be taught best by case method.
2. Theories of management can be developed by studying larger number of expreiences because some sort of generalisation can be possible.
3. Managerial experience can be passed from one practitioner to another or to students of management for continuity in the knowledge of management.
4. It is a study of successes and failures in the application of management techniques by managers in their practice. Thus techniques used by successful managers in the past can be used by future managers.

USE AND LIMITATIONS

This approach offers the most conventional way of acquiring skills in managemnet, that is, learning through the experience of others. In fact, in the beginning, this approach offered considerable help in developing management principles. This approach also helps in classroom situations for developing diagnostic and analytical skills in management students. Case method as a tool of teaching management is a positive indication in this direction. However, development of management litrature through scientific researches has put the question about the validity of this approach in modern day. Following limitations of this approach are quite obvious:

1. This empirical approach, basing its generalisations on cases and past experiences has not contributed anything fundamental to the development of management as a discipline because of obvious contradictions in various management experiences.
2. The proposition that a successful technique applied in the past will be good for future is untenable. Management is not based on precedents and no two situations can be exactly identical. Therefore, what was a right approach in a particular situation is the past may not be so in a situation occuring in the future. For example, Koontz has cautioned against the use of empirical approach as such. "Management, unlike law, is not a science based on precedents, and the situtation in the future exactly comparable to the past are exceedingly unlikely to occur. Indeed, there is a positive danger in relying too much on past experience and on undistilled history of managerial problem-solving for the simple reason that a technique or approach found right in the past may not fit a situation of the future."

PRINCIPLES OF MANAGEMENT

According to Terry, 'Principles of management are to a manager as a table of strength of materials is to a civil engineer.' The utility of principles lies in foundation they provide for its effective conduct, by making out the basic features that must characterize the practice of management, irrespective of where it is occuring. By means of principles of management a manager can avoid fundamental mistakes in his job and foretell the results of his actions with confidence. According to Koontz, principles help in the following ways:

1. **To Increase Efficiency.** Principles aid thinking and action. The need for guess work, haphazard activities is reduced. The problems brought out by rapid changes in the environment can be solved easily. For example, the principles of span of control tells a manager that he can manage only

a limited number of subordinates, say 8 to 10, and thereby helps him to predict the results if the principle is not applied.

2. **To Attain Social Goals.** Management principles play an important role in improving the quality of life of people and the standard of living. They bring order out of chaos. Managers are able to commit resources to best advantages and employ them in a judicious fashion.
3. **To Crystallize the Nature of Management.** Principles crystallize the ever-increasing knolwedge and thinking in the field of management. Without principles it is not possible to impart knowledge and provide training to managers.
4. **To Improve Research in Management.** Management deals with human beings whose behaviour is highly unpredictable. Principles provide a canopy of broad generalisatons which help in testing behaviour, understanding it and predicting the outcomes for future. They help in improving the fund of tested knowledge and promoting further research in human behaviour.

CHARACTERSITICS OF MANAGEMENT PRINCIPLES

Management principles are characterized by the following:

1. **Dynamic.** Management principles are flexible in nature and are continually changing. Most of the principles of scientific management and bureaucracy have been replaced. Refinements take place continuously. This is made possible by the ever-increasing research activity in the field of management. Management principles change with the changes in the environment in which the organisation exists. As such they must be accepted as flexible and dynamic guidelines and not as rigid and static rules. They can be accepted at best as 'diagnostic guides'.
2. **Relative.** As pointed out earlier, Management principles are relative and not absolute laws which can be applied blindly in all situations. They must be applied carefully

depending on organisational requirements and situational demands. In the words of Terry, management principles are 'capsules of selected management wisdom to be used carefully and discreetly'. Lawrence and Lorseh along with the work of James Thompson have clearly shown how the environment affects the sturcture of an organisation. In his book, TVA and the Grass Roots, Seznik had shown how various other organisations and interest groups in the outside environment of the Tennessee Valley Authority influenced managerial decisions. In his book, Organizations in Action, Thompson had outlined the importance of achieving the co-alignment of environmental factors with the internal technology, human resources and organisational structure. After studying twenty firms representing various industries in UK, Burns and Salker found that when the technological and market environments were uncertain, a flexible organisation structure was adopted. They have also found that successful firms in stable environments were mechanistic in structure. Another English study reported by Woodward showed that there were definite relationships between technology and structure of an organisation. found that detailed procedures, centralisation of decision-making process, controls etc. would work effectively in organisations operating in a stable environment.

SCHOOLS OF MANAGEMENT THOUGHT

Management is one of the oldest arts dating back to the beginnings of civilisation. Excepting some attempts to study the art of administration of management systematically in some of the leading civilisations of the world, the management discipline or science is relatively of recent origin. Beginning with an examination of the functions performed by the executives, the process of management has been studied by the scholars drawn from a number of disciplines. The stream of management has swelled with rich contributions from all the various disciplines. As a result, different management theories have emerged. Each of these reflects a specialist angle of the contributors from a particular discipline. For a long time, there was no communication among the various disciplines on the concept and process of management. As a result, there is a great measure of confusion leading to a situation which Harold Koontz has described as the "management theory jungle". The various approaches to the study of management as propounded by specialists from different disciplines have come to be called the schools of management thought. Attempts have been made by writers on management to identify the major schools of thought in management.

According to Ernest Dale, management writers may be divided into Classicists and behaviourists.

Newman, Summers and Warren refer to the various schools as productivity approach, behavioural approach, rationalistic model approach and institutional approach.

According to Harold Koontz, the major schools of management thought are:

(a) Management process school
(b) Empirical school
(c) Human behaviour school
(d) Social system school
(e) Decision school
(f) Mathematical school.

Taking into account the above classifications, we may identify the major schools of thought in management as follows:

(i) Management process school
(ii) Empirical school
(iii) Human behaviour or human relations school
(iv) Social school
(v) Decision theory school
(vi) Mathematical or quentitative management school
(vii) Systems management school
(viii) Contingency school.

1. Management Process School or the Operational Approach. This approach is known by various labels such as the traditional approach, the universalist approach or the classicist approach. The father the this school of thought was the noted French management thinker and practitioner Henri Fayol. According to this school, management can best be studied in terms of the process that it involves. The management process consisting of five broad categories of functions, *viz.*, planning, organising, starting, directing and controlling is in evidence in all managerial situations. Following this, this school of management thought has evolved some universal principles of management. Those subscribing to this school are of the view that management principles are universally applicable. They could be equally well applied to business, government or any other type of organisation. However, they do recognise the distinctions between the different types of enterprises.

In short, the main features of the management process school are:

(i) The study of management school focuses on the role and functions of managers.

(ii) The functions of managers are the same irrespective of the type of organisation.

(iii) The five functions, *viz.*, planning, organising, startign, directing and controlling are the core of management.

(iv) The conceptual framework of management can be built through an analysis of the processes of management and identification of principles.

The management process school is criticised on three main grounds:

(1) This school is losing ground as hardly any significant contribution has been made after what Henri Fayol contributed at the end of the nineteenth century.

(2) With all these criticisms, the management process school does provide a concept on framework which could be usefully utilised in understanding the basics of management.

(3) The so called universal principles of management do not always stand the test of empirical scrutiny.

(4) Organisations function under dynamic conditions and, therefore, searching for universal principles may not always be a fruitful exercise.

2. The Empirical School or the Management by Customs School. Those subscribing to this school of thought believe that management is a study of the experiences of managers. If managerial experiences can be studied closely, management knowledge would emerge and grow out of it. This knowledge can be utilised by other managers in making their own decisions and solving managerial situations faced by them. But this school of thought depends heavily on the historical methods of study.

The basic assumption of this approach to the study of management is that the of actual business situation contributes to the development of managerial skills. The study school treats the case methods of study and analysis as the best methods of imparting management education. By studying management situations which are unique, the manager gets an idea about what could be good managerial decisions and what makes for poor managerial decisions. He also develops the analytical and problem-solving abilities which are so very essential for the successful practice of management in actual life.

The main features of this school of thought may be summed up as under:

(a) Management is the study of experience.

(b) The managerial experience can be passed over to the practitioner and students.

(c) Theoretical research has to be based on practical experience.

(d) The success and the failure of management in the process of decision-making could provide guidance to the manager in a similar situation.

The empirical school of thought goes mainly by precedents in so far as. It studies the managerial situations handled by the managers and their own experience. However, the exponents of this school do not fully realise that a manager has to work under dynamic conditions and that history does not exactly repeat itself. The situations of the past may not be exactly the same as of the present. There is definitely a certain amount of danger in transferring the insight gained from a particular case relating to the past to a situation facing the manager at a point of time in the present. In the words of Harold Koontz : "Management unlike law is not a science based on precedents and situations in the future exactly comparable to the past are exceedingly unlikely to occur. There is a positive danger in relying too much on past experience and on undistilled history of managerial problem solving for the simple reason that the technique or approach found right in the past may not fit a situation of the future."

The principal tool of study for the empirical school of thought is the case method. The case is considered to be the most convenient way of acquiring skill in decision-making. However, this method is not necessarily the best method in imparting training for decision-making. In decision-making, there are several complex variables which change under dynamic conditions.

3. The Human Relations or the Human Behaviour School. Management could rightly be thought of as the process of getting things done through or with people. If that be so, any organisation could be compared to a building that is made up of bricks of people. The relationships among these people are the cementing force that bind them together in pursuit of common objectives. According to this school of thought, management is the study of behaviour of people at work. The school had its origins in a series of experiments conducted by Professor Alton Mayo and his associates at the Harvard School of Business at the Western Electric Company's Hawthorne Works, near Chicago. These studies brought out for the first time the important relationships between social factors and productivity. Hitherto productivity of the employees was considered to be a function only of physical conditions of work and money wages paid to them. For the first time it was realised that productivity depended heavily upon the satisfaction of the employees in work situations.

Following the Hawthorne experiments, a great deal of work has been carried on by behavioural scientists belonging to a variety of disciplines including psychology, sociology, anthropology and philosophy in studying the behaviour of people at work in organisations. Those who subscribe to the Human Relations or the Human Behaviour School of thought are of the view that the effectiveness of any organisation depends upon the quality of relationships among the people working in the organisation. Therefore, the management, according to them, must concern itself with an analysis or organisation behaviour, that is, intereaction of people with the organisation. The basic assumption of this school still remains that the goals of the organisation are accomplished throught and with people. Apart from the study of formal organisation and techniques used by such organisations, this school studies the psychological processes in the organisations, group dynamics, informal organisations, conflict, change, motivation and relationship and the various techniques of achieving organisational development by improving the relationships among the various groups of people constituting organisation and the climate of the organisation. Thus, it may be said in summary that this school concentrates on people and their behaviour within formal and informal organisations. The main features of the Human Behaviour School of thought are:

(1) Since management is getting things done through and with people, a manager must have a basic understanding of human behaviour in all its aspects, particularly in the context to work groups and organisations.

(2) Motivation, leadership, communication, trading, participative management and group dynamics are critical to the study of management.

(3) Management must study inter-personal realtions among people.

(4) Greater production and higher motivation can be achieved only through good human relations.

(5) The study of management must draw upon the concepts and principles of various behavioural sciences like psychology and social psychology.

The main thinkers subscribing to this school of thought are Elton Mayo, Roethlisberger, McGregor and Keith Davis. The school has also benefited from the contributiosn of psychologists like Maslow, Argyris, Herzberg and McClelland.

4. The Social Systems School. This school of thought is closely related to the human behaviour or the human relations school of thought. According to this view, an organisation could be considered as a social system consisting of various groups of people. The founding father of this school of thought. Chester Barnard, viewed an organisation as a co-operative system involving collaboration and co-operation among a number of groups. If the groups in an organisation do not co-operate together in pursuit of a common objective, the effectiveness of an organisation will be jeopardised. The focus of this school of thought is, therefore, on the study of the organisation as a co-operative or collaborative system. It may be mentioned here that a system is an entity or unit consisting of various parts called sub-systems which are inter-related or inter-dependent. A social system is, therefore, a unit or an entity consisting of various social sub-systems called the groups.

The major constribution of this school of thought is in the development of concepts and theories related to the formal organisation, that is, the organisation as formerly planned by the entrepreneurs or the top management. Another area is which valuable contribution has been made by the pioneers belonging to this school is that of the informal organisation.

An important aspect of the Social Systems School of Thought in management is its focus on the cultural factors in the working of an organisation. It is recognised by the exponents of this school that people working together in groups have their own norms and values which have a bearing on the contribution that they are likely to make towards the goals of the organisation. Further the organisation has its own cultural environment made of norms and values. The norms and values of the organisation are in turn affected by the culture in which the organisation operates. For example, when an organisation is functioning in a culutre that places a great value on industry and social responsibility, the organisation's own culture is likely to be affected by these values. In turn, the culture of the organisation will have a bearing on the norms, values and mores of the various groups that form part of it.

The main features of the Social Systems School of Thought in management are as follows:

(1) An organisation is a social system, *i.e.*, a system on cultural relationship, and management concerned with the effectiveness of an organisation must study it as such.

(2) Formal organisations represent cultural relationship of the social groups working within the organisation.

(3) Co-operation of the members working and the groups is essential and is the core of good management.

(4) Relationships exist between internal and external environments and change.

(5) Management has to direct its efforts towards establishing harmony between the goals of the organisation and the needs, aims and aspirations of the people comprising the various groups in the organisation.

The main pioneers and contributors to this field are Max Weber, Moreno, Simon and Rensis Likert.

5. Decision Theory School. The essence of management lies in decision-making. Whatever a manager does is the outcome of a decision made by him from out of a set of alternatives available to him. The Decision Theory School of Management Thought concentrates its attention on decision-making and treats the various aspects of decision-making as constituting the scope of the study of management.

This school of thought has its origins in the theory of consumer's choice which has been the favourate preoccupation of the economists since early 19th century. Economists have been trying to determine the process through which a consumer makes a rational choice from among a number of alternative commodities or products available to him. It also takes into account some of the relatively irrational or logical aspects of consumer's choice.

While the Decision Theory School of Thought accepts the basic assumption that decisions are taken through rational choice from among different alternatives given different constraints, it does not confine itself of the process of decision-making. It fact, the analysis of this school includes the behaviour of the persons or organisational groups making the decision. Going further into the question of decision-making, the exponents of this school also concern themselves with the various factors involved in decision-makers including the implementation of the decisions, the psychological and sociological foundations of decision and even the cultural background of the decision-makers. In so far as the writers belonging to this school touch upon the social and cultural factors relating to the decision-makers and bearing on the decision-making process, this school gets very close to the Social Systems School of Thought in Management.

The main features of this school of thought may be summed up as under:

(1) Decision-making is central to the study of management.

(2) The field of management theory is, in essence, the fielf of decision making.

(3) Management information system and the process and technique of decision-making form the subject-matter of the study of management according to the decision theory school of thought.

(4) The members of any organisation are essentially decision-makers and problem-solvers. Hence, management is the study of the process of decision making and the personalities and behaviour of the decision-makers.

The main contributors and thinkers belonging to this school are Chester Bernard, James March, Herbert Simon, Forrester and Richard Cyert.

Decision-making is certainly a very central and critical aspect of management. However, the advocates of this school do not always concern themselve with the actual practice of decision-making. In fact, they miss the point that decision-making cannot be treated as an independent function. It is after all only one of the tasks that the executive performs. In some cases, it takes only a small fraction of the time of the executive. In view of this, it is open to question whether the decision theory school can do justice to the various aspects of management which include besides decision-making such important functions as co-ordination, organisation and implementation of decisions.

6. The Mathematical School. If there is one discipline which has made inroads into practically all disciplines, it is mathematics. Universally recognised as an important tool of analysis and a language for precise expression of concepts and relationships among the concepts, mathematics has now entered the field of management in a big way. It is sometimes said that modern economics is more than half mathematics and less than half economics. Perhaps the same could be said about the writings of the mathematical school of thought in management.

The scientific and technological developments and the introduction of computers have brought management and mathematics closer to each other. Mathematics is now being used in management to study various problems and analyse them as also to find out suitable rational solutions to these problems. In this respect, the mathematical school is closely related to the decision theory school of management.

The exponents of the mathematical school of thought believe that effective solutions to the problems of management can be achieved through application of suitable simulation and the use of analytic and synthetic mathematical techniques. The contributors to this school of thought have been using mathematical and quantitative techniques in developing mode of the various kinds of decision and problems involved in managing organisations with a view to understading them and also finding solution to them. The major form that this school of thought has taken is Operations Research.

Basically, the Mathematical School or the quantitative method school dates back to the Scientific Management propounded by Frederick Taylor and his associates. It would be recalled that it was Taylor who for the first time suggested that a scientific study of work must be made before the management sets about the task of allocating work among the employees. The thinkers and writers belonging to this school are branded as maangement scientists.

The main features of the mathematical school of thought in management are:

(1) Management is concerned with problem-solving and it must make use of mathematical tools and techniques for the purpose.

(2) The different factors involved in management can be quantified and expressed in the form of models, *i.e.*, in the form of equations which can be solved with the help of mathematical techniques.

(3) Operations Research, mathematical tools, simulation and model building are the basic methodologies developed by this school of thought.

(4) Management problems can be described in mathematical symbols.

The main contributors to this school are Taylor, Gilbreth, Gantt, Joel Dean, Newmann, Ackoff and Hicks. The contributions of mathematics in the field of management are undoubtedly quite impressive. Mathematics has certainly helped management is systematising thinking and has lent a certain measure of exactness to the management discipline. The contribution of mathematics to the development of management can hardly be over-emphasised. However, it will also be necessary to take note of the major limitations of this school of thought.

In the first place, we must remember that mathematical models cannot be considered as a substitute for sound judgment. They can at best be treated as tools and techniques for purposes of analysis. Secondly, there are still certain phases of the management process which cannot be expressed in mathematical symbols and formulae.

Perhaps the danger with the mathematical school is that it leads us to believe that complex management problems involving people and other resources can be reduced to formulae or mathematical formulations which is not a very correct approach.

7. The Systems Approach School. Major contributions in the development of management thought since 1960 have come basically from the quantitative and behavioural science schools of thought. However, a new direction in management thought has been given by what has come to be commonly called as the Systems Approach. The Systems Approach is not new to the natural and the physical sciences where its application began about a quarter of a century ago.

To briefly recapitulate, a system in composed of related and interdependent elements which form a unitary whole. It may be viewed as an assemblage or a combination of things of parts forming a complex whole. Every system is made up of a number of sub-systems arranged in a hierarchy. From this point of view, an organisation may be viewed as a system made up of different parts in the form of departments. Each of the deparments like Finance, Personnel, Production of Marketing is also a system comprising various other systems.

According to the traditional schools of management thought developed before the Systems Approach, each department or function of management has to be studied separately, However, with the introduction of the Systems Approach, this approach or method of study has to be changed. In an organisation, for instance, a project management approach may be introduced by forming teams drawn from different specialisation, coordinated by a project manager.

The Systems Approach has been applied to various other approaches developed in the management thought. For example, in operations research, the systems approach has led to emphasis on computer application and operations management techniques. Similarly, in the field of organisational behaviour, a formal organisation is viewed as a system consisting of structure, processes and technology. In a similar way, the human being is conceived of as a system containing biological, physiological and psychological processes and personality.

Systems could be simple or complex. Simple systems can be studied more easily in terms of input, the processes and the output. In addition, feedback from the output could be linked with the input so that improvements could be brought about in terms of input, process and output. But when it comes to complex systems, it is not easy to study large number of factors involved in such systems. It is here that the application of computer technology becomes important. Given the help of computers and various mathematical techniques, the model building approach is being used to produce simulations of actual systems. This helps a great deal in analysing and designing organisational systems. However, this is an approach that has yet to be fully developed even though it holds out tremendous possibilities.

The major features of the Systems Approach to the study of management may be summed up as under:

(1) A system consists of inter-related and interdependent parts.

(2) The systems approach emphasises the study of the various parts in their inter-relationships rather than in isolation from each other.

(3) The Systems Approach to management brings out the complexity of a real life maangement problem much more sharply that any of the other approaches.

(4) The Systems Approach can be utilised by any of the other approaches including the process approach, the mathematical or the quantitative approach, the decision theory or the behavioural science or human relations appraoch. We have already seen how the social study approach also makes use of the systems study of management.

(5) The Systems Appoach has been utilised in studying the function of complex organisations and has been utilised as the base for new kinds of organisation like the project management organisation.

The Systems Approach has an edge over the other approaches in so far as its closeness to reality is concerned. However, the peoblem with the systems approach is its utter complexity, particularly when it comes to a study of large and complex organisations or for that matter the whole management concept and function.

8. The Contingency Approach School of Management. As one surveys the whole scene, it appears that the whole field of management is divided into two camps:

(a) Behavioural Camp, and

(b) Quantitative Camp.

Quantitative approach works in some situations while the behavioural approach works in others. Those who have grounding in disciplines like psychology, sociology, anthropology and philosophy have been in the behavioural science camp and have provided useful insights into the field of management from their respective viewpoints. On the other hand, those who have come from disciplines like mathematics or natural or physical sciences have been trying to apply quantitative techniques of analysis to an understanding of management problems. The main problem, however, has been that while quantitative people could not overcome behavioural problems, the behavioural people could not cope with operational problems adaptable to quantitative solutions.

In view of these deficiencies in both the behavioural and quantitative approaches, reliance has recently been placed more and more on what has been described as the Systems Approach to management. However, the problem with this approach is that it is still not complete in spite of all the advances made in the development of general systems.

According to the Contingency Approach, management is situation. Study of management, according to this approach, lies in identifying the important variables in the situation. The approach has been used in important sub-systems of management like organisation, design, leadership, behaviour change and operations.

The major contributors to this school of thought in management are Joan Woodward. Fiedler, Lorsch and Lawrence.

At the present stage, the contingency Approach to management seems to be the only practicable way to studying management, applying as it does to various other approaches including the latest among them, that is, the Systems Approach.

PRINCIPLES OF PLANNING

Planning is a well-knwon fact in which many facts are analysed and planning is made. Planning is a process in which various principles are followed. The various principles of management planning are as follows:

1. Principle of Contribution in Objectives. Every plan and sub-plan of the institution should help in the achievement of general objectives of the institution. All resources of the institution should be so utilised that objectives of the instituion may be achieved in fixed time. It is necessary for achieving the good results and development of organisation that planning should be based towards desired goals.

2. Principle of Primacy of Planning. This principle of planning attracts the attention towards that planning of various managerial activities to achieve the set goals is a primary need. Without planning, all activities either they are related to organisation or related to direction, or they are related to establish co-ordination they are like motor without driver. Planning gives proper direction for the people working in the organisation.

3. Principle of Efficiency. This principle of planning makes it clear that group objectives should be achieved on least efforts and least investment. The success of planning depends how easily objectives are achieved. The attempts are made to systematise the working in planning.

4. Principle of Assumptions of Planning. For the success of planning it is necessary to set the assumptions of planning earlier.

This principle throws light on the the person who is responsible for the execution of planning should understand planning properly and the assumptions should be agreed by all.

5. Principle of Pervasiveness. This principle emphasises that planning is needed in organisations of every field as religious, political and social. This work of planning is made at every level of business management as top level, middle level and lower level. So planning should be according to levels of management.

6. Principle of Policy Making. If more and more policies are capable of guiding the way to achieve the objectives of enterprise if they are clearly defined and are understood properly by managers, the framework of planning of an enterprise will be more firm and effective. So, according to this principle firm and solid policies should be formulated to make the planning effective.

7. Principle of Change. According to this principle of planning a manager should always check his work like a navigator and should bring changes accordingly to achieve the objectives. It means that he should replan to achieve the set objectives.

8. Principle of Limited Factors. The resources of the enterprise are limited and they are utilised more. In the planning for enterprise, limited resources or limited factors should be determined. Environmental factors should also be kept in mind along with limited factors at the time of planning.

9. Principle of Alternatives. Planning is based on decision. It means that managers have to take many decision at the time of planning. Hence, at the time of decision making, best alternative among various is selected. This principle of planning makes it clear that best alternatives is only that which contributes most in achieving the set objectives.

10. Principle of Promise. Managers of the enterprise make some promises for the organisation. These promises mean the important decisions of the enterprise. The principle of promise also believes that managers should make the planning to fulfill these promises in time. So such decisions should be made as may be achieved without much difficulty. For this short term planning should be made.

11. Principle of Simplicity. This principle of simplicity tells that planning should be simple. Planning should be so simple that may be understood by all workers of the enterprise. For the best utilisation of all human and physical resources, planning should be simple and clear.

12. Principle of Competitive Strategy. According to this principle of planning, when an enterprise works under various competitive conditions or enterprise have many competitive organisations, planning should be according to this—what should be done or what should not be done. So, this principle emphasises the fact that at the time of planning for the enterprise, technique of competitive organisation should be also kept in mind.

13. Principle of Continuity. Planning is a continuous process. Planning are made for all the activities of the enterprise either big or small. The principle of continuity tells that planning should be always evaluated and amended form time to time so that planning may be coordinated.

14. Principle of Flexibilty. According to this principle of planning, planning should be flexible so that losses due to unexpected factors may be minimized.

❑

2

Aspects of Planning and Controlling

Generally what is to be done in future? The predetermination of it is called planning. In other words, planning answers the six pertinent questions *i.e.* what, why, where, how, who and when. Thus planning is a process of thinking before doing. Planning is deliberate and conscious research to formulate the design and sequence of actions through which it is expected to help reach its objectives. In the field of business management, the selection of best in alternative policies, objectives and programmes is called business planning.

Though to define the planning is very difficult, some authors have tried to give its definitions—

According to **E. Harley**, "Planning is deciding in advance what is to be done. lt involves the selection of objectives, policies, procedures and programme from among alternatives."

According to **The Haimann**, "Planning is deciding in advance what is to be done. When a manager plans, he projects a course of action for the future attempting to achieve a consistent, co-ordinated structure of operations aimed at the desired results."

According to **Louis A. Allen**, "Management planning involves the development of forecasts, objectives, policies, programmes, procedures, schedules and budgets."

According to **George R. Terry**, "Planning is the selecting and relating of facts and the making and using of assumptions regarding the future in the visualisation and formulation of proposed activities, believed necessary to achieve desired results."

Thus planning is an intellectual exercise of looking into future. *i.e.*, to decide in advance the activities to be undertaken in future and also to visualise the best course to achieve the desired goal, leading to decision making and controlling.

CHARACTERISTICS OF PLANNING

Planning has a number of characteristics:

1. Foundation. Planning is the foundation of management. It is a parent exercise in management process. It is a preface to business activities. Terry supported the view that without the activities determined by planning, there would be nothing to organize, no one to motivate and no need to control. Planning, logically speaking, precedes the execution of all other management functions. It provides point and purpose and incentive to the efforts of those in the organisation. Planning is the means for organised action, an essential prerequisite for success in all other areas. Without it work becomes aimless and wasted. The ideal of primacy of planning emphasizes the fact that planning takes precedence over other managerial functions like organizing, directing and controlling because none of these functions can come into being until there is a plan. Of course, it should be noted that the various functions of management are interrleated in that no one function can exist without the other.

2. Flexibility. Good planning helps an organisation adapt to its individual circumstances. Planning must help the organisation do what it needs it to do. Because circumstances can and often do change, plans should possess built-in flexibility. To be useful, a plan must be both stable and reasonably flexible. Too little planning (to permit flexible behaviour) can mean missed opportunities and inadequate direction. Too much planning (where everything is specified in a rigid manner) can prevent the flexible behaviour necessary to cope with novel situations. A plan must reflect and meet current needs.

3. Pervasive. Where is planning done? Plans can be centralized or decentralized. When planning is centralized, the planning work is done from a central point, such as a corporate planning department. In decentralised planning, each division or department is responsible for planning all its own operations, without regard to the central planning unit. Irrespective of the policy adopted, planning is a function of all managers. It is needed and practised at all managerial levels. Every manager has a planning function to perform within his particular area of activities. Planning is inherent in everything a manager does. Managers have to plan before launching a new business. They have to plan whenever things change; they have to plan in order to organize the business.

4. Continuous. Planning is continuous, it is a never-ending activity of a manager. However, this does not mean that a manager never completes work on a specific plan. The budget for a specific period may be adopted, but the manager who approves it must immediately shift his attention to other planning activities and must soon begin consideration of the budget for the next period. Planning, actually, is an ongoing process of adjustment and readjustment to change. Planning creates the criteria for control which itself creates the information for new planning. Planning sets action in motion and control, monitors the results to see that the plan is actually translated into action. Thus, one plan begets another and at any point of time there are several plans operating in the organisation.

5. Action orientation. Plans must be formulated in a precise way and expressed in realistic terms. They must be framed in an intelligible manner indicating organisational preferences. They should be neither impossible to attain nor too easily to be reached. As rightly pointed out by Duncan, "if they are impossible or unrealistic or both, incentive is lost. If they are too easy, exceptional performance is not necessary." To ensure satisfactory performance, plans must be understood by those who must accomplish them.

5. Unity. To ensure consistency and unity of action, it is necessary to have unified focus in planning operations. The focus must be clearly on objectives, policies and procedures etc, by all organisational sub-units (sales, production, finance departments etc). For example, efficiency would suffer if sales department pursues a liberalized credit policy while the accounting department adopts a programme to reduce bad debts. The activities of various departments in the organisation must complement one another rather than be in conflict.

7. Participation. Planning activity is not the exclusive prerogative of top management. Traditionally, the manager is accepted as the complete planner for his part of the organisation. Information was supplied to him and framed the plans in isolation. This has created problems of loyalty, commitment on the part of subordinate managers. Modern planning discounts these ivory tower exercises totally. Nowadays plans are formulated, as pointed out by Koontz and O'Donnel, in an atmosphere of close participation and a high degree of concurrence'. Operating personnel are also involved in the planning activities so that they can submit their view on organisational efforts and recommend improvements in future programmes.

OBJECTIVES OF PLANNING

The objectives of planning are as follows:

1. **To Help in Forecasting.** Forecasting is the essence of planning. Really speaking, planning is to prepare the plans for the organization on the basis of forecasting. Planning helps in effective forecasting.
2. **To Establish Co-ordination.** Planning is an important tool of co-ordination. Policies, objectives, procedures and programmes of an enterprise are co-ordinated with the help of planning.
3. **To Provide Certainty in Activities.** Planning decides the policies, defines the procedures and makes the rules for the activities of all the employees of the organisation. This helps in bringing certainty in the activities of the organisation.
4. **To Give a Specific Direction.** Planning gives a specific direction to all the activities of an organisation by preparing the outlines of these activities well in advance.
5. **To Forecast the Risk.** Planning helps in forecasting the risk that may appear in future. By forecasting the risks, the strategies may be designed to treat with them effectively and successfully.

6. **To Provide Economy in Management.** Planning establishes the co-ordination among all the activities of the organisation. It guides the management and all the employees of the organisation in their activities. It helps in maintaining effective control and discipline.

7. **To Help in Accomplishment of Budgets.** Planning helps the management in accomplishing the pre-determined budgets of the enterprise in a planned way.

8. **To Provide Important Information.** All the employees and all the outsiders dealing with an organisation can get all the important information regarding objectives, policies and programmes of the organisation.

9. **To Maintain Healthy Competition.** Planning helps in creating a healthy competition among the employees of the organisation and also among all the activities. It creates healthy competition among the employees in their efforts towards the achievement of pre-determined objects of the organisation.

Importance of Business Planning

As an aimless or directionless person can not succeed in life, in the same way an industrial organisation without planning cannot succeed. Without planning a business management becomes directionless sailor who is incapable of achieving the objectives. Planning provides direction to business, directs the group efforts towards objectives and makes possible the control of business activities. The significance and importance of planning may be explained under the following heads:

1. **For Facing the Future Uncertainty and Changes.** Future is uncertain and changeable. Planning helps in reducing uncertainties of future.A significant aspect of it is to obtain information to forecast conditions in future. Another set of action shall be undertaken conforming to the changed conditions. Due to continuous changes in the environment the organisation has to work in the accelerating change.

Change may be of two types. Tangible changes may be in the form of changes in technology, market forces, government regulations etc. Intangible changes may reflect in changes in attitudes, values, cultures etc. In order to cope with the requirement of such changes, the organisation must look ahead for its future course of action which is basically provided by planning process.

2. **For Future Co-ordination.** No organisation can achieve its objectives until the co-ordination is established among group efforts, interests, policies, etc. Managerial functions in an organisation require co-ordination for which beginning is made at planning stage. Planning determines the actions taken at each level of organisation to accomplish the objectives. The action plan unifies interdepartmental activites. It restricts the area of freedom in the development of purely departmental plans. Various departments work in accordance with the overall plans to achieve harmony.
3. **For Focussing Attention on Objectives.** Organisations exist to pursue and achieve certain objectives. Planning focusses on these objectives. It directs action for achieving objectives. Sometimes due to lack of clarity people in the organisation may not be specific about organisational objectives. Planning defines these objectives more clearly. It determines the course of action to achieve them. In a company the organisational objective is to earn profits which is to be persued. Planning as to how much profit is to be earned and how to be divided, requires looking into all supporting and limiting factors.
4. **Minimising Costs of Performance.** In planning, knowledge of present situations and their impact on future activities, help in setting of goals, objectives and deciding future of action. It involves the selection of only one profitable course of action that would yield the best result at minimum cost. It introduces an even flow of work without any friction or dissipation of energy for consistency and balance

of efforts. In removes hesitancy, avoids crisis, eliminates false steps and protects against improper deviation.

5. **Providing the Basis For Control.** Planning expresses the goals, objectives and targets in numerical data. These present standards for subsequent work performance and the time to be taken in completing the different jobs. Within the time limit actual performance is compared to the standards fixed by the plans. Any deviation is located and corrected. There can be no real control without planning. Some control is necessary to see that events conform to plans. It is exercised in the context of planning.
6. **For Improving Competitive Strength.** Planning in an enterprise gives it a competitive edge over other enterprises that do not believe in planning. This is so because, planning enables the organisation to discover new opportunities and thereby shape its own future. It ensures an orderly progress of the organisation. It provides added strength to the business for its continuous growth and steady prosperity. Earnest Dale has rightly pointed out that organisation continually monitors the environment for new ideas and development as corporate leader and dynamic in the real sense of the term.
7. **Increasing Organisation Effectiveness.** Planning ensures organisational effectiveness. Effectiveness ensures that the organisation is in a position to achieve its objectives with the help of available resources. Resources should be put to use in the best possible way so that the organisational objectives are achieved. Planning helps in proper utilization of resources. Each resource of the organisation has a specific use at a particular time. Along with control function planning ensures that resources are put in a way in which these have been specified in the plan.
8. **Path of National Progress.** Planning is a unique path for national progress and development. Because it makes possible the proper use of resources of the country, prevents

the business cycles, washes away the financial inequality, establishes balance between utilisation and production and provides employment. Our five years plans are the live example of importance of planning.

It is clear from the above discussion that business planning is the basis of business management. Management can do nothing in the absence of planning. So planning is a necessity of business and non-business fields.

PLANNING PROCESS

Determining objectives and outlining the courses of action needed to achieve these objectives is referred to as the planning process. The actual steps in the planning process are difficult to specify for all organisations because of wide differences in size and complexity. It is not necessary that a particular planning process is applicable for all organisations and for all types of plans because the various factors that go into planning process may differ from plan to plan or from one organisation to another. For example, planning for a major action will take more serious evaluation of various elements necessary for planning but this may not be true for a minor one. Similarly in a small organisation, planning process may not be taken in the same way as in a large organisation. Here is given a process of planning which is applicable for a major programme like opening of a new product line or acquisition of a major plant. With minor modifications the process is applicable to all types of plans. Planning process is presented in the following figure.

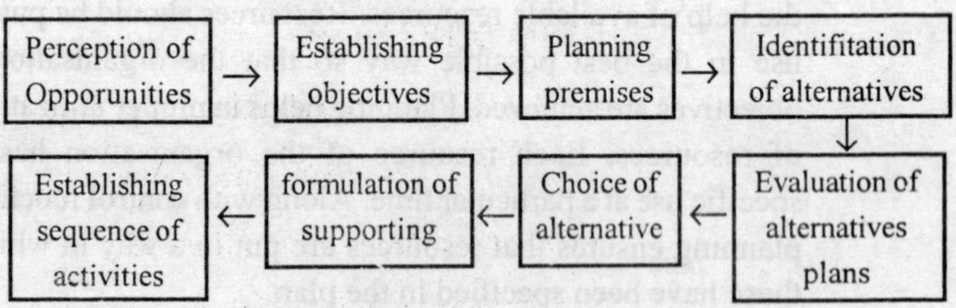

Fig. Planning process

The sequences of various steps in planning are in such a way that they lead to the translation of an idea into action by reaching to the state of establishing of activities. Each stage contributes in plan formulation in the following way:

1. Preception of Opportunities. Perception of opportunities is not strictly a planning process. However, this awareness is very important for planning process because it leads to formulation of plans by providing clue whether opportunities exist for taking up particular plans. From this point of view, it can be considered as the beginning of planning process. Perception of opportunities includes a preliminary look at possible opportunities and the ability to see them clearly and completely, aknowledge of where the organisation stands in the light of its strengths and weaknesses, an understanding of why the organisation wants to solve uncertainties, and a vision of what it expects to gain. This provides an opportunity to set the objectives in real sense because the organisation tries to relate itself with the environment. In doing so, it takes the advantages of opportunities and avoids threats.

2. Establishing Objectives. At this stage, major organisational and unit objectives are set. Objectives specify the results expected and indicate the end points of what is to be done, where the primary emphasis is to be placed, and what is to be accomplished by the various types of plans. The organisational objectives should be specified in all key result areas. Key result areas are those which are important for organisation in achieving its objectives. For example, for an organisation, key result areas may be profitability, sales, research and development of manufacturing, and so on. Once organisational objectives are identified, objectives of lower units and sub-units can be identified in that context.

3. Planning Premises. After determination of organisational goals, the next step is establishing plannings, the conditions under which planning activities will be undertaken. Planning premises are planning assumptions, the expected environmental and internal conditions. Thus planning premises are external and internal. External premises include total factors in task environment like political, social, technological, competitors' plans and actions, government policies, etc. Internal factors include organisation's policies, resources of various types, and the ability of the organisation to withstand the environmental pressure. The plans are formulated in the light of both external and internal factors. The more individuals charged with planning understand and utliise consistent planning premises, the more coordinated planning will be.

The nature of planning differs at different levels of planning. At the top level, it is mostly externally focused. As one moves down the organisation hierarchy, the composition of planning premises changes from external to internal. The major plans, both old and new, will materially affect the future against which the managers at lower units must plan.

4. Evaluation of Alternatives. Various alternatives which are considered feasible in terms of preliminary criteria may be taken for detailed evaluation. At this stage, an attempt is made to evaluate how each alternative contributes to the organisational objectives light of its resources and constraints. This presents a problem because each alternative may have certain positive points on one aspect but negative on others. For example, one alternative may be most profitable but requires heavy investment with long gestation period; another may be less profitable but also involves less risk. Moreover, there is no certainty about the outcome of any alternative because it is related with future and future is not certian.

5. Identification of Alternatives. Based on the organisational objectives and planning premises, various alternatives can be identified. The concept of various alternatives suggests that a particular objective can be achieved through various actions. For example, if an organisation has set its objective to grow further, it can be achieved in several ways like expanding in the same field of business or porduct line, diversifying in other areas, joining hands with other organisations or taking over another organisation, and so on. Within each category, there may be several alternatives. For example, diversification itself may point out the possibility of entering into one of the several fields. The most common problem with alternatives is not that of finding of alternatives only but to reduce the number of alternatives so that most promising ones may be taken for detailed analysis. Since all alternatives cannot be considered for further analysis, it is necessary for the planner to reduce in preliminary examination the number of alternatives which do not meet the minimum perliminary criteria. Preliminary criteria can be defined in several ways, such as minimum investment required, matching with the present business of the organisation, the criteria in terms of size of investment in new project and may not consider any project involving investment of less than Rs. 40 crores.

6. Choice of Alternative. After the evaluation of various alternatives, the most fit one is selected. Sometimes evaluation shows that more than one alternative is equally good. In such a case, a planner may choose more than one alternative. There is another reason for choosing more than one alternative. Alternative course of action is to be undertaken in future which is not constant. A course of action chosen keeping in view the various planning premises may not be ready with alternative, normally known as contingency plan, which can be implemennted in changed situations.

7. Establishing Sequence of Activities. After formulating basic and derivative plans, the sequence of activities is determined so that plans are put into action. Based on plans at various levels, it can be decided who will do what and at what time. Budgets for various periods can be prepared to give plans more concrete meaning for implementation.

TYPES OF PLANNING

The plans employed by various levels of management can be classified in a number of ways:

1. (a) Operational Planning. Operational plans are short range plans. They are usually made in a specific and detailed manner. They provide content and form to lone range plans. Operational planning is usally done at lower levels. Its primary concern is efficiency (doing things right) rather than effectiveness (doing the right things). Operational planning involves gathering information, evaluating alternatives, and choosing the most effective courses of action. It is usually guided by a set of standing single use and standing plans. Standing plans focus on organizational situations that recur repeatedly. Standing plans include policies, procedures and rules.

Single use plans are also used to guide managerial decisions and to obtain uniformity of action, but these purposes only for a specified period of time. They are specially developed to implement courses of action which are relatively unique and are unlikely to be repeated are designed to deal with novel situations and may never be major types of single use plans.

Operational planning is concerned with day to day operations and the focus is one short-run operating periods, that is, usually a year or a season. Without operating plans, the big picture provided by strategic plans would remain a blank outline. Usually the functional aspects of the production of goods and services are converted in operational plans. Market plans, production plans and financial plans are typical examples of operational planning.

(b) Tactical or Coordinative (Intermediate) Planning. Tectical plans are less detailed than the short range plans. They are concerned with implementing strategic plans by coordinating the work of different departments in the organization. They try to integrate various organizational units and ensure commitment to strategic plans. Based on the results obtained by implementing short range plans, a mid-term review is undertaken. A moving average is usually obtained and the success or failure of operational plans is assessed and the need for readjustment is indicated.

(c) Strategic Planning (Long-range Planning). The determination of how the organizational objectives will be achieved is referred to as long range strategy planning. Essentially, strategy is a plan of action that will define the way in which goals can be accomplished. Strategy determining the organization, overall character, missions and directions. It links the human and other resources of an organization, on the one hand, with the challenges and risks nosed by the outside world. On the other, strategic planning, generally speaking, cover a time frame extending five years or more into the future. In India companies in cement, petroleum, paper, petrochemical industries plan for a period of five years whereas tyre, chemicals and textile industries plan for three years.

2. Proactive *vs.* Reactive Planning. The statement that 'the best laid plans of mice and men often go astrays is certainly applicable in todays business world. Even before a plan sees the light of the day external and internal disturbsances force its modification of rejection. Intelligent managers recognize that unforeseen events can occur and they must attempt to anticipate these disruptions, and deal effectively with the new conditions these disruptions create. Proactive planning fills the holes created by unforeseen events, it forces managers to be dynamic, active and creative. Through proactive planning managers take the initiative, attempt to shape the future and create a more desirable environment.

Proactive planning is a philosophy, a way of thinking about managing the future. Research and experience have shown that organization that plan do and plan will, are more effective, efficient and profitable. In reactive planning we do not give consideration to what we desire the future to be like and as a result the future of the organization is left to the vagaries of societal forces.

3. Formal *vs.* Informal Planning. A formal plan can be defined as a written, documented plan developed through an identifiable process. When planners do not record their thoughts but carry them around in their minds. informal plans result in. In informal planning managers do not plan for contingencies and there is no provision for unanticipated situations. They merely wait for the lightning so strictly. Formal planning is hard mental work and it forces managers to observe the rule 'look before you leap' strictly. Informal planning promotes unhealthy tendencies like carelessness, and result in ineffective and inefficient employee performance.

4. Corporate Planning *vs.* Functional Planning. Functional planning is segmental in nature. Coordination problems often arise if productions, finance, marketing, manufacturing departments prepare their separate plans without a unified focus. Further, functional planning promotes 'components' mentality in executives; they fail to see the big picture and the impact of external forces on various activities of the departments. Corporate planning is integrative in nature. It has both micro and macro aspects *i.e.* provides for internal and external disturbances. It tries to integrate corporate goals with the individual goals. It takes the broad interests of the organization as a whole; integrates the various functional plans and provides meaningful direction to enterprise activities. The main purpose of corporate planning is "to determine the long term goals of a compnay as a whole and then to generate plans designed to achieve these goals bearing in mind probable changes in its environment." The above definition brings out four essential features of corporate planning: *(1)* Corporate planning is proactive planning; it provides for future contingencies. It tries to match organizational resources with environmental opportunities/threats (macro aspect). The primary purpose of corporate planning is to help the organization to affect rather than accept the future. *(2)* Corporate planning is concerned with long term goals of the organization. *(3)* It is planning for over all organizational perspective. It takes a long term view, and has an overall organizational perspective. It discourages *ad hocism* in executive thinking and action. It discourages "tunnel vision" on the part of functional heads and forces them to think and act in broad way taking the overall intersts of the organization into account. (4) The corporate plan is the synthesis of various functional plans.

NATURE OF PLANNING

As has been discussed in the foregoing section, planning invovles an attempt on the part of a manager to fix his mind on the course of action that he would adopt for the realisation of organisational objectives. From this the following points emerge highlighting the nature of planning:

(a) **Planning is an Intellectual Process.** 'Think before you leap' is a maxim that every manager is asked to take to heart. The emphasis on thinking before action points to the need for thorough planning before starting with any operation. The manager has to get at the relevant facts, marshall them and organise them and use them as the jumping board to envisage how best the objectives of the organisation can be attained. How far into the future a manager can see and with how much clarity will depends on his intellectual calibre. In thinking of objectives, and the alternative courses of action and above all in making decisions choosing certain alternatives, the planner goes through an intellectual process. The quality of planning will vary according to the quantity of the mind of the manager.

(b) **Planning is a Primary Function of Management.** Planning has been described as the most basic of all managerial functions. This is so because the manager decides upon the policies, procedures, programmes, projects, etc., before proceeding with the work. The other functions of management, *viz.*, organisation, staffing direction and control, can be performed only after the manager has done the necessary planning. In performing the function of controlling, the manager compares the actual performance with the plan and tries to analyse the reasons for such deviation. This helps him in revising and readjusting his plans. This means that the management process is a circular process beginning with planning and returning to planning for improvement and adjustment.

(c) **Planning is Goal-oriented.** All planning is linked up with certain goals and objectives. It follows therefore, that every plan "must contribute in some positive way to the accomplishment or group objectives." Planning has no meaning without being related to goals and objectives; it becomes an empty mental exercise if it does not keep the objectives of organiged activity in view.

(d) **Planning is Directed Towards Efficiency.** The concept of efficiency is implicit in planning. A plan is a course of action that shows promise of optimising return at the minimum expenses of inputs. In planning, the manager evaluates the alternatives of on the basis efficiency. A good plan should not only attain optimal relationship between output and input but should also bring the greatest deal of satisfaction to those implementing it.

(e) **Planning Pervades all Managerial Activity.** Planning is a function of every manager. Whatever be the nature of activity, management starts with planning. The character and sweep of planning will, of course, vary from one job to another depending upon his authority and the policies of the superiors. None, who does not plan, can really be called a manager. On this basis, some writers make a distinction between management (goal-setting and policy-making) and administration or supervision (execution and implementation). "The scope, extent, and imiportance of the nature of planning tend to decrease as we descend towards the lower levels of management and approach the point of execution of the plan."

Planning Premises

All managerial plans are based on certain assumptions which may be called 'planning premises'. Such premises constitute the group on which plans will stand. The suitability of the plans will depend upon the extent to which the management is able to formulate the premises correctly and realistically. If the premises of plans change, the plans too will have to be modified. In the context of business management the planning premises may be classified as *(a)* non-controllable premises, *(b)* semi-controllable premises, and *(c)* controllable premises.

(a) **Non-Controllable Premises.** These are assumptions about the economy, the political situations, the tastes of the people and such other factors as cannot be influenced and controlled through management policies and decisions. Even though the management cannot do anything about these factors, it must take them into account while planning for expension of the existing capacity. It must take into account the fact that the command policy in this regard is becoming increasingly restricted. If such a factor is not considered the plans will remain mere wishes.

(b) **Controllable Premises.** In chalking its plans, the management has also to decide what policies, procedures, rules, etc., it will be following over the future period and how these are likely to affect the plans of the enterprise. These factors could be called 'controllable premises' because these are subject to decisions of the management.

(c) **Semi-Controllable Premises.** These include assumptions about those factors which are only partially controllable through suitable management policies and deicsions but cannot be full controlled by the management. For example, industries demand the firm's share in the market, union-management relations or factors which must be considered partially as being given and partially as being subjected to decision-making on the part of the management. The plans for any business enterprise will naturally have to be based on proper assumptions with regard to these factors.

LIMITATIONS OF PLANNING

Planning as a management function is essential to every manager and every organisation but there are some practical problems in proper planning. Managers can do better if they are aware of these limitations so that they can take adequate precautions against them. Below are the major limitations to effective planning:

1. **Difficulty of Accurate Premising.** Planning exercise is undertaken under certain assumptions of future events which are determined by large number of factors in the environment. Thus a limiting factor in planning is the difficulty of formulating accurate premises. Since the future cannot be known with accuracy, premising is subject to a margin of error. Though this margin of error can bed minimised by making suitable forecast of future events, perfection cannot be expected. It is often suggested that since long-range planning requires peeping into the distant future and distant future is not certain, it is useless to undertake long-range planning. In fact this is a true to some extent and specially under two situations long-range planning cannot be undertaken : first, in the formative stage of the organisation; second, when the environment in

which the organisation operates is unstable and uncertain owing to social, technological and other changes.

2. **Problems of Rapid Change.** In a complex and rapidly changing environment, complications that make planning extremely difficult often magnify the succession of new problems. The problem of change is more complex in long-range planning that is short-range planning. Present conditions tend to weight heavily in planning, and by overshadowing future needs may some times result in error of judgment.

3. **Internal Inflexibilities.** Managers while going through the planning process have to work in a set of given variables. These variables often provide less flexibility in planning which is needed to cope up with the changes in future events. Such inflexibilities may be either internal to the organisation or may lie outside.

   (i) ***Policy and Procedural Inflexibility.*** Another internal inflexibility emerges because of orgainsational policies and procedures. Once these are established, they are difficult to change. Though these policies, procedures, and rules are meant to facilitate managerial actions by providing guidelines, they often tend to be too exacting and numerous that they leave very little scope for managerial initiative and flexibility. Since managers have to plan for future which is not static but changing, they often find themselves in great constraints. Such problems are more prominent in bureaucratic organisations where rules and procedures become more important than results.

   (ii) ***Psychological Inflexibilities.*** Psychological inflexibility is in the form of resistant to change. Managers and employees in the organisation may develop patterns of thought and behaviour that are hard to change. They look more in terms of present rather than future. For them, present is not only more certain but is also more

desirable and more real. They believe that 'if they do not take care of present, future will not be there'. For them, planning tends to accelerate change and unrest. Thus this approach works against planning because planning often depends on changes.

(iii) Capital Investment. In most cases, once funds are invested in fixed assets the ability to switch future course of action becomes rather limited, and investment itself becomes a planning premise. During the entire life of the fixed assets, this inflexibility continues unless the organisation can reasonably liquidate its investment or change its course of action, unless it can afford to write off the investment.

4. **External Inflexibilities.** Besides the internal inflexibilities, managers are confronted with many external inflexibilities and they do not have control over these. For example, managers have little or no control over social, economic, technological, and political forces. Whether these change quickly or slowly, they do stand in the way of effective planning. Three environmental factors generate infliexibilities for an organisational planning : political climate, trade unions, and technological changes.

(i) Technological Changes. The rate and nature of technology changes also present very definite limitations upon planning. An organisation is engaged in its process with a given technology. When there is a change in technology, it has to face numerous problems resulting into higher cost of production and less competitive competence in the market. However, the organisation cannot change its technology so frequently.

(ii) Trade Unions. The existence of trade unions, particulary those organised at the national level, tends to restrict freedom of planning. Apart from wages and other associated benefits, they affect the planning process by putting limitations on the work that can be undertaken by the organisation. They set up the work rule and productivity. To that extent, managers are not to make decisions of their choice.

(iii) ***Political Climate.*** Every organisation, to a greater or lesser degree, is faced with the inflexibility of the political climate existing at any given time. Attitudes of government towards business, taxation policy, regulation of business, etc., generate constraints on the organisational planning process. Government being the major supplier of certain raw materials, finances through financial institutions may affect the business organisations considerably.

5. **Failure of People in Planning.** Apart from the above factors, sometimes, people involved in planning process fail to formulate correct plans. There are many reasons why people fail in planning at the formulation level as well as implementation level. Some of the major reasons for failure are : lack of commitment to planning, failure to formulate sound strategies, lack of clear and meaningful objectives, tendency to overlook planning premises, failure to see the scope of plan, failure to see planning as a rational approach, excessive reliance on the past experience, lack of top management support, lack of adequate control techniques, etc. These personnel factors are responsible for either inadequate planning or wrong planning in the organisation.
6. **Times and Cost Factors.** Planning process is quite a costly and time consuming process. The various steps of planning may go as far as possible because there is no limit of precision in planning tools. Managers can spend unlimited amount of time in forecasting, evaluating alternatives, developing supporting plans, or attending other aspects of planning, if they do not have limitations of time and money. Planning process suffers because of time and cost factors. Time is a limiting factor for every manager in the organisation.

Besides times factor, planning is also limited because of cost factor. Planning cost increase if planning becomes more elaborate and formalised. Additional staff is to be appointed. Looking at the cost aspect, many people have commented that planning consumes more but contributes less. Thus planning cannot be undertaken beyond a certain level. It should be taken at a level where it justifies its cost. Apart from direct cost involved in manager's time, financial compensation for those who are involved in paper work, planning etc., planning may be costly to the organisation indirectly.

Factors for Making Planning Effective

Various limitations of planning as enumerated above should not lead one to believe that planning is unnecessary in the organisation, or it is the luxury that only few large organisation can afford. The fact is otherwise. It must be accepted that planning is an essential managerial function and should be given adequate emphasis. The question is not whether to plan or not, but the question is how well to plan. Therefore, managers should take adequate precautions to make planning acitvity more effective to gain its real contributions in realising organisational objectives. However, it is not sufficient to say that managers should take action to make planning effective, but they should be clear about what actions can be taken in this regard. following factors are important to make planning exercise more effective:

1. Initiative at Top Level. Planning to be effective must originate at top level. It must be supported by top management. In fact, in any organisation, the role of top management in planning process is quite unique and important. It is the top management which is responsible for the success or failure of any organisational process, and planning is no exception. For planning process, basic goals from which others stem must be organisation-wide and, therefore, goals must be set at the top management level. The example and drive of top management are the most important single force in the planning process. When top management rigorously reviews subordinates' programmes, it naturally stimulates planning interest throughout the organisation. Effective planning may start at the top level and get support from lower level managers. But this should not mean that subordinate managers can do nothing in initiating the planning process.

2. Communication of Planning Elements. Many planning efforts fail because managers do not really understand their goals and other planning premises which affect their planning efforts. Similarly lack of proper under-standing of organisational policies and strategies affects planning, particularly at the lower levels. In order to avoid this impediment, it is highly desirable that these aspects of planning are communicated properly. If planning division has been created, it can communicate planning aspects to various level managers. If no such division exists, there should be direct communication between various level managers whose planning efforts are directly related. While communicating, it should be borne in mind that information about planning should be specific and clear.

3. Establishing Climate for Planning. Managers should create a climate where every person in the organisation takes planning action. Every superior manager should remove obstacles to planning and present facilities for planning. This can be done by setting goals, establishing and publishing planning premises involving all managers in planning process, reviewing subordinates' plans and their performance, and ensuring that managers have appropriate staff assistance and information. All these steps add to recognising that planning will not occur unless it is forced and the facilities required to undertake planning are provided.

4. Participation in Planning Process. No doubt, top management can initiate planning process by providing goals and planning premises, effective planning can take place by the participation of subordinate managers. The best planning is likely to be done when managers are given opportunities to contribute to plans affecting areas over which they have authority. Participation in planning affecting managers' areas of authority at all levels through their being informed, contributing suggestions, and being consulted leads to their commitment, loyalty to planning, and enthusiasm to implement the plan.

5. An Open System Approach. Planning can be made effective by taking it as an open systems approach. It suggests that managers must take into account interactions with their total environment in every aspect of planning. Objective, a starting point in planning, should be set taking into account the various environemntal forces. Planning premises represent a clear recognition interfaces and interactions of plans with every element of the conditions and influence surrounding an organisation are many and complex. This fact should be recognised in the planning process.

STEPS INVOLVED IN PLANNING

Planning is a scientific process which is needed in every enterprise either small or big. The following steps are followed in the process of planning:

1. Determination of Objectives. To set the objectives is first step of business planning. The planning process starts with the setting of objectives. First of all, overall objectives are set, they are split into departmental, sectional and individual objectives. Overall organisational objectives give defections to the nature of all other plans of the major departments. Departmental objectives conform to the overall objectives. Thus, there is hierarchy of objectives in the organisation. As a guide the objectives decide the future course of action.

2. Determination of Limits of Planning. The third step of planning process or to fix the limits of planning. These limits should be determined by dividing into three parts. First those limits should be decided which can be controlled as policies of company development programme etc. Second, those limits should be decided which cannot be controlled as government policies, business circle, copulation of the country etc. Third, those limits should be decided which cannot be controlled halfly as price policy, selling field etc.

3. Forecasting. Forecasting is the second step of planning process. Forecasting is the basis of planning. So, to establish the basis is necessary for planning. These basis are established by forecasting. There are many things to be forecasted in the business as. what will be the situation of market, what will be the ratio of demand and supply, what will be investment cost of production, what will be the selling price? Whose will be the sale, what will be the wayes of workers, what will be the dividend policy, what will be the possibility of dearness and cheapness etc.

4. Developing Plans. After formulating the basic plan, various plans are derived for each department of the company so as to support the main plan. The derivative plans are developed in each area of the business to integrate objectives with all relevant policies, procedures, programmes and budgets, within the framework of basic plan. Examples of various directive plans are planning or buying raw material, for selling finished product, recruitment and training of personnel, developing new product etc.

5. Selection of Best Alternative. This is the fifth step of planning process, where best alternative is selected. The selection of best alternative is a very difficult task so it should be done with great care. This step is the step of decision in the planning process. After this, the work of planning starts, Sometimes, evaluation shows that more than one alternative is equally good. In such cases, more than one alternatives may be chosen for execution. If the situation changes and the plan chosen do not prove to be the best, the other alternative may be tried.

6. Establishing Sequence of Activities. Timing and sequence of activities are determined after reformulating basic and derivative plans, so that plans may be put into action. Timing is essential consideration in planning. It gives practical shape and concrete form to the programme. The starting and finishing times are fixed for each piece of work, so as to indicate when and within what time that work is to be commenced and completed. Bad timings of programmes result in their failure. To maintain a symmetry, bad timings of programmes result int heir failure. To maintain a symmetry the performance and a smooth flow of work, the sequence of operation shaped are arranged carefully by giving priorities to some work in preference to others.

7. Follow up Action. Formulating plans and chalking out of programmes are not sufficient, unless follow up action is provided to see the plans so prepared and programmes chalked out are being carried out in accordance with the plan and to see whether these are not kept into cold storage. It is also required to see whether the plan is working well in the present situation. If conditions have changed, the plan should also be modified accordingly to meet the changed situation. If the current plan has become outdated or inoperative it should be replaced by another plan.

8. Formation and Execution of Policies-Methods. In this step of planning process, policies and methods are formulated keeping in mind the changing canditions and human behaviour. These policies coordinate the planning with the changing conditions and needs. These policies generally are used in short term planning.

The plan should be communicated to all persons concerned in the organisation. Its objectives and course of action must be clearly defined leaving no ambiguity in the minds of those who are responsible for its execution. Planning is effective only when the persons involved work in a team spirit and all are committed to these objectives, policies, programmes, strategies envisaged in the plan.

PLANNING PREMISES

Plans are prepared for future. But future is uncertain. Therefore, management makes certain assumptions about the future. These assumptions should not be based upon hunch, or guesswork. Rather these should be developed through scentific forecasting of future events. The assumptions about future derived from forcasting and used in planning are known as planning premises. According to Koontz and 'Donnel' "Planning premises are the anticipated environment in which plans are expected to operate. They include assumptions or forecasts of the future and known conditions that will affect the course of plans, such as prevailing policies and existing company plans that control the basic nature of supporting plans."

Planning premises are the building blocks on which the super-structure of planning is based. These premises relate to the strategic or crucial and limiting factors. Consistent and coordinated plans can be prepared on the basis of good planning premises. One of the major purposes of premises is to facilitate the planning process by guiding, directing simplifying and reducing the degree of uncertainty in it. Premises guide planning. Developing sound premises is vital for successful planning.

Planning premises may be classified as under:

1. **Controllable and Uncontrollable Premises.** Those premises which are entirely within the control and realm of management are known as controllable premises. These include the policies, programmes and rules of the enterprise. Premises over which an enterprise has absolutely no control are uncontrollable premises. War, natural calmities, new inventions population trends, etc. are examples of such premises. Some premises are such over which the management has partial control, *e.g.*, union-managemnet relations, supply position in the industry, etc. Such premises are called semi-controllable premises.
2. **External and Internal Premises.** External premises are those which lie outside the firm. These are of many kinds: *(a)* General busines environment including economic, technological, political and social conditions, *(b)* product market consisting of the demand and supply forces for the product or service, and *(c)* the factor market for land, labour, capital, etc. Internal premises refer to the factors within the enterprise. These include sales forecast, capital investment in plant and equipment, competence of management personnel skill of labour force, etc.
3. **Tangible and Intagible Premises.** Tangible premises are those which can be quantified *e.g.*, money, units of production etc. On the other hand, intangible premises refer to the qualitative factors like pubic relations, company's reputation, employee morale, etc. These cannot be expressed in quantitative terms. However, such premises play an important role in planning.

TYPES OF MANAGEMENT PLANS (COMPONENTS OF PLANNING)

Depending on their use, management plans may be classified into two broad categories as shown in the following figure:

Plans

- Multi-use plans
  - Objectives
  - Strategies
  - Policies
  - Procedures
  - Rules
- Single-use plans
  - Programmes
  - Budgets
  - Schedules
  - Projects
  - Methods

Fig. Type of Plans

Multi-use or standing plans are used repeatedly in situations of a similar nature. They are long term in nature and represent standing answer to recurring problems. They serve as ready guides to action. These plans help in trafining of employees and in job rotation. They enable the performation of work by persons with less experience. These plans help to save time and effort of executives. They facilitate delegation of authority, co-ordination and control. Objectives, strategies, policies, procedures and ruels and standing plans or repeated use plans. Standing plans facilitate delegation of authority to lower levels. Standing plans help to operationalise goals of an organisation. They provide a ready reference for executive. If well-communicated and well understood, they ensure uniformity of action. Standing plans become the habit pattern for guiding and specifying human behaviour in organisations.

Single-use or ad hoc plans are formulated to meet novel, unique and non-repetitive situations. A single use plan is used up once the objectives are achieved. It is of short duration and non-recurring in nature. Programmes, budget, schedules, projects and methods are examples of single-use plans.

DECISION-MAKING

Management is compulsorily a process of Decision Making. To take the decisions is a very important responsibility of a manager. Therefore, management is also called the process of decision Making. A manager is faced with many alternatives for the solution of a given problem. To decide the best alternative from these alternatives is called Decision Making. The success of a Manager depends to a great extent upon his ability to take the decision under different conditions. The term 'Decision Making' has been defined as under:

According to **G.L.S. Shackle**, "Decision Making is the focal creative physic event where knowledge, thoughts, feeling and imagination are fused into action.

According to **George R. Terry**, "Decision Making is the selection based on some criteria from two or more possible alternatives."

According to **D.E. Mc. Farland**, "A decision is an act of choice wherein an executive forms a conclusion about what must be done in a given situation."

According to **R.S. Davar**, "Decision Making can be defined as the selection based on some criteria of one particular alternative from two or more possible alternatives. To decide means "to cut off" or in practical context, "to come to conclusion."

On the basis of above definitions, it may be concluded that Decision Making is the selection of best possible alternative from among the various alternatives available for the solution of a given problem. It is an act wherein a manager arrives at a conclusion about what must be done in a particular situation. It involves the choice of a course of action to achieve pre-determined objectives.

CHARACTERISTICS OF DECISION MAKING

A careful study of the above noted definitions of Decision Making reveals the following characteristics:

1. **A Job of Top Manager.** Decision Making is the responsibility of Top Manager of a business enterprise.

Although various decisions are taken at different levels of Management in the course of business activities but the most important decisions are taken by the Top Manager.

2. **Selection of Best Alternative.** Decision Making is a process of selecting the best possible alternative from among the various alternatives available for the solution of a given problem. Thus, the need of decision arises only when more than one alternatives are available for a particular action.
3. **A Human and Social Process.** Decision Making is a human and social process. It involves all the human activities which are necessary for taking a decision on an aspect. It involves making discretion and judgment.
4. **Uncertainty and Risk.** Decision Making involves uncertainty and risk also because the decisions are taken in regard to the activities which will take place in future. It is very difficult to forecast the future activities with complete accuracy. Therefore, the decisions cannot be cent percent correct and accurate.
5. **Rational Selection.** Decision Making is the process to select the best alternative in a rational manner. It involves the evaluation of available alternatives and then to select the best possible alternative.
6. **Decisions are Means.** A very important characteristic of decisions is that the decision are not an end in themselves, they are only the means of end. The object of Decision Making is to achieve the pre-determined objectives of the business and industrial enterprise.
7. **Decisions may be Positive or Negative.** A decision is not necessary to be positive. It may be negative also. A decision may be taken to do or not to do a particular activity.

NATURE OF DECISION MAKING

The process of Decision Making involves the selection of best possible alternative from among the available alternatives for doing a particular work. Ultimate object of Decision Making is to ahcieve the pre-determined targets of the business and industrial enterprise. A decision is generally expressed as a policy or as a rule or as an order or as a directive of the enterprise. A decision may also be expressed as to consider a problem or not consider it or to consider it after sometime. Nature of Decision Making can be expressed as follows:

1. **Commitment.** A decision reflects the commitment of the person who takes the decision. The person taking the decision is committed to implement it and to prepare the plans according to the decision taken. All the business activities are performed in accordance with the decision taken by the Top Management of the business enterprise.
2. **Birth to New Decisions.** Some are the decisions which create the need of many other decisions. Some decisions are taken to overcome the defects of the decision taken earlier. Sometimes, the decisions are taken to remove the variations of actual results from decisions.
3. **Process of Continuity.** Every incident of past, present and future affects the decision in one way or the other. If some problems have arisen in the past, the alternative solutions of that problem may be considered at present and the best alternative is selected, the alternative so selected is used in the future. Not only this, a decision creates many other decisions. In addition to this, sometimes a decision in the result of some other decisions. Thus, decisions are inter-related and inter-dependent. Thus, it is said that Decision Making is a process of continuity.
4. **Rationality.** Decision Making process is a mental process which involves the rationality of best possible alternative from among the available alternatives. It involves the choice of best possible course of action and it is performed only by human beings.
5. **Evaluation.** It is not sufficient and enough to take the decisions. Decisions must be followed and actual results

must be evaluated so that the implementation of decision may be ensured. If the decisions are not followed and evaluated, the objects of enterprise may not be achieved, however, the best decisions might have been taken.

TECHNIQUES OF DECISION MAKING

Decision Making is the most important task of a manager in a business and an industrial enterprise. If Decision Making process is divorced from the functions of Management, the management process will be meaningless, useless and impractical. The fact is that a manager is a person who takes decision.

While establishing the business enterprise, many decisions have to be taken as to. What will be the nature of business? What will be the amount of capital invested in the business? What will be the area of activities of business? etc. After the establishment of business enterprise, many decisions are required to be taken for the successful operation of enterprise as to. What should be the quantity of production? What should be the quality of production? What should be the quantity of raw-materials to be purchased? Where the sales must be made? What price should be fixed? What should be the policy of credit sales? How many and of what qualifications should the employees be appointed? What should be personnel policies? etc. In addition to all these, some more decisions are to be taken as to. Whether the production of a particular commodity should be discontinued? Whether a particular branch should be closed? Whether a particular area of sales should be dropped? Whether the business should be dissolved? etc.

According to Peter F. Drucker,"Every activity of Management depends upon decisions." Prof. Earnest Dale has connected upon the Importance of Decision Making in the words, "Management decisions mean the decisions which are taken in the course of managerial activities such as planning, organisation, direction, staffing, renovation and control etc." Briefly speaking, main function of a manager is to take the managerial decisions and the structure of managerial activities depends upon the managerial decisions. In the words of Melvin T.

Copeland,"Management is essentially a decision making process and authority is responsibility for making decisions and for ascertaining that the decisions are carried out. In business, whether the enterprise be large or small, changes in conditions occur, shifts in personnel take place, unforeseen contingencies arise. Moreover, just to get the wheel started decisions must be made.

Techniques of Decision Making

There are two techniques of Decision Making: *(I)* Traditional Method; and *(II)* Scientific Method. These methods are described in detail as follows:

(I) Traditional Method. This method of Decision Making is based upon the method of symptomatic diagnosis. As in the old time a doctor used to treat his patients on the basis of symptoms of disease. In the same manner, the business managers decide some definite solution for some definite problems on the basis of their experiences. Whenever that situation arises, they take the decision according to their pre-determined solution. But this method of Decision Making is based on scientific analysis. Now-a-days this method has become unpopular.

(II) Scientific Method. Under this method of Decision Making, a scientific process is applied for taking decisions. Drucker has described this process as under:

1. ***Ascertaining the Problem.*** The problem must be ascertained carefully before deciding its solution. Therefore, the very first task in the process of Decision Making under this method is to understand the problem fully and thoroughly because unless we understand our porblem, we cannot solve it. For example, if the sales of an enterprise are decreasing and the decisions are to be taken to increase the sales, it becomes necessary that the reasons for the fall in sales must be diagnosed. There may be many reasons for this fall as. fall in quality of the products, increase in price, fall in customer services, lack of advertisement, lack of cooperation of salesmen, heavy competition, etc. Before

taking any decision for this problem, the reason for the fall in sales must be established and then the efforts must be made to solve the problems. Therefore, before making decisions, the problem and the reasons of problem must be carefully examined.

2. ***To Analyse the Problem.*** After understanding the problem second important step of the decision making process is to analyse the problem. For the analysis problem, the cooperation of research and development department should be taken. Analysis problem involves the following:

   (i) How the decision must be made?

   (ii) Who should take the decision?

   (iii) What information would be required for taking decision?

   (iv) Who must be consulted before making decision?

   (v) Who must be informed of the decision?

   (vi) How can the required information be obtained?

3. ***Development of Alternative Solutions.*** After ascertaining and analysing the problem, all the possible alternatives are developed for the solution of problem. All the possible alternatives may be as follows:

   (i) To discontinue the product.

   (ii) To reduce the selling price of product.

   (iii) To improve the quality of product.

   (iv) To change the look or packing of product so that it may attract the attention of customers.

   (v) To arrange for more effective distribution of the product.

   (vi) To provide better sale service to the consumers.

   (vii) To advertise the product incentively.

4. ***Selection of the Best Alternative.*** This is the most important step of the process of Decision Making. After developing

all the possible alternatives and studying them thoroughly an attempt is made to select the best possible alternative. While making such selection, some certain points must be considered. Peter F. Drucker laid down the following criteria for such selection:

(i) *Economy of Efforts.* We must try to choose the alternative in which we can get the maximum results by putting our minimum efforts.

(ii) *Risk.* Risk is an essential part of the business activities and every decision involves some or the other risk. The only thing we can do and we must do is to minimise the risk.

(iii) *Limitation of Resources.* While making a decision the availability of resources to implement the decision must be duly considered. If we take a decision which cannot be implemented because of the lack of resources it is the limitation of resources that must be considered and the decision must be taken keeping in view the available resources.

(iv) *Timing.* Timing is a very important factor while making a decision. We must take the right decision at the right time. A decision taken at a wrong time is useless even if it is best. Therefore, the time element must be considered.

5. ***To Convert the Decision into Effective Action.*** A decision is not an end in itself. It is only a means to achieve an end. It is of no use to take even the best possible decision if it is not implemented. Therefore, all the efforts must be made for getting the decision implemented. For such implementation, the following procedure may be adopted:

(i) The acceptance of employees must be obtained on the particular decision so that they may contribute their whole-hearted efforts to implement it. All the necessary steps must be taken to implement it.

(ii) Managerial executive should be delegated required authority to implement the decisions.

(iii) Effective communication system must be adopted to communicate the decision to the concerned employees.

6. ***Following-up the Decision.*** Decision Making process is not completed if the decisions are not effectively followed. It will be of hardly any use to the enterprise if the decisions are taken and implemented but not followed. The effectiveness and the uses of decisions can be evaluated only if it is properly followed. Actual results must be compared with the decision made and the points of variations must be determined.

DECISION-MAKING THEORY

Decision making is a kind of commitment, a resolution to do or not to do, an act to adopt or to reject an attitude. Decision making is a part of everyday life. Whether you are at a board meeting or in the play ground, you are almost constantly making decisions, sometimes working on several at the same time. There may be major or minor but some of these might have proved to be effective decisions, viz, appropriate, timely and acceptable. Some of your decisions might have been wrong, but you knew that there was something worse than a few wrong decisions and that was indecision. It could probably be shown that if the manager of a telephone company ordered ten telephone poles removed and an underground system installed using different locations, The carrying out that order could involve 10 thousand decisions made by 100 workers located at 15 points. The decision to move the poles would probably also require some consideration of the social, legal, economic and physical facts of the environment.

In the decision process the attitudes are always involved because attitudes often develop unconsciously, they are hard to see part of the decision-making process until decisions are actually made. For example, many men in the business world today resist the idea that women should hold managerial or executive positions. Social and legal pressures currently being brought to bear on such resistance have had something to do with changes in business attitude and organisational policy. If attitudes continue to change, we can expect to see many more women in top managerial positions in near future.

While taking decisions we should keep the six fundamentals *i.e.* ACTION.

A - Analyze the problem and gather data

C - Consider the alternative solution

T - Take action; select a solution

O - On going evaluation of the solution.

N - Need for change; consider the need for modification of the original decision.

(1) Analyse the Problem. Problem can be defined as obstacles that prevent the achievement of goals or purposes. Often, the surface problem is only a symptom of a more important problem. For example having a fever is a symptom of something more serious. perhaps a cold, the flu, or even pneumonia. Similarly, in a company with rapid employee turnover, The turnover itself is not the real problem; it is a symptom of more serious trouble. The question that-needs to be asked is; why is there so much employee turnover? Attempting to cure a symptom usually does not cure the cause. An asprin may bring down the fever, but it will not cure the illness. Similarly, a retirement programme may encourage some employees to stay on the job, but it will not cure their desire to leave. It is also necessary to delve deeply into a situation to locate the real problem and define it. For example, a supervisor may believe that he or she is confronted with a problem of conflicting personalities in the department. After checking into the situation, the supervisor may find that the problem is not one of personalties at all; rather, the work functions and specific responsibilities of each employee have been outlined clearly. Once the problem is defined, it must be analyzed in order to be solved. Collecting information for use in analysis is sometimes recommended as the first step in good decision making, but untill the problem has been identified and defined, you will not know what to look for. What somtimes happens is that the problem has to be redefined and reanalyzed as more information is found, because the new information casts so much light on the nature of the original problem that its original boundaries are no longer accurate. First of all look to find out the problem not the solution.

(2) Consider the Alternative Solution. During decision making there is need to learn, to think about all possible alternatives. Even when one of the available alternatives is desirable, it is better to have choices than to be left with no choice at all. Doing nothing is also a decision, it can be worthwhile or it can be fatal. The auto industry's failure: *(1)* to make design changes, *(2)* to reduce production during an economic slow down and *(3)* to reduce the number of plants are examples of doing nothing. Brainstorming is one of the best known methods for developing alternatives to problems. The free wheeling, receptive atmosphere of a brain-storming session often produces workable solutions.

When more than one person is involved in making decision, it is often a challenge to arrive at a solution with a minimum of conflict. For example, suppose that the sales personnel of a cosmetics firm insists on a particular kind of packaging for a new product because of its eye-catching appeal. The production department, however, is firmly opposed to this packaging on the grounds of expense and difficulty of manufacture. Both groups are right, at least within their respective areas of concern. Solution to this kind of conflict are usually plentiful as soon as the parties involved agree to explore alternative choices together.

(3) Take Action. After the alternative solutions have been developed, the probable desirable and undesirable conseqences of each should be tested mentally. The selection must be the best solution from the point of view of time and energy as well as money. The decision makers selection will probably be based on a combination of factors, such as experience, intuition, advice, experimentation and computer forecasts. Many decisions are based on experimentation. When experimentation is not too costly, it is worth following. Even on a small scale, experimentation is almost always justified by good results. Moving employees around according to specific skills, changing work schedule or changing the location of desks in a department to see if production rises or falls are examples of small scale experimentation, which can sometimes yield surprising results. When experimentation is not possible the decision maker must select an alternative based on the most objective forcasting possible. the premise of strategic analysis, for example that decisions are different because the initial objectives, assumptions and expectations are defferent.

(4) Ongoing Evaluation. All ramifications of a chosen solution can not be seen readily until the plan is put into action. Even as the solution is being tried, you and your subordinates will see ways in which to improve the implementation plan. On going evalution is a necessity in developing a plan and the key word in this stage is "feed back". You will need to solicit feed back or advice, openly from employees working on the project as well as from your peers and your superiors.

(5) Implement a Solution. When a plan has been accepted, it must be put into action carefully and watched closely to ensure that it works.

General Foods Corporation provided a good example of planning for implementation when it decided to close down four plants in four states and combine operations in one new, larger plant in yet another state. About 2000 employees were notified of the move by letter a year before the move was scheduled to take place. A few months later, a policy statement on transfer and termination was calculated to all employees, indicating the company's intention to transfer those employees who wish to move. Transferred employees were given job preference over newly hired people.

(6) Need for Change. After the solution has been tried, it must consider the need for modifying the original decision. New information, experience and new ideas will help to shape the project into a better plan. However, after the plan has been tried and improved, the final analysis may be that the decision was a poor one. We must be ready for that possibility, profit from the mistake and move on to another solution.

As much time can be spent in refining our decision as we spend in analyzing the problem and collection of data. Whether it involves a professional goal or new methods of routing manufactured goods, a decision can have a long-lasting effect on us. The time spent on the refinement of the decision is often well worth it. Remember when you have a big decision to make, think of ACTION, analyze the problem, consider alternatives, Take action, implement the soultion, make the on going evaluation, and make necessary changes.

STEPS IN CONTROLLING PROCESS

According to Allen, "Controlling refers to the evaluation of the performance of those who are responsible for executing the plans agreed upon" and includes controlling adherence to plans and appraising performance against predetermined yardsticks or criteria. The work of the manager in controlling involves four specific activities or there are four basic steps in control process. They are:

(i) Setting performance standards or criteria

(ii) Measuring work in progress or checking on performance

(iii) Evaluating and interpreting results or performance

(iv) Taking corrective action.

1. Setting Performance Standards or Criteria. The first step in the direction of performing the controlling function is to set standards or criteria against which to judge results or one's performance. A criterion is an evaluative standard which can be used to measure a person's performance, attitudes, motives, etc. For example, the criterion to measure a person's performance might be sale figures, quantity of output, profits earned, readership or an advertisement or any other measure of accomplishment. A performance standard is a measure of acceptable performance and helps in differentiating between good work and poor work.

We have read that while performing planning function, a manager is required to determine objectives and goals, decide policies, procedures and course of action to be followed to achieve those overall goals. Again, these objectives are split and divided into subgoals and targets to be accomplished by various departments or individuals and are expressed in terms of quality, output, sales, costs, time schedules or desired results etc. These can be used as standards to assess the performance. In other words, the performance standards are based on objectives, policies, programmes and budgets as envisaged in planning. Thus objectives and goals set up in the planning become standards for evaluating performance in the control process.

The performance standards may be tangible or intangible. Tangible standards are those criteria which can be masured physically, that is, which are expressed in physical or monetary terms such as quantities, time spent, expenses, costs, sales, profits. Intangible standards are the standards which cannot be expressed in physical or numerical terms such as image of the company, goodwill of customers, a high morale etc. The performance standards may be tangible or intangible, specific or vague but every one concerned must understand well what results are desired. For effective controlling, the performance criteria or standards must have certain characteristics such as :

(1) Standards should be simple, understandable and acceptable yardsticks for measurement of work. These should be discriminating.

(2) Standards should be valid, reliable and representative.

(3) Standards should be relevant and consistent with the overall objectives of the enterprise.

(4) Standards should be realistic and achievable.

(5) These should be acceptable to job analyst, employees, management.

(6) Standards should be flexible and not rigid.

(7) Standards should be identified with individual reponsibility. Only then, they can serve as standards of accountability.

(8) Standards should be uncontaminated and bias-free.

(9) Standards should be interrelated and consistent from one situation to another.

It must be noted that a manager has got his own limitations and he cannot assess all aspects of performance. Therefore he needs to select only a few standards that may give him adequate information about he progress of the work. Thus he needs to set certain standards at strategic control points. While selecting strategic standards, a manager must also determine the time when these standards are to be used or applied. Timeliness and inexpensiveness are other characteristics affecting performance. Checking of work at proper time promotes performance whereas belated checking or exercise of control can adversely affect the performance as corrective action cannot be taken when the time has passed. '*A stitch in time saves nine*', so goes the saying.

2. Measuring Work in Progress or Checking on Performance. The second step in controlling process is measuring the work in progress, recording it and comparing it with the predetermined goals or desired results. This step involves checking the performance and comparing actual performance with the standards expected. Measurement, in fact, in the communication medium for keeping management informed of performance against standard. This step consists of checking whether established methods, procedures and techniques are complied with. Checking is done by direct observation and personal contact, by inspection, by check lists, or with the help of written reports or summaries. Effective measurement of actual performance also requires its accurate reporting. The actual performance must be reported to be persons who can take corrective steps.

Measuring work in progress or assesing performance in the light of established standards or desired results is a continuous function of a manager which he may have to perform periodically, say weekly or monthly or quarterly, as may be the case.

3. Evaluating or Interpreting Results or Performance. This step is an extension of the second step and consists of comparing the actual performance or observed results with the established standards or set goals and finding the deviations, if any. This suggests that while checking performance, a manager should concentrate on those cases where performance deviates from the establsihed standard. Exceptional cases need more attention.

In this step, a manager is required to analyse and interpret performance and results. Evaluation requires comparison of actual performance and results with the predetermined standards, identification of deficiencies or discrepancies, and also of the cases of such deviations. Interpretation of results also includes why variances have occurred in the results. Corrective action cannot be taken unless reasons for deviation between actual perfomance and desired performance and found out. The cause of deviation may be wrong premises or errors in planning. Again causes may be controllable *i.e.* which can be rectified by the management and uncontrollable, that is, which are beyond the power of management.

4. Taking Corrective Action. The fourth step in the process comprises of taking corrective action. When the acutal performance or results achieved are not in conformity with the desired standards that is, when there is deviation between the actual performance and standard performance evisaged in the plan, it calls for corrective action so as to accomplish enterprise goals. It is very important that performance is evaluated regularly so that timely action may be taken to rectify the situation. No specific corrective action can be suggested unless reasons for the occurrence of deviations are known. The reasons for gaps between the actual performance and desired performance may be errors in planning, wrong premises, faulty forecasts, improper issuance of directions or instructions, negligence of laxity on the part of employees, poor quality of raw materials, machine breakdown, power failure or short supply of power, employees grievances or long standing demands, so on and so forth. It is the responsibility of the manager to take necessary action to put the work to the desired course. Corrective action closes the gap between planning and controlling and leads to a higher level of performance. Corrective action may consist of revision of plan, changes in organisation, changes is staffing, improvement of working conditions, provision of positive incentives, supply of good raw material, immediate repair or replacement of machinery, changes in methods, or even establishment of new feasible standards, depeneding upon the requirements of the prevailing situation. If deviations occur again, additional corrective steps will have to be taken. Thus controlling is an ongoing process.

6. Integration of Long-term and Short-term Plans. To be effective, it is necessary that both long term and short-term plans are fully integrated in which short-term plans should be taken as contributing to long-term plans. If managers emphasise only short-term plans, they cannot set direction for their future course of action. Long-term and short-term plans can best be integrated if the latter is prepared in the light of the former.

FEATURES OF MANAGERIAL CONTROL

1. Controlling is Based on Planning. Planning and controlling are interrelated functions. It is planning which provides base for controls. Planning sets objectives, goals, policies, programmes and courses of action to be followed and fulfilled. Controlling is essential to ensure that these are implemented and accomplished properly in accordance with what is planned. Without effective controlling, plans will remain pipedreams or hollow hopes. Effective implementation of plans requires effective controlling. Controlling is essential counter part to planning. Without corresponding control, plans cannot be effective.

2. It is an Important Function of Management. The management process is not complete without it. A manager is given the responsibility of showing desired results of activities entrusted to him. For this purpose he has been given the responsibility and authority to use organisation's resources, both men and material and he is accountable for their efficient use in the achievement of the desired goals. This requires effective controlling. It is intrinsically interwoven with all other functions of management. It is an essential part of total managerial process and affects other managerial functions as well.

3. Controlling is Pervasive Function. It is not merely the function of chief executive only. It is the duty of every manager to see that the activities entrusted to him are accomplished properly as expected and yield desired results. For reaching desired goals, a manager needs to exercise control over things and actions under his charge. This function is to be performed by managers at all levels.

4. Controlling is a Forward-looking Process. Its main aim is to assess the work in progress against expected standards, to find deviations, if any, and to take corrective action for future. It can rectify the past failings or under-achievements. Past is a thing of the past. Controlling helps in reporting current deviations so that proper and effective action is taken in time to correct the situation. Providing post-mortem report is not its functions. However, a manager can learn a lot from the past experience and failings, and about the reasons for the same. This may help in taking corrective action in the circumstances in future. Control is thus forward-looking.

5. Controlling is Action-oriented. In performing this function, a manager is required to measure the work in progress against expected performance, find the deviations and take corrective action to reach the goals. Therefore, control cannot be obtained without action. It is a process which guides activity towards predetermined goal. It involves a number of activities. It is a dynamic process.

6. Controlling is a Continuous Process. A manager requires regular periodic reports and information regarding status of work and the results that have been achieved and may have to take corrective action frequently. Moreover there is need of continuous review of results and standards. It is a never-ending process. Machines, tools, and equipment and frequent inspections.

ELEMENTS OF CONTROL

Managerial control involves four basic steps. The manager establishes the standard of performance to ensure that performance is in accordance with the plans. Then the manager will measure the performance and compare it with the predetermined standards. This will lead the manager to know whether the performance has come up to the expected standards or if there is any deviation. Following are the elements of control:

(a) Establishing Standards.

(b) Measurement of Performance.

(c) Performance Appraisal.

(d) Corrective Action.

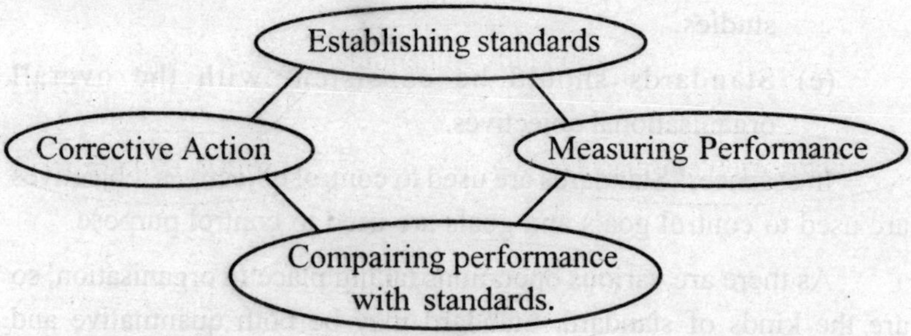

Fig.

(A) Establishing Standards. Standards represent criteria for measurement of performance of different departments or individuals. They are expressions of goals of the enterprise or the department in such terms that the actual accomplishment of assigned duties can be measured against them. Standards may be tangible or intangible, vague or specific. But they must be so expressed that people concerned understand them, and that accomplishment of assigned duties can be measured against them. Standards relating to factors like employee morale, loyalty, results expected of a training programme and public relation cannot be generally stated in quantifiable terms.

Standards should be accurate, precise, acceptable and workable. Standards should be flexible, *i.e.*, capable of being changed when the circumstances require so. Standards should not be based merely on past performace. A standard is bound to fail if it based on records of past performance which show either too high or too low achievement. Therefore, standards should be based on scientific analysis. In addition, they should possess the following characteristics:

(a) Standards should be capable of achievement with reasonable amount of cost effort and time.

(b) Standards should not be rigid. They should be capable of being changed whenever the need arises.

(c) Standards should concentrate at results and not at procedures.

(d) As far as possible, standards should be expressed in quantitative terms and based on the result of work measurment carried with the help of time and motion studies.

(e) Standards should be consistent with the overall organisational objectives.

In essence, "Standards are used to control objectives, objectives are used to control goals and goals are used to control purpose.

As there are various operations taking place in organisation, so are the kinds of standard. Standard may be both quantitative and qualitative. Performance standards may be generally summarized into four categories. quantity, quality time and cost. Standards therefore are expressed in physical and monetary terms, sometimes are expressed in intangible forms like objective of fair growth, goodwill, high morale etc.

Basic steps in establishing standards is to identify and locate the strategic control points. These have a number of salient features:

(i) Central points must be comprehensive and economical. They are comprehensive in the sense they include all sub-operations in the operation. Economy is also sought because each and every item produced need not be checked or verified.

(ii) A central point is established for every key operation or event. For example in a factory timekeeper should check the time of a worker's entry into the factory. As far as the punctuality is concerned the gate is the strategic and central point.

(iii) Strategic points are genrally balanced in the sense equal importance is given to both qualitative and quantitative factors. Marketing and leadership should receive equal weight in setting standards.

(B) Measurement Performance. The second element of control is concerned with the measurement of actual performance of the unit under control. Without having information about the current operations or actually performance, a manager cannot exercise control. It is the actual performance which is to be compared with standards of performance to decide about further action. The management should not depend upon guess-work as far as meeting of standards is concerned. It should measure the actual performance and compare it with the standards. The quantitative measurement should be done in cases where standards have been set in numerical terms. This will make evaluation easy and simple. In other cases, the performance should be measured in terms of qualitative factors. In case of industrial relations manager, performance can be measured in terms of attitude of workers, frequency of strikes and morale of workers. Again, attitude and morale of workers are not capable of being measured quantitatively. They have to be measured qualitatively.

(i) What to Measure. It is the performance that has to be measured. Manager has to measure that work against which appropriate standards are set. Before proceeding he should check himself whether he is on the right track.

(ii) How to Measure. Measurement sometimes poses a threatening challange to the managers. It may be quick simple to establish standards and measure easily the performance in highly technical tasks. But as the task becomes less technical it is not easy either to set standards or to measure the performance, less technical activities are hard to measure.

(iii) The Technique of Measurement. The generally used techniques are personal observation, management by exception, sampling managerial accounting and appraisal by results:

(a) Personal Observation. This method is widely used. According to Henry Sisk "a supervisor is able to judge output by observing the pace of his workers quality and an estimate of moral and attitudes results from

seeing employees, listening to their spontaneous remarks and obtaining responses to questions.

(b) *Sampling.* Manager picks certain items at random and ensures the place of work and supervises at random the work operations. Sampling simplifies the managers task.

(c) *Management by Exception.* The essence of the management by exception is that only exceptional matters are brought to the attention of the executives. It is a system of identification and communication that signals the manager. When his attention is needed; conversely, it remains silent when his attention is not required.

(d) *Managerial Accounting and Computer Science.* Management accounting besides providing information for purposes; is now a days entering into the control evaluations. Managerial accounting generates much objective information and it has become a major method of measurement in control process.

(e) *Appraisal by Results.* It is relatively soft approach, and if carefully implemented, combines the behavioural, contingency and modern management into an effective evaluation approach in controlling the organisation. Appraisal by results is diagnostic in character and concentrates on ends rather than means.

(iv) ***How to Solve the Problem of Measurement in Less Technical and Qualitative Jobs.*** Managers are to resort to certain vague standards in qualitative jobs. For example, to measure the performance of a financial advisor, a standard may be the financial health; similarly, the task of labour relations officer can be measured in terms of dealing and behaviour of trade union, absence of strikes, increased enthusiasm and productivity etc.

(v) ***When to Measure.*** It is a matter of general principle that measurement and evaluation are done in the past sense, *i.e.*, after the task if accomplished. Always this is not so however. Measurement of work may be done even during the performance, and certain adjustments are made in the case of production of certain commodities. Sometimes performance may be checked on the completion of each phase in the production. In the case of assembling task, each part is checked before assembling.

(C) Performance Appraisal. Performance appraisal for the purpose of control involves comparing of actual performance with the predetermined standards. Comparison is easy where standards have been set quantitatively as in production and marketing. In other cases, where results are intangible and cannot be measured quantitatively, direct personal observation, inspection and reports are a few methods which can be used for evaluation. The evaluation will reveal deviations from the set standards. The evaluator should point out the defects or deficiencies in performance and investigate the causes responsible for these.

All deviations need not be brought to the notice of top management. Those deviations should be brought to the notice of top management which are too high. A range of deviations should be established beyond which the attention of top management is warranted. Only such cases should be reproted up which pinpoint exceptional situations. This is what is known as 'management by exception'. According to Dale, the control reports should meet three criteria. Firstly, control reports must produce figures that are truly comparable from one period to another and from one section of the business to another. Secondly, they must be coordinated so that they not only portray the results in different sections of the business, but also make plain the reasons why the business is or is not doing so well as could be expected. Finally, they must be presented in such form that the manager can get the bird's eyeview.

(D) Corrective Action. When significant deviations from standards are detected, corrective action is obviously called for. This involves taking certain decisions by the management like replanning or redrawing of goals or standards, reassignment or reclassification of duties. It may also necessitate reforming the process of selection and training of workers. Thus, control function may require change in all other managerial functions. If the standards are found to be defective, they will be modified or set up again in the the light of observations. Joseph Massie has pointed out that a manager may commit two types of mistakes at this stage: *(1)* taking action when no action is needed, and *(2)* failing to take action when some corrective action is needed. A good control system should provide some basis for helping the manager estimate the risks of making either of these types of errors.

Managerial control can't be so instantaneous as thermostat system or any other mechanical or electronic system. There always exists a time-lag between recording deviations and taking corrective actions even when sophisticated system of information collection used. The collected information needs to be analysed properly before suggesting any corrective action.

IMPROTANCE OF CONTROL

Control is an important function of management. Without control, a manager cannot complete his job of managing. All other functions are the preparatory steps for getting the work done and controlling is concerned with making sure that there is proper execution of these functions. Control is necessary whenever a manager assigns duties and delegates authority to the subordinates. He must exercise control over the actions of his subordinates so as to ensure that the delegated authority is used properly.

The road signals at a road crossing appropriately illustrate the significance of control. Just as road signals are essential to ensure accident-free and smooth traffic, management control devices are necessary in any organisation for its smooth functioning. By controlling, the management ensures that resources are obtained and used economically and efficiently for the achievement of organisational objectives. A good control system provides timely information to the manager which is very much useful for taking corrective actions. Control simplifies supervision by pointing out the significant deviations from the standards of performance.

The advantages of control are listed below:

(1) Control brings order in the organisation. Absence of control means anarchy. Control ensures business operations in the desired direction.

(2) It helps in improving the performance of subordinates.

(3) Control increases the effectiveness of planning. In fact, controlling and planning go hand in hand. Control is the only means to ensure that the plans are being implemented in the real sense. Control points out the shortcomings of not only planning, but also other functions of management such as organising, staffing and directing.

(4) It facilitates the process of delegation. Authority can be safely transferred if effective control exist in organisation.

(5) Control provides the basis for future action. It will reduce the chances of mistakes being repeated in future by suggesting preventive steps.

(6) It brings about better utilisation of resources—human and material, and thus increases productivity and profit, and contributes to the progress of business.

LIMITATIONS OF CONTROL

The control process in an organisation may suffer from the following limitations:

(1) Measurable yardsticks are essential to control; but many aspects of business, *e.g.*, employee morale and public realtions cannot be expressed in quantitative terms.

(2) Control may stifle the intiative of subordinates and dampen their spirit.

(3) The success of control depends on personal responsibility. But this cannot be fixed in all cases.

(4) Control is an expensive process because sufficient attention has to be paid to observe the performance of the subordinates. This requires an expenditure of a lot of time and effort.

(5) The effectiveness of controls mainly depends on their acceptance by the subordinates. They may resist controls if they feel that these will reduce or curtail their freedom. Control also loses its significance when it is not possible to fix the accountability of the subordinates.

(6) An enterprise cannot control the external factors such as government policy, technological changes, fashion changes, etc.

CLASSIFICATION OF CONTROL

Controls are of three types which are as follows:

(a) **Historical Control.** It measures results after the happening of an event. It tells management to what extent objectives are actually accomplished. It is also known as feedback control. Income statement and position statements are examples of this type of controls. Here control is seen as a post mortem of events the purpose of which is to improve in the future. The measured activity has already occured and it is impossible to go back and correct performance to bring it up to the standard. Examples of feedback controls are disciplinary action, performance appraisal interviews, financial and budgetary results and final inspections.

In all physical and biological systems, some massage is transmitted in the form of mechanical transfer of energy, a chemical reaction, or any other means which is known as 'Cybernetics'. In social systems also, some information is sent back to exercise control. And good managerial system controls itself by information feedback which discloses errors in accomplishing goals and initiates corrective action. Feedback is the process of adjusting future actions based upon information about past performance. Though feedback is 'after the fact', it is still vital to the control process. Sometimes, input variables are unmeasurable (*e.g.*, the values an employee brings to the job) or are not detected at the feedforward control point. Feeback is vital in any control system as it ties together all the elements of the control mechanism. Feedback covers both measurement of performance and its evaluation. The manager receives feedback information regarding actual performance against the planned objective. If the feedback reveals accomplishment of objective, the manager must command and congratulate subordinates through open recognition and appreciation. This will enhance the employee morale. However, if the feedback reveals significant deviations from the set standards, the manager will have to take some form of corrective action to improve performance in the future.

Managerial control is somewhat akin to the thermostal system of a refrigerator. Thermostat is a control device of closed loop type that makes control instantaneous. The thermostat records the actual temperature inside the refrigerator, compares it with the required temperature and instantaneously intiates corrective action to bring the actual temperature to what is required. Similarly in an organisation, management needs continuous flow of information about actual performance so that deviations may be promptly corrected.

(b) **Concurrent Control.** It is also known as 'real time' or 'steering' control. It is concerned with the adjustment of performance before any major damage is done. For instance, the navigator of a ship adjusts its movements continuously or the driver of a car adjusts its steering continuously depending upon the direction of destination, obstacles, and other factors. In a factory control chart is an example of concurrent control . It enables the production supervisor to take immediate corrective action before additional products of inferior quality are produced.

(c) **Predictive Control.** Here the control systems anticipates problems the management encounters in future. Cash budget is an example of this type. Where the finance manager is in a position to estimate the next year's flow of cash. If there is a shortage of funds in a particular month, he can arrange for bank loans or some other alternatives. Predictive Control is also frequently termed as 'feedforward control'. This control attempts to anticipate problems or deviations from the standard in advance of their occurance.

Feedforward control may be used with greater advantage if the following guidelines are followed:

1. Through planning and analysis must be done.

2. Careful discrimination must be applied in selecting input variables.

3. Data on input variables must be regularly collected and assessed.

4. The feedforward system must be kept dynamic.

5. Corrective action must be taken as suggested by feedforward control.

PRINCIPLES OF EFFECTIVE CONTROL SYSTEM

The control process is not automatic. It is deliberate. An effective control system should have the following principles:

1. Controls Must be Understandable. The individuals must understand what the control system is attempting to do. Sophisticated control tools are increasingly used now-a-days in the system and the managers must have a thorough knowledge of these before operating. They must first understand the usefulnes of the control advices before they use them. It requires proper training and employment of competent people in the execution of control system. Without proper understanding if managers use the recently innovated control devices it would be catastrophic to the organisation and have adverse consequences.

2. Controls must be Economical. Control should be worth its costs. This requirement is deceptively simple. It is because a manager may have a difficulty in finding out what is 'worth' or what are the cost involved in it. As a matter of fact, economy is a relative concept because costs and benefits vary for different operations. Control system however becomes economical if appropriately tailored to the job task, and the size of organisation. A big organisation may afford sophisticated and high cost technique of control in its system whereas a small organisation may not afford that. The important limiting factor in control system therefore is cost.

3. Controls Must be Objective. The effective control system calls for objectives, accurate, suitable and definite standards or plans. If controls are subjective then a manager's or subordinate's personality may influence judgments and hence there may be any element of bias in decisions leading to ineffective performance. No doubt, management of things in an orgasnisation, contain many subjective elements but for effective performance, controls must be objective and clearly quantifiable and verifiable.

4. Controls Must be Flexible. Flexibility is another essential thing in the wake of rapidly changing and widely fluctuating economic and organizational environments. Standards and plans on which controls are based frequently need modification or revision when underlying circumstances change. Flexibility in control is generally achieved through flexible budgets. For example, in the case of economic prosperity a particular type of budget is suited to the organization, whereas in the context of economic depression such budget is unsuitable and an altogether different budget may be called for. If the organisation rigidly follows the budget that suits prosperity, it cannot operate with it under depression and ultimately organisation will be doomed to failure.

5. Control Dystem should Provide Useful, Understandable Information. Information that is valuable to some individuals may be totally useless for others. An effective control system provides information to the right people who can use them in correcting deviations and fostering growth. Further, some people like information in complex tables of data or voluminous computer printouts, some others like chartwise presentation. Mathematicians and statisticians like the information in the mathematical form. An effective control system must have the characteristics of supplying the information in the required form for the purpose of analysis.

6. Control should Recognize the Importance of the Time Element. Timeliness is one very important factor that cannot be ignored in controlling. Effective control system attaches great importance to the time element. Controls should quickly report deviations. Appropriate actions should be taken without much loss of time, or delay. Time is precious in some matters like cash management, inventories etc., Wrong decision taken in right time is far better than right decision taken too late.

7. Controls should be Selective. For every organisation there are certain key determinants of efficiency and effectiveness. An effective control system considers management be exception as an important concept to be practised in reality. Also management should concentrate on certain control points which are key of organisation's success. It is, in fact, the secret of success of an organisation. It should be pointed that these key points differ in different organisations and hence control system will also be different and must be tailored to the situations existing. Sometimes it so happens that managers and employees may spend much of their time trying to control activities that are relatively unimportant to organisation's success while possibly ignoring, neglecting or paying inadequate attention to the key point.

8. Control should Lead to Corrective Action. Merely discovering deviations in the performance of operations is not enough, an effective control system must lead to appropriate and corrective action. The system must also disclose the key areas of concentration where are the problem areas, who are responsible for that etc. Management control system must also provide various alternative courses of action for different problems. Control system must also suggest the ways of improving the performance, evaluating and implementing these suggestions is then the task of management.

9. Control should be Forward-looking. It is misconception that control is a post mortem of events or things. An effective control system is always aiming at future. Control aids in further planning. It is rightly said that the starting point of planning is control. Control through feedback provides a framework within which planning on new lines can be undertaken. Control system must also have a feedforward subsystem that helps in correct and accurate planning. 'Planning is looking ahead and control is looking back' is an outdated concept nowadays. In fact, control always looks forward, of course, through planning. To say it in simple words, planning and controls are inseparable twins.

REQUIREMENTS OF EFFECTIVE CONTROLLING SYSTEM

Control is necessary in every organisation to ensure that everything is going properly. Every manager, therefore, should have an effective and adequate control system to assist him in making sure that events conform to plans. However, control does not work automatically, but it requires certain design. While the basic principles involves in designing a control system in organisations may be universal, the actual system in an organisation requires some specific design. In this tailoring of control system, there are certain requirements which should be kept in mind:

(a) **Strategic Point Control.** It is not sufficient merely to look at exceptions. Some deviations from standards have rather little impact while others have a great deal. Small deviations in certain areas may have greater significance than larger in other areas. For example, a deviation of 5 percent in the budgeted labour cost may be more troublesome to a manager than a deviation of 20 percent in the budgeted postal charges. Therefore, the principle of exception must be accompanied by the principle of strategic point control which states that effective control can be achieved if critical or strategic points can be identified and close attention directed to adjustment at those points. It is not enough just to look for exceptions, a manager must look for deviations at all critical points.

(b) **Remedial Measures.** Controlling should lead to corrective action. The purpose of control is to keep the system on its predetermined track by preferably preventing deviations from occurring or by enabling the managers to correct deviations immediately after they occur as the second best proposition. Deviations from standards should be immediately reported to the concerned managers for explanation and, wherever necessary, for corrective action.

(c) **Controls must be Flexible.** Flexibility is another essential thing in the wakė of rapidly changing and widely fluctuating economic and organizational environments. Standards and plans on which controls are based frequently need modification or revision when underlying circumstances change. For example, in the case of economic prosperity a particular type of budget is suited to the organisation, whereas in the context of economic depression such budget is unsuitable and altogether different budget may be called for. If the organisation rigidly follows the budget that suits prosperity, it can not operate with it under depression and ultimately organization will be doomed to failure.

(d) **Responsibility for Control.** Controls are to be designed and related to managerial positions at various levels of the organisation to facilitate correction of deviations from standards. Centres for collection of cost data on production should be related to the production department's organisational structure. In other words, each manager in the production department should be accountable for only those costs over which he has control by virtue of his organisational position.

(e) **Prompt Reporting.** Controls should report deviations promptly. Timeliness is the essence of control. Ideally, deviations should be anticipated and preventive action should be taken. More realistically, information on deviations should be monitored and fed back to the system immediately so the corrections are effected with minimum cost and inconvenience.

(f) **Suitability.** Controls should be appropriately designed to suit the nature and needs of the activities being controlled. This means that different types and scales of activity need different types of controls. The control techniques should be tailored to reflect accurately the preformance of particular segments of activity. In production cost control, certain cost standards like direct and indirect costs per unit produced, labour cost per unit or per hour, material cost per unit, machine hour, costs, etc. are illustrations which attach monetary values to the cost of operations.

(g) **Self Control.** Units may be planned to control themselves. If a department can have its own goals and control system, much of the detailed controls can be handled within the department. These sub-systems of self control can then be tied together by the overall control system.

(h) **Controls must be Economical.** Control should be worth its costs. This requirement is deceptively simple. It is because a manager may have a difficulty in finding out what is 'worth' or what are the costs involved in it. As a matter of fact, economy is a relative concept because costs and benefits vary for different operations. Control system however becomes economical if appropriately tailored to the job task and size of organisation.

(i) **Consideration of Human Factor.** A good system of control should be employee centered rather than work-centered as control is exercised on the performance of workers. It must find the persons accountable for results whenever large deviations take place and they must be guided and directed, and reprimanded, if necessary. Thus, human factor must be given proper attention while controlling.

(j) **Controls should be Selective.** For every organisation there are certain key determinants of efficiency and effectiveness. An effective control system considers management by exception as an improtant concept to be practised in reality. It is, in fact, the secret of success of an organisation. It should be pointed that these key points differ in different organizations and hence control system will also be different and must be tailored to the situation existing.

(k) **Controls must be Objective.** The effective control system calls for objective, accurate, suitable and definte standards or plans. If controls are subjective then a manager or subordinate's personality may influence judgements and hence there may be an element of bias in decisions leading to ineffective performcance. No doubt, management of things in an organisation, certain many subjective elements but for effective performance, controls must be objective and clearly quantifiable and verifiable.

(l) **Control should be Forward Looking.** Control is a post-mortem of events or things. An effective control system is always aiming at future. Control aids in further planning. It is rightly said that the starting point of planning is control. Control through feedback provides a framework within which planning on new lines can be undertaken. Control system must also have a feedforward subsystem that helps in correct and accurate planning. 'Planning is looking ahead and control is looking back' is an outdated concept now a days.

(m) **Controls should Lead to Corrective Action.** Merely discovering deviations in the performance of operations is not enough, an effective control system must lead to appropriate and corrective action. The system must also disclose the key areas of concentration, where are the problem areas, who are responsible for that etc. Management control system must also provide various alternative courses of action for different problems.

Action is the essence of control. The comparison of actual performance against the standards reveals the deviations which serve as guide for future action. This may lead to improvement of planning, organising, staffing and directing. It may be pointed out that top managers cannot carry on the control function minutely themselves. They have to delegate a portion of their authority of controlling. The task of regulation of operational action plans can be delegated to the middle level managers and first line managers. They may be asked to report only exceptional matters to the top management.

The effectiveness of control systems is influenced to a great extent by the accuracy of the information on which these are based. Information is a guide to controlling. Therefore, it is necessary that sufficient information of right type is available to the management for taking corrective steps in time. If a control mechanism does not transmit such information to the management, it is not going to last long.

CONTROL AND HUMAN FACTOR

It is vital in every organisation to know the reaction of employees for various types of controls imposed on them. It is a fact that unless a certain amount of control over the human element is exercised, organizational personnel would tend to pursue their own goals, needs and most likely to adversely affect the organizational efficiency and economy of operations. The subordinates often resist controls which are likely to restrict their freedom and obstruct the achievement of their personal goals. They may react to control in the following ways:

- **(a) Absenteeism.** Some employees may absent themselves from the work place to escape the controls temporarily. They may proceed on long leave to avoid problems.
- **(b) Resignation.** Some employees who are not willing to accept controls may leave the organisation, if they get suitable jobs somewhere else.
- **(c) Transfer.** Some employees may seek tranfer to other departments or units to escape controls.
- **(d) Group dynamics.** Employees may form small informal groups to resist the pressures brought upon them by various controls.
- **(e) Compliance.** The employees cooperate with the management and offer their compliance willingly.
- **(f) Unionisation.** Employees may join labour unions to take up their grievances against the management controls. Unions try to nullify the adverse effects of controls on employees through the process of collective bargaining and other weapons such as strike, gherao, picketing, etc.

(g) **Deliberate Deviation.** The employees may devise innovative ways of deviation from controls and keep the deviations from being discovered.

(h) **Aggression.** The employees may show aggressive behaviour against controls. They may try to sabotage the controls to render them ineffective.

(i) **Apathy.** The employees may adopt an attitude of indifference against the imposition of controls.

"The control of human behaviour has always been unpopular. Any undistinguised effort to control usually arouses emotional reaction. We hesitate to admit, even to ourselves, that we are engaged in control, and we may refuse to control, even when this would be helpful, for fear of criticism. Control creates problems not only for the subordinates but for the superiors also. Subordinates resist controls because it restricts their freedom and some managers may not like to impose controls on their subordinates for fear of criticism.

Exercise of control may have some serious behavioural implications for the management. Generally, management uses both planned and unplanned controls to regulate the behaviour of employees. Some sort of resistance is generally offered by the employees against both types of controls. But there might be serious repercussions of unplanned controls because they are unplanned and the subordinates are not mentally prepared to accept them, Behaviourists consider this as an evidence of ineffective management . But it is difficult to rule out exercise of unplanned controls in modern organisations for meeting competition, for reducing costs, or for increasing productivity. Whatever may be the situation, management should try to perceive the behavioural implications of control beforehand if it is to exercise control effectively. But it is not always possible to recognise behavioural dysfunctions of controls because of the following reasons:

(i) Sometimes, human behaviour is unpredicatable. It is difficult to analyse unexpected and uncoventional responses from the employees.

(ii) Many a time, there is a time lag between exercise of control and surfacing of negative reactions of the people. Relating of slow reactions with a particular type of managerial behaviour may be a difficult task.

(iii) Information system in an organisation might not be able to sense or isolate factors which cause resistance to controls on the part of the workers.

(iv) Controls may slowly lead to deterioration of organisational relationships and performance and these occurrences may not come to the knowledge of the management.

Employees resist controls because of the following factors:

(i) The controls may be perceived as unnecessary curbs to the freedom of individuals.

(ii) The controls may suppress the creative and innovative urges of the individuals.

(iii) The standards of performance may be imposed from the top and the subordinates have no say in their determination. The standards of performance may be rigid and unrealistic.

(iv) The performance appraisal may concentrate on fault-finding rather than guiding the people for better results.

(v) The controls may be administered in a discriminatory, arbitrary and whimsical manner.

IMPORTANCE AND SIGNIFICANCE OF CONTROLLING

Controlling is an important function of management. It enables the manager to measure progress and decide whether it is satisfactory or not and in the latter case what corrective action is needed. Controlling is the core of management process and forms the nervous system of management. The importance and significance of controlling function of management can be summarised as follows:

1. It Helps in Achieving the Objectives. Controlling involves measuring work in progress or performance, comparing it with the goals set up in the plan, finding out the deviations if any and taking corrective action to ensure that goals are achieved as envisaged in the plan. Controlling not only makes it sure that the objectives are being achieved but also aims at taking effective steps to achieve them if there is a shortfall. Thus controlling helps in effective implementation of policies, procedures and plans, and in achieving the desired results and objectives.

2. It Facilitates Coordination. Controlling system serves as a tool to integrating efforts of various limbs of organisation. Controlling ensures that actions are in accordance with the plan and results are achieved as desired, and in pursuance of this purpose it helps in creating a harmonious working environment and promoting coordination between various units of the organisation.

3. Controlling Stimulates Action. Through controlling a manager determines the deviation between the actual performance and standard performance and devises corrective action to fill the gap. It points out errors in planning, flaws in materials or methods and suggests what action can be taken to set the things right. The effectiveness of controlling depends on that timely corrective action is taken to solve the problem.

4. Controlling Helps in Better Planning and is Basis for Future Planning. Controlling involves identification of the reasons for the deviation between the performance and desired results and checking whether the plans had been framed correctly, whether results expected were attainable or whether there have occurred some errors in planning, and it needs to be reviewed and revised. This leads to better planning. Again by providing useful feedback and information, it provides the basis for future planning.

5. Controlling Ensures Efficient Use of Resources. Controlling helps the manager to achieve desired results and targets. For this purpose, controlling involves checking whether or not the work is being done according to schedule, whether or not plant, machines and materials are being put to proper use, whether or not the quality is being maintained, whether or not money is being spent as intended. Controlling helps in preventing misuse or wastage of resources and ensures efficient utilisation of human and material resources. In this way, it improves overall efficiency.

6. Controlling Facilitates Decision-making. Controlling involves assessing of performance against established standards, identifying gaps between them, finding causes of the deficiencies, and deciding what action can be taken to solve the problem in hand to get desired results. All this calls for decision-making on the part of the manager. It is he who has to decide the appropriate action to achieve the objectives. In this way, controlling helps in verifying whether policies have been properly framed and have helped in taking right decisions to achieve organisational decisions.

7. Controlling Facilitates Delegation. An effective control sytem will induce the manager to delegate some of its authority to subordinate at lower level, as this would enable him to judge whether the subordinate employee is using the delegated authority properly or not, or whether or not the objectives are being achieved as planned. With necessary feedback from his subordinates he can take proper corrective action. In this way, controlling facilitates delegation and decentralisation. The better the controls, the greater the scope for delegation.

8. Controlling Puts Psychological Pressure on the Employee to Show Good Performance. Controlling makes the employee understand what results he is expected to achieve, that his performance will be evaluated against the established standards and that his position in the organisation will be dependent on his performance. This puts a psychological pressure on the employee to work assiduously towards achieving the set standards. Controlling regulates the work and gives a feeling of security.

9. Controlling Improves Employee Morale. Controlling brings order and discipline in the organisation. It helps and guides employees to reach desired goals and to have job satisfaction and a feeling of achievement. Controlling inculcates positive attitudes among employees towards improving their performance and hence improves their morale.

TECHNIQUES OF CONTROLLING

Controlling can not be effective without effective planning and effective controlling is essential for implementing the plan effectively. Thus planning and controlling are interdependent processes. Effective controlling calls for integration of planning and controls. Therefore, controlling techniques are the tools or devices which integrate planning and controls and aid in ensuring achievement of results as projected in the plans.

Control techniques can be divided into two categories, traditional and modern. Traditional techniques or devices are further categorised as budgetary and non-budgetary.

(A) BUDGETS AND BUDGETARY CONTROL

In simple words, a budget is a financial statement of expected expenses and anticipated revenue or income for a future period. In management, budgets are the monetary evaluation of resources, that is of time, men, materials, money and other units, required to perform work and to achieve the organisational objectives stated in terms of end results or anticipated income. You have read that a budget is a plan that specifies allocation or resources necessary to carry out a programme within time limits and to achieve the desired result. Budgeting implies estimating manpower, money, materials, equipment, tools and facilities required to implement a programme effectively according to the schedule. These requirements need to be stated or quantified in terms of money. Again, the expected performance or end results also need to be converted into money units.

Budgeting means budget planning and budget preparation. It is a formal expression of objectives and goals set up in advance for the company. From the above study, it is evident that a budget is a plan which starts with setting and projecting both long term and short term goals and specifies the expected money costs of the resources like manpower, materials, tools and equipment, and other facilities required to achieve these goals and end-results also expressed in terms of money. According to Allen, a budget is "an appraisal of expected expense projected against anticipated income for a future period." In a budget, a manager presents financial statements of estimates of expenditures to be incurred, in order to carry out the plan and estimates of incomes (*i.e.* revenue) that would arise out of the planned performance or accomplished work. In order to maximise return or the capital employed, it is necessary to ensure that expenses are kept within the limits specified in the budgeted plan and at the same time end-results are achieved as planned. Budget can thus surve as effective tool of controlling. A budget is an instrument of control which enables a manager to plan expenditures correctly and to check the actual performance against the budgeted standard.

Budgetary Control is a device of using budgets to control day-to-day operations and to check whether or not the performance is being achied as planned. Financial budgeting is a widely accepted control technique. Use of budgets helps in controlling individual operations as well as administering the entire business. Budget can be used as a tool for appraising operating results and can serve as a device for effecting financial controls on expenditure, investment and cash position. Actual performance or income can be compared with the budgeted performance or income and corrective action can be taken, if needed. In short, budgetary control implies preparing a financial plan and then making control decisions on the basis of known and emerging facts.

We know that in planning, the overall objectives of the enterprise are split further into sub-objectives or sub-goals to be achieved by various departments or individuals. Therefore, budgets will have to be prepared for all aspects of the operations namely sales, production, materials, manpower requirements, capital expenditure, cash etc., separately. The budget for an enterprise as a whole is the sum of the budgets for all functions or operations.

Elements in Budgetary Control

Terry has defined budgetary control "as a process of comparing the actual results with the corresponding budget data in order to approve accomplishments or to remedy differences by either adjusting the budget estimates or correcting the cause of the difference." Thus basically, budgetary control involves three steps:

1. Expressing in money terms (*i.e.* in rupees, dollars, pound sterlings, yens etc.) the anticipated results of plans or the performance targets in a future period. The budgets will show how the accounts of the enterprise would look like if

the plans are implemented effectively. These data will become a standard for evaluating actual performance.

2. Coordinating the budgeted estimates into a well-balanced programme. It must be ensured that the budget estimates of various components of the plan or programme, namely of sales, production, inventory, advertising, personnel research are in consonance with the overall objectives, and that the targets set in the budgets are financially feasible. They must be adjusted accordingly to fit in the overall programme.
3. The third step in budgetary control comprises of comparing actual results with the programme estimates as evolved in step 2. The budgets become the basis of measuring progression of activities or performance in the organisation.

We have seen that budgetary control requires preparation of budgets for all aspects of planning *i.e.* for all operations of the enterprise. After these budgets have been developed, they are summarised and presented in the form of balance sheet and profit and loss account. We will discuss budgeting of some important operations here.

SOME IMPORTANT BUDGETS

Budgeting is a logical activity of planning which involves setting up of objectives and desired goals and devising way and means to achieve them. In modern business, the ultimate goals or desired results are expressed in terms of sale targets to be achieved over a time. Planning would mean working out details of resources allocation to various operations to produce necessary produce to reach the planned goals or targets. This would require developing a number of budgets for various operations and functions such as sales, finished goods or inventory, production, materials, personnel or labour, capital expenditure, cash etc. etc. A few of them are being discussed here:

1. **The Sales Budget.** The first step in planning is establishment of enterprise objectives and goals. Obviously the initial step

in budgeting is developing sales budget. A business enterprise generally forecasts estimates of volume of sales of its product or products over a period of time. These sale targets can be further split into small sales targets product wise and areas wise. The periodwise targets are prepared taking into consideration the seasonal fluctuations and other factors. Thus total sales estimates to be achieved at the end of a year are broken down into twelve monthwise sales estimates. Sales budget shows the monetary value of anticipated sales units of the product or products. Sales budgets is a forecast of total volume of sales with its break-up productwise, areawise and periodwise, *i.e.* quarterly or monthly, as converted into money. It is prepared on the basis of past experience of sales performance, anticipated market trends and conditions, economic climate or nature of competition, price trends, extent of advertisement etc. Seasonal fluctuations are also kept in view while preparing monthly sales budgets. Sales budgets throw light on many aspects such as estimated number of units to be sold monthwise, periodwise or monthwise inflows of cash, inventory of finished goods requirements to effect the sales etc. Sales budget serves as the basis for developing other budgets like finished good budgets, production budget, cash budget and so on.

2. **Materials and Material Purchase Budgets**. The main objectives of materials and materials purchase budgets is to maintain an adequate supply of right type of needed raw materials to produce goods according to the production schedule. Obviously materials budgets are based on production budgets. The quantity of raw materials is expressed in terms of physical quantities but is converted into money terms by the materials purchase departments of the enterprise. It will show purchase schedules, funds requirements for maintenance of inventory control limits of all types of raw materials, provisions of storing facilities and issuing facilities etc. Production cannot take place

unless requried raw materials of needed quality and specifications are made available to the production department, according to the production schedules drawn by it. It is the responsibility of the materials department to ensure it.

3. **Finished Goods Budget.** Goods need to be produced before they can be sold. An enterprise, therefore, must carry some inventory or finished product to meet demand orders quickly. The objective here is that the enterprise must maintain an adequate supply of the required finished product. Shortcomings in this area can considerably affect profitability. Finished goods budget shows the plan of monthly opening inventory and monthly closing inventory and in prepared keeping is view the seasonal fluctuations and monthly demands of the product. It is very important to maintain desired inventory levels of finished product. Finished goods budget helps in achieving this aim. The sales budget and fininished goods budget serve as a base for developing the production budget and to keep up production schedules, so as to reach the sale targets.

4. **Production Budget.** The production budget will show the number of units of finished product that are to be produced to meet the sales targets and finished goods inventory limits, according to the drawn up production schedules. The main purpose of developing a production budget is twofold *i.e.* of optimum use of production facilities and of matching output with finished goods inventory and sales requirements.

5. **Personnel and Labour Budgets.** As the name suggests, personnel and labour budgets are the estimates of personnel and labour requirements for performance of various functions in the organisation. These budgets will specify the type of personnel or labour required *e.g.* engineer, skilled, semi-skilled, typist, salesman etc., their number and when they are required. These are prepared on the

basis of production budgets, sales budgets or other concerned budgets. The main aim is that right types of persons and labour may be made available at right time to achieve the desired goals. These budgets also give the estimates of salarly bill, cost of training and other allied expenses. These budgets are prepared keepng in view the seasonal fluctuations in the labour requirements and help the department in devising their employment policies. For example, curtailment in production will result in reduction of the number of workers required.

6. **Capital Expenditure Budgets.** These budgets indicate the estimates of expenditures on plant, machinery, equipment replacements, and items of fixed capital. These budgets are projected over a long time, say 5 to 10 years and represent plans for expansion and growth of the enterprise and are of vital importance. The budget for the current year will include that proportion of long-term capital expenditure budget which is to be spent during the particular year. These budgets are of importance not only to the particular enterpise but also for the growth of economy as a whole.

7. **Overhead and Other Expenses Budget.** Besides wages and costs of materials, an enterprise has to incur expenses on a number of other items. These include administrative and selling expenses, heat, light, expenses, repair, depreciation, travel allowances, commissions, interests, loss of bad debts, taxes, insurance, and the like. All these expenses are accounted for in the budgets and form a part of the overall budget programme.

8. **The Cash Budget.** The cash budget forecasts the estimated cash flows over a period of time. It shows the estimated cash receipts and cash disbursements and cash position of the enterprise during the budgeted period. For smooth running of the enterprise, cash must be available when needed. The cash budget indicates the cash requirements at various times and anticipated receipts. It must be noted

that sale of products on credit at a time does not bring in cash flow at the point of time and cannot be shown as receipt in the cash budget. Again there may be certain expenses which may not require cash to be paid. Cash is also required for meeting financial commitments. Cash inflow forecasts include bank balances, cash receipts from sales, debtors or other sources. Cash outflow forecasts include cash payments for materials, purchases, wages, other operating costs, loan repayments, taxation and for capital expenditure. The cash budget will help the manager to know the cash position of the organisation, *i.e.* when it is going to fall short and when it would be surplus and the management can take necessary steps to deal with the situation well in time. The cash can be obtained by borrowing at the time needed. Cash budget is in fact one of the most important types of the budget.

9. **Budgeted Profit and Loss Statement (Income Statement).** From the data provided by the above budgets, an enterprise can make estimates of its income for the budgeted years. The budgeted income statements is in the form of a profit and loss statement, consolidated on the basis of various budgets for the year. They can be prepared for the whole year or on monthly or quarterly basis. These statements will show the anticipated performance of the organisation at the end of the budgeted period. Monthly or quarterly profit and loss statements can be used as effective control devices. They help not only in detecting seasonal variations but also in identifying variations in expenses in time so that corrective action is initiated in time. Again, if the income or profit and loss statements suggest highly unsatisfactory results, the budget estimates of various operations can be reviewed and revised and necessary modifications can be made in the plans to achieve the desired results. Generally, Profit-and-Loss statement or income statement contains estimates of new sale proceeds, expenses on materials, labour, supervision, administration,

commissions, debt servicing, operating profit, taxes and net profit for the budgeted year.

10. **The Budgeted Balance Sheet.** A balance sheet of a company shows its assets, liabilities and network. A budgeted balance sheet gives its financial position as it would look at the end of the budgeted period. The balance sheet based on various budgets can be prepared by the finance or accounts department of the enterprise at the beginning of the budgeted period. It helps the management in knowning in advance what would be the financial position of the enterprise as a result of the operation of various budgets during the budgeted period. Comparison of final balance sheet with the budgeted balance sheet becomes possible and necessary lessons can be learnt.

    The main purpose of controlling is to attain maximum efficiency of operations and hence maximum returns on capital employed. The budgets help in controlling use of resources and costs effectively and hence in achieving maximum returns for the enterprise. Budgeting is an effective and important instrument of integrating planning and control. It is in fact a mechanism that aids planning, coordination as well as control.

ADVANTAGES AND LIMITATIONS OF BUDGETING (BUDGETARY CONTROL)

From the above discussion on budgets and budgetary control, we can enlist the following advantages and limitations of budgeting or budgetary control.

Advantages

(i) Budgeting makes planning meaningful and improves its quality. In fact, budgeting is the very instrument of planning and reduces its objectives to concrete numerical goals giving it reality and a sense of purpose. It aids sound planning. It involves participation of all levels of management.

(ii) It aids coordination and promotes balanced operation of activites or functions among various departments. It is not merely a tool of planning but an instrument of coordination as well. It helps in coordinating the efforts of various individuals and departments and directing them towards realisation of organisational goals. It promotes cooperation among various sub-units in the organisation.

(iii) Budgeting leads to democratic management. It requires delegation of authority and responsibility to subordinates by the top hierarchy without losing overall control.

(iv) Budgeting improves communication process. It requires free flow of information among various departments and coordination to make a good budget. Budgeting thus encourages exchange of information between various departments and in the process develops an effective communication system.

(v) Budgets prepared in consultation with the employees serve as approved and accepted standards of performance and motivate them to work more diligently to accomplish them. Budgeting improves motivation.

(vi) Budgets permit comprehensive control and budgetary control is an important technique of controlling.

The budgets provide standards of performance. As a controlling technique, budgeting provides means of checking results, and comparing performance, of identifying weakness and their causes, and making corrections in time. Budgets keep expenditures in check and effect cost control at the points at which costs are incurred. They enable the management to assess whether or not the performance is being accomplished as budgeted and to take necessary corrective action, if needed, in time.

Limitations. Though budgetary control improves planing, coordination and motivation and is a useful device of exercising control over various operations in the organisation yet it is not a foolproof system. If suffers from many limitations and shortcomings and a manager should be aware of the dangers and problems that one can face in budget making or is using this device. Some important limitations are given below:

(1) Budgets are estimates prepared on the basis of anticipated conditions. With the change in conditions or environment, they may not prove reliable. The effectiveness of budgets depends to a large extent on accuracy of the estimates.

(2) Another danger is that of overbudgeting. A manager while developing a budget may try to give the minutest details for sake of better control and may make it so rigid that it may permit no freedom of action to his subordinates. The budget in this case becomes cumbersome and delegation of authority becomes meaningles. They could get far better results, had they been given more freedom of action to spend.

(3) Danger of inappropriateness of items—The budget may include some items that might have lost their appropriatenees of usefulness long ago. There go into budgets by custom or as a matter of routine. These need to be looked into.

(4) Budgets become the basis for future course of action. It is possible that budgeting may jeopardise the effectiveness of other managerial functions like organising, staffing, training etc. in the sense that it may prevent the manager from performing these functions properly.

(5) Budgeting is a cumbersome, time consuming and expensive process. It may not yield quick or desired results.

(6) Budgetary controls are usually restrictive in nature and are considered as pressure devices. Obviously they are not liked by the subordinates. They are regarded as barriers to spending with the result that they prove demotivators rather than motivators. Budgets limit the role of the manager. Spending even a little extra amount to achieve desired results may invite censure. The most serious limitation of budgeting is its rigidity and inflexibility. Often it becomes an end it itself.

It must be understood that a budget is a tool of management and not a substitute for it. Yet inspite of these shortcomings and problems, budgeting is the most important instrument of planning and control.

(B) NON-BUDGETARY CONTROL TECHNIQUES

Besides the budgetary technique, many other traditional control devices are in use. Sometimes they are used alongwith the budgets. Some of the popualr techniques are personal observation, statistical data or the chart system, operational audit or internal audit, control section or unit, and break-even-point analysis. A brief description of these techniques is given here.

1. Personal Observation. Personal observation is the most effective control device to assess and check the activities of subordinates. In this technique, conrol is exercised by personal observation of the performance of the subordinates and it involves face-to-face contact. The superior can know at first hand whether the work is being performed accoding to established standard or not. The deficiences can be detected early and corrective action, if needed, can be taken qickely Personal observation exerts a psychological pressure on the workers and induces them to work hard to come upto the expectations of the management. This technique thus ensures that goals are realised as planned.

Personal observation necessitites presence of the sueppervisor at the plae of operation and so is time-consuming and expensive. It may discourage initiative on the part of the subordinates or the observer may have a personal bias against the subordinate. Yet it cannot be denied that personal observation is rather the most meaningful and effective controlling technique.

2. Internal Audit or Operational Audit Technique. In simple words, internal auditing is concerned with accouting and financial matters and is a device to check whether or not the expenses are being spent according to laid out procedures and regualtions or whether or not the results ar being achieved as expected or desired. This encompasses the whole gamut of business operations. Therefore this technique is being used to appriase the overall performance of all the operations of the enterprise, and its field is not limited to checking accounts and finances only.

Internal or operational auditing is the device of appraising performance or results and accounts of various operations or departments of the organisation by a staff of internal auditors by checking whether or not the employees are following the company's policies, procedures or work methods as intended. In this sense, it serves as a control to measure effectiveness of other types of controls, checking in the process, the appropriateness and adequacy of other controls. Internal auditing evaluates the various operations and activities on day-to-day basis to see whether or not results are being achieved as planned. Internal audit is continuously concerned with operations in other deparments such as purchasing, advertising, personnel, prodcution etc.

3. Statistical Data or the Chart System. Statitsical information or data provide a popualr conrolling technique. Statistical infromation can be presented in the form of tables of figures, charts and graphs. In this technique, the actual performance or results are shown in the charts or graphs against the desired performance or the performance in previous years. Thus charts are used to compare with previous year's performance. These charts are prepared periodically sectionwise or departmentwise. This is a popular control device with many big companies. Charts help in comparing performance at a glance. Poor performance can be noted immediately and source of trouble can be detected quickly. Though charts speak for themselves, yet statistical information in the form of tables is available to supplement the process and explain things.

4. The Control Unit or the Control Cell. The establishment of a control unit or control department in large comapnies is of recent origin. A control unit is a fact-finding and recommendation section reporting to the higher echelons of management. It has no administrative or operating responsibility. Neither it has any authority to control or direct. It performs a staff function and provides to the higher echelons of management necessary information and recommendations so as to enable them to take necessary corrective action.

5. Break-Even Point Analysis. Break-even chart or analysis is another controlling technique available to management. An enterprise is concerned with the maximisation of the return on the capital employed. The profitablity of a business depends on the volume of output or sales, cost, and revenue. Break-even point is that level of volume at which total revenue is equal to total cost. Volume beyond that point will result in profit and volume less than this level will result in loss for the business because break-even point represents no-profit, no-less level. It is a point where operations pass on from loss to profitablity or from being profitable to the position of loss. Therefore this point can help the management in controlling the performance. The efficacy of effectivness of this technique depend on the accuracy of the decisions regarding the anticipated or planned break-even point.

Break-even point is not a rigid point. It will change with change in costs, change in selling prices, change in operating efficiency, change in sales volume or product mix and change in management decisions. Therefore break-even analysis is based on certain assumptions *e.g.*, that the costs will remain at the anticipated level, the sales mix will not vary, the volume will remain within the anticipated range etc.

The break-even diagram shows the relationship of different volumes, costs, revenues and sales mix to profit. Costs are generally categorised as (i) fixed costs, and (ii) variable costs. Fixed costs are costs which do not change with the change in output. They are rent and interest payments, depreciation charges, wages and salaries of the permanent staff. Fixed costs have to be incurred by the company even if it stops production temporarily. These costs are also described as overhead costs or supplmentary costs or standly costs. Variable costs are those costs which change with the change in company's output. More output will require large inputs of labour, raw materials, power, fuel etc. resulting in increased expenses. In case of reduction in output variable costs also diminish. These are called prime costs.

In a break-even diagram, the volume of ouput is shown along horizontal axis and revenue an costs is shown along the vertical axis.

The fixed costs line is drawn parallel to the horizontal axis, reflecting fixed costs of the company. The total cost line starts from the fixed costs point aboe the origin. The revenue line or sales line reflects the anticipated revenue from sale of different units of output. The break-even point is the point where the revenue line and total cost line interself each other. At this point, the total revenue will be equal to total cost and there will be no profit or loss. If the output is less than the break-even point, the firm will not be doing well and is likely to incur losses. The above relationships are shown in Figure.

Break-Even Chart

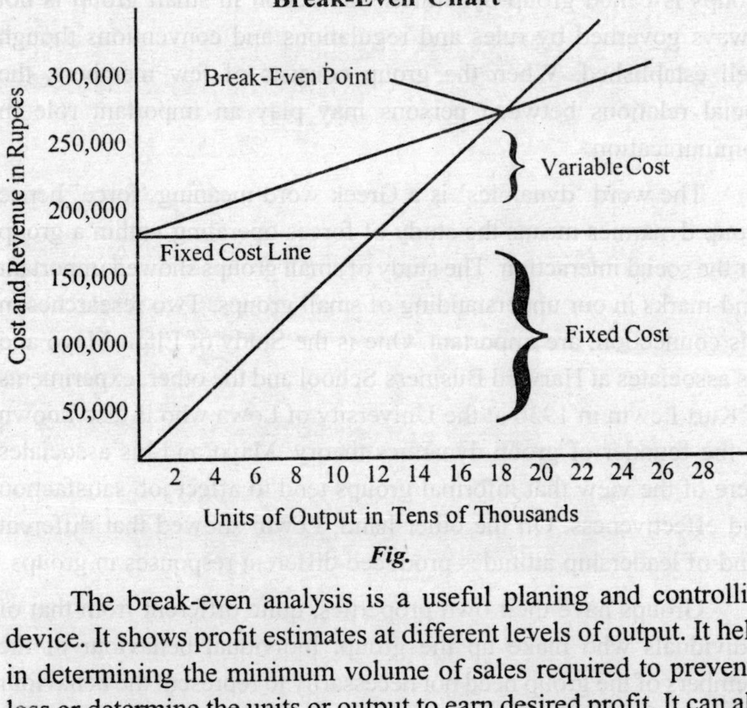

Fig.

The break-even analysis is a useful planing and controlling device. It shows profit estimates at different levels of output. It helps in determining the minimum volume of sales required to prevent a loss or determine the units or output to earn desired profit. It can also help in knowing the impact of variation in costs, price or management decisions on the volume of sales and profits. It helps in comparing actual profits with planned profits. If the actual breakeven point does not lie close to the anticipated break-even point, it will mean that the control was weak or the operations were not efficient enough. ❐

3

Group Dynamics

The social process by which people interact face to face in small groups is called group dynamics. Interaction in small group is not always governed by rules and regulations and conventions though well established. When the group consists of few members, the social relations between persons may play an important role in communication.

The word 'dynamics' is a Greek word meaning 'force' hence group dynamics means the study of forces operating within a group for the social interaction. The study of small groups showed important land-marks in our understanding of small groups. Two researches in this connection, are important. One is the Study of Elton Mayo and his associates at Harvard Business School and the other, experiments of Kurt Lewin in 1930 at the University of Lowa who is also known as the founder of group dynamics theory. Mayo and his associates were of the view that informal groups tend to affect job satisfaction and effectiveness. On the other hand, Lewin showed that different kind of leadership attitudes produced different responses in groups.

Groups have their own properties, quite different from that of individuals who make up the group. Individual behaviour of the members of the group need not necessarily to represent the behaviour of the whole group or *vice versa*. Simply two members do not represent a group, the force of relationship is a must to make them a group.

IMPORTANCE OF GROUP DYNAMICS

There are so many problems of human behaviour which have disturbed the man from the very beginning. There are certain questions which are asked about the human relations and the group behaviour that are very difficult to answer. Some of the questions are like-How should we consider the relationship between individuals and the group? Are the needs of the group, the individual needs? and if so, then what are the properties of the group? Do groups learn? Have they goal? Do they feel frustration? Do they develop? Are they formed or deformed? Are the all properties found in individuals? Are groups good or bad ? How do individuals behave with the group? Researches have been done or are being done to answer these related questions of human and group behaviour.

In this age of behavioural science we think we should be rational and unbiased in the study of the human behaviour but can we? No it is not absolutely possible because still there are certain prerequisites about the realities or unrealities, qualities and evils of groups that guide us. Generally these preconceptions are integral parts of an individual's personal philosophy. Such preconceptions may be positive or negative.

First, we shall consider the negative viewpoint. The people having negative view point are of the view that: *(i)* Groups do not exist and these and the product of distorted thought processes generally known as abstractions, *(ii)* Groups are not good. They like that their members must be loyal to the groups without their head and brain.

There is another view, *i.e.*, positive view. Followers or positive view say that: *(i)* groups do exist. Acceptance or non-acceptance of an individual by a group counts much to that individual and it proves the existence and importance of groups. *(ii)* Groups are not bad, they are good. They satisfy the higher order needs of an individual such as affection, recognition and self-esteem. Groups provide the means to get such things through mutual interaction that a person can never attain them individually.

The characteristics of the positive attitude may be called the characteristics of so called group dynamics movement. The intention of the promoters and group dynamics is that the work should be done in group. Individual responsibility and man to man supervision are bad. Individual problem solving and individual theory are bad. Committee-meetings, group decisions, collective problem solving and group therapy are the index of the group prosperity.

Though group dynamics studies the relationship of individuals, yet we forget the every individual in the group is different in attitude and behaviour. The manager of an organisation must not forget that each member of a positive group does not have similarity in views in a particular situation and they are quite different in views and have their own self-respect.

Management can't wish away the existence of informal groups since it does not create them. Therefore, the management should identify their existence, goals, structure, norms and leadership to understand the behaviour of groups. This will enable it to find ways of making use of groups for the achievement of organisational objectives. For instance, it can have support with the informal leaders and achieve their cooperation in the performance of organisational tasks. A manager can have favourable relationships with an informal leader in several ways. He can consult with the leader and seek their advice on technical matters or human relations problems. He can take his help to train the workers. The informal leadership can be a useful medium of two-way communication in the organisation.

Informal communication can also be used by the management to fill gaps in the formal communication system. A manager can use informal contacts to encourage workers, impart them guidance and to give them counselling. Informal communication can also be used for getting better results from the workers.

Group solidarity or cohesiveness may produce resistance to change or acceptance of it. It is the responsibility of management to use group dynamics in such a way that the solidarity of the group contributes to a favourable attitude towards high standards of performance. The management should not try to finish the groups, rather it should nourish them so that the group members tend to identify themselves with the group and form a cooperative work-team.

Introduction of change in the organisation is a big challenge before any management. Changes can be introduced with the help of groups. For this, the following techniques may be suggested:

1. The goals of the group should be set in such a manner that they are in conformity with the organisational goals. The whole group should be motivated and convinced about the need to achieve the organisational goals. If the group feels that achievement of organisational goals will be instrumental in the realisation of group goals, it will feel highly committed to the organistional goals.
2. The group should be kept fully informed about the need for change, plans for change and consequences of change. The workers will accept a change which is in accordance with their group norms and which does not clash with the group goals.
3. The group which is to be used as a medium of change must be strengthend adequately. Its members must develop a strong sense of belongingness to the group. Cohesive groups are more useful for introducing change than the casual groups.
4. Strong pressure for changes in the group can be established by creating a shared perception by the members of the need for change, thus making the source of pressure for change lie within the group.
5. The management should try to help the groups in evolving norms which are favouable to the organisation. For this, it can use informal leaders for modifying the behaviour of group members. The informal leaders should be given due recognition and they should be kept fully informed.
6. The groups should be encouraged to participate in organisational processes such as making policies, designing plans, preparing budgets, establishing controls, etc. Because of their participation, the groups will feel committed to such changes

7. Changes in one part of a group produce strain in other related parts which can be reduced only by eliminating the change or by bringing about readjustment in related parts.
8. Adequate checks should be maintained on the informal communication. Special care is needed for not allowing rumour to originate and if it has already originated, not to allow it to spread. To curb rumour, supply of full facts is essential. The cause of the rumour should be properly analysed and steps should be taken to prevent its recurrence.

GROUPS AND GROUP DYNAMICS

In simple words, group means a number of people placed together or connected in a particular way. We know that in an organisation, some individuals may have common ties, common interests and even common threats. The commonality of interests, needs, attitudes, threats, and identity unites them into a group and makes them work in cohesion to serve their common ends.

A group is thus a cluster of persons related in some way or united by common ties, needs, inerests or threats over a time. In the process they interact with each other and develop strong interpersonal relations with the result that there develops a feeling of belongingness among the members of the groups.

Clovis Shephered has defined group as having "two or more persons who are interacting with one another in such a manner that each person influences and is influenced by each other." In a group the members form a kind of relationship which persists over a period of time and there is a feeling among them of the mutual awareness and belongingness to that group. Interaction between members and mutual belongingness bind them into a group.

A group is thus a cluster of individuals who have common goals or interests to serve, have interacted with each other over a period of time have developed a pattern of conduct and behaviour, and each of them has a feeling of belongingness to the group.

The groups may be formal or informal. Studies of such groups in an industrial situation have shown that:

(1) There is difference in the structures of various groups.

(2) These groups are rarely distinct, rather, they overlap.

(3) There are certain individuals who determine the group behaviour.

(4) The behaviour of certain individuals is determined by group behaviour.

(5) The group generates a climate that transcends individual feelings.

(6) A group has a strong influence on individuals and hence on group dynamics.

(7) Members in a group contribute to group structure and behaviour in different degrees.

Groups dynamics refers to complex forces operating within a group. Group dynamics means forces that determine and influence internal nature of groups, their formation (*i.e.* size and structure) and processes, interaction or behaviour, conflict and cohesiveness. Kurt Lewin explained the concept and developed it into a distinct technique and discipline of study in the field of management and organisational behaviour.

Group Dynamics refers to study of forces operating within a group *i.e.* sutdy of forces affecting group attitude and behaviours and their influences on the functioning of individuals, groups and organisation as a whole. Group Dynamics deals with the study and predictions of group attitudes and behaviour and how these can be changed to the advantage of the organisation in particular and of individuals and groups in general. Thus group dynamics has given us new techniques which can be helpful in making groups to work whole-heartedly in a cohesive manner towards realisation of organisational objectives.

Studies have shown that as a result of proper and encouraging group formations, it is possible to:

(1) Change the objectives of groups.

(2) Change the structure of groups.

(3) Change the personality *i.e.* attitude and behaviour of indivdiuals in a group.

(4) Improve morale, and

(5) Solve problems by reducing conflict, mistrust and hostility.

(6) Promote an understanding of the motives *i.e.* needs and interests of other individuals in the group.

What is needed most is to harness group dynamics to serve the purpose of the individuals, group of the organisaton as a whole.

CHARACTERISTICS OF WORK GROUP

Following are the characteristics of work group:

1. Norms. There are certain norms of the group that represents its culture. Every groups has its own culture and a level of behaviour by which it is recognised within the society. These norms are fixed by the group itself and are followed by each and every member of the group. These norms may be in writing or oral.

2. Informal Leadership. There must be a informal leader among the members of the group. It is nominated by the members of the group taking into consideration the age, experience, technical knowledge, etc. He has no formal power but he obtains the power from the members of the group. A group may have more than one leaders for different purposes.

3. Cohesion. A group develops because it satisfied certain needs of its members. The more needs it satisfies, the more it attracts the members. This attraction or belongingness may be called cohesiveness. Group cohesiveness implies consensus, unanimity or agreement among members on major issues. Members of the group feel highly attached to the group and attract towards each other.

4. Confirmity. There must be confirmity between the individual and group goals. If these two confirm, there will be a group cohesiveness. Cohesive group demands confirmity from its members so that it can attain its goals and may enjoy the security in the society.

5. Activities. Almost all the group do something. Work groups may be busy in activities on the work while friendship groups may talk each other, go to a place, take lunch together. The group must be active but it is not necessary that all of its members are active. Some may be active while others may be quite inactive.

6. Interaction. A very common characteristic of a group is inter-action between the members of the group. In a wider term, interaction is a communication. Such communication may be oral or by gesture or by nodding the head. People or members of the group are closely associated with one another and adjust themselves among them only through interaction. They know each other and their behaviour through interaction.

REASONS FOR FORMING GROUPS

Here are some important factors which explain why the groups are formed:

1. Socialisation. Man is a social being. He wants to socialise with others. Being a member of a number of informal groups allows him to satisfy his social needs on the job. He can interact with others rather than working in isolated loneliness.

2. Sense of Identification. Many people have an urge to be identified as members of a district group. So they form special groups as cricket club, literary society, etc. This might also help in increasing their status.

3. Goal Achievement. People form groups to pool talents, knowledge and resources to achieve a common goal or interest. People doing a common task confront similar types of problems. To remove such problems, they can constitute a separate group.

4. Monotonous Jobs. Workers performing standardised routine jobs often feel bored. In order to reduce their mental fatigue at work, they may form informal groups and have interaction with each other at the workplace at frequent intervals.

5. Security. There is strength in numbers by joining a group, a person can reduce the insecurity of standing alone. Groups help the members to meet pressures effectively. Further, they feel secured against the managements arbitrariness.

6. Source of Information. Informal group is a source of information to its members. Informal communication is very fast. A piece of information available to a member will reach nearly all the members of the group in a short span of time. The group may develop a special (code) language for speedy communication. Psychological barriers to communication are also overcome by the group.

The work groups are formed to enjoy the following benefits through the groups:

1. Communication and Information. A work group is a media of communication for its workers. It gets its member acquainted with the news and information. Facts and rumours spread very quickly within the group. It has the abonormal capacity to carry the information and rumour. Communication within the group is necessary for the adjustment of individuals in changing work situations.

2. Better Work Situations. The people form work-group to advance group position for improving their work conditions, an organisation. Most probably the people unite themselves under informal leadership, show their strength and demand for better conditions.

3. Companionship and Friendship. An individual gets companions and friends in the group with whom one can interact and mutually communiate one's experiences and ideas. One cannot live alone for long. He needs companions and friends to pass time or to achieve the individual's objectives. Group develops oneness and cooperation among its members. Members share feelings of each other.

4. Security and Protection. Group provides security and protection to its members. There may be difference of opinions among members but they forget differences when they feel themselves insecured from certain outside forces. They jointly protect themselves. Each member of the group expects other members that they could save him in odd times.

5. Satisfaction of Needs. Work groups are formed because members get their needs especially self-esteem or self-actualisation needs, satisfied through groups for which they are formed. A person may be a member of different groups which serve his various interests. They promote self-confidence among members.

6. Help with the work. Work situations require help of others in day to day working. He consults, seeks advice for performing his job efficiently and expect removal of any impediment in the way of performing his job. So, group removes difficulties of the members and help with the work.

Thus groups are formed to serve the above purposes.

DIFFERENCE BETWEEN INFORMAL GROUPS FROM FORMAL GROUPS

We have explained explicitly the meaning and nature of formal and informal groups. Now in this question, we shall make an attempt to distinguish these two groups on the basis of their basic characteristics. These two groups differ from each other on the following grounds:

1. Origin. A formal group is deliberately structured and planned to subserve organisational interest. The manager decides about the activities of each individual and his interaction with others. They come together because of the interdependence of their operations or their mutual dependence on their common boss. An informal group, on the other hand emerges voluntarily and spontaneously. In fact, the formal organisation itself contains the seeds for the emergence of informal groups. It allocates people in different departments, work locations and time-schedules and while performing their tasks, the members develop their activities, interaction and sentiments towards each other which are not cared for by the formal organisation.

2. Sanctions to Members. Members are suitably rewarded or punished for their work done in a formal group according to the formal rules and regulations of the group. Rewards or punishments may be financial or non-financial. But in an informal group, the efforts of the person are recognised mainly through non-financial rewards or punishments generally in terms of feelings, status, and prestige.

3. Nature of Group. Formal groups are stable in character and continues for a longer period. Informal groups are quite unstable because they are subject to sentiments and feelings of the group members. A particular informal group ceases to exist as soon as its purpose is sloved.

4. Authority. The authority to a formal group is given by the institution according to the position on the organisation chart. It is given to the position and not to the man concerned. Whosoever be in that position, will enjoy the authority. Authority in such groups is acquired through delegation from the above to the downward. Contrarily, the authority in an informal group is earned or given permissively by the members of the group.

5. Communication. All message-upward or downward–pass through the chain of command strictly as given on the organisation chart. In an informal group, all messages are passed through informal channel because there is no such chain of command. People remain in mutual contact with each other, they learn about every person of group what is going on in the organisation.

6. Purpose of the Group Formation. The main purpose of formal groups is to serve the organisation as means to formal ends, while the informal groups provide social satisfaction and stability to work groups.

7. Size. Formal groups are quite large because personal relations have no concern there while the informal groups tend to remain smaller so as to keep it within limits of personal relations.

8. Abolition of the Group. As formal groups are subject to management control, they can be abolished at the discretion of the proper authority while a particular informal group cannot be destroyed because any attempt to destroy it may lead to formation of several other groups because there is no management control over it.

9. Control on Behaviour. Behaviour of the people of the formal group is regulated by the rules and regulations framed with an intention to attain rationality and efficiency. Violation of any rule attracts penalty and punishment. In an informal group, on the other hand behaviour of the members is controlled through norms, values and beliefs of the group. The members of the informal group may compel any member of the group to disassociate himself from the group.

10. Number of Groups. The whole organisation (formal group) is divided into several units and sub-units working for thte common cause but a large number of informal groups are found in an institution and some ever outside the institution. An individual may be the member of a number of informal groups for different purposes. So, there is overlapping membership and multiple groups.

Thus formal groups can very easily be differentiated with informal groups on the basis of the above grounds.

TYPES OF GROUPS

Basically two types of groups are found in every organisation. One is formal group and another is informal group.

Formal Groups. Such groups are a part of the organisation structure. They are created deliberately by the management to perform the assigned duties. The examples are work groups, committees and quality teams. These groups are characterised by clear-cut authority-responsibility relationships. The pattern of communication is also well defined. Rules are laid down to regulate the behaviour of group members. The formal groups are also known as official organisation.

Informal Groups. Informal groups arise spontaneously in the organisation because of social interaction between the people. They are created by individuals rather than by management. They are natural groupings of people in response to the need for social interaction. They may be based on common interest, language, taste, caste, religion, background, etc. Thus, informal groups are alliances that are formally planned. These groups are natural formations in the work environment.

The informal organisation represents unofficial groups which have focus on person rather than position. Every group develops norms to regulate the behaviour of its members. There is no fixed pattern of communication between the members. That is why, informal groups are more flexible than the formal groups. Since they concentrate on personal contacts between the members, they represent the human side of enterprise as compared to technical side represented by the formal groups. Formal groups are formed by the management of an organisation, so they are controlled and can be abolished by the management at any time it likes. The formal groups can be classified as follows:

1. Permanent and Temporary Formal Groups. On the basis of permanency formal groups may be permanent or temporary. Permanent formal groups are formed by the organisation on the permanent basis and more or less exist till the organisation exists. Board of directors, depratmental units, staff groups, standing committees are some of the examples of formal groups.

Groups formed by the organisation to carry the particular work or to perform the specific task are temporary formal groups. A committee or study groups, appointed to analyse or review the pay structure in the organisation are examples of temporary formal groups. These groups come to an end as soon as the tasks assigned to them are over.

2. Functional Groups. Functional groups are those groups whose primary task is to carry on the operations. In many cases, the functional groups may be congruent with the authority groups. Thus, a single department in the organisation would probably be both command group and a functional group. The department is a command group within the authority structure but the staff working in that department engaged in a particular activity and directed and coordinated by the same superior may form a functional group such as typists, clerk, salesman, etc.

3. Status Group. Status groups involve the member of the same status in an organisation. The term is ambiguous in the sense that it includes a number of different rankings of positions which are frequently inconsistant with each other. Moreover, the formally prescribed status distinction is extremely hazy. It makes distinction on a functional basis between manager and workers, on an authoritarian basis between superiors and subordinates, and on a paymen' basis between salary and wages earners. In some cases status distinction is made on the basis of facilities or amenities to be enjoyed by the members.

4. Command and Task Groups. Formal groups may be sub-classified into command and task groups. The command group is composed of subordinates who report directly to a given boss. A supervisor and the operative employees reporting to him form a command group. The task group, on the other hand, represents those working together to complete a given task. The boundaries of a task group are not confined to its immediate superior. It can cross command relationship. A task group or team, say for the introduction of a new product of service, is usually formed to complete an assignment that involves a number of departments.

INFORMAL GROUPS

An informal group arises voluntarily and spontaneously and they are generally satisfying the social needs of the members of the groups. Each informal group has its own informal leader who is elected among the members of the group not on the basis of authority he possesses in the formal group but on the basis of age, seniority, technical knowledge respect etc. So authority is to be earned from members of the group. Authority in the informal group is given to the person and not to the position. As soon as the members lose their confidence in him, he will no more be the leader of the group.

Communication in informal groups possess through informal channel, mostly verbal or by gesture. Behaviour of members are regulated by norms, values and beliefs of the group. Violaters of norms are punished through non-financial modes such as social boycott, loss of prestige and status within the group.

Informal groups, unlike formal ones, cannot be abolished. Any attempt to destroy them causes several others to emerge. Informal groups may exist within or outside the organisation.

The informal group is of following types:

1. Interest and Friendship Groups. Informal alliances may take the shape of interest and friendship groups. An interest group consists of people having a specific objective and not aligned to common command or task groups. For instance, employees who group together to pressurise the management for subsidised transport constitute an interest group. But a friendship group includes close friends or relatives. These relations even extend outside the organisation. The group members know each other very well and have good relations.

2. Cliques. A clique consists of those people who have frequent interactions and observe certain norms and standards. Its purpose is to gain and control power. The number of members of a clique is restricted to five or six organisational members. Some members of a clique may form another group consisting of some persons who are not members of the organisation. Thus, this group known as sub-clique is partially external to the organisation.

Dalton identified three types of cliques as follows:

(i) ***Vertical Clique.*** It consists of people working in the same department drawing membership regardless of ranks. For example, superior may be a member in a group consisting mainly of subordinates. Such groups cutting across hierarchical lines develop because of the earlier acquaintance of people or because the superior is dependent upon his subordinates for some fromal purposes like filling gaps in his abilities.

(ii) ***Mixed or Random Clique.*** Such a group draws members from different ranks, departments and physical locations who come together for a common purpose. The members may be residing in the same locality and travelling by the common bus or may be members of the common club.

(iii) ***Horizontal Clique.*** It consists of people of more or less the same rank and working in the same unit. This is the commonest kind of informal groups. The members have certain common interests for whose achievements they follow certain norms and standards.

3. Sayle's Classification. On the basis of pressure tactics adopted by small groups, Sayles identified four finds of groups in organisation which are discussed below:

(i) ***The Apathetic Group.*** These groups are the least likely to develop the grievances or engage in any pressure tactics. Although incidents occur on various occasions but workers are mostly disinclined to challenge the decisions or attempt to gain something extra for themselves. There are evidences of workers' discontent but often it is not focussed in terms of any specific demands but often it is not focussed in terms of any specific demands or grievances. In the group no one emerges as an acceptable leader and therefore there is lack of clearly identified leadership.

These groups do not engage in union activities and generally are jealousies and interpersonal problems within the group. Group cohesiveness is absent as a primary characteristics of the group. The members are generally low paid and from the low skilled job. Thus there are four behaviour characteristics of these groups:

(i) Relatively few grievances or use of pressure tactics.

(ii) Lack of clearly identified or accepted leadership.

(iii) Internal disunity and frictions over petty matters.

(iv) Evidence of suppressed discontent.

(ii) The Erratic Group. Members in the erratic group are easily inflamed and easily pacified. The employees themselves are not very much serious about their problem raised and they take the grievance as minor. Sometimes they infuriate with the management without working into a major conflagration, mass demonstration or a wild-cat strike etc. They may be pacified even in no time gaining nothing from the management.

Any active member within the group may assume the leadership. Management puts these groups in the very dangerous list because the time and the energy of management and union officials in evolving a grievance procedure are lost in solving the problems of these tension areas. There is cooperation and unity in the group. Internally these groups have autocratic leadership that keeps them in line.

(iii) ***The Strategic Group.*** The strategic group refers to member's ability to prepare a strategy and not the location of the group. These groups have a well planned and consistent grievance activity and exercise continuous pressure. They seem to be shrewdly calculating pressure groups which never tire of objecting to unfavourable management decision, seeking loopholes in existing policies and policies that redowned to their benefits and comparing their benefits with those of other groups in the plant. The demand constant attention for their problems and have the ability to reinforce their demands by group action. The amount and kind of pressure the strategic groups exert are carefully measured, so the degree of their behaviour is predictable and this consistency in their behaviour seems as a virtue.

Members of such groups are generally performing technologically independent job and are well placed. They are highly united and maintain cohesiveness within their group. The leadership of these groups is consisted of highly active and influential group members each of whom specialise in such function as dealing with the management, dealing with the union, maintaining internal unity or taking the lead in voicing dissatisfaction.

(iv) ***Conservative Group.*** The conservative group consists of persons who possess critical or scarce skills. They are in the strong position in the organisation and the management is also worried about them but they are least active in union politics and certainly there was little chance of using concerted action without warning. These are strong hence are most stable among informal groups. Such groups excercise restrained pressure for highly specified objectives

and display internal unity and self-assurance. Thus these groups are much more conservative in their grievance activities. There are very little evidences of turmoil, trouble or concerted activity.

GROUP FORMATION AND GROUP DEVELOPMENT

Individuals form groups for economic, psychological, sociological and cultural reasons. They form groups on account of physical proximity, or conmmon interests, threats, and attitudes. Groups are also formed to

(1) reduce tensions

(2) take united stand against organisational and outside pressures

(3) solve problems

(4) derive benfits of association and affiliation with a group

(5) satisfy various needs ranging from basic physiological to esteem and self-actualisation needs.

Groups are categorised as formal groups and informal groups

(a) Formal Groups. The complexities of modern production require the combined efforts of a variety of people. Managements deliberately create formal groups to meet such requirements. Formal groups are those groups which are consciously created to meet certain requirements and are generally of permanent nature whose members can be substituted. Some examples of formal groups are Board of Directors, Standing Committees, Staff groups, Work groups. Formal groups may also be formed for some specific purposes and may be abolished once the purpose is served *e.g.* task force, adhoc committees etc. Managements also compose work groups by combining jobs.

A work group is a set of people who see one another on the job almost daily, whose work is usually independent in some respect and whose output is viewed by outsiders as a single achievement. The groups may be functional or compound.

(i) ***Functional Groups.*** In functional groups operators perform the same kind of work and their supervisor or manager is a specialist in the field.

(ii) ***Compound Groups.*** In compound groups operators perform different but related work and their supervisor manager is more of a generalist concerned with coordination. They help in local coordination.

Work groups tend to be close-knit social groups as they can either be a great source of strength for an oganisation or can harm its interests seriously. So care is needed in the formation of such groups.

Groups decisions are generally more balanced, acceptable and practical.

(b) Informal Groups. It is individuals themselves who form informal groups. These groups are formed because of some social and psychological factors operating a the work place. We have discussed in detail in the fomation of informal groups as a natural phenomenon and consequence of personal and social interaction between people working together in an organisation. The members of those informal groups ar generally more akin to each otehr because of their common social needs and interests, habits, attitudes, caste, culture or language. These informal groups provide their members a social satisfiaction which formal groups cannot provide them.

GROUP COHESIVENESS AND PRODUCTIVITY

Group dynamics necessitates setting of norms and standards of behaviours to which all members of the group must conform. The extent and degree of conformity to group norms and standards reflects the group cohesiveness. The more the conformity to group norms, the more is the cohesiveness of the group. Encouraging and powerful group dynamics results in greater group cohesiveness.

Hawthorne Studies show that association and human affiliations are primary work motivators and that the degree of cooperation and cohesiveness in one's primary group is very critical to a successful organisation and greatly influence their behaviour and productivity or performance. Informal relations have stronger influence than formal relationships. The group approach to a problem provides a promising means of increasing morale, besides solving the problems. Hawthorne Studies showed that social relationship among workers and the willingness of the workers to cooperate with the management were significant factors responsible for improved output *i.e.* productivity. It has been found that a highly cohesive group under proper leadership will have the highest possible productivity. We have studied how OD seeks to improve group processes and techniques to cope with the change situation, and to get the best desired results. It would require group development as reflected in development of inter personal skills so that the group or team charged with implementing plans of action works as a cohesive group. Manager as a leader has a special role in creating such an environment in which group is motivated to work towards improved performance resulting in benefits to all in the group and the organisation as well.

Renis Likert has studied relationship between group solidarity and productivity. According to him. "work groups with high group pride and loyalty are more productive. One reason is that the workers cooperate more and help one another in getting the work done. Work groups with high group loyalty shows more team work and more willingness to help each other than those with low group loyalty." The willingness to help one another displayed by the group loyalty seems to come from a better team spirit and better inerpersonal relationships that were developed by the foreman. Another factor contributing to the higehr productivity is their lower rate of absance from the job. Group solidarity thus contributes to higher productivity, greater job satisfaction, less absense and less turnover.

PROBLEMS OF MANAGING GROUPS

Every managers has to deal with groups and shape their behaviour in such a way that the groups have favourable attitude towards the organisational objectives. But this is not an easy task because the groups may create the following problems for the management:

1. Conformity of Group Norms. The informal group exerts strong pressure on its members for conformity. The members may become so loyal to their group that following the group norms becomes a part of their life. This implies that members become subject to wilful control of the group leader who may lead the group towards selfish ends.

2. Role Conflict. Every member of the informal group is also a member of the formal organisation. Sometimes, there may be role conflict because what the informal group requires of a member is just the opposite of what is expected of him by the formal organisation. In such a situation, groups member may conform their social norms. And if an individual member wants to follow the formal instructions of his boss, he may be snubbed bythe informal leader and compelled to conform to informal group norms.

3. Spreading of Rumours. Informal communication may give rise to rumours which is not desirable for the organisation. A rumour is a piece of information which lacks authenticity and which is false and misleading. The rumours may prove to be very dangerous for the organisation. The workers may feel insecure and unhappy with the organisational policies. This may lead to lower productivity. A sudden break out of a rumour may even lead to stoppage of work by the employees. Having a check on the origin of rumours is a very challenging problem for the management.

4. Negative Attitude of Informal Leader. The informal leader may turn out to be a troubleshooter for the organisation. In order to increase his influence, he may work against the policies of management and manipulate the behaviour of his followers. Thus, he can be a source of conflict between the management and the workers. He may induce the followers to work against the interests of the organisation.

5. Resistance to Change. Informal groups generally have a tendency to resist change. Change requires group members to make new adjustment and acquire new skills. But groups want to maintain status quo. Sometimes, groups react violently to the proposed changes being brought by the management.

GROUP DEVELOPMENT IN BRIEF

Groups are formed and developed through several stages. They do not form overnight. The process of developing from a group of strangers to a unit of cohesive and well coordinated team members requires time and a great deal of interaction among group members.

It has been pointed out that groups pass through a standard sequence of five stages forming, storming, norming, performing and adjourning.

In **Forming stage** there is a great deal of uncertainty about the group's purpose, structure and leadership. The stage is complete when interpersonal relationships are established and when members have begun to think of themselves as part of group.

In **Storming stage** conflict arises because of interpesonal behaviour. Additionally there is resistance to group influence and task requirements. Occasionally, groups split.

In **Norming stage**, a single leader emerges and this results in groups cohesion. There is now a strong sense of group identify and comaraderie. New groups standards and roles are formed for members.

Performing stage is marked by teamwork, role clearity and task accomplishment. Group energy has moved from getting to know and understand each other to the job of performance.

Performing happens to be the last stage in permanent work groups. But for temporary work teams, task forces, and similar groups that have a limited task to perform, there is an adjourning stage. In this stage, the group prepares for its disbandment. Task performance is no longer the group's top priority. Instead, attention is directed towards wrapping up activities. Responses of group members vary in this stage. Some are upbeat, basking in the group's accomplishments.

There is an alternative theory of group development. Accoding to this, group development proceeds on four stages:

(1) **Mutual Acceptance.** In the mutual acceptance stage of group development, members get to know about each other by sharing information about themselves. They discuss

subject, often not connected with the group, such as politics, wheather, prices rise, deteriorating morals, sports or recent events within the organisation. Some aspects of the group's task, such as its formal objective, may also be discussed at this stage.

As the members get to know one another, disicussion may turn to more sensitive issues, such as the organisation's politics or recent controversial decisions. In this way, the participants explore one another's reactions, knowledge, and expertise. From the discussion, members may learn one another's views on a variety of issues, how similar their beliefs and values are, the extent to which they can trust one another. Eventually, the conversation will turn to the business of the group. When this discussion becomes serious, the group is moving to the next stage—communication and decision making.

(2) **Communication and Decision Making.** Once group members have begun to accept one another, the group progresses to the communication and decision making stage. Here, the group members discuss their feelings and opinions more openly. They may show more tolerence for opposing view points and explore different ideas to bring about a reasonable solution or decision. Members discuss and eventually agree on the group's goals. Then they are assigned roles and tasks to accomplish the goals.

(3) **Motivation and Productivity.** In the motivation and productivity stage, emphasis shifts away from personal concerns and viewpoints to activities that will benefit the group. Members co-operate and actively help others accomplish their goals. The members are highly motivated and may carry out their activities creatively. In this stage, the group is accomplishing its work and is moving towards the final stage of development.

(4) **Control and Organisation.** In the final stage, control and organisation, the groups work effectively towards

accomplishing its goals. Tasks are assigned by mutual agreement and according to ability. In a mature group, the members' activities are relatively spontaneous and flexible, rather than subject to ·rigid structural restraints, Mature groups evaluate their activities and potential outcomes and take corrective actions if necessary. The characteristics of flexibility, spontaneity, and self-correction are eseential if the group is to become productive and last long.

INTER-GROUP CONFLICT MANAGEMENT

Inter-group conflict, also called organisational conflict, refers to the conflict between two groups, departments, or sections in an organisation. Conflict between groups is frequent and highly visible. The reasons for inter-group conflict are many. The most important of them are explained below:

1. Task Inter-dependence. Task inter-dependence refers to the extent to which two departments depend on each other for assistance, information, compliance, or other coordinative acts in the performance of their respective tasks. Task dependence may be pooled dependence, sequential dependence, or reciprocal dependence.

Pooled inter-dependence exists when two groups function with relative independence but their combined output contributes to the overall performance. Sequential inter-dependence occurs when one group's performance depends on another group's prior performance. In reciprocal inter-dependence departments exchange outputs, and hence are mutually inter-dependent in accomplishing their tasks.

In all the three types of inter-dependence, conflict arises from differences in performance expectations. In general conflict as a result of task inter-dependence will be worse when: *(a)* the more the activities of one group affect the performance of other groups; *(b)* the wider the range of activities in a group that are affected by another, and *(c)* the more unstructured the work flow is.

2. Competition for Limited Resources. Yet another source of inter-group conflict relates to competition for resources which are limited in their supply. These resources may be tangible such as money, materials, and other physical facilities, or they may be intangible, such as power, status, and prestige. Each department tries to secure a larger share in the resources, and this will result in conflict.

3. Task Ambiguity. Another important source of inter-group conflict arises when it is not clear which group is responsible for performing certain activities; "things fall between the cracks", and both groups are upset with each other. Task ambiguity arises when the organisation is growing or its environment is changing fast. Task ambiguity can also occur from unstructured and non-directive leadership.

4. Goal Incompatibility. Goal incompatibility leads to inter-group conflict. However hard managers try to avoid incompatible goals for different organisational units, they do exist, leading to conflict. The main objective of the quality assurance department, for example, is to ensure uniform quality of all the units of output. This might clash with the production department which desires somehow to push through the units, minor deviations in quality notwithstanding.

5. Line and Staff. The traditional organisational structure which has line officers being assisted by staff officers at different levels has inherent potential for conflict. One reason for conflict lies in the background of line and staff personnel. The line manager, for example the work manager, may either rise from the lower ranks and reach his position after some years of loyal service, or he may be technically qualified and may enter the industry straight from university. He is not a status keeper or an empire-builder, but is concerned with preserving this present status and authority within his own empire. The staff specialist, on the other hand, is better qualified educationally. He is more loyal to his profession than to his employers. He may see his future depending on mobility within the profession as opposed to internal promotion.

6. Competitive Reward Systems. Managers seem to believe that better performance can be achieved through competition, and this belief is reflected in their reward systems. Competition can indeed increase the level of performance in work situations where tasks can be performed independently. However, when tasks require high levels of inter-dependence, competition can hurt cooperation among members and work groups. For example, conflict occurs when the personnel department is rewarded for achieveing cost reduction or the production department is given an award for better industrial relations.

7. Intra-personal and Inter-personal Conflicts. Intera-personal and inter personal sources of conflict discussed earlier are reasons for inter-group conflict also.

GROUP COHESIVENESS

In case of informal groups, authority, responsibility, relationship, channnel of communication, pattern of coordination, etc. are not pre-determined. Informal groups operate in an unstructured way. An informal group interacts with the formal organisation quite frequently. It affects and is affected by the formal organisation. If we observe the working of any informal group, we shall come across the following important elements:

Authority. There is a network of relationships in an informal organisation and it is not surprising if these relationships may be contradictory to the formal prescribed pattern of relationships. An informal organisation has set of unique characteristics. It has its own codes of conduct, system of communication and system of reward and punishment. The authority in informal organisation is personal rather than positional as in case of formal organisation. Power in informal organisation is earned or given by group members, rather than delegated; therefore, it does not follow the official chain of command. It is more likely to come from peers than from superiors in the formal hierarchy; and it may cut across organisational lines into other departments. It is usually more unstable than its subjective nature, informal organisation cannot be controlled by management in the way that formal organisation is.

Objectives. Groups evolve their own goals reflecting their special interests. Group members are dedicated to group goals. Group cohesivenss results in the group acting in a unified manner. This cohesiveness is a result of the degree to which the group goals help in satisfaction of the individual's needs. An important management problem, therefore, is to relate the group's objectives to the individual needs of the members of the group. If the goal congruency does not take place, organisation will have to pay a price of this goal conflict as the group goals will take precedence over the organisation's goals.

Communication. Informal organisation comes into existence because of the deficiencies of the formal channels of communication. The formal channels of communication may be inadequate and they may be show. The need for speedier communication may give birth to informal channels of communication. Infomal communication is very fast, but its greatest danger is that it may give rise to rumours. Rumours may prove to be detrimental to the interests of the organisation. It is the responsibility of the management to maintain informal channels of communication properly by feeding the necessary information, whenever necessary.

Leadership. The informal group has its own leader. An informal leader may not be the superior under whom the group members are working. An informal group leader performs the following functions: *(i)* he facilitates a consensus among group members, *(ii)* he initiates action, and *(iii)* he provides link with the outside world. If the formal leader is able to perform these functions, he may be accepted as an informal leader also. Workers will go to him for their personal problems, counselling, etc. The important factors which determine informal leadership are age, seniority, work location, technical competence, etc. It may be noted that persons who emerge as informal leaders are perceived by the other group members as being the best people who can satisfy the goals of the group. The group may have a number of leaders for different purposes.

Group Cohesiveness. Group cohesiveness represents the degree of attachment of the members to their group. The greater the degree of attachment, the greater is the likelihood that all members will conform strictly to the group standards and greater the likelihood that its leader will represent the feelings of all members. Cohesive groups are more powerful and are more likely to act in union when their expectations do not come to be realised.

The degree of group cohesiveness is determined by the following factors:

(i) Nature of the Group. Heterogeneous groups, whose members have different interests and backgrounds, are often less effective in promoting their own interests than groups whose members are homogeneous. Homegeneous groups, whose members are alike on such factors as age, education, status, experience, background, etc., are better when the task or goal requires mutual cooperation and conflict-free behaviour. For example, where people with sharp differences in their scales of pay and job responsibilities work near one another, the resulting informal group is generally less cohesive.

(ii) Status of the Group. Status of a group determines the degree of group cohesiveness to a great extent. A high status group receives greater loyalty from its members which in turn makes the group more strong. That is why, people are generally more loyal to high status groups.

(iii) Size of the Group. The effective group is relatively small. Small groups are more closely knitted than the large ones. When the group is small, its members have constant face contacts.

(iv) Communication. Groups whose members are located close together and can interact frequently and easily are likely to be more cohesive and effective than those whose members are scattered. Such groups tend to develop their own language, symbols and codes to communication with the group members. Even scattered groups like maintenance crews may become tightly knitted if the technology of work requires or permits them to interact frequently with one another. In fact, one of the determinants of group cohesion is the speed with which message can be transmitted through the group.

(v) Leadership Style. The different styles of leadership influence the group cohesiveness differently. An effective leader keeps the members of the group close by helping them satisfy their social needs.

(vi) Autonomy. A group may be dependent or independent of other groups and, thus, have a different structure. When each member of a group has independent and different activities, the cohesiveness among members of the group will be less as compared to the group whose members are dependent upon each other.

(vii) Outside Pressure. Groups provide a sense of security for the individual members from pressures from other groups. The group members work together when they are threatened by a common danger, *e.g.*, a group of employees may forget their personal differences and also ranks against a new supervisor who is regarded as a threat to the group. It may also happen that the group is unable to bear the excessive pressure and cohesiveness cannot be created to withstand the pressure from outside.

(viii) Management Behaviour. The behaviour of management has a direct influence on the degree of cohesion that exists within a group. By creating competition among employees and by constantly comparing one empolyees with another, a manager may make closer relations difficult. A manager can also build solidarity by rewarding cooperative behaviour.

GROUP COHESIVENESS AND PRODUCTIVITY

As revealed by Hawthorne studies group, norms may encourage either high or low performance by group (such as bricklayers, assembly-line workers, and typists) whose individual members' output can be accurately measured. These studies have found that the output of members of a cohesive group tends to be more uniform than that of members of less cohesive groups. That is, incohesive groups, individual's productivity will stay within a narrow range. Groups with low cohesion will have a much wider range of output among their members, reflecting the groups' weaker social control.

Some research studies have shown that highly choesive groups are more effective than those with less cohesiveness, but the relationship is more complex than merely allowing us to say high cohesiveness is good. First, high cohesiveness is both a cause and outcome of high productivity. Second, the relationship is moderated by the degree to which the group's attitude aligns with its formal goals or those of the larger organisation of which it is a part.

Cohesiveness influences productivity and productivity influences cohesiveness. Cohesiveness reduces tension and prodvides a supportive environment for the successful attainment to group goals. But as already noted, the successful attaintment of group goals and the members' feelings of having been a part of a successful unit, can serve to enhance the commitment of members. For instance, a football team may win beacuse of team work and the successful performance may lead to increased inter-member attractiveness.

The relationship of cohesiveness and productivity depends on the alignment of the group's attitude with the formal goals, or those of the larger organisation of which it is a part. The more cohesive a group, the more its members will follow its goals. If group norms or attitudes are favourable (*i.e.*, high output, quality work, cooperation with individual outside the group), a cohesive group will be more productive than a less cohesive group. But if cohesiveness is high and group norms are unfavourable, there will be decreases in productivity. If conhesiveness is low and there is support of goals, productivity increases but less than in the high cohesiveness-high support situation.

High cohesiveness tends to have a positive impact on satisfaction, and the reduction of absenteeism, tardiness, and turnover among group members. However, it may or may not affect productivity, depending on the co-alignment between the group's goals and the organisation's goals.

The above findings are important for managers because cohesive groups commonly set their own production standards. If the group is antagonistic to management, it will restrict output to a level well below management standards. In factories, this sort of restriction often occurs in a workgroup assigned the job for which piece rates have been established. Members of such groups often believe that if management standards are reached or surpassed, higher standards or lower piece rate will be forthcoming; they therefore restrict their output. The group members may also feel that if their actual output stays below the set level, management may offer a more favourable rate as an inducement to increase productivity.

❒

4

Motivational Process

Motivation has come from motives which are the expression of human needs by a human being. In fact, the activities of human beings are caused, and behind every action there is particular motive or need. The need can be defined as feeling of lackness for something and human being tries (activities) to get lackness removed (satisfaction). Here, we can differentiate between needs and wants. While needs are more comprehensive and include desires—physiological or psychological, wants are expressed in narrow sense and include only those desires for which a person has money and also the desire to spend money for satisfyng the wants. There are many psychological needs, *e.g.*, to get status in the organisation, which do not come under the category of wants. Thus human behaviour (activities) is caused by motives or needs, and motivtion is the process of inducing persons to experience needs for certain desired behaviour so that organisation efficiency is achieved. Many a persons have defined motivation in their own words; however, the basic contents are the same. For example, Scott has defined motivation as follows:

"Motivation means a process of stimulating people to action to accomplish desired goals."

As against this, McFarland has defined it as follows:

"Motivation refers to the way in which urges, drives, desires, aspirations, strivings, needs direct, control or explain the behaviour of human beings"

On the analysis of these definitions, we can derive the following two characteristics of motivation:

1. Motivation is an Internal Feeling. Motivation is a psychological phenomenon which generates within an individual. Needs are feelings in the mind of a person that he lacks certain things. Such feelings affect the behaviour of the person.

2. Person in Totality, not in Part, is Motivated. Each individual in the organisation is a self-contained and inseparable unit and his all needs are interrelated. These affect the behaviour in different ways. Moreover, feeling of needs is a continuous process, as such these create continuity in human behaviour.

Motivation is the product of anticipated values from an action and the perceived probablity that these values will be achieved by the action. The anticipated value is called 'valence' and it is defined as the strength of a person's preference for one outcome in relation to others. The perceived probablity is called 'expectancy' and it is defined as the strength of belief that a particular act will be followed by a particular outcome. Thus, motivational relationship can be expressed in the following formula:

$$\text{Motivation} = \text{Valence} \times \text{Expectancy}$$

ELEMENTS OR CHARACTERISTICS OF MOTIVATION

1. Psychological Concept. Motivation is a psychological concept. It develops the mental power of an individual and motivates him to do more and better.

2. Unending Process. Motivation is an unending process. Human needs are unlimited and a person always feels a need. To satisfy these needs, the persons, must always be inspired with the incentives to work. Satisfaction of one need leads to the feeling of another one and this process never ends.

3. Increase in Morale. Morale is a group feeling. Motivation motivates the employees to work with the co-operation of others. Thus, the motivation is helpful in increasing the moral of the employees.

4. Incentive. Motivation is the incentive of employees. It is a personal and natural feeling of the mind of the employees. This feeling is in the mind of an individual. In fact an individual is inspired to make his efforts to satisfy the needs of his life.

5. Increase in Efficiency. Motivation increases the efficiency of an individual. He uses his ability and efficiency to the best possible extent because of motivation which increases his efficiency. Motivation increases the quality of a production, improves the quality of a production.

6. Power to Act. Motivation is a power to act. It inspires an individual to work. Feeling of a needy creates tension and a person wants to work to satisfy his need. When the need is satsfied, the person feels motivated to work for the achievement of common goals.

Koontz & O'Donnel has described four elements of motivation: *(1)* Productivity; *(2)* Competition; *(3)* Comprehension; and *(4)* Flexibility.

OBJECTS OF MOTIVATION

The aims and objects of motivation may be described as under:

1. To motivate the employees to do more work.
2. To satisfy the economic, social and psychological needs of the employees.
3. To achieve the objects of enterprise.
4. To develop human relations in the enterprise.
5. To get the co-operation of employees.
6. To establish sweet relations between labour and capital.
7. To increase the moral of employees.
8. To increase the efficiency of employees.
9. To get the maximum exploitation of human resources.

IMPORTANCE OF MOTIVATION

Motivation is one of the most important factors determining organisational efficiency. All organisational facilities will go waste in the lack of motivated people to utilise these facilities effectiviely. Every superior in the organisation must motivate his subordinates for the right types of behaviour. Diagnosing human behaviour and analysing as to why people behave in a particular way is of prime importance in motivating them irrespective of the nature of the organisation because individual is the basic component of any organisation. The importance of motivation in an organisation may be summed up as follows:

1. Optimum Utilisation of Resources. Motivation inspires employees to make best possible use of different factors of production. They work wholeheartedly to apply their abilities and potential in minimising waste and cost. The enterprise can make maximum use of its physical and financial resources.

2. Reduction in Labour Turnover. Higher motivation leads to job satisfaction of workers. Opportunities for need satisfaction make employees loyal and committed to the organisation. As a result labour absenteeism and turnover are low.

3. Higher Efficiency. Motivation is an effective instrument in the hands of management to maximise efficiency of operations. A worker may be very competent but no activity can take place until the individual is willing to perform that activity. What employees do, depends largely on how much and why they want to do. Motivated employees give greater performance than demotivated ones.

4. Better Industrial Relations. Increased labour productivity in turn results in higher wages for employees. Motivational schemes create integration of individual interests with organisational objectives. There arises a sense of belonging and mutual co-operation at all levels. Motivation will foster team spirit among workers. This will reduce labour unrest and create better relations between management and workers.

5. Easier Selection. An enterprise that offers abundant financial and non-financial incentives enjoys reputation in the labour market. Therefore, it can easily attract competent persons for filling various vacancies.

6. Facilitates Changes. High motivation helps to reduce resistance to change. An organisation has to incorporate changes to cope with environmental changes. Properly motivated employees accept, introduce and implement these changes keeping the organisation effects.

Thus, the motivation is an eminent factor in management process. The basic objective of studying the organisation behaviour is related with observing, comprehending, analysing, predicting and influencing human behaviour in the organisation.

MOTIVATION PROCESS

A critical analysis of the various motivational models reveals that there is wide scope of variability in the facors of motivation. As such, management will be in dilemma as to how to motivate their employees to get best results. Moreover, the models have been given by foreign contributors which are more applicable to their industrial system. In our country, because of different socio-economic conditions, these models are applicable with certain reservations. Thus, while adopting a motivational model, some important considerations should be kept in mind like.

1. Simplicity in Motivational System. The system should be simple both in terms of its understanding by the employees and its applicability in the organisation. Employees' efforts are directed to goal only when they preceive that a particular goal exists and this requires a particular type of effort. The system should be simple to be adopted by the organisation at various levels.

2. Adequate Motivation. The motivation system should be adequate covering the entire human force in the orgnisation and it should cover entire activities of the working force. Sometimes, the presence of a motivational factors fails to produce any effective result, particularly when its amount is too small. In such a case, its energetic force should be increased so that it motivates strongly.

3. Analysis of Motives. A good motivation system also attempts at analysing the factors which motivate the employees in the prevailing organisational environment. Study of the various needs of the employees degree of intensity and the prospective consequence of satisfying them or continuing them dissatisfied on output should be conducted.

4. Productive. This motivation system must be of motivating the employees to do the maximum work of best quality. It follows that the motivation system must be productive.

5. Healthy Competition. Motivation System must be prepared in the manner that it may develop healthy competition among the employees so that they may be motivated to work more and more.

6. Increase in the Goodwill of the Enterpirses. The motivation system must be prepared in the manner that it may increase the goodwill of the enterprise.

7. Flexibility. Management is a dynamic science dealing with the human problems. No principle or approach of the management can be rigid. The motivation system must also be flexible so that the necessary changes may be made in it according to the need of time.

8. Maximum Satisfaction. Motivation system must be of the nature that it may satisfy the economic, social and mental needs of the employees so that the employees may feel maximum satisfaction from the motivation system.

9. Based on Certain Principles. The motivation system must be based on some certain rules and principles of the enterprise. It must be prepared keeping in view the objects of the enterprise.

10. Complete Knowledge. Motivation scheme must be properly communicated to all employees of the enterprise. If properly communicated, the scheme may become effective.

11. Economic. Motivation schemes of the enterpise must be prepared keeping in view the budget of enterprise. It must be within the reach of enterprise. The expenses on motivation scheme should not exceed its benefit.

12. Implementation of Plan. The rights, duties and responsibilities of all the employees must be clearly and specifically determind and defined. The liability of the implementation of motivation schemes must be assigned to responsible person of the enterprise so that the succeessful implementation of the plan may be assured.

THEORIES OF MOTIVATION

From the very beginning, when human organisations were established people had tried to find out the answer to what motivated people maximum. The satisfactory and generalised answer is yet to be found out. Right from the very beginning, when F.W. Taylor gave the concept of 'scientific management' and more particularly differential peice rate system for motivating workers, many researchers and managers in the field have given their views on the subject. Many new reserches are being carreid on and motivation, however, they all emphasise that due to complex nature of human beings no generalisation is possible. Moreover, the findings of research studies and theories are not universally applicable and these are affected by time, country, and circumstance. In this context it is imperative to have a knowledge about various theories of motivation and how these affect the behaviour of human beings.

Since various people have been engaged in finding out the answer of the question relating to what motivates people, their approaches have differed resulting into a number of theories concerning motivation. Though all these theories try to focus attention on the basic issue, they differ considerably. These theories may be grouped into some categories, though this grouping may not truly reflect the basic nature of each theory suggesting that any attempt to group various theories into some categories may be for simplication. Thus, there may be overlapping in any such grouping. Notwithstanding, the various theories can be grouped into three categories; theories associated with human needs—theories by Maslow, Herzberg, and Mc Clelland and theories associated with expectancy of individuals—theories of Vroom and Porter and Lawler. The major ingredients of these theories are presented in brief in that order.

MASLOW'S NEED HIERARCHY

The behaviour of an individual at a particular moment is usually determined by his strongest need. Pscyhologists claim that needs have a certain priority. As the more basic needs are satisfied, an individual seeks to satisfy the higher needs. If his basic needs are not met, efforts to satisfy the higher needs should be postponed. A.H. Maslow, a famous social scientist, has given a framework that helps to explain the strength of certain needs. According to him, there seems to be hierarachy into which human needs are arranged as shown in Fig below.

1. Physiological Needs. The physiological needs are shown at the top of the hierarchy because they tend to have the highest strength until they are reasonably satisfied. Until these needs are satisfied to the degree needed for the efficient operation of the body, the majority of a person's activities will probably be at this level, and the other levels will provide him with little motivation. A famous saying ' man can live on bread alone if there is no bread' suggest that human beings first try to acquire necessities for their survival.

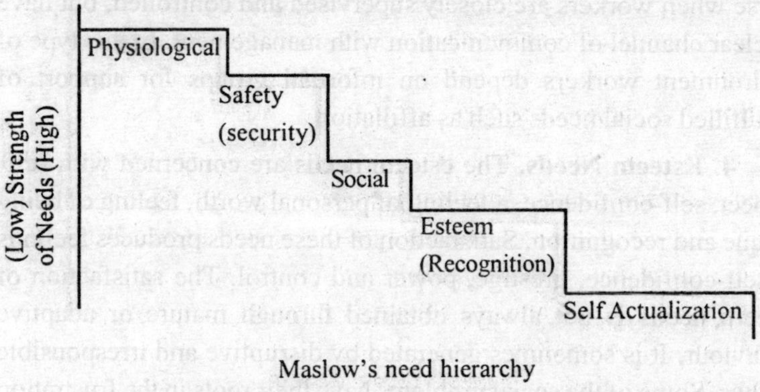

Maslow's need hierarchy

2. Safety Needs. Once the physiological needs are satisfied to a reasonable levels—it is not necessary that they are fully satisfied and degree of reasonableness is subjective—other levels of needs become important. In this hierarchy comes the needs for safety, that is needed for being free of physical danger or self-preservation. In the industrial society, safety needs may take considerable importance in the context of the dependent relationship of employees to employers. As pointed out by McGregor, the safety needs may serve as motivators in such circumstances as arbitrary management actions, behaviour which arouse uncertainty with respect to continued unemployment and unpredictable administration of policy. Peter F. Drucker has suggested that one's attitude towards security is an important consideration in choosing a job. Organisation can influence these security needs either postively—through pension plan, insurance plan, etc—or negatively by arousing fears of being fired or laid off, demoted.

3. Social Needs. After the first two needs are satisfied, social needs become important in the need hierarchy. Since man is a social being, he has a need to belong and to be accepted by various groups. When social needs become dominant, a person will strive for meaningful relations with others. If the opportunity for association with other people is reduced, men often take vigorous action against the obstacles to social intercourse. In the organiation, workers form informal group environment. Such environments develop where the work is routine, tedious or over-simplified. This situation is made worse when workers are closely supervised and controlled, but have no clear channel of communication with management. In this type of environment workers depend on informal groups for support of unfulfilled social needs such as affiliation.

4. Esteem Needs. The esteem needs are concerned with self-respect, self-confidence, a feeling of personal worth, feeling of being unique and recognition. Satisfaction of these needs produces feelings of self-confidence, prestige, power and control. The satisfaction of esteem needs is not always obtained through mature or adaptive behaviour. It is sometimes generated by disruptive and irresponsible actions. Some of the social problems have their roots in the frustration of esteem needs.

5. Self-actualisation Needs. Self actualisation is the need to maximise one's potential, whatever it may be. This is related with the development of intrisinc capabilities which lead people to seek situations that can utilise their potential. This includes competence which implies control over environmental factors, both physical and social, and achievement. A man with high intensity of achievement needs will be restless unless he can find fulfilment in doing what he is fitted to do.

Maslow suggests that the various levels are interdependent and overlapping, each higher level need emerging before the lower-level need has been completely satisfied as shown in Fig. Since one need does not disapper when another emerges, all needs tend to be partially satisfied in each area. When the peak of a need is passed, that need ceases to be primary motivator. The next level need then begins to dominate. Even though a need is satisfied, it still influences behaviour because of interdependent and overlapping characteristics of needs.

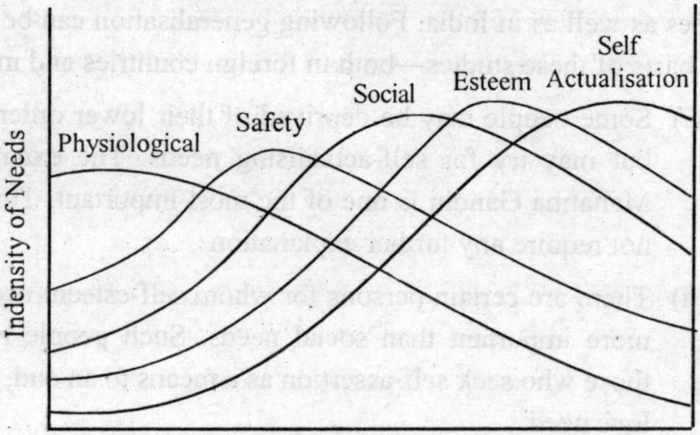

Relationship of new levels

CRITICAL ANALYSIS OF MASLOW'S THEORY

Maslow's theory has reasonable support for the hypothesis that human needs have some hierarchical order. The theory is based on the assumption, it is true also, that man is continuously wanting. His all needs are never fully satisfied. As soon as one need is reasonably satisfied, its prepotency diminishes and another need emerges to replace it. Thus at last some needs remain unsatisfied which serve the man to strive to satisfy. Thus it presents a very simple solution of managerial problems, that is, managers can try to satisfy the needs of people in this particular order. But this raises a basic question: Is need hierarchy rigid? Does every person try to satisfy his needs according to this model? If the answers are in postive, there is no problem in motivating people. However, it is not so. The hierarchy is not so rigid for all the individuals and all the times. Below are identified few problems which are not adequately solved by this theory.

1. There is lack of hierarchical structure of needs as suggested by Maslow, though every individual has some ordering for his need

satisfaction. This is based on the assumption that man has limited resources which he can use alternatively. Resources, here, cannot be taken only in a physical way rather, it is used in more comprehensive way. Naturally, every person has to satisfy his needs in some order. However, this order may not follow Maslow's need hierarchy. This has been demonstrated by large number of researches both in foreign countries as well as in India. Following generalisation can be drawn on the basis of these studies—both in foreign countries and in India:

(i) Some people may be deprived of their lower order needs but may try for self-actualising needs. The example of Mahatma Gandhi is one of the most important. This does not require any further explanation.

(ii) There are certain persons for whom self-esteem needs are more important than social needs. Such people may be those who seek self-assertion as a means to an end, that is, love need.

(iii) For certain people, many of the needs may not form part of their own need hierarchy. Thus there is not only question for reversal of hierarchy but also descontinuity of hierarchy. For example, there may be people who might be deprived of social need from their childhood. They may develop apathy towards such needs, though it is just possible that they may develop high order for such need.

(iv) There is considerable disordering among physiological needs, safety needs, social needs, and esteem needs, particularly in organisational context. For example, many people do not care for job security (security need) but care for social need. Similarly, many people may not care for social need but for self-esteem need.

2. There is another problem, which is common with many other theories also, that there is often a lack of direct cause-effect relationship between need and behaviour. Thus a particular need may cause behaviour in different ways in different persons. Similarly, one particular behaviour may be the result of different needs. For example,

if a person is thirsty, he may take water, or some soft drink, or some juice. Similarly, people may earn money to satisfy their several types of needs, not only physiological needs.

3. There is another problem in applying the theory into practice. A person tries for his higher level need when his lower order need is reasonably satisfied. What is this reasonable level is a question of subjective matter. Thus the level of satisfaction for particular need may differ from person to person. In fact needs and their satisfaction are mental feelings. Sometimes even the person concerned may not be aware about his own needs. The question is how can a manager know the needs of others?

There are some basic problems involved in the application of Maslow's need hierarchy model. At every level of point, it can be seen that the role of individual is very important. Since individuals differ, it may not be quite possible to prescribe one standard action for solving motivational problems of all persons, rather, a contingency approach has to be applied.

ERG THEORY

Clayton Alderfer of Yale University has reworked Maslow's need hierarchy to align it more closely with the empirical research. His revised need hierarchy is labeled ERG theory.

Alderfer argues that there are three groups of core needs—existence, relatedness, and growth—hence, the label: ERG theory. The existence group is concerned with providing our basic material existence requiements. They include the items that Maslow considered to be physiological and safety needs. The second group of needs are those of relatedness—the desire we have for maintaining important interpersonal relationships. These social and status desires require interaction wih others if they are to be satisfied and they align with Maslow's social need and the external component of Maslow's esteem classification. Finally, Alderfer isolates growth needs—an intrinsic desire for personal development. These include the intrinsic component from Maslow's esteem category and the characteristics included under self-actualization.

Besides substituting three needs for five, how does Alderfer's ERG theory differ from Maslow's? In contrast to the hierarchy of needs theory, the ERG theory demonstrates that *(1)* more than one need may be operative at the same time, and *(2)* if the gratification of a higher level is stifled, the desire to satisfy lower-level need increases.

Maslow's need hierarchy follows a rigid, steplike progression. ERG theory does not assume that there exists a rigid hierarchy where a lower need must be substantially gratified before one can move on. A person can, for instance, be working on growth even though existence or relatedness needs are unsatisfied; or all three need categories could be operating at the same time.

ERG theory also contains a frustration-regression dimension. Maslow, you'll remember, argued that an individual would stay at a certain need level until that need was satisfied. ERG theory counters by noting that when a higher-order need level is frustrated, the individual's desire to increase a lower-level need takes place. Inability to satisfy a need for social interaction, for instance, might increase the desire for more money or better working conditions. So frustration can lead to a régression to a lower need.

In summary, ERG theory argues, like Maslow, that satisfied lower-order needs lead to the desire to satisfy higher-order needs; but multiple needs can be operating as motivators at the same time, and frustration in attempting to satisfy a higher-level need can result in regression to a lower-level need.

ERG theory is more consistent with our knowledge of individual differences among people. Variables such as education, family background, and cultural environment can alter the importance or driving force that a group of needs holds for a particular individual. The evidence demonstrating that people in other cultures rank the need catgeories differently—for instance, natives of Spain and Japan place social needs before their physiological requirements—would be consistent with ERG theory. Several studies have supported ERG theory, but there is also evidence that it doesn't work in some organizations. Overall, however, ERG theory represents a more valid version of the need hierarchy.

STACY ADAMS EQUITY THEORY

Equity plays an important role in motivation. Employees make comparisions of their job inputs and outcomes relative to those of others. We perceive what we get from a job situation (outcomes) in relation to what were put into it (inputs), and then we compare our outcome-input ratio with the outcome-input ratio of relevant others. If we perceive our ratio to be equal to that of the relevant others with whom we compare ourselves, a state of equity is said to exist. We perceive our situation as fair—that justice prevails. When we see the ratio as unequal, we experience equity tension. J. Stacy Adams has proposed that this negative tension state provides the motivation to do something to correct it.

The referent that an employee selects adds to the complexity of equity theory. Evidence indicates that the referent chosen is an important variable in equity theory. There are four referent comparisions that an employee can use:

1. **Self-inside.** An employee's experiences in a different position inside his or her current organization.
2. **Self-outside.** An employee's experiences in a situation or position outside his or her current organization.
3. **Other-inside.** Another individual or group of individuals inside the employee's organization.
4. **Other-outside.** Another individual or group of individuals outside the employee's organization.

Employees might compare themselves to friends, neighbours, co-workers, colleagues in other organisations, or past jobs they themselves have had. Which referent an employee chooses will be influenced by the information the employee holds about referents as well as by the attractiveness of the referent. This has led to focusing on four moderating variables—gender, length of tenure, level in the organization, and amount of education or professionalism. Research shows that both men and women prefer same-sex comparisions. The reasarch also demonstrates that women are typically paid less than men in comparable jobs and have lower pay expectations than men for the same work. So a female that uses another female as a referent tends to result in a lower comparative standard. This leads us to conclude that employees in jobs that are not sex segregated will make more cross-sex comparisons than those in jobs that are either male or female dominated. This also suggests that if women are tolerant of lower pay, it may be due to the comparative standard they use.

Employees with short tenure in their current organisations tend to have little information about other inside the organisation, so they rely on their own personal experiences. On the other hand, employees with long tenue rely more heavily on co-workers for comparison. Upper employees, those in the professional ranks, and those with higher amounts of education tend to be more cosmopolitan and have better information about people in other organizations. Therefore, these types of employees will make more other-outside comparisons.

Based on equity theory, when employees perceive an inequity they can be predicted to make one of six choices:

1. Change their inputs (for example, don't exert as much effort).
2. Change their outcomes (for example, individuals paid on a piece-rate basis can increase their pay by producing a higher quanity of units of lower quality).
3. Distort perceptions of self (for example, "I used to think I worked at a moderate pace but now I realise that I work a lot harder than everyone else.")
4. Distort perceptions of others (for example, "mike's job isn't as desirable as I previously thought it was.")
5. Choose a different referent (for example, "I may not make as much as my brother-in-law, but I'm doing a lot better than my Dad did when he was my age.")
6. Leave the field (for example, quit the job)

Equity theory recognizes that individuals are concerned not only with the absolute amount of rewards they receive for their efforts, but also with the relationship of this amount to what others receive. They make judgemnts as to the realtionship between their inputs and outcomes and the inputs and outcomes of others. Based on one's inputs, such as effort, experience, education, and competence, one compares outcomes such as salary levels, raises, recognition, and other factors. When people perceive an imbalance in their outcome—input ratio relative to others, tension is created. This tension provides the basis for motivation, as people strive for what they perceive as equity and fairness.

Specifically, the theory establishes four propossitions relating to inequitable pay:

1. Given payment by time, over rewarded employees will produce more than will equitably paid employees. Hourly and salaried employees will generate high quantity or quality of producton in order to increase the inputs side of the ratio and bring about equity.
2. Given payment by quantity of production, overrewarded employees will produce fewer, but higher-quality, units than will equitably paid employees. Individuals paid on a piece-rate basis will increase their effort to achieve equity, which can result in greater quality or quantity. However, increases in quantity will only increase inequity, since every unit produced results in further overpayment. Therefore, effort is directed towards increasing quality rather than increasing qantity.
3. Given payment by time, under rewarded employees will produce less or poorer quality of output. Effort will be decreased, which will bring about lower prodcutivity or poorer-quality output than equitably paid subjects.
4. Given payment by quantity of production, under rewarded employees will produce a larger number of low-quality units in comparison with equitably paid employees. Employees on piece-rate pay plans can bring about equity because trading off quality of output for quanity will result in an increase in rewards with little or no increase in rewards with little or no increase in contributions.

These propositions have generally been supported, with a few minor qualifications. First, inequities created by overpayment do not seem to have a very signficant impact on behaviour in most work situations. Apparently, people have a great deal more tolerance of overpayment inequities than on underpayment inequities, or are better able to rationalize them. Second, not all people are equity sensitive. For example, there is a small part of the working population who actually prefer that their outcome-input ratio be less than the referent comparison. Predictions from equity theory are not likely to be very accurate with these "benevolent types."

It's also important to note that while most research on equity theory has focused on pay, employees seem to look for equity in the distribution of other organisational rewards. For instane, it's been shown that the use of high-status job titles as well as large and lavishly furnished offices may function as outcomes for some employees in their equity equation.

In conclusion, equity theory demonstrates that, for most employees, motivation is influenced signficantly by relative rewards as well as by absolute rewards, but some key issues are still unclear. For instance, how do employees handle conflicting equity signals, such as when unions point to other employee groups who are substantially better off, while management argues how much things have improvted? How do employees define inputs and outcomes? How do they combine and weigh their inputs and outcome to arrive a totals. When and how do the factors change over time? Yet, reagrdless of these problems, equity theory continues to offer us some important in sights into employees motivation.

APPROACHES TO MOTIVATION

There are two main approaches to motivation. These are as follows:

I. Carrot and Stick Approach to Motivation

This approach is based upon the old belief that the best way to get work from a person is to put a reward (carrot) before him or to hold out the threat of punishment (stick). Carrot is the reward for working and stick is the punishment for not working. Under carrot and stick approach employees who perform the task well are given rewards in the form of bonus, pay rise, promotion, etc. While the employees avoiding work (showing undesired behaviour) are given punishment in the form of demotion, termination from service, transfer to an unpleasant job, etc. Employers who adopt this approach believe that a person seeks employment because he expects to earn money with the help of which he can satsify the needs of himself and of his family. He knows that if he does not perform his job satisfactorily he will lose his job. Stick pushes people to engage in positive behaviour or to avoid negative behaviour.

F.W. Taylor and his associates evolved incentive plans of wages payment. Under these plans workers who produced more than the standard output were given rewards while those producing less than the standard were punished in the form of wage cut. This system became very popular in the United States and in the United Kingdom.

Carrot and stick apporach began to fail after sometime. Workers became well organised into powerful trade unions who resisted fines, suspension, dismissal and other forms of punishment. Government in many demorcartic countries enacted laws to protect the interests of the working class. As a result threat of punishment lost much of its force. Carrot and stick approach helps to influence only the internal environment of an organisation. But motivation is affected by many other (external) forces. The following steps may be taken to make the carrot and stick approach more effective:—

1. Reward (carrot) is a more effective motivator when it is directly linked with performance.
2. The mixture of reward and punishment should be judiciously applied to reinforce desirable behaviour patterns.
3. Punishment should be administered with extreme care so that it does not become a reward for undesirable behaviour.

4. Punishment (stick) is more effective if applied at the time when the undesirable behaviour actually occurs.
5. Punishment should be used to modify the behaviour and to force the person to adopt desirable behaviour which is rewarded.

II. Motivation Through Job Enrichment

Job enrichment is a non-financial technique of motivation. It is an outgrowth of Herzberg's two-factors theory of motivation. It is based on the assumption that the factors surrounding the work are not effective motivators of behaviour. In order to motivate employees the job itself must provide opportanities for achievement, recognition, responsibility, advancement and growth. The nature of modern technology (division of labour, assembly line, job simplification) has made the jobs dull and monotonous. Workers do not get job satisfaction and, therefore, they are not fully motivated despite fair wages and fringe benefits. In order to overcome these problems, the IBM Corporation of USA made an experiment in job enlargement.

Job enrichment is an extension of job enlargement technique. The difference between job enlargement and job enrichment lies in the nature of additions to the job. Job enlargement involves a horizontal expansion of the job, *i.e.* addition of more tasks. On the other hand, job enrichment involves vertical loading of the job to make it more challenging and interesting. Job enrichment may be defined as an attempt to design jobs in such a way as to build in the opportunity for achievement, recognition, responsibility and personal growth. It provides a worker greater autonomy and responsibility in carrying out a complete task and with timely feedback on his performance. Horizontal loading (job enlargement) does not enrich the task. But job enrichment involves designing jobs with variety of work content that requires a high level of knowledge and skill. It provides meaningful work experience and greater responsibility for planning and controlling his own performance. Job enrichment requires decentralisation of decision-making authority to the worker.

Dr. Robert N. Ford reported that the process of job enrichment consists of three stages involving systematic changes in:

(a) **Work Module.** Work elements are defined to ensure each employee has a natural area of responsibility.

(b) **Control of the Work Module.** As a person gains experience, the supervisor turns more responsibility over to him.

(c) **Feedback.** Performance evaluation reports are sent directly to the worker to enable him to correct his behaviour.

Job enrichment is said to be a key to higher motivation and productivity. It removes the labour management distinction. It creates a self-managed job where the worker himself plans and controls his task. It offers job satisfaction to the whole man. According to Ford, A T & T Co. Job enrichment led to a cost saving of $ 5,58,000 in one year.

Inspite of its benefits, job enrichment has been criticised on the following grounds:

(i) Job enrichment may have little value for workers who do not seek satisfaction in the work place. Some jobs cannot be enriched beyond a certain point.

(ii) Job enrichment is based on the assumption that workers want more responsibility. In reality some workers (*e.g.*, uneducated persons) may prefer less responsible jobs with good social interaction. Such workers may show feelings in inadequacy and fear of failure to job enrichment.

(iii) job enrichment may have negative effects in the short run. Workers take time to adjust to the challenging demand made by job enrichment. Job enrichment helps individuals grow slowly and steadily. Job enrichment is an individual theory of work motivation. Its success depends ultimately on how work groups implement it. Trade unions may not accept it.

(iv) Job enrichment is basically limited to non-managerial jobs. In managerial and professional jobs there is little scope for applying job enrichment. Such jobs can be enriched more by techniques like MBO, participative management and delegation of authority.

(v) Supervisors may feel that their power and prestige is being undermined when greater authority is delegated to workers. Thus, job enrichment is not a panacea for motivational problems and it is not a substitute for good management. Sucessful implementation of job enrichment requires a supporting climate for innvoation and change.

(vi) When managers use their own scale of values of responsibility and challenges, workers may resists job enrichment. Similarly, the tendency to impose job enrichment leads to resistance from employees.

PROCESS OF MOTIVATION

Incentives are the inducements which are offered to employees in order to direct their behaviour towards enterprise objectives. These are the objects perceived to satisfy needs. Incentives are attention-getting and effort-producing mechanisms. Incentives can broadly be classified into two categories—(i) pecuniary incentives, and (ii) non-pecuniary incentives. Pecuniary or financial incentives are payments directly or indiectly in money. Wages, salaries, bonus, profit-sharing, retirement pay, vacation pay, etc., are examples of pecuniary incentives. Financial incentives can be of two types: (a) individual incentives refer to all such plans which induce an individual to achieve higher performance to earn higher financial rewards. Piece rate wages, Halsey's plan, Rowan's plan, Emerson's efficiency plan, Gantt's bonus plan and Tylor's differential plan are examples of individual incentives: (b) Group incentive plans include profit-sharing, production bonus, pension plan, etc., wherein employees are rewarded collectively.

Non-financial incentives provide psychological and emotional satisfaction rather than financial rewards. Status, reponsibility, recognition of work, job security, challenging job, team spirit, competition, participation are examples of non-financial incentives. These incentives are very important for the satisfaction of socio-psychological needs which cannot be satisfied by money alone.

These are certain inducements which serve as both financial and non-financial incentives.

FINANCIAL INCENTIVES

In the context of existing system money has become a means not only to satisfy the physical needs of daily life but also of obtaining a social position and power.

It should be borne in mind that money has its speical significance in the motivational scheme since money is not an end but a means of purchasing ends, it can gratify both physical and safety needs, the lower-order needs. Thus, to some people, money is not important, whether they have a lot or little. Others no matter how much money they have are continuously driven by the desire to acquire more money, possibly to satisfy thier desire for status or their goal of being rich. Thus, money is a factor by which a person can satisfy his various types of needs.

Economists and some managers tend to put the special emphasis on money as motivator while behavioural scientists do not recognise this. From organisation's point of view, the fact may be in between this is , the role of money as a motivating force must be seen in organisational context. Thus, following points are important for analysing the role of money as motivator:

1. If the money is to act as motivator, it is necessary to assume a relationship between performance and reward in terms of money. Those who seek money will be motivated only if they can clearly link higher performance to the reward of money. Moreover, people are concerned not only with absolute amount of money they are paid for their efforts, the relationship of this amount to what others are paid is also important. This is based on equity theory.
2. The type of organisation also determines the importance of money to the people. For example, Gellerman points out that in most kinds of business organisation, money is actually used as a means of keeping an organisation adequately staffed and not as a motivator. This can be seen

INCENTIVES

- **Financial Incentives**
  - **Individual**
    - Various premium plans by Taylor, Halsey, Rowan, Gantt, etc.
  - **Collection**
    1. Equal wage rates
    2. Wages increase based on ability
    3. Pension Plan
    4. Production bonus
    5. Profit-sharing
    6. Co-partnership
- **Non-Financial Incentives**
  - **Individual**
    1. Status
    2. Promotion
    3. Responsibility
    4. Pleasant and interesting job
    5. Recognition of work
    6. Job security
  - **Collective**
    1. Social importance of work
    2. Team spirit
    3. Competition
    4. Informal groups
  - **Institutional**
    1. Human Relations in industry
    2. Participation
    3. Communication
    4. Building morale
    5. Discipline

Figure: Financial and Non-financial Incentives

in the practice of making wages and salaries competitive between various organisations so as to attract and hold people.

3. Economic conditions necessarily affect the importance of money as a motivator. Money is an urgent means of achieving a minimum standard of living, although this minimum has a way of expanding upward as people become more affluent. However, this cannot be taken as generalisation because for some people, money will remain important irrespective of their economic conditions, while for others, it is not important afte. a certain level.

4. Money to act as motivator in the organisation should be given insufficient quantity to the people. Gellerman suggests that money can motivate only when the prospective payment is large enough relative to a person's income. The people will try to earn money by their higher performance if they feel that additional money earned by their efforts is significant portion of their income.

5. The social attitude towards wealth plays an important role in determining whether, within a given culture, money will be actively sought and used to satisfy human needs. In some societies, the personal acquisition of wealth has been looked upon as evil, or as being beneath the dignity of man.

These financial incentives may classified into two parts, viz, individual and collective.

1. Individual Financial Incentives. This group of incentives tries to motivate individuals collectively. The basic idea of these incentives is the same as above; however, the employees are given these collectively. Examples, are bonus, profit-sharing, pension plan, etc.

2. Individal Financial Incentives. This group of incentives includes all such plans which induce an individual to achieve higher output to earn higher financial rewards. Piece-rate wages, Taylor's differential piece-rate system, Halsey's efficiency plan are example of such incentives. The basic assumption behind this incentive is that an individual will be motivated for higher output to earn more moeny which satsifies his needs.

NON-FINANCIAL INCENTIVES

Financial incentives are used to motivate employees for higher work. However, individuals have various needs which they want to satisfy while working in the organisation. Poeple at compartively higher level of management hierarchy attach more importance to socio-psychological needs which can not be satisfied by money alone. This management, in addition to the finanacial incentive, provides non-financlia incentives to motivate people in the organisation. The connotation of non-financial incentives does not mean that organisation has nothing to spend on these. However, the emphasis of non- financial incentives is to provide psychological and emotional satisfaction rather than financial satisfaction.

1. Individual Incentives. These incentives motivate people on individual basis. The incentives exist, but only certain individuals may get them, though on individual basis not group basis, *e.g.*, making job more pleasant. The various forms of individual non-financial incentives are as follows:

(i) ***Status.*** Status, in general term, is the ranking of people in the society. in the organisational context, status means the ranking of positions, right and duties in the formal organisation structure. The status system is an instrument of motivation because it is extremely important for most of the people. The status system should be closely related to the abilities and aspirations of people in the organisation.

(ii) ***Making Job Pleasant and Interesting.*** The work can be made enjoyable and pleasant if it is so designed that it allows the employees to satisfy their natural instincts. This creates interset in the work and emplyees take it as natural as play. Job enlargement—a method of making job more complicated and varied—makes the job more pleasant and interesting.

(iii) ***Promotion.*** Promotion is defined as a movement to position in which responsibilities and presumably prestige are

increased. Promotion satisfies the needs of human beings in the organisation. Since the promotion depends upon capabilities and good performance, people will try for that if the avenues of promotion exist.

(iv) ***Job Security.*** Employees want that their job is secure. They want certain stability about future income and work so that they do not feel warried on these aspects and they can work with greater zeal. In India, this aspect is more important considering the inadequate job opportunities and too many aspirants for these. However, there is one negative aspect of job security. When people feel that they are not likely to forfeit jobs they become complacent.

(v) ***Responsibility.*** Most of the people prefer challenging and responsible jobs rather than monotonous and routine type jobs. If the job is responsible, it satisfies people's natural and inherent characteristics and they put more effort for completing the job.

(vi) ***Recognition of Work.*** Most people have a need for a high evaluation of themselves. They feel that what they do should be recognised by others concerned. Recognition means acknowledgement with a show of appreciation. When such appreciation is given to the work performed by employees, they feel motivated to perform work at similar or higher level.

2. Collective Incentives. People may be motivated in groups also. They perform their duties in groups and are affected by the group. If the group in general is efficient, an individual tends to become efficient. Some of the collective non-financial incentives are as follows:

(i) ***Social Importance of Work.*** People generally prefer to work which is socially acceptable. If the society gives importance and praise to the work, people like it to perform. Sometimes, people prefer a job of high social importance even though the financial compensation would be less. The reason is simple. People have to live in the society and by

performing a job of high social importance they derive satisfaction of being important in the society.

(ii) ***Informal Groups.*** When people work together they develop some sort of affiliation among themselves. These relationships are not officially prescribed, but created on the basis of certain factors, both personality factors of the employees and other social factors. The creation of these informal groups provides social satisfaction to employees at workplace. People feel to achieve a sense of belongingness and security. Management should provide the way for creational of such informal groups so long as they are not detrimental to organisation efficiency and objectives because sometimes, the informal groups may go against the interest of the organisation.

(iii) ***Competition.*** Sometimes, for providing incentives to employees, competitions are organised between different individuals or different groups. There may be a case of self-competition where an individual tries to improve his earlier performance. When an individual performs very well because of any such competition, he should be given some advantages, not necessarily in terms of money, but it may be in terms of recognition, prestige, praise, etc. However, this method has a negative consequence also. Though all the employees to put in their maximum efforts all of them cannot win.

(iv) ***Team Spirit.*** The management should encourage team spirit, that is, to work in co-operation and coordination. Team work is a coordinated action by a co-operative small group in regular contact wherein members contribute responsibly and enthusiastically toward task achievement. If there is team spirit among the employees, they will try to put in maximum efforts to achieve the objectives.

3. Institutional Incentives. These incentives are related with the environmental factors in the organisation. Conducive and congenial atmosphere of the organisation motivates employees to produce better results. Following incentives fall in this category:

(i) ***Human Relations in Industry.*** Human relations in the industry is related with the policy to be adopted in the organisation to develop a sense of belongingness in the employees, improve their efficiency and treat them as human beings and not merely a factor of production. The emphasis is on providing greater satisfaction, both psychological and physiological, by creating such environment in the organisation where employees are able to work efficiently. In such an environment, employees are motivated to stay with the organisation and they also adopt more productive behaviour.

(ii) ***Building Morale.*** Though there are various definitions of morale, it can be defined as the attitudes of individuals and groups towards work environment and towards voluntary co-operation to the full extent of their ability in the best interest of the organisation. Generally, high level of morale results in high productivity. High morale of employees depends on the various facilities provided to them to satisfy their physiological and psychological needs, latter being more important. However, management should attempt to measure employees' morale.

(iii) ***Participation.*** The superior-subordinate realtionship emphasises that superior takes the decisions and subordinates implement them. However, in such a decision-making process, subordinate does not feel very enthusiastic in implementing the decisions. As such, the subordinate should also be associated with decision-making process. This not only motivates a subordinate to take prompt and proper action on decision implementation, but also makes him responsible for anything which goes worng.

(iv) ***Discipline.*** The quality of an organisation's climate is reflected in the discipline of its employees. Discipline is in essence obedience, application, energy, behaviour and

outward marks of respect shown by employees. It is employees self-control to meet organisation standards and objectives. Management has primary responsibility of developing and maintaining discipline. It maintains discipline by applying standards in a consistent, fair and flexible manner. This provides employees to behave in a particular direction as any employee whose behaviour is inconsistent with standards invites disciplinary action. However, discipline does not means in a negative term only as putting constraints over employees behaviour, it has a positive role to satisfy them by providing them proper atmosphere.

(v) ***Communication.*** Communication is the lifeblood of an organisation. Complex nature and big size of organisations require greater specialisation and division of work. Thus, for a particular goal, total activities are divided into parts and sub-parts to share the information about their functioning among themselves. This is done through communication as communication is the process of passing ideas and understanding from one person or group to other person or group. A free and adequate flow of communication is necessary. This, besides providing base for successful organisational functioning, provides satisfaction to individuals in the organisation as they want to be informed properly about the matters concerning their interests.

In an organisation, both these incentives are used and should be applied according to need. All the incentives have different roles. Moerever, even a single incentive motivates in different ways. This depends upon the level of an individual in the managerial hierarchy, attitudes, interests, family background, etc. While choosing an incentive careful study should be made in respect of these factors.

MCCLELLAND'S NEED THEORY

Shortly after World War II, a group of psychologists led by David C. Mclelland of Harvard University began to experiment with TAT (Thematic Apperception Test) to see if it were sensitive enough to detect changes in motivation that were caused by simple attmepts to sway the individual's attitudes. In order to simplify their task, the group decided to select one particular motive for intensive analysis. For, it was not long before the implications of the achievement motive were recognised that it became the subject of intensive investigation in its own right.

McClelland has identified three types of basic motivting needs. He classified these as need for power(n/PWR), need for affiliation (n/ AFF), and need for achievement (n/ACH). Considerable research work was done by McClelland and his associates in this respect, particularly, on achiveemnt motive.

Power Motive. The ability to induce or influence behaviour is power. Power motive has been formally recognised and studied for a relatively long time. The leading advocate of the power motive was Alfred Adler. To explain the power need, the need to manipulate others or the drive for superiority over others. Adler developed the concepts of inferiority complex and compensation. Accordingly, the individual's life style is characterised by striving to compensate for the feeling of inferiority which are combined with the innate drive for power. McClelland and his associates have found that people with a high power need have a greed concern for exercising influence and control. Such individuals are generally seeking positions of leadership; they involve in conversation; they are forceful, outspoken, hard headed, and demanding.

Affiliation Motive. Since people are social animals, most individuals like to interact and be with others in situations where they feel they belong and are accepted. Sometimes affiliation is equated with social motives.

However, the affiliation motive is not so broad. Affiliation plays a very complex but vital role in human behaviour. The study of affiliation is complicated by the fact that some behavioural scientists believe that it is an unlearned motive. However, the fact is partly true. McClelland has suggested that people with high need for affiliation usually derive pleasure from being loved and tend to avoid the pain of being rejected. They are concerned with maintaining pleasant social relationships, enjoying a sense of intimacy and understanding, and enjoy consoling and helping others in trouble.

Achievement Motive. Over the years, behavioural scientists have observed that some people have an intense desire to achieve. McClelland's research has led him to believe that the need for achievement is a distinct human motive that can be distinguished from other needs. It can also be isolated and assessed in any group. McClelland has identified four basic characteristics of high achievers.

(i) Moderate Risks. Taking moderate risks is probably the simple most descriptive characteristic of the person possessing high achievement need. This is against the commonsense that a high achiever would take high risks.

(ii) Immediate Feedback. Person with high n/ACH desires activities which provide immediate and precise feedback informtion how he is progressing toward a goal.

(iii) Accomplishment. Person with high n/ACH finds accomplishing a task intrinsically satisfying in and of itself, or he does not expect or necessarily want the accompanying material rewards. Though he likes to earn moeny a lot but not for the usual reason of wanting money for its own sake or for the material benefits that it can buy.

(iv) Preoccupation with the Tasks. Once a high achiever selects a goal, he tends to be totally preoccupied with the task until it is successfully completed. He will not feel satisfied unless he has put his maximum effort in completing the task. This type of dedicated commitment often reflects on his outward personality, which frequently has a negative effect on those who come in contact with him.

Implications of the Theory

Because any organisation and every departmemnt of it represents groups of individuals working together to achieve goals, the need for achivement is of paramount importance. According to the research conducted by McClelland and others, managers show high on achievement and power and low on affiliation. The research finding also indicates that chief executive of smaller compainies show higher achievement motive as compared to those of large compainies. Similarly, middle level managers have higher n/ACH as compared to the chief executive. This seems to be contradictory but McClelland feels that it is quite understandable because chief executives have already arrived, and those below them are striving to advance.

Acheivement motivated people can be the backbone of most organisations because they progress much faster. However, when they are promoted where their success depends not only on their work but on the activities of others, they may be less effective. Since they are high task oriented and work to their utmost capacity, they expect similar results from others. As a result, they sometimes lack human skill and patience of being effective managers, specially of those persons having high affiliation motive. Thus such persons can be better managers in production, research and development as compared to personnel activity. Thus an organisation may need managers with varying degree of achievement and affiliation motives.

Development of Achievement Motive. Achievement motive can be developed not only at early age, but also at later stage. Experimenting with people from the U.S.A., Italy, Poland and India, McClelland and his group found that in all cases training programmes were successful in increasing individual need for achievement. Their achievement development course has four primary goals.

1. To teach participants how to think, talk and eat like a person with high achievement.
2. To stimulate participants to set higher, but carefully planned and realistic work goals over the next two years.
3. To give the participants knowledge about themselves.
4. To create group espirit de corps from learning about each other's hope and fears, successes and failure, and from going through an emotional experience together, away from everyday life, in a retreat setting.

It was found that after two years, who had taken the course made more money; were promoted faster and expanded their business faster than comparable men who had not taken some other management course. For example, in India, he subjected a group of fifty-two entrepreneurs to the concentrated achievement motivation course. Two-thirds of them were found unusally active in the post-training period. Some of them actually started new business, others investigated new product lines, increased their profits and expanded their present business. This has another implication and that is in the training programmes such courses may be added to develop achievement motive in individuals where it is needed.

CONTINGENCY APPROACH OF MOTIVATION

The appraisal of various theories of motivation and resultant motivational strategies suggested by these fails to provide any concrete result as how a manager can be sure about the way he can motivate people in the organisation. The various theories suggest that there is no universal device applicable to everyone. What motivates people is situational. This is the basic theme of contingency approach of motivation. This shows the complexity of human behaviour and consequently the inability to predict his behaviour. Since individuals differ, as discussed earlier, it is not possible to motivate them by a single method. Thus universality of motivational strategy is out of question. However, it does not mean that various theories do not offer any help. In fact, the contingency approach is derived out of these theories which merely suggests that in motivating people, all the contextual variables must be specified and their inter-relationship should be established. When this is done, it may be easy to find out what would be the best motivational strategy. Followinσ factors seem to be important in this respect; individual personality, organisational climate, and type of incentives available.

1. Individual Personality. Individual differences suggest that all people do not like the same things. Consequently, their need pattern will be different. This is the reason that research studies show conflicting results when a particular theory is tested in the field. Thus the analysis of individuals will give a clue as to what a person wants.

2. Organisational Climate. A person's needs are determined by his initial needs as well the needs which he develops through the interaction with the organisation. It means many of individual's needs are modified by organisational factors. The various organisational factörs may be termed as organistional climate. Since there is a relationship between organisational climate and arousal of individual needs, organisational climate can be used to motivate people.

3. Available Incentives. No doubt, organisational climate will affect human behaviour, what is more important for motivating people is the availability of various types of incentives through which they can be motivated. Availability and applicability of incentives are determiend by various factors, both internal and external. For example, an organisation is considerably restricted by its environment in distributing financial incentives. It cannot fix its salary and wage structure in total disregard of its internal and external factors. Thus people's motivation will be decided by these factors.

When all these factors are considered, a manager can get some insights of how in each case, he should go for motivating people. Thus rather than going for a universal framework of motivation, he should decide this on the basis of situational factors.

HERZBERG'S MOTIVATIONAL MAINTENANCE MODEL

We have noted that needs such as esteerm and self actualisation seems to have became more important as people matūre. Maintenance Factor—This was another set of factors, the presence of which did not significantly motivate them but the absence of such factors caused serious dissatifaction. The presence of such factors prevents dissatisfaction and maintains a certain level of motivation but any reduction in the availabilities of these factors is likely to affect motivation and bring down the level of performance. For example, an increase of Rs. 10 in the salary of a person does not mean much but a reduction of Rs. 10 from his salary may upset him and is likely to cause dissatisfaction. Maintenance factors mostly are related to environment, outside the job. Herzberg called these factors hygiene or maintenance factors or dissatisfier because they produce nothing to the workers' capacity but they help maintain or prevent losses to the worker-performance due to work-restriction.

Herzberg named 10 maintenance factors as: *(i)* Company policy and administration, *(ii)* technical supervision, *(iii)* interpersonal relations with subordinates, *(iv)* salary, *(v)* job security, *(vi)* personal life, *(vii)* working conditions, *(viii)* status, *(ix)* interpersonal relations with supervisors, and *(x)* inter-personal relations with peers.

INTRINSIC AND EXTRINSIC FACTORS

Intrinsic motivations are internal rewards that occur at the time of performance of work. So, there is a direct motivation to perform work because the act of performance is itself rewarding. In this situation employee is self-motivated. Extrinsic motivators are external rewards which are not directly related to the performance of work and occur after or away from the work such as retirement plans, leaves, health insurance etc.

Prior to Herzberg's research organisational manager paid their attention to extrinsic maintenance factors often proved poor results. Now, they had better understanding and insist more on intrinsic motivational factors, because of their superior possibilities for the workers society and organisation.

MOTIVATORS

Motivators are associated with feelings of employees about the job. They are related to the content of the job. They make people satisfied with their job. If managers wish to increase motivation and performance above the average level, they must enrich the work and increase a person's freedom on the job. Motivators are necessary to keep job satisfaction and job performance high. On the other hand, if they are not present they do not prove highly satisfying.

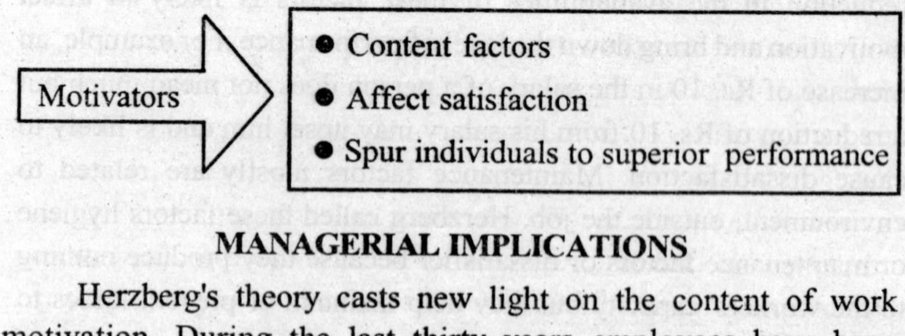

MANAGERIAL IMPLICATIONS

Herzberg's theory casts new light on the content of work motivation. During the last thirty years employees have been paternalistically maintained too much and enthusiastically motivated too little. Managers have been focussing their attention on hygiene factors often with poor results. They were preoccupied with the environment of work rather than work itself. The distinction of motivational and maintenance factors will help managers in spurring individuals to peak performance. The most basic implication of the motivation-maintenance theory is that in order to maximize human productivity it is absolutely necessary to satisfy employee's maintenance needs and provide the opportunity to gratify their motivation needs. The key to motivation lies in structuring meaningful jobs, jobs that are challenging and rewarding that provide increased opportunities for achievement, responsibility, growth and recognition.

Criticism to Herzberg's Theory. Herzberg's theory was subjected to several serious criticism. Some of the criticisms are:

(i) Herzberg model is based on two factor theory of motivation and job satisfaction. It suggests job satisfiers and dissatisfiers as two different qualitative factors. This was objected by others on the ground that job-satisfaction and dissatisfaction are two opposite points.

(ii) Some others cirticised the theory on the ground that it is easier to get results favourable to the model by using the Herzberg method. Other methods failed to produce the similar results.

(iii) According to some others, model does not give sufficient emphasis to the motivating qualities of pay, status and inter-personal relations. Admittedly, these are important employee-motivators. The model gives credit primarily to their maintenance capabilities.

(iv) The terminology used in the model is confusing and the difference between motivational and maintenance factors is very thin. Items designated as maintenance factors may serve as motivational factors to some and *vice-versa*.

In spite of the criticism , the theory is useful in distinguishing factors that motivate people on the job and factors that primarily maintain employees ready to be motivated. In this manner, the model provides new insights in organisational behaviour.

In his studies, he tried to understand the motivation problem and felt that knowledge about human behaviour, nature, motives and needs could be invaluable to organisation and individuals. In his efforts to uncover the circumstances where a person felt satisfied or dissatisfied with his work, he conducted a study and interviewed about 200 engineers and accountants from 11 industries in the Pittsburgh area. He asked these engineers and accountants to think to describe the conditions that led to those feelings. Herzberg found that employees named different types of conditions for good and bad feelings. The study revealed that the factors responsible for job satisfaction are quite different from the factors that led to dissatisfaction. These two feelings were not obverse of each other. If a person was satisfied with his job in a particular condition, the absence of such condition would not mean job dissatisfaction but it might be called no job-satisfaction. Similarly opposite of job-dissatisfaction is not job satisfaction but it might be no job dissatisfaction.

The factors so identified were classified by him into two categories: *(i)* Motivational factors, and *(ii)* Hygiene or Maintenance factors.

MASLOW'S NEED PRIORITY MODEL

Maslow's need priority model is one of the most popular theories of motivation in the management and organizational behaviour literature. The model presents the student of work motivation with an interesting paradox; the theory is widely accepted but there is little empirical evidence to support it, it is largely tentative and untested. Part of the appeal of Maslow's model is that it provides both a theory of human motives by classifying basic human needs in a hierarchy and a theory of human motivation that links these needs to general behaviour. Maslow's theory is a clinically derived theory. The essential elements in the model, as adopted by McGregor for use in management, are presented below:

1. Adult Motives are Complex. No single motive determines behaviour, rather, a number of motives operate at the same time.

2. Needs form a Hierarchy. Lower level needs must atleast partly be satisfied before higher level needs emerge. In other words, a higher order need cannot become an active motivating force until the preceding lower order need is essentially satisfied.

3. A Satisfied Need is not a Motivator. A need that is unsatisfied activates seeking behaviour. If a lower level need is satisfied; a higher level need emerges.

4. Satisfaction of Higher Level Needs. Higher level needs can be satisfied in many more ways than can the lower level needs.

5. People Seek Growth. They want to move up the hierarchy of needs. No person is content at the psysiological level. Usually people seek the satisfaction of higher order needs.

IMPORTANCE OF MOTIVATION IN AN ORGANISATION

Motivation is one of the important methods of inducing man on the job to get work done efficiently and to have the best results out of minimum efforts. Motivation is necessary for the better performance. The good results of motivation are:

1. **Improvement Upon Skill and Knowledge.** All the members will try to be as efficient as possible and to improve upon their skill and knowledge so that they may be able to contribute to the progress of the organisation as much as possible because they know that they, in turn, will get what have been promised and ultimately they will be able to satisfy their personal as well as social needs.
2. **Proper Utilisation of Human Resources.** Motivation induces men to work and it results in increased production and productivity because men try to put their efforts to produce more and more for the benefits of the organisation and thus their efficiency increases. Moreover the inherent qualities of workers are developed by employing different techniques in the interest of the organisation so that they are able to use the methods, systems and technology effectively.

3. **Builds Human Relations.** Motivation builds human relations because the human concept of labour has changed and now labour is treated as human being. He is behaved as a man and not as a commodity. This attitude contributes towards motivating the people at work. Now workers are invited to participate in the decision making function of the management. Thus motivation builds human relations.

   In nut shell, in order to achieve the organisational and individual goals in an economical and efficient manner, motivation is an important tool in the hands of management to direct the behaviour of subrodinates in the desired and appropriate drection and thus minimising the wastage of human and other resources.

4. **Best Utilisation of Other Resources.** All other resources except human resource can produce no results unless the men try to put them in action. Men should be motivated to carry out plans, policies and programmes laid down by the organisation by utilising the order resources to the best of their efforts. In other words, utilisation of resources is not possible to their fullest extent unless the men is induced to contribute their efforts towards attaining the organisation goals.

5. **Basis of Cooperation.** In a zeal to produce more the members work as a team to pull the weight effectively, to get their loyalty to the group and to the organisation, to carryout properly the activities allocated and generally to play an efficient part in achieving the goals which the organisation has undertaken. Thus motivation is the basis of cooperation, to get the best results out of the efforts of the men on the job.

ROOM' EXPECTANCY THEORY

This theory is developed by Victor H. Vroom. The theory attempts to show how the characteristics of individual combine to create a reason for the person to make the necessary efforts to complete a sequence of action. It states that motivation is an outcome of the interaction of the values one seeks and one's estimate of the probability of certain actions leading to those values. His model is built around the concept of two variables – valence and expectancy. The relationship between these two variables can be put in the following mathematical formula:

$$\text{Motivation} = \text{Valence} \times \text{Expectancy}$$

Let us now discuss these two variables:

Valence. Valence refers to the strength of person's preference for a particular outcome in relation to others. It is an expression of the amount of one's desire for a goal. For example, if an employee wants promotion, it can be said that he has high valence for the promotion. Valence arise out of a person's internal self as conditioned by experience, so it differs from person to person.

Valence may be positive or negative depending upon his preferences for an outcome. When a person prospects for attaining a thing, the valence is positive or it may be negative if he prefers not attaining an outcome such as fear of demotion or transfer to a less important job.

Expectancy. Expectancy is the perceived belief concerning the likelihood that a particular act will be followed by a particular outcome. It represents employee judgement of probability of an outcome from an action. Mostly it is based on past experience. Since expectancy is an action-outcome association, it may range from zero to one. If an employee sees no probability of an outcome from an action, the expectancy would be zero. If the probability of outcome is certain from an action, then expectancy has a value of one.

An important point is that the expected outcome must be under the control of someone else and not under the employee himself. So, probability of a particular outcome is always uncertain because the behaviour of a person cannot be forcasted.

Features

1. Expectancy theory is one of the most ambitious theories developed in the area of organizational behaviour. It accommodates a number of motivational determinants in its theoretical framework.

Recognizing its complexity, Miner remarked, "it is primarily a theory for the scholar and the scientist rather than for the practitioner".

2. It is one of the most complete theories for detailing not only how people feel and behave but also why they react as they do.

3. It is a congnitive model *i.e.*, it is based on conscious thoughts about the situation. Individuals are viewed as thinking, reasoning beings who have beliefs and anticipations concerning future events in their lives. When people are faced with number of behavioural options leading to need satisfaction, they will evaluate the potential outcomes of these options and select the one that promises the optimum result. The motivational relationship may be expressed in the form of a formula:

Motivation = V × E × 1 (Valence, expectancy, instrumentality).

The theory assumes, basically, that individuals are largely autonomous beings who independently determine expectancies, instrumentalities and valences for various types of behaviour.

4. It is a predictive theory of motivation, a heuristic decision tool to guide managers in dealing with the complexity of employee motivation in organizations.

5. It is sufficiently general so as to be useful in a wide variety of situations. It considers employee needs, organizational rewards, and task performance, as well as their contingency relationships in particular work situations.

6. It is a theory based on self-interest, wherein each individual seeks to maximize his expected satisfaction. It is a "form of calculative, psychological hedonism in which the ultimate motive of every human act is asserted to be the maximization of pleasure and/or the minimization of pain".

7. The expectancy model is a choice-based model, for the individual chooses to behave according to the expectancy process (also knows as Instrumentality theory).

KEY VARIABLES IN THE MODEL

In general the expectancy theory is based upon a relation-economic view of people. It views people as having their own needs and expectations of what they desire from their work (obviously rewards). They use these to decide on which company to join and how hard to work on the job. The theory assumes that people are decision-makers who choose among alternatives by selecting the one that appears most desirable at the time. Thus, motivation depends on the situation facing people and how it satisfies their desires. Both individual and situational differences are given due consideration. The expectancy theory is built around three concepts: Valence, Expectancy and instrumentality.

(a) Valence. People have preferences (valences) for various outcomes or incentives that are potentially available to them. Valence refers to the personal value workers place on the rewards they believe they will receive for performing. It is the importnace that the individual places on the potential outcome or reward that can be achieved on the job. It reflects the strength of a person's desire for or attraction to the outcome of a particular course of action. It can be defined as the strength of person's preference for one outcome in relation to others. In the words of Hunt and hill, valence is the strength of an individual's desire for a particular outcome.

(b) Expectancy. People have expectancies about the likelihood that an action or effort on their part will lead to the intended performance. Workers will be motivated by the belief that their performance will ultimately lead to payoffs for them. Expectancy refers to the perceived relationship between a given level of effort and a given level of performance. It refers to the extent to which the person believes that his efforts will lead to the first level outcome, that is, performance.

Expectancy = Efforts to First level outcomes (the belief that effort leads to performance).

People must expend some effort to achieve a goal. Usually people have certain expectations about whether their behaviour will be successful or not. If they see odds as zero, they will not even try. Expectancy is subjective. People attach various expectancies to an outcome. Competent and secure individuals tend to perceive expectancy more positively than incompetent and pessimistic individuals. Managers can influence the employee's expectancies positively by matching people to jobs.

(c) **Instrumentality.** It refers to the relationships between performance and reward. It providés answer to such questions "Will I be rewarded if I perform the job well?" Instrumentality refers to the degree to which a first level outcome will lead to a desired second level outcome. Perceived instrumentality is also a subjective feeling. If people perceive that their performance is adequately rewarded the perceived instrumentality will be positive.

On the basis of the concepts of expectanacy, valence and instrumentality, it is possible to build the general model of behaviour as presented above. Vroom's concept of force is essentially equivalent to motivation. Expectancy and valence combine multiplicatively to determine motivation. If expectancy, valence or both equal zero, motivation will be zero. The model shows motivation as the force on individuals to expend effort. However, effort will be expended only if the individual believes or feels confident that effort will lead to some performance level (performance-outcome expectancy indicated by the arrow). The level of performance is highly important in obtaining desired outcomes.

Thus, willingness to expend effort depends on the negative or positive valence attached to an outcome. Generally speaking. The more likely people feel that a performance level will lead in desired outcomes, the more likely they will be to expend efforts to perform at that level (effort-performance expectancy).

EVALUATION

Expectancy theory emphasizes expected behaviours, concerned with expectations. It is irrelevant as to what is realistic or national. It makes a strong argument in favour of having rewards contingent upon successful performanace.

Managerial implications as follows:

1. It emphasizes payoffs, People make choices based upon what they think they will get, not what they got in the past.
2. Rewards should be tied to performance.

3. Rewards should be equitable.
4. Emphasizes expected behaviour. Does the individual know what is expected of him and how he will be appraised?

Vroom's expectancy theory appears to be the most popular motivation theory in terms of amount of research being done. Unfortunately, in spite of its usefulness, the apparent complexity of the model discourages many would be users. The findings of expectancy research are mixed:

1. It has not been fully tasted empirically. It is complex and thus its validity is difficult to test in its entirety. Most studies that have attempted to test its validity have been only marignally successful.
2. It is overly rational. Not every one is willing or able to expend the energy to calculate probabilities. "People rarely sit down and list their expected outcomes for a contemplated behaviour, estimate expectancies and valences, multiply, and adds up the total unless, of course, they are asked to do so by a researcher".
3. The predictive accuracy of the theory leaves much to be desired. The amount of effort individuals are willing to put on the job is influenced by many factors.

HERZBERG'S TWO FACTOR THEORY

Needs priority to a great extent, characterises the types of behaviour. It will be either directed towards achieving desirable positive goals, or conversely, towards avoiding other undesirable, negative consequences. Thus a question may arise as to what variables are preceived to be desirable goals to achieve, and conversely, undesriable conditions to avoid. In this connection, a research study was conduct by Frederick Herzberg and his associates. This study consisted of an intesnive analysis of the experiences and feelings of 200 engineers and accountants in nine different comapnies in U.S.A. During the structured interview, they were asked to describe a few previous job experiences in which they felt 'exceptionally good' or 'exceptionally bad' about jobs. They were also asked to rate the degree to which their feeling were influenced—for better or worse-by each experience which they described.

In concluding the information from the interview, Herzberg concluded that there were two categories of needs essentially independent of each other affecting behaviour in different ways. His findings are that there are some job conditions which operate primarily to dissatisfy employees when the conditions are absent, their presence does not motivate them in a strong way. Another set of job conditions operates primarily to build strong motivation and high job satisfaction, but their absence rarely proves strongly dissatisfying.

Hygiene Factors

Accroding to Herzberg, there are ten maintenance or hygiene factors. These are company policy and administration, technical supervision, inter-personal relationship with supervisors, inter-personal relationship with peers, inter-personal relationship with subordinates, salary, job secruity, personal life, working conditions, and status. There are not intrinsic parts of a job, but they are related to conditions under which a job is performed. They produce no growth in a worker's output; they only prevent losses in workers' performance due to work restrictuions. These maintenance factors are necessary to maintain a reasonable level of satisfaction in employees. Any increase beyond this level will not provide any satisfaction to the employees; however, any cut below this level will dissatisfy them. As such, these are also called as dissatisfiers. Since any increase i n these factors will not affect employees' level of satisfaction, these are of no use for motivating them.

Motivational Factors

These factors are capable of having a positive effect on job satisfaction often resulting in an increase in one's total output. Herzberg includes six factors that motivate employees. These are: Achievement, recognition, advancement, work itself, possibility of growth, and responsibility. Most of these factors are related with job contents. An increase in these factors will satisfy the employees; however, any decrease will not affect their level of satisfaction. Since these increase level of satisfaction in the employees, these can be used in motivating them for higher output.

Table

Hygiene factors	*Motivating Factors*
Company Policy and Administration	Achievement
Technical Supervision	Recognition
Inter-personal relationship with peers	Advancement
Inter-relationship with supervisors	Opportunity for growth
Inter-relationship with subordinates	Responsibility
Salary	Work itself
Job Security	
Personal life	
Working conditions	
Status	

Herzberg maintains that potency of various factors is not entirely a function of the factors themselves. It is also influenced by the personality characteristic of the individuals. From this point of view, individuals may be classified into two parts—motivation seekers and maintenance seekers. The motivation seekers generally are individuals who are primarily motivated by the 'satisfiers' such as advancement, achievement and other factors associated with work itself. On the other hand, the maintenance seekers tend to be more concerned with factors surrounding the job such as supervision, working conditions, pay etc. by the nature of the task and has high tolerance for poor environmental factors. On the other hand maintenance seeker is motivated primarily by the nature of his enviroment and tends to avoid motivation opportunities. He is dissatisfied with maintenance factors surrounding the job.

Critical Appraisal

Herzberg's theory has received a great deal of attention and it has become popular among managers. One striking conclusion of Herzberg's theory is that one cannot achieve higher performance simply by improving wages and working conditions. The conclusion should be an eye opener to managers who go on improving wages and fringe benefits with the hope of improving efficiency. Herzberg stressed upon the job as an intrinsic motivating factor. The key to job satisfaction and high performance lies in job enrichment. Herzberg's two factor theory has made a significant contribution towards improving manager's basic understanding of human behaviour. His theory is simple and based on empirical data. It offers specific actions for managers to improve motivation and performance. This theory has exercised tremendous impact in stimulating thought, research and experimentation in the area of work motivation.

Traditionally, job satisfaction and dissatisfaction were viewed as opposite ends of a single continum. Herzberg's findings indicate that dissatisfaction is not simply the opposite of satisfaction or motivation. Satisfaction and dissatisfaction are independent rather than opposite ends of the same continum.

Motivating	Factors
Satisfaction (Motivation)	No satisfaction (no motivation)

Hygiene	Factors
Dissastisfation	No satisfaction

Herzberg's theory has been criticised on the following grounds:

(i) The theory is based on a small sample of 200 accountants and engineers which is not a representative of the work force in general. Other researchers have drawn different results from similar studies. The theory is most applicable to knowledge workers. Studies of manual workers are less supportive of the theory.

(ii) Hezberg's model is method bound and is limited by the critical incident method used to obtain information. When satisfied people attribute the causes of their feelings to themselves. When they are dissatisfied they attribute their failures to outside forces. People tend to tell the interviewer what he would like to hear rather than what they really feel.

The interview method used by Herzberg suffers from bias. The methodology has the bias of being able to recall the most recent job conditions and feelings. The method is faught with procedural deficiencies also. The analysis of the responses derived from this approach is highly subjective.

(iii) The theory focuses too much attention on satisfaction rather than on performance level. There is no direct link between satisfaction, motivation and performance. Therefore, Herzberg's two-factor is a grossly oversimplified portrayal of the process of motivation.

(iv) The distinction between maintenance factors and motivating factors in not fixed. What is a maintenance factor (*e.g.*, pay) for a worker in the United States may very much be a motivator for an Indian worker. The theory ignores the dominating influence of the situational variables. Motivational and maintenance factors are not wholly unidimensional. They operate primarily in one direction but also partly in other direction.

COMPARISION BETWEEN MASLOW AND HERZBERG MODELS

Herzberg's theory is an extension of Maslow's need priority model. The two models are basically compatible or complementary. There is a close similarity between survival needs (physiological, safety and social needs) and dissatisfiers on the one hand and between growth needs (esteem and self-actulization needs) and satisfiers on the other.

Both Maslow and Herzberg models tends to over-simplify the motivational process. Maslow's model is formulated in terms of human needs while Herzberg's model is in terms of rewards or goals. Herzberg has attempted to refine and reinforce on the need prioirty model and has thrown a new light on the content of work motivation. Herzberg has suggested the use of hygiene factors to avoid dissatisfaction and the use of motivators to improve motivation and job performance. Maslow has given a hierarchical or sequential arrangement suggesting that any unsatisfied need whether of lower order or higher order will motivate individuals. Despite these apparent differences, the two models show marked similarities. Both models fail to take account of individual differences in motivation.

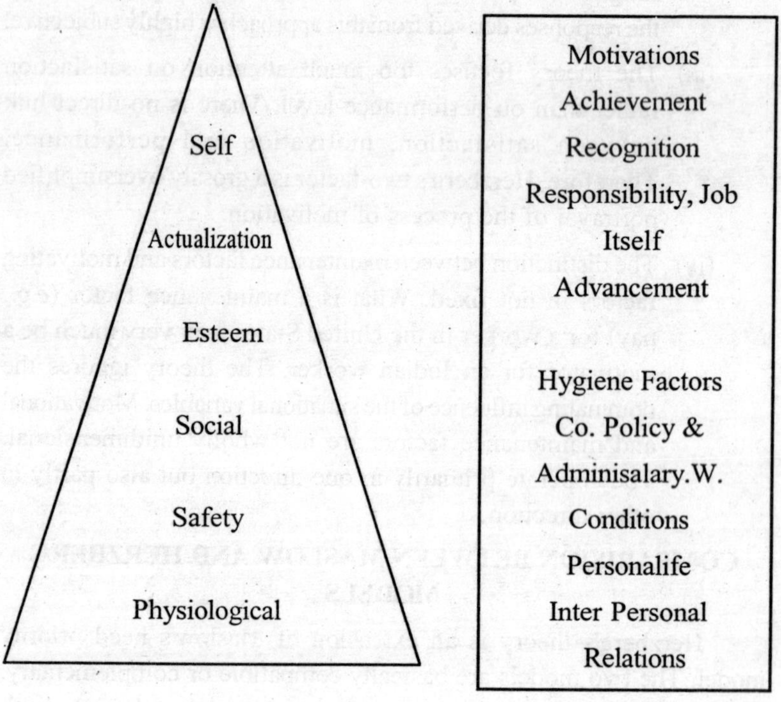

PORTER AND LAWLER MODEL OF MOTIVATION

Built in large part on expectancy model, Porter and Lawler have derived a substantially more complete model of motivation and have applied it in their study primarily to managers. They propose a multivariate model to explain the complex reltionship that exists between job attitude and job performance. Their model encounters some of the simplistic traditional assumptions made about the positive relationship satisfaction and performance. Porter and Lawler explain their choice for the expectancy approach as under: 'The emphasis in expectancy theory or rationality and expectations seems to us to describe best the kinds of cognition that influences managerial performance. We assume that manager operate on the basis of some sort of expectancies which, although based upon previous experience, are forward oriented in a way that does not seem to be as easily handled by the concept of habit strength. The various elements of this model are as follows:

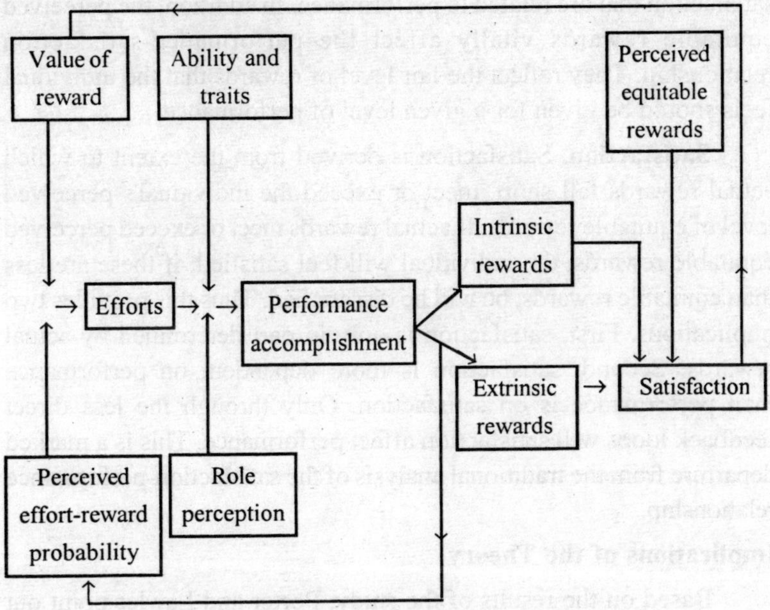

Porter and Lawler motivation model
(adapted from Porter and Lawler, op.cu., p.195)

Effort. Effort refers to the amount of energy exerted by an employer on a given task. Perceived-reward probability refers to the individual's perception of the probability that differential rewards depend upon differential amounts of effort. These two factors—value of reward and perception of effort-reward probability—determine the amount of effort that the employee will put in.

Performance. Effort leads to performance but both of these may not be equal, rather performance is determined by the amount of effort and the ability and role perception of the individual. Thus, if an individual has little ability and/or inaccurate role perception, his performance may be ineffective in spite of his putting great efforts.

Rewards. Performance is seen as leading to intrinsic rewards (such as a sense of accomplishment and actualisation) and extrinsic rewards (such as working conditions and status). However, the intrinsic rewards are much more liekly to produce attitudes about satisfaction that are related to performance. In addition, the perceived equitable rewards vitally affect the performance-satisfaction relationship. They reflect the fair level of rewards that the individual feels should be given for a given level of performance.

Satisfaction. Satisfaction is derived from the extent to which actual rewards fall short, meet or exceed the individual's perceived level of equitable rewards. If actual rewards meet or exceed perceived equitable rewards, the individual will feel satisfied; if these are less than equitable rewards, he will be dissatisfied. Thus this provides two implications. First, satisfaction is only in part determined by actual rewards. Second, satisfaction is more dependent on performance than performance is on satisfaction. Only through the less direct feedback loops will satisfaction affect performance. This is a marked departure from the traditional analysis of the satisfaction-performance relationship.

Implications of the Theory

Based on the results of the study, Porter and Lawler point out that 'these variables presumed to affect performance turned out to show relations to performance and those variables presumed to result from performance also typically were related to performance.' After the review of related research studies, they conclude that 'over all the evidence on the relationship between expectancy attitudes, importance attitudes, and performance provides rather impressive support for our model. The models, although more complex than other models of motivation, explains fully the different variables underlying in motivation. In practice, too, motivation is not a simple cause-effect relationship rather it is a complex phenomenon. The model suggests that managers should carefully assess their reward structures and that through careful planning and clear definition of role requirements, the effort performance reward satisfaction system should be integrated into an entire system of managing.

5

Leadership Theories and Behaviour

Leadership is most important means of direction. Leadership is a process by which an executive directs his subordinates and influences the work and behaviour of others for the common benefit of the organisations as well as its members. To lead means to guide, to direct, and to integrate the efforts of people of an organisation towards the common goal. An effective leader directs the activites of his followers and integrates their activities for the accomplishment of some pre-determined objectives. He motivates them to work more and better. The success of an enterprise largely depends upon the quality of its leadership. The term leadership has been defined by many authors as under:

Chester I Koontz and O'Donnel, "Leadership may be defined as the influence, the art or the process of influencing people so that they will strive willingly towards the achievement of group goals."

Mooney and Reiley,"Leadership is regarded as the form which the authority assumes when it enters into a process."

Bernard, "Leadership refers to the quality of the behaviour of the individuals whereby they guide people on their activities in an organisation."

Theo Haimann, "Leadership can be defined as a process by which an executive directs, guides and influences the works of others in choosing and attaining specified goals by mediating between the individual and the organisation in such a manner that both will obtain maximum satisfaction.

Ordway Tead, "Leadership is that combination of qualities by the possession of which one is able to get something done by others, chiefly because, through his influence they become willing to do so."

On the basis of analysis of above definitions, it may be concluded that leadership is an ability to direct, and motivate other persons of an organisation so that they may contribute their efforts towards the success of organisation.

NATURE OR FEATURES OF LEADERSHIP

The definitions given above reveal the following salient features of leadership:

1. A leader must have followers. Lead who? Leadership does not exist in vacuum. Leadership cannot exist without a group of followers. A person can be called a leader only when people accept him and agree to be influenced. He must receive habitual obediance from his team of followers. Leadership cannot be imagined without followers.

2. Leadership is a working relationship between the leader and his followers. This means that the leader must be an active participant in the activities of the group. There must be community of interest betweeen the leader and his followers.

3. The purpose of leadership is to achieve some common goal or goals. The process of influence and interaction is rational in the sense that it is goal-directed. A leader seeks to make the followers strive willingly to accomplish group objectives.

4. Leadership is a social interaction-influence process between the leader and his followers. It is an interpersonal process of influencing behaviour. A person's leadership position exists only in relation to people not things. A leader is one who holds a sway over the attitudes, actions and behaviour of a group of persons. Followers may also influence the attitudes and behaviour of the leader to some extent by interacting with him.

5. A leader influences his followers willingly not by force or coercion. Leadership is not bossism. A leader shows the way by his own example. He is not a pusher but sets an ideal before his followers

by his personal conduct. According to Urwick, "It is not what a leader says, still less what he writes that influences subordinates. It is what he is. And they judge what he is by what he does not how he behaves." Leadership is the ability to secure desirable actions from a group of followers voluntarily, without the use of coercion.

6. Leadership is exercised in a given situation. It is a function of the leader, the followers and other situational variables

$$L = f(L,f,s)$$

where l, f and s stand for leader, followers and situation respectively.

7. Leadership is a power relationship in which power and influence are unevenly distributed. The person holding powers over other members of the group becomes the leader. A leader is at the centre of the group's power structure. He derives his power from superior knowledge or experience, formal authority, charisma, distinct personal traits, resources for rewards and punishment.

8. Leadership is a continuous and dynamic process of influencing behaviour. It is also a psychological process, it is complex and multidimensional in character.

FUNCTIONS OF LEADERSHIP

The main function of leadership is to explain the importance or cooperative efforts and direct those efforts towards the attainment of the goal. The following are the functions of leadership:

(1) Integration. One of the main functions of leadership is to integrate the efforts of his followers and to direct them towards organisations goals. The leader integrates the efforts of the group and without that, common objectives cannot be achieved and coordination is not possible. In this age of specialisation, each individual does a part of the whole work and integration of the parts of the whole is of paramount importance for a leader.

(2) Organisation -Organising capacity of a leader is an important trait. In organising the activities of a group, he is to decide who will do what and how? He provides necessary inputs to get the work done effectively. If he fails in organisation function, he will lose his confidence among the workers and also the organisation.

(3) Evaluation of Performance. A leader must evaluate the performance of his subordinates. If a worker does well he should be adequately rewarded and if he fails in discharging his responsibility, he should be punished. Both reward and punishment must aim at motivating people to improve the situation.

(4) Representation. A leader respresents the organisation and its objectives before those who work for it and before those who are outsiders. He represents workers before the higher management and outsiders. He represents management before the workers and thus he provides link between his leader (management) and subordinates.

(5) Fraternity. Leadership should promote fraternity among the subordinates. Leadership approach and its style play an important role in developing industrial harmony. He should develop a climate of cooperation among workers in the organisation to achieve the success.

(6) Production Emphasis. A leader should follow the production oriented supervisory style of leadership but not at the cost of human relations and he should do all to increase the production and productivity of the organisation.

(7) Domination. Leader dominates his followers. He holds authority and some organisational power and use his power anyway constructively or distructively. He can ignore his followers wishes but he should not do that. He should be participative and must use his power in the interest of group of which he is a leader.

(8) Initiation. A leader must take initiative to introduce changes, wherever necessary, in the organisation and the group's efforts. He should communicate the changes and reasons behind them to convince the workers from its rationality.

(9) Communication. In order to integrate the efforts of the members of the group, communication of organisational policies, procedure and programmes is necessary. A leader communicates authority and responsibility of each individual so that he may come to know what he is to do and what not.

IMPORTANCE OF LEADERSHIP

An organisation, howsoever good it is, is quite inactive without effective leadership. An effective leader can only pull out the organisation from darkness to light, push it to the path of development by resolving the various genuine difficulties. Without leadership, an organisation is but a muddle of men, machines and materials because all these factors of production remain idle unless. They are engaged in a coordinate manner to produce more towards the accomplishment of goal of the organisation.

Success or Failure of an organisation depends very much on the leadership provided to it. Leadership is still an art and there is no substitute alternative to it. We can present the following points in support of its importance:

1. Developing Good Human Relations. Human relations represent the relations between the leader (manager) and the subordinates (workers). An efficient leadership develops the talents of the individuals, promotes self confidence in them, provides an opportunity to demonstrate their ability apart from the motivation towards the accomplishment of goal. This the leader emphasises the coorperative attitude of workers and it creates an environment of good human relations which in turn increases the productivity of the organisation.

2. Fulfilling Social Responsibilities. An effective leadership only can be able to get the work done effectively. It is a well known fact that a well satisfied worker will help serving the organisation interest in his first preference under a good leadership. Good management or leadership is always concerned with the need satisfaction of its workforce which in turn, provides higher standard of living to workers, higher productivity and production to the organisation, lower price to consumers, higher national product, and increased revenue to the nation, and a fair return to the investors.

3. Source of Motivation. Efficient leadership is a source of motivation to the subordinates. Leadership does not mean simply the existence of leadership traits in a person but it is to utilise those traits in motivating the people at work towards the desired goal by applying a leadership style most suited to the situation. Motivation is an element of dynamic leadership and in absence of that organisation success is doubtful.

4. Promoting the Spirit of Coordination. The activities of members of a group and those of different groups must be coordinated in order to achieve the desired goal. A leader promotes the spirit of coordination among workers. A dynamic leadership provides all that by following human behaviour approach.

5. Better utilisation of Manpower. The first management function of a leader is to make plans, policies, and programmes and to carry them out because plans, policies, and programmes cannot work themselves. He mobilises the work force, engage them to get higher performance and coordinates their efforts and it is all to utilise the available manpower effectively so as to get highest output with minimum human cost.

VARIOUS TYPES OF LEADERSHIP

The behaviour exhibited by a leader during supervision of subordinates is known as leadership style. There are probably as many different styles of leadership as there are leaders. Basically three styles are listed out-autocratic, democratic and free-rein.

(i) Directive Autocratic/Authoritative Style. An autocratic leader centralizes power and decision making in himself and exercises complete control over the subordinates. He holds over the head of his subordinates the threat of penalties and punishment. He runs his own show. The leader gives orders and the subordinates are to follow them ungrudgingly and unquestioningly. The problem with this style is that subordinates are made aware of what to do but not why. It may be satisfying for the leader to dictate terms to others continuously but for subordinates this may be totally frustrating. He breathes so closely down the necks of his subordinates that he makes effective action impossible. Subordinates are compelled to follow the leader's directions to the letter even though they may be wrong. Later when errors creep in, subordinates will aviod responsibility since they were merely obeying. In autocratic situations, frustration, low morale and conflict develop easily. Subordinates are induced to avoid responsibility, initiative and innovative behaviour.

Autocratic style permits quick decision-making and hence can be applied with success in situations where:

(i) The subordinates lack knowledge of company goals.

(ii) There is little room for error in final accomplishment.

(iii) The subordinates are inexperienced or lack in training.

(iv) The leader prefers to be active and dominant in decision making.

(v) The company endorses fear and punishment as accepted disciplinary techniques.

Again under conditions of stress, or when great speed and efficiency are required autocratic leadership can yield positive outcomes. It can increase productivity and somewhat more surprising it can also enhance morale.

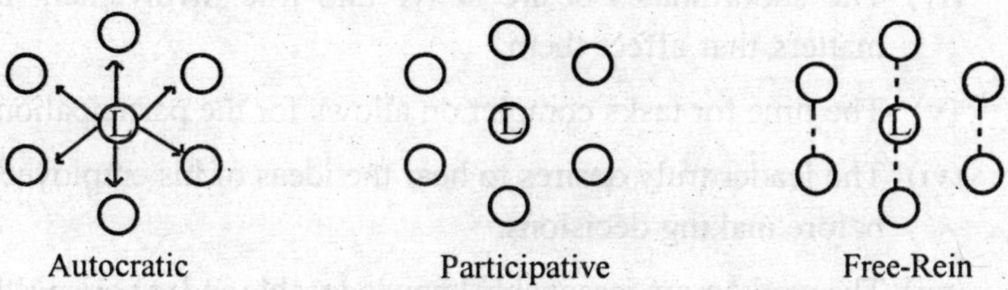

Fig. Leadership Styles

(ii) Democratic/Participative Style. In contrast to the autocrat, the democratic leader practices leadership by consultation. He is like a Theory Y Leader and invites decision sharing. Here authoritiy is decentralized. The subordinates are also encouraged to exploit their potential and assume greater challenging responsibilities. The participative leader attaches high importance to both work and people. This style improves job satisfaction and morale of employees. It helps in gaining the services from a more satisfied and cohesive group. In fact, no manager can perform effectively over an extended period of time without some degree of employee participation.

However, there is no evidence that participation is good for everybody, when subordinates prefer minimum interaction with the leader, participative style may not yield positive results. Furthermore, over a period of time group members develop a frustrating habit of expecting to be consulted on every issue, even those to which they cannot contribute. When they are not consulted, they feel slighted, insulted and become resentful and uncooperative.

Participative leadership style is appropriate where:

(i) The leader wishes to develop analytical and self-control abilities in his subordinates.

(ii) The organization has communicated its goals and the objectives to the subordinates and the subordinates have accepted them.

(iii) Rewards and involvement are used as the primary means of motivation and control.

(iv) The subordinates desire active and true involvement in matters that affect them.

(v) The time for tasks completion allows for the participation.

(vi) The leader truly desires to hear the ideas of his employees before making decisions.

(vii) The workers are reasonably knowledgeable and experienced.

Participative style is appreciated on the following that grounds:

(i) The leader seriously listens to and thoroughly reviews the ideas of his subordinates and accepts their contributions wherever possible and practical.

(ii) The leader cultivates the decision-making abilities of his subordinates. Participative leadership style is not always a bed of roses. It is attacked on the following grounds:

(a) Participative style is a misleading term. There is always a danger of misinterpretation of decision sharing. Subordinates may view the leader as incompetent to handle crisis independently. Participation may also be interpreted as a sign of inefficiency on the part of the leader to deal with the problems and taking decisions.

(b) For some leaders, participative style is an effective way of passing the buck to others. It is a means of abdication of the responsibility for them.

(c) Participative leadership is time consuming. It is a tough job for the leader to provide a relaxed atmosphere to the subordinates so that they actively participate in decision-making.

AUTHORITARIAN VERSUS DEMOCRATIC STYLES

The distinction between authoritative and participative leadership styles is made quite often by the social scientists.

Is Participative Style Superior?

Many people now-a-days unassailably acknowledge that effective leadership is a function of the situation. But surprisingly some people still cling on to the old age that participative style is superior to the authoritarian one. It is beacuse of the two reasons:

(1) The democratic, participative approach may be more compatible with the prevailing value system in 'Post-Hawthorne' America. The feeling that a person should wish and be able to set his own goals and monitor his own activities suggest that such behaviour is a criterion of good mental health. Furthermore, democratic leadership is frequently associated with subordinate satisfaction, not performance.

Table

Authoritative	*Participative*
1. Manager exhibiting this style is labelled as a 'Theory-X' leader.	Manager exhibiting this style is labelled as a 'Theory-Y' leaders.
2. Leader structures the task, strives to find out better methods, and keeps the employees busy on task.	Leader is conciderate of his subordinates recognizes their needs and respects their human dignity.

Contd.

Authoritative	Participative
3. Leader is autocratic, task-oriented and restrictive.	Leader is democratic follower oriented and permissive.
4. Communication is one-way traffic; threads of control swielded by one individual.	Two-way communication.
5. Decision-making is centralized, and quick decisions are taken.	Decentralized decision-making, and slow process of making decisions
6. Because of greater resistance change winning over employee confidence and obtaining comm-itment to task is difficult.	Because resistance to change is minimum, leader gains a contented and cohesive group confidence.

(2) Participative leadership may be a result rather than a cause of a satisfied or high performance group.

In a study it has been found that democratic leadership results in higher job satisfaction to the employees and autocratic leadership results in greater productivity. The choice of leadership style thus depends on the goals: if the immediate goal is to increase output autocratic style is appropriate and if the leader is willing to build a stable and highly motivated work force, democratic approach may be called for.

The choice of leadership style also depends on the employees. Some employees have a liking for autocratic leadership as they have high needs for structure and low needs for independence. For instance, Vroom found that participative leadership has a positive effect only on these individuals with strong non-authoritarian values or high need for independence. Some researchers have found that employees considered the participative leadership style to be legitimate or proper.

(iii) Free Rein Leadership Style. Free-rein leadership is a rather complete delegation of authority into the hands of the subordinates so that they must plan, motivate, control and otherwise be responsible for their own actions. The free-rein manager avoids power and relinquishes the leadership position. Then the question arises as to why certain leaders opt out of the leadership role? In a gerneral sense we can state that leader perceives that the costs associated with leadering are greater than the benefits. More specifically the reasons may be lack of self-confidence, fear of failure etc.

Free-rein style would seem to be appropriate under the condition where:

(a) The subordinates themselves are well-trained and hightly know-ledgeable concerning their tasks and are ready to assume responsibility.

(b) The organizational goals have been communicated well and are acceptable to the subordinates.

(c) The leader is interested in delegating decision-making fully.

The problem with this style is that it tends to permit various units of an organization to proceed at cross purposes and can deleberate into chaos. Hence it should be the rare exception not a general rule.

LEADERSHIP

Leadership is a personal quality of an individual who organises the efforts of the followers and directs their activities towards the attainment of organisational goal. Leadership is, therefore, regarded as the process of influencing the activities of an individual or a group in efforts towards goal achievement in a given situation. Leadership is a function of the leader, the follower and other situational variables. One who is in a position of influencing others (followers) whether a manager of a formal organisation or an informal leader of an informal group or a head of family, may be called leader.

According to Ordway Tead "Leadership is that combination of qualities by the possession of which one is able to get something done by others, chiefly because through his influence they become willing to do so." George R. Terry said that leadership is the activity of influencing people to strive willingly for group objectives.

According to these definitions here we get some important points:

(a) Leadership is a function of the leader, the follower and other situational variables. It is a matter of removing barriers in a situation so that subordinates work with freedom and independence.

(b) Leadership is essentially a continuous process of influencing behaviour. A leader breathes life into the group and motivates it toward goals. The lukewarm desires for achievement are transformed into a burning passion for accomplishment.

(c) Leadership is a relationship between two or more people in which influence and power are unevenly distributed.

(d) Leadership is something a person does, not something he has. Leadership is something that emerges, that grows and that is achieved.

(e) Leaders do not flourish in vacuum. The essence of leadership is followership. Leadership implies that followers must consent to being influenced. They must suspend their judgment and allow another person to make decisions in specific situations. Leaders gain their authority over a group by group consensus alone.

A leader has to do a lot such as, make initiate change, help in decision making, help the groups to achieve their objectives and to solve the difficulties and create a good atmosphere between employees. The function may also be much more complex at times, such as serving to integrate the groups needs with outside realities, satisfying interpersonal needs within the groups, creating an atmosphere free of conflict for groups members. In the wake of vast, rapid technological changes leader has to perform multifarious functions.

FUNCTIONS OF A LEADER

Leader is an Appropriate Counseller. Quite often people in the work place need counselling to eliminate the emotional disequilibrium that is created sometimes in them. Leader removes barriers and stumbling blocks to effective performance. For instance, frustration that result from blocked need drive keeps an employee derailed of the working track.

Strives for Effectiveness. Quite frequently the managers are workabolic and too busy with petty things to address to major details of effectiveness. To fill the gap, sometimes leader throws his concerted effort to bring effectiveness by encouraging and nurturing teamwork, by better time management and by the proper use of power. Further, leader provides an adequate reward structure to encourage performance of employees. Leaders delegates authority where needed and invites participation wherever possible to achieve the better results. He also provides the workers with necessary resources. By communicating to workers what is expected of them leader brings effectiveness to organization.

Leader Manages the Time Well. Time is precious and vital but often overlooked in management. Therefore, three dimensions of time, bossimposed-time, system-imposed-time and self-imposed-time, that are prominent in literature. Because the leader has thorough knowledge of the principles of time management such as time preparing charts, scheduling techniques etc., he is in a position to utilize the time productivity in the organizations.

Leader Develops Team Work. The three vital determinants of teamwork are the leader, subordinates and the environment. These factors are interdependent. It is the leader's responsibility to make the environment conducive to work. He studies the employee individually and instils interest in them. By encouraging the inquisitive employees and by prohibiting insidious elements he creates hyegenic environment. He inculcates the sense of collectivism in employees to work as a team. The resultant output will then be efficiency.

Leader is a Representative of Subordinates. He is an intermediary between the work groups and top management. They are called linking pins by Rensis Likert. As linking pins they serve to integrate the entire organization and the effectiveness depends on the strength of these linking pins. Leader shows personal consideration for the employee. As representatives they carry the voice of the subordinates to the top management.

Uses Power Property. If a leader is to effectively achieve the goals expected of him, he must have power and authority to act in a way that will stimulate a positive response from the workers. A leader, depending on the situation exercises different types of power, *viz.*, reward power, coercive power, legitimate power, referent power and expert power. Besides the formal basis the informal basis of power also have a more powerful impact on organizational effectiveness. No leader is effective unless the subordinates obey his orders.

QUALITIES FOR LEADERSHIP

Different thinkers have suggested different qualities for leadership. According to Henry Feyol good leader should have the following qualities:

(a) Sound health and physical fitness
(b) Knowledge of work
(c) Managerial ability
(d) Intelligence and mutual vigour
(e) Moral qualities

According toChester I. Bernard the following are essential:

(a) Intellectual Capacity
(b) Decisiveness
(c) Knowledge
(d) Vitality and Endurance
(e) Stability
(f) Persuasiveness

According to F.M.V. Shim a leader should have:

(a) Courage
(b) Will power
(c) Flexibility
(d) Integrity
(e) Knowledge
(f) Judgement

According to Ordway Tead he should have:

(a) Techincal Mastery

(b) Sense of purpose and direction

(c) Physical and nervous energy

(d) Enthusiasm

All the above qualities are needed for a good leader to achieve the goal. We may group all the qualities into the following categories:

(1) Qualities of Character

- (a) Selfdiscipline
- (b) Fair in dealing
- (c) Humanism
- (d) Integrity
- (e) Willingness to accept responsibility

(2) Psychological Qualities:

- (a) Tactful
- (b) Forcefulness
- (c) Co-operation
- (d) Ability to inspire
- (e) Enthusiasm

(3) Intellectual traits:

- (a) Open minded
- (b) Ability to teach
- (c) Scientific approach
- (d) Capability of sound judgement
- (e) Intelligent

(4) Physical Qualities:

- (a) Sound health
- (b) Vitality and Endurance.

FIEDLER'S CONTINGENCY MODEL OF LEADERSHIP

Fiedler's contingency model is one of the most serious and elaborate situational theories in leadership literature. Fiedler is probably the first researcher who recognized the need for a broader explanation of leadership phenomena anchored on situational variables. The major problem with the earlier Trait and Behavioural Approaches is that they are universalistic approaches; they search for magic key to leadership that is devoid of situational context and follower behaviour and personality. The contingency model attempts to rectify these inherent deficiencies in behavioural theories.

Fiedler's model is called a 'contingency' model because the leader's effectiveness is partially contingent upon three major situational variables. They are: *(1)* leader-member relations, *(2)* the task structure, and *(3)* the leader's position power.

(1) Leader-member Relations. It refers to the degree of confidence, trust and respect follower have in the leader. It indicates the degree to which group members like the leader and are willing to accept the leader's behaviour, as an influence on them. If followers are willing to follow because of charisma, expertise, competence or mutual respect, the leader has little need to depend on task structure or position power. If, on the other hand, the leader is not trusted and is viewed negatively by followers the situation is considered less favourable.

(2) Task-structure. It may be highly structured or highly unstructured. If task is highly specific, can be done only in one and rules and procedures are well defined, and there is no scope for different interpretations, it is said to be highly structured. On the other hand, if task is completely non-routine, there are many rotes to reach the goal or rules and procedures are not clear, then the task is regarded as highly unstructured. In a highly structured tax, leader's ability to influence the group is restricted because the tax dilutes the leaders potential influence.

(3) Leader's Position Power. The most obvious manner in which the leader secures power is by accepting and performing the leadership role. Position power in the contingency model refers to the power inherent in the leader's organizational position.

It refers to the degree to which the leader has at his disposal various rewards and sanctions, his authority over group's members, and the degree to which this authority is supported by the organization.

Fiedler has considered eight possible combinations of these free variables in addition to Cader's employee-orientation ranging from a highly favourable position to a highly unfavourable situation for a leader.

A favourable situation is where the leader-member relations are good, the task is highly structured and the leader has enormous power to exert influence on the subordinates. The first cell in the table is identified with this high degree of favourableness.At the other extreme, an unfavourable situation is where the leader's power is weak, relations with members are poor and the task is unstructured and unpredictable. The last cell represents this situation. Between these two extremes lies the situation of intermediate difficulty. Fiedler arouses that a permissive, relationship-oriented style is best when the situation is moderatly favourable or moderately unfavourable. When the situation is highly favourable or highly unfavourable a task-oriented style produces the desired performance.

Fiedler Classification of Situational Favourableness.

Leader-Member relation	Good				Poor			
Task Structure	High		Low		High		Low	
Leader position power	Strong	Weak	Strong	Weak	Strong	Weak	Strong	Weak
Cells	I	II	III	IV	V	VI	VII	VIII

Favourable ——————————————————— Unfavourable

Leader gets better group performance in the conditions of moderate or intermediate favourableness in which the task is structured and leader is disliked or the leader is liked and the task is unstructured and the leader depends upon the willingness and creativity of group's members to accomplish the goals.

THEORIES OF LEADERSHIP

Leadership is crucial ingredient in organisational effectiveness. It is a complex inter personal process of influencing behaviour. There are five theories of leadership:

1. Trait Theory
2. Behavioural Theory
3. Situational Theory
4. Acceptance Theory
5. System Theory

The first approach views leadership as a conglomeration of a set of personality traits. The oldest tradition in these studies of leadership has been the search for a cluster of traits, attributes, or other types of individual differences, which set leaders apart from their followers or which discriminate effective leaders from ineffective ones. Trait theorists tried to unearth a pure prototype of leadership personality. The second approach to study of leadership attempts to identify the individual behaviour of leaders associated with effective leadership. Of course, one fundamental assumption underlying these trait and behavioural theories is that an individual who possesses the appropriate traits or displays appropriate behaviours will emerge as the leader in whatever the group situation he is.

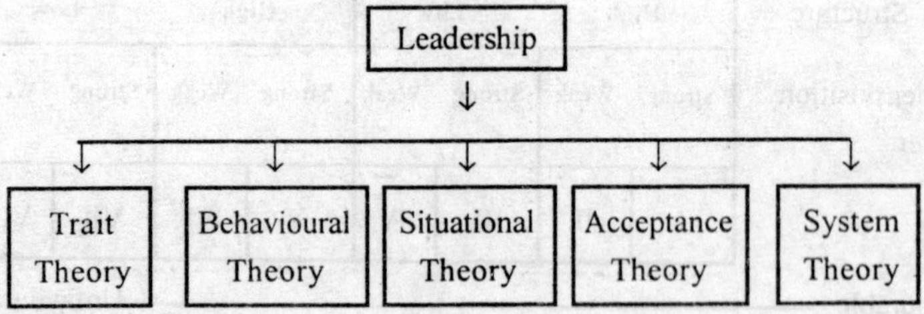

(1) Trait Theory. In an attempt to develop a quick and easy test for assessing leadership potential, early writers concluded that leadership is largely a matter of personality, a function of specific traits. Trait theorists suggest that leaders differ from followers with respect to a small number of key traits and these traits remain unchanged across time.

The trait theory attempts to isolate the attributes of successful and unsuccessful leaders and, using this list of traits, predict the success or failure of potential leaders. If traits can be measured in some way, most of the organizations can easily select for leadership only persons well suited by their personality or temperament for such roles.

A number of traits have been identified by various researches to distinguish successful leaders from unsuccessful one or followers. A successful leader is supposed to have the following traits: *(i)* Good personality, *(ii)* Tirelessness, *(iii)* Ability to quick decision, *(iv)* Courage, *(v)* Persuasion, *(vi)* Intelligence, *(vii)* Reliability, *(viii)* Imagination, *(ix)* Physically fit, *(x)* Intellectually sound etc. The psychologists have grouped the various traits of a leader into four categories: *(a)* Physical, *(b)* Psychological, *(c)* Intellectual, and *(d)* Qualities of character.

Weaknesses of the Theory

1. ***No Consideration for Situational Factors.*** Traitists do not consider the situational factors for leadership which influence the leaders more than their inner traits. Traits come to light only when a situation arise and they are helpful in facing a particular situation but without a situation, traits are useless.
2. ***The Approach Ignores Other Variables of Leadership.*** Such as acts of leader, followers and their acts, situation, and their effects on the leader.
3. ***No Common or Universal Traits.*** Neither leadership traits are comman in nature nor universal. It is, therefore, very difficult to indicate what mix of traits is necessary to make an effective leader. Its measurement is problematic.
4. ***Traits of an Individual cannot be Known.*** Unless situation arises. When an individual faces a problem, then only the

presence or absence or absence of the trait required otherwise traits remain unknown.

5. ***No Room for Developing Future Leaders.*** The theory stresses the inborn qualities of an individual which cannot be developed or acquired but it was later accepted that such inborn traits can be developed or acquired through experience or training. Earlier it was assumed that leaders are born and therefore, it left no scope for development of future leader.

6. ***Different Roles Require Different Traits.*** Even in the same organisation. At lower managerial level, where there is direct contact between a worker and the supervisor, technical knowledge is of paramount importance. At middle management level, where policies are elaborated and interpreted, human relations skills are of prime importance. At higher management level where policies are framed, planning is undertaken, conceptual skill gains pre-eminent position. Leadership, in a large organisation has a limited role while in a small organisation it demand multiplicity of roles.

Leaders who fail as leaders and individuals who never achieve leadership positions often possess some of the same traits as successful leaders. From example, although taller people may generally be more successful as leaders, many tall people have neither the inclination nor the capabilities to be the leaders. Trait theroy is severely criticised on the following grounds:

1. The list of personality traits is painfully long and exhaustive. Although over one hundred personality attributes of successful leaders have been identified, no consistent pattern / patterns have been found.

2. Researchers often disagree over which traits are the most important for an effective leader. There is no universal list of traits for successful leaders.

3. Leaders cannot be markedly different from their followers. Extremes in personality are not usually associated with leadership.

4. It is difficult to define traits. When posed with the question of defining a trait, executives often come out with a bewildering variety of explanations, making a mockery of the trait theory.
5. Effective leadership is not a function of traits alone. Executives often behave in a way they think is appropriate for their job. There is a wealth of scientific evidence pointing the significance of situational factors as determinants of leadership behaviour. Trait theory fell into disfavour because it did not consider the whole leadership environment.
6. It is often difficult to measure traits. The measurement tools employed to quantify traits (in ways that will make them useful to executives) are open to doubt. For example, some of the psychological attributes (intelligence initiative) cannot be observed but can only be inferred from the behaviour.
7. How much of a trait a person should have remains a puzzling question. It is not clear how high score a person must achieve on a given trait to make it effective.
8. Finally, leadership skills vary according to the type of work a person performs in the organization. A leader may employ three different types of skills at different levels in the organization technical.

(2) Behavioural Approach or Theory. It was apparent from the traitists theory that traits fail to explain the leadership phenomenon and the theorists diverted their attention to the study of leader behaviour. This approach was much in current during 1950s—1960s. The basis of this theory lie in how the management viewed the workers.

Under classical management approach, man or worker was regarded no more than a commodity or just an appendage to a machine. Management coerced directed and motivated workers through the offer of economic rewards and attempted to increase efficiency or productivity by reducing wastes of times and material and no consideration was given to men as an asset. The basic assumption under this theory was taken that the people, by nature, were lazy, uncreative and irresponsible and therefore leader (manager) should be directive.

This approach developed various leadership styles such as autocratic or democratic or supervisory style which produce different and conflicting results because behaviour of leader and followers differ in different situations.

The theory endeavoured to explain the leadership phenomenon in terms of the behaviour of the leader. What the leader does was the main concern therefore the investigators examined the style followed by the leader, *i.e.*, authoritarian or democratic. It may be a mix of the two.

Weaknesses

The main limitation of this approach is questionnaire which has its own limitations. Scientific tests cannot be applied in studies which are likely to be affected by perceptual differences and a variety of interpretations of questions. However no measurement methodology, *i.e.*, questionnaire, observation, or interviews has been universally accepted by behavioural researchers. This is, therefore, an unavoidable limitation.

(3) Situational Theory. Both the Trait and Behavioural approaches proved to fall short of a comprehensive and adequate theory of leadership style. Each of the theories attempted to isolate broad dimensions of leadership behaviour and indulged profusely in oversimplification. The logic behind such fallacious reasoning appears to be that multidimensions confound that interpretations of leadership behaviour and complicate the research designs developed to test the particular theory. These theories have tried to construct a theoretical edifice based on controversial questionnaire methods. There is no attempt on the part of the eminent researchers to link leadership with important performance indicators such as production, efficiency and satisfaction. Practising managers who are primarily interested in procedures, basic guidelines and results to improve their styles were clearly disenchanted with these approaches. As pointed out by Tannenbaum and Schmidt "the successful manager often can be primarily characterized neither as a strong leader nor as a permissive one. Rather, he is one who maintains a high batting average in accurately assessing the forces that determine what his most appropriate behaviour at any given time should be and in actually being able to behave accordingly.

The theory advocates that leadership is strongly affected by the situation in which he works. The theory believes that it is a situation that helps developing leadership and from which leaders emerge. Traits or behaviour may be supportive elements. A person may be good leader in a particular situation or set of circumstances but it may be possible that he may be quite ineffective in a different situation.

The theory further believes that there exists an interaction between a group of workers and its leader. The people (followers) tend to follow the person (leader) who is capable of fulfilling their aspirations. For acquiring such a position, the leader is to recognise the needs of situation and the aspirations of the followers and to act accordingly.

Limitations

The theory suffers from the following short-comings:

(i) It overemphasises the situational aspect of leadership. Situation may affect the decision of a leader in a particular situation but it is not everything.

(ii) It completely overlooks the traits and behaviour of a leader which play an important role in the emergence of a particular leader. The head and heart of a leader, definitely plays a decisive role in every situation.

(4) Followers' Theory or Acceptance Theory. The theory assets that followers are important in deciding whether a person is a leader or not. If followers accept a person their leader he is leader irrespective of his traits or behaviour. According to this theory, followers must form groups. The theory cannot be applied without group of followers. The theory based on the assumption that groups have certain basic needs which they want to be fulfilled through their leader. A person who is successful in satisfying their basic needs, is assumed to be their leader on the contrary, if he does not succeed in getting their needs satisfied he can neither be said to be a good leader nor he will be allowed to function as such.

The major weakness of the theory is that it ignores the quality aspect of leadership. But modern managers are of the opinion that it is the followers' theory that is now playing a significant role in managing the people today.

(5) System Theory. Leadership is governed by a person's act rather than by his traits which influences the followers most. It follows that leadership is a sole behaviour which co-ordinates the efforts of the people and stimulates them towards the achievement of their goal in a particular situation. This approach is called system approach because it considers all the variables present at the same time, *i.e.*, leader, followers, situation, goals, leadership traits, environments and group's nature, characteristics and needs, role, behaviour of the leader and his coordinating efforts.

This theory is recognised as the modern theory of leadership. In the modern world, this theory is rather more acceptable to followers.

❒

6

Organisation and Effectiveness

The organisation structure, being abstract, is not visible in the same way as a biological or mechanical structure, though it can be inferred from the actual operations and behaviour of the organisation. The biological or mechanical system, such as organism and machine, can be identified even when it is not working because it has both anatomy and physiology The study of the anatomy is basically the study of the structure of the organism whereas the physiology deals with functions of living organism. The biological and mechanical systems can be studied in both these terms–structure as well as functioning. However, this is not the case with social systems which do not have both anatomy and physiology. As such, it is very difficult to study the organisation structure separately from its functioning. For example, Katz and Kahn observe as follows in this context:

> "A social system is a structuring of events or happenings rather than of physiological parts and it, therefore, has not structure apart from its functioning."

Organisation structure is basic framework within which the managers' decision-making behaviour takes place. Structure basically deals with relationships. It is an important scientific concept. All sciences try to discover the structural relationships in the phenomena in which they are interested. For example, biologist wants to know the structure of cells; the astronomer wants to know the structure of the universe; the physicist studies the structure of the atom or molecule; the economist seeks to discover the structure of a labour market or of money-flow patterns. Similarly in management, we need to understand how organisations are structured and how these structures are created and maintained.

Basic Structure and Operating Mechanism

The problem of identifying structure from organisational processes does not mean that there is no difference between the two. There is a basic difference between the two this distinction is important in understanding the concept and design of organisation structure. The structure of a system is the arrangement of its subsystems and components at a given moment of time. Process is dynamic change in the matter, energy, or information of the system over time. Thus the concepts of structure and process can be viewed as the static and dynamic features and both of these aspects are related rather than opposite. Thus organisation structure can be viewed as established pattern of relationships among the components of the organisation. In large and complex organisations, structure is set forth initially by the design of the major components or subsystems and then by establishing relationships among these subsystems. It is the patterning of these relationships with some degree of permanancy which is referred to as organisation structure.

Design of basic structure involves such issues as how the work of the organisation will be divided and assigned among various positions, groups, divisions, departments, etc. and how the coordination necessary to accomplish total organisational objectives will be achieved. Besides the formally established organisation structure, people create relationships independent of the formal relationships known as informal relationships or organisation. Thus organisation structure, truly speaking, the totality of both formal and informal relationships. Operating mechanism or organisational process, on the other hand, includes such factors as control procedures, information systems, reward and punishment systems, rules and procedures, and so on. These structural variables, both basic structure and operating mechanism, can be used to identify what is required of organisational members to motivate them to do their assigned part of the organisational objectives, and encourage them to take collective activities.

Differentiation and Integration in Designing

Organisation structure refers to the differentiation and integration of activities and authority, role and relationship in the organisation. Thus, there are two considerations in organisation design problem: differentiation and integration. Differentiation is defined as 'the differences in cognitive and emotional orientations among managers in different functional departments, and the differences in formal structure among these departments,' and integration as 'quality of the state of collaboration that are required to achieve unity of effort by the environment." Since various departments are the parts of the whole system, they should not be considered in isolation of others as affecting the economics and efficiencies of work performance. However, since each unit is interacting in a different way with the environment, various units are likely to develop differentiation to some degree or other, depending upon the specific environment. The extent of organisation differentiation depends upon the certainty or uncertainty of environment and its diversity or differentiation depends upon the certainty or uncertainty of environment and its diversity or homogeneity. Thus designing of one unit may be different from that of other. Applying the concepts of differentiation and integration to organisation design requires various activities in sequence: identification, grouping, and authority relationships among individuals and groups. Thus designing of basic structure involves the following steps:

1. **Grouping of Activities.** Closely related and similar activities are grouped together to form departments, divisions, or sections because co-ordination of numerous activities can best be achieved by grouping them into basic and derivative departments. Grouping may be done on several bases depending upon the situational requirements, Grouped activities in the from of departments, divisions, or sections are assigned to various positions. These positions are occupied by various individuals. The assignment of activities creates responsibility and ensures certainty of work performance, These job assignments are made to different management members who, in turn, distribute the jobs to

their subordinates. This process goes on till the last level of the organisation.

2. **Delegation of Authority.** Since the assignment of the job to an individual creates responsibility on his part, he must have corresponding authority to discharge his obligations. Authority and responsibility are correlated and are taken to be constant companions, because authority without responsibility is a dangerous thing, and responsibility without authority is an empty vessel. Through the process of delegation, authority structure in organisation is created defining who will interact with whom in an official way.
3. **Identification of Activities.** In designing the strcuture, managers must identify the various necessary activities that must be performed in order to achieve the organisational objectives. While identifying the various activities, the deductive method is followed which suggests that in order to achieve a particular goal, which steps and functions should be undertaken. It provides a classificatory system that omits nothing and guards against the activities which are unrelated to the goals. the major activities are then classified into a number of sub-activities. While classifying and reclassifying the activities, it should be borne in mind that: *(i)* all the necessary activities are performed; *(ii)* there is no unnecessary duplication in performing various necessary activites; and *(iii)* the various activities are performed in a synchronised or co-ordinated way.

Before proceeding to the first aspect of organisation designing, it is desirable to identify the features and importance of a good organisation structure so that various activities of designing are related with these to make it more effective. Moreover, understanding of organisation chart and manual also contribute towards this effectiveness.

ROLE OF ORGANISATION STRUCTURE

Organisation structure is capable of serving many functions at the same time but can not serve all functions equally well over unlimted time. Structure created for one purpose may not serve other purposes well. Therefore, it is important for managers to determine the outcomes desired from organisation structure, and to match the organisation with changing needs. With multiple needs or roles of organisation structure, a balance will have to be struck and priorities established in the operation of the organisational mechanism. In general, there can be following roles of organisation structure:

(i) **Encouraging Efficiency.** Organisation structure is the framework within which an organisation functions. In this functioning, efficiency is the major criterion. Therefore, organisational members try to maximise the output of goods or services resulting from a given input of resources, or at least make a respectable showing in that direction. Since chaos or disorganisation works against the ideal of efficiency, there is pressure to develop some measure of systematic, orderly, rational and coordinated effort, and to control waste and loss. In fact, various models of organisational design try to achieve efficiency in organisational operations.

(ii) **Facilitating Management Action.** When large number of people work together, some sort of formal structuring is required to place them according to the needs of the organisation. All of them perform various functions which are interdependent and interrelated. As such, there must be plan for systematic completion of the work of each specialised job so that total activities accomplish common objectives. Further these activities should be completed in coordinated way. Organisation structure is the mechanism through which management directs, coordinates, and controls the organisational activities. It is indeed the foundation of management. A properly-designed organisation structure facilitates both management and operation of an organisation. Management actions take place with certainty and continuity only if appropriate functional groups are provided to help managers. The grouping and arrangement of activities directly affect operating results. If the important activities are overlooked or subordinated, the results would be detrimental to the organisation. Need for updated organisation structure can be gauged from the fact that many organisations create separate unity for organisational analysis which looks after the various aspects affected by the organisation structure such as delegation of authority, communication, control, coordination, etc. and tries to find ways for improving them to make suitable for organisational needs.

(iii) **Communication.** Organisation structure provides the pathways for communication among organisational members as well between the organisation and its environment. In fact, when we say that organisation structure establishes relationships, we mean that it creates reporting relationships, that is, who will communicate with whom. Similarly, when the organisation interacts with its environment, a communication process is involved. Thus structure serves the purpose of communication. Within organisational boundary, communication is required in horizontal, vertical, and lateral directions, organisation structure, if designed properly, provides lines of communication in all these directions.

(iv) **Job Satisfaction.** Organisation structure is a source of satisfaction to people. Since organisation provides relatedness among tasks and responsibilities and among people, those who work for an organisation sooner or later come to evaluate the nature of those relationships and of their own relationships to the organisation and to their jobs. Organisation structure provides for each person a place of status which confers a certain standing among his fellows. This works as motivating factor for them. Most of the people spend a large part of their lives at work associated with organisation.They expect their jobs and work to provide a reasonable degree of job satisfaction, and the framework for this is in the structure of the organisation itself.

(v) **Stimulating Creativity.** A sound organisation stucture based on specialisation stimulates creative thinking by providing well-defined area of work with provision of development of new and improved ways of working. For creativity, it is essential that one is well conversant with the problem on hand. Organisation structure tries to put people at places where they are required. When they work on a job for considerably long time, they are in a position to suggest something new. Many practitioners have contributed to the development of management thinking which shows the results of their creativity which has come because of organisation stucture itself.

(vi) **Optimum Use of Organisational Resources.** Organisational structure tries to make optimum use of organisational resources by ensuring their allocation to points where these are needed. Organisational structure gives higher place to activities which are more important to the achievement of organisational objectives. Thus placing of activities according to their importance provides guidelines for resource allocation. While efficiency in the use of organisational resources is necessary for organisational units is equally important.

The above roles of organisation structure are important. All these roles can be performed by the structure only when it is properly designed. Further, organisation structure should be viewed as a means towards specific ends. As such, it can be used as a tool, not an end. Like any tool, results depend on the skill with which it is used. Managers need not go out of their way to equip themselves with out-of-date or inadequate organisational tools.

FEATURES OF GOOD ORGANISATION STUCTURE

The contingency approach of organisational design suggests that there is no one best way of designing an organisation structure. The good structure is one which meets the demands of various contextual variables namely environment, technology, people, and size. However, certain features of organisation structure can meet all these demands. These features can be obtained in an organisation structure if properly designed. If the following criteria are taken into account while designing an organisation structure, it is likely to meet the demand of various factors.

1. Clear Line of Authority. Whatever the form of structure is adopted, there should be clear lines of authority running from top to bottom or in horizontal directions. The concept of clear line of authority implies that one should be very clear about what he is expected to achieve or contribute and what relationships should be maintained by him at his official level. The failure to clarify lines of authority results into frictions, politics, and inefficiencies. Often in bureaucratic structure followed by government organisation, the problem of jurisdiction of a department or division arises and work suffers. The problem arises because authority and responsibility for action are critical in the organisation, and lack of clarity means lack of knowledge on the part of a manager to perceive his role clearly.

2. Simplicity. An organisation structure should be basically simple. The concept of simplicity implies that various organisational relations should be kept minimum possible. Provisions of various networks is essential but it should not lead to confusion and ambiguity. Every person in the organisation should be clear about to whom he has to consult in a particular matter. Too many levels, too many communication channels, multiplicity of commands, or too many committees often cause more problems than solving these. Ideally speaking their numbers and places in the organisation should be based on organisational needs rather than on personal whims or mere decorative needs.

3. Application of Ultimate Responsibility. The concept of ultimate responsibility suggests that although a superior manager assigns some of the work to his subordinates, he is ultimately responsible for performance of total work. Thus he is responsible for his own work as well as for the work performed by his subordinates. In this concept, no superior can absolve himself from the responsibility of non-performanace of work by his subordinates. If this concept is applied, it ensures that every body carries dual responsibility; responsibility for his work and that for his subordinates' work.

4. Flexibility. An organisation structure should be flexible enough so that changes can be incorporated whenever needs arise. The structure is designed not only for a time period but for a distant future also. As such continuity must be maintained in the organisation structure over the period of time. However, since organisation structure is based on circumstances and these are not fixed but change over the period of time, there is a need for incorporating changes in organisation structure also. These changes can be incorporated easily if the structure is flexible. Thus the concept of flexible structure is that it provides opportunity to incorporate changes where these are needed without adversely affecting the other parts. However, if change in one part of the structure necessitates changes in other parts also, suitable changes should be made in those parts also.

5. Minimum Possible Managerial Levels. As far as possible, there should be minimum managerial levels. Greater the number of managerial levels longer is the line of communication in the chain of command and the communication has to travel along the line creating problems of delay and distortion. Further, more managerial levels means that they increase cost in the organisation as ratio of managers to non-managers (operatives who actually work) goes in favour of managers. Though it may not be possible to suggest how many managerial levels should be kept by an organisation because the number of levels is affected by so many variables, the principle of minimum levels can be followed.

6. Proper Delegation of Authority. The concept of ultimate responsibility can work only when there is proper delegation of authority at various levels of the organisation. Delegation of authority refers to authorisation of a manager to make certain decisions. He can discharge his responsibility properly if he has commensurate authority. A common problem in the organisational life is that managers often fail to delegate adequate authority and suffer with various problems. Such problems may be in the form of decision bottlenecks, delay in decision implementation, more pressure on higher-level managers for making decisions, and less motivation to subordinates. All these factors affect organisational efficiency adversely. These problems can be overcome by proper delegation of authority.

7. Principles of Unity of Direction and Command. Unless absolutely essential, principles of unity of direction and unity of command should be followed. As discussed earlier, unity of direction refers to the concept of one plan one man. Every work in the organisation having same objective must be assigned to a single person. Thus activities and functions of same type can be grouped together or geographical areas having same characteristics can be grouped together, and so on. This provides clarity in carrying out the activities. A combination of ill-related assignments may work only so long as a particular person holds the position. It is not a good sign of an organisation structure and often creates more confusion and role conflict leading to inefficiency. Similarly, unity of command principle should be followed and should be allowed multiple command only as exception. Unity of command suggests that one person should receive others and instructions from one superior only. Unity of command again provides clarity in role while multiple command provides opportunity to avoid responsibility.

8. Provision for Top Management. In corporate form of organisation, it is imperative to provide some means by which shareholders and members of the board of directors participate in management process. Normally shareholders are indifferent so far as day-to-day management affairs of the company are concerned. Similarly board of directors also do not meet on regular basis. However, these two groups affect the organisational functioning. Therefore, a link should be provided between regular management team and members of board and shareholders. The organisation structure should clearly specify how these top management groups will participate in management of the company, how they exercise control over the functioning of the company, and so on.

9. Proper Emphasis on Staff. Line functions should be separated from staff functions and adequate emphasis should be placed on important staff activities. This is important particularly in large organisation. The line and staff activities are required because both serve different objectives in the organisation. A line activity is that which serves the organisational objectives directly, for example, production activities in a manufacturing organisation. On the other hand contributions of staff activities are indirect, that is, they help in carrying out the line activities so as to achieve organisational objectives. Staff activities may be personnel, accounting, etc. Both of these activities should be clearly spelled out to make organisation work smoothly. Similarly line and staff authority should also be made clear so that no conflict or ambiguity arises.

NATURE, CHARACTERISTICS AND IMPORTANCE ORGANISATION

The term organisation is used in a business or industrial enterprise in two different meanings. **As a structure** and as process: As a structure, organisation is the structure of human relationships. It includes all formal, informal relationships which affects the behaviour of employees. It is systematic combination of people, functions and facilities. It is the mechanism or framework within people live and work together for the achievement or predetermined objectives. **As a process**, organisation is an important function of management. It is a process of establishing harmonious relationship between different departments activites and factors of production of an enterprise. Organisation defines the functions of all the employees of organisation, decides their authorities and establishes relationship among them. The term Organisation is the process which aims at obtaining mamixum production at minimum cost. The definitions of Organisation can be divided into two parts:

(I) Definitions on the Basis of Object

J.N. Schulze, "Organisation is a combination of necessary beings, materials, tool, equipments, working space and apparatuses, brought together in a systematic and effective correlation to accomplish some desired objects."

Mc Farland, An identifiable group of people contributing their efforts towards the attainment of goals is called organisation.

L.H. Haney, "Organisation is a harmonious adjustment of specialised parts for the accomplishment of some common purpose or purposes."

(II) Functional Definitions

L.F. Urwick, "Organisation is to determinre the activities to accomplish a job and to arrange the distribution of the activities among the people."

Oliver Sheldon, "The Process of so combining the work which individuals or groups have to perform with the faculties necessary for its execution that the duties, so performed, provide the best channels for the efficient, systematic, positive and co-ordinated application of the available efforts."

Kmball and Kimball, "It embracs the duties designating the departments and personnel that are to carry on the work, defining their functions and specifying the relationship that are to exist between departments and individuals.

In brief, it can be concluded that organisation is a process to carry on the activities of an enterprise in a efficient manner and to have proper control over those activities so that the pre-detrermined objectives of enterprise may be accomplished.

NATURE OF ORGANISATION

Nature of organisation is as follows:

1. **Authority Structure.** There is an arrangement of positiosn into a graded series. The authority of every position is defined. It is subordinate to the position above it and superior to the one below it. This chain of superior-subordinate relationships is known as chain of command.
2. **Common Purpose.** Every organisation exists to accomplish some common gaols. The strcuture must reflect these objecives as enterprise activities are derived from them. It is bound by common purpose.
3. **Co-ordination.** There is a mechanism for coordinating different activities and parts of an organisation so that it

functions as an integrated whole. Co-operative effort is a basic feature of organisation.

4. **Division of Labour.** The total work of an organisation is divided into functions and sub-functions. This is necessary to avoid the waste of time, energy and resources which arises when people have to constantly change from one work to another. It also provides benefits of specialisation.

5. **People.** An organisation is basically a group of persons. Therefore, activity groupings and authority provision must take into account the limitations and customs of people. People constitute the dynamic human element of an organisation.

6. **Environment.** An organisation functions in an environment comprising economic, social, political and legal factors. Therefore, the structure must be designed to work efficiently in a changing environmnet. It cannot be static or mechanistic.

7. **Rules and regulations.** Every organisation has some rules and regulations for orderly functioning of people. These rules and regulations may be in writing or implied from customary behaviour.

8. **Communication.** Every organisation has its own channels of communication. Such channels are necessary for mutual understanding and co-operation among the members of an organisation.

CHARACTERISTICS OF ORGANISATION

On the basis of above definitions, it can be concluded that the following are the characteristics of organisation:

1. **Objects.** Sound and effective organisation is possible only when the business or industrial enterprise has clearly defined objectives. Therefore, the objectives of enterprise must be clearly defined.

2. **Attainment of Goals.** Effective organisation helps in the attainment of pre determined goals of a business and

industrial enterprise. Really speaking, it is a tool of attaining such objectives.

3. **Operation of Activities.** Organisation defines activites of an enterprise also. It defines as to what activites are to be done, who are to do these activities, how and when are these activities to be done, etc. Organsiation also defines the responsibilites and authorities of all the employees of an enterprise.
4. **Co-ordination.** Organisation establishes harmonious co-ordiantion and adjustment among different fctors of production.
5. **Combination.** Harmoniuos adjustment between different factors of production is also necessary for effective oragnisation. If harmonious adjustment is not established among different fctors of production the organisation cannot be fruitful.

IMPORTANCE OF ORGANISATION

According to L.A. Allen, sound organisation can contribute greatly to the continuty and success of enterprise in the following ways:

1. Facilitates Growth and Diversification. Sound organisation permits organisational elaboration. Under the traditional fucntional organisations growth and diversification of activities is facilitated by clear division of work, proper delegation of authority etc. As the organisation balloons to a reasonsable proportion the functional type can be replaced by a more flexible decentralised organisation.

2. Facilitate Administration. If the organisation plan is ill-designed, if it is merely a makeshift arrangement, then management is rendered difficult and ineffectie. Poor organisation leads to waste motion and expensie overlap in work. Imp[ortant work may be subordinated or may be overlooked totally. Sound organisation allows management to relate resources flows continually to overall objectives; it provides an appropriate platform from where management can perform the functions of planning direction, controlling etc. in a smooth way.

3. Stimulates Creativity. Specialisation provides individuals with well defined duties, clear lines of authority and responsibility. Where there is no sound organisation, work is divided by force and agressiveness affecting the morale of the employees seriously. Sound organisation structure enables managers to turn over routine and repetitive jobs to supporting positions and concentrate on important issues where they can exploit their potential better.

4. Permits Optimum Use of Resources. Sound organisation structure permits optimum use of technical and human resources. The organisation can take note of the latest technological improvments and incorporate, for example, computers, electronic data processing machines wherever necessary. Similarly, sound organisation structure permits optimum use of human efforts through specialisation. Right persons are placed in the right positions on the basis of their knowledge and experience. It also develops people by creating appropriate training and promotion opportunities. An ideal organisation plan, in short, would give a company the greatest possible strength for meeting predicted needs-changing conditions

However, sound organisation structure by itself does not guarantee success. It is not a sure bet. In the words of Drucker, 'good organisation structure does not by itself produce good performance. just a good constitution does not guarantee great presidents, or good laws or a moral society. But a poor organisation structure makes good performance impossible, no matter how good the individuals may be.'

PROJECT ORGANISATION STRUCTURE

The major reform in the traditional functional structure has come from a group of closely related structure having titles such as project management, programme management, systems organisation, product management, brand management, and matrix structure. All these have in common that they provide a horizontal grouping together of a number of functions which might otherwise be labelled functional departments and exercising staff and functional authority. Out of these, project organisation structure and matrix organisation structure have become quite popular. The basic idea behind these structures is that since environment changes very rapidly, the organisation must take up various activities on project basis, that is, adding the required ones and deleting the unnecessary ones. Thus the organisation can be organic-adaptive one. The project work can be managed in two forms of organisation; pure project organisation and matrix organisation. The pure project organisation is suitable for taking small number of larger projects with long duration so that a separate division can be created for each project. Matrix organisation, on the other hand, is suitable for taking large number of smaller projects and the activities of various projects can be accomplished through temporary departments.

Project organisation appears very like to divisional structure except that in the latter various divisions are created on permanent basis while in the former, they are created only for the life time of a project. When a particular project is completed, the concerned division may disappear. However, since a project may continue for quite long time, a project may become a sort of permanent. For example, Middleton observes that "a project organisation can also be the beginning of an organisation cycle. The project may become a long term or permanent effort that eventually becomes a programme or branch organisation. The latter, in turn, may become separated from the parent organisation and be established as a full-feledged division, functionally organised."

The establishment of project organisation calls for appointment of a project manager who is responsible for the completion of the project. He coordinated the activities of the project. He prescribes what is to be done, when it is to be done, and how much resources are required. The functional personnel are drawn from various functional departments and functional managers decide who in their department will perform the task and how it will be done. Thus project manager is a unifying and focal point for the project activities.

A Project manager really does not have vertical authority on the personnel drawn from various functional departments unlike a dvisional manager who has line authority over the people working in various functional departments assigned to his division. In the absence of any vertical authority, the project manager must convince the functional people so that they help him to finish the undertaking within the time. In reality, project manager faces an authority gap. He has responsibility for completing the project but does not have direct authority over the people associated with his project.

Suitability of Project Organisation

For activities which are undertaken on project basis, project organisation is the most suitable. Such an activity has following features:

1. It is one- time task and is definable in terms of a single, specific goal.

2. It is infrequent, unique , and unfamiliar to the present organisation. Unfamiliarity usually leads to a disagreement as to how the activity should be managed.

3. It is complex and calls for a high degree of interdependence among the tasks.

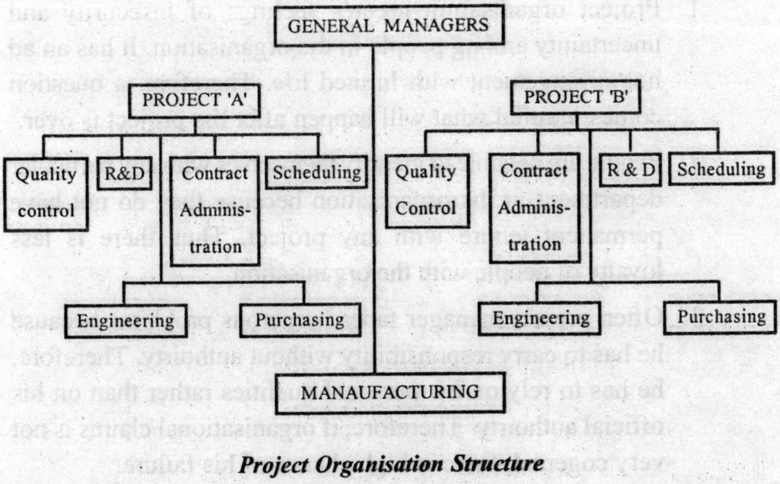

Project Organisation Structure

4. There is a high degree of stake in the successful completion of the project. The time factor is critical because if the project is not completed within the stipulated time, the organisation may lose heavily because of fine provision due to delay.

When project organisation structure is adopted for this type of activity, following advantages emerge:

1. Project organiation allows maximum use of specialised knowledge which is available to all projects on equal basis. Knowledge and skills can be transferred from one project to another project.
2. It provides more flexibility for the utilisation of resources in the organisation by allocating them to the projects where these are needed.
3. It enables the organisation to adapt to environment demands particularly when environmental factors are fast changing.

PROBLEMS IN PROJECT ORGANISATION

In fact, many of the flexibilities of project organisation may turn into problems if proper arrangement is not made for overcoming these problems. A project manager has to face unusual problems resulting from the project management. Following problems are usually experienced in project organisation.

1. Project organisation creates feelings of insecurity and uncertainty among people in the organisation. It has an ad hoc arrangement with limited life. Therefore, a question comes in mind what will happen after the project is over.
2. People are not able to identify themselves with any particular department in the organisation because they do not have permanent tenure with any project. Thus there is less loyalty of people with the organisation.
3. Often project manager faces numerous problems because he has to carry responsibility without authoirty. Therefore, he has to rely on his personal qualities rather than on his official authoirty. Therefore, if organisational claims is not very cogenial, there is high chance of his failure.
4. There is lack of clarity among memebers about their role in the organisation. For example, project relationships are not based on the principles of clarity of authority and responsibility and fixed amount of authority. Thus only

those persons can work better who have high level of tolerance for ambiguity.

These problems are real and a challenge lies before the project manager. If he believes in traditional system of organisation, he may not be able to work. He has to change the total philosophy of managing. For example, Cleland and King stress that a project manager has to take a new approach to his job. Such approach may be: *(i)* he must become reoriented away from the functional approach to the management of human and non-human resources; *(ii)* he must understand that purposeful conflict may very well be a necessary way of life as he manages his project across many vertical organisational lines; and *(iii)* he must recognise that project management is a dynamic activity where major changes are almost the order of the day.

MATRIX ORGANISATION STRUCTURE

Matrix organisation structure is essentially a violation of unity of command and, therefore, whole classical concept related to the principle of unity of command are violated. Matrix structure is the realisation of two-dimensional structure which emanates directly from two dimensions of authority. Two complementary structrues. pure project structure and functional structure—are merged together to create matrix structure. Thus matrix structure not only employs a multiple command but also related support mechanism and associated organisational culture and behaviour. Thus it shows many organisational overlaps not only in terms of command system but also in terms of whole organisational processes and behaviour. For example, Davis and Lawrence have presented matrix structure as follows

Martrix Organisation = Matrix Structure + Matrix Systems + Matrix Culture + Matrix Behaviour

Sometimes, matirx and project structures are considered to be the same. However, there is a difference between two. In project organisation, separate identificable units are created for taking and managing projects, and complete responsibility for the tasks as well as all the resources needed for their accomplishment are usually assigned to one project manager. In a large project with long life, the project division resembles a regular division, reltively independent of any other division. In matrix organisation, project manager is usually not assigned complete responsibility for resources. Instead, he shares them with others in the organisation. Project organisation is preferred when the organisation has small number of major projects. For projects of major magnitudes, a project type organistion can be established, but rest of the organistion can be managed through functional structure. In such a case, there are well-established functional departments which have skills and capabilities for the performance of a variety of programmes. Essentially, programmes flow through the functional complex and receive the services of these specialised departments.

Design of Matrix Structure

In matrix organisation structure, a project manager is appointed to coordinate the activities of the project. Personnel are drawn from their respective functional departments. Upon completion of the project, these people may return to their original departments for further assignment. Thus each functional staff has two bosses—his administrative head and his project manager. During his assignment to a project, he works under the coordinative command of the project manager and he may be called upon by his permanent superior to perform certain services needed in the project. Thus a subordinate in matrix structure may receive instructions from two bosses. Therefore, he must co-ordinate the instructions received from two or even more bosses. Similarly, matrix, superior has to share the fcilities with others. He reports in a direct line to the up, but does not have a complete line of command below, A matrix organistion structure can be presented in.

Suitability of Matrix Structure

Matrix structure is of recent origin but its use has spread in various fields. For example, Davis and Lawrence have observed that matrix structure can be successfully applied to the following types of activities; manufacturing activities—aerospace, chemcials, eletronics, heavy equipment, industrial project and pharmaceutical; service activities—banking, brokerage, construction, insurance, and retailing; professional activies-accounting, advertising, consulting, and law; and non-profit organisations- government agencies, hospital, united nations, and universtities. They emphasise that this list is suggestive and not exhaustive. In fact, matrix structure has been evolved to overcome the limitations of traditional organistion structures.

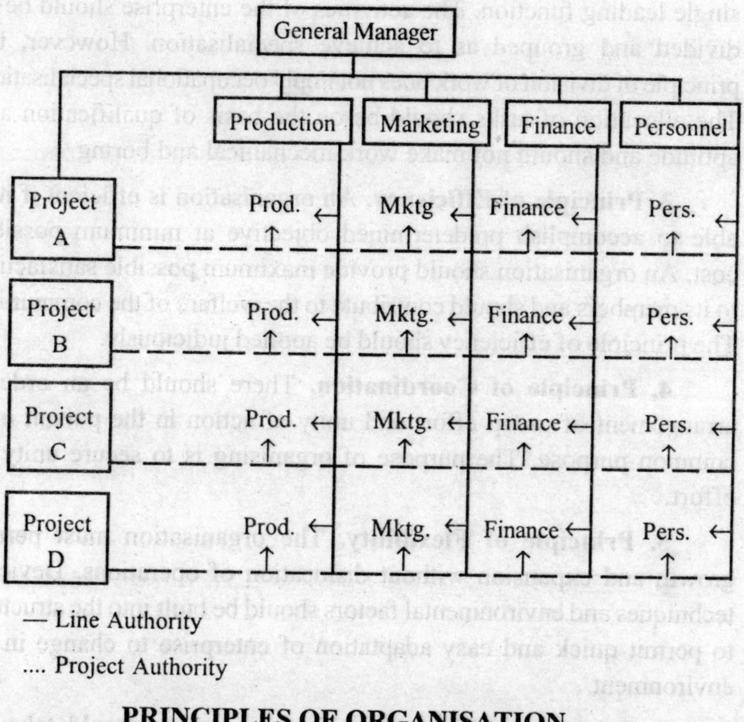

PRINCIPLES OF ORGANISATION

In order to create a sound organisation, the following principles are very useful:

1. Principle of Objective. An organisation and every part of it should be directed towards the accomplishment of basic objectives. Every member of the organisation should be well familiar with its goals and objectives. Common objectives create commonness of interests. In the words of Urwick, "Every organisation and every part of the organisation must be an expression of the prupose of the undertaking concerned." The application of this principle implies the existence of clearly formulated and well understood objective. An organisation structure must be measured against the criterion of effectiveness in meeting these objectives.

2. Principle of Division of Work. The total task should be divided in such a manner that the work of every individual in the organisation is limited as far as possible to the performance of a single leading function. The activities of the enterprise should be so divided and grouped as to achieve specialisation. However, the principle of division of work does not imply occupational specialisation. The allocation of tasks should be on the basis of qualification and aptitude and should not make work mechanical and boring.

3. Principle of Efficiency. An organisation is efficient if it is able to accomplish predetermined objective at minimum possible cost. An organisation should provide maximum possible satisfaction to its members and should contribute to the welfare of the community. The principle of efficiency should be applied judiciously.

4. Principle of Coordination. There should be an orderly arrangement of group effort and unity of action in the pursuit of a common purpose. The purpose of organising is to secure unity of effort.

5. Principle of Flexibility. The organisation must permit growth and expansion without dislocation of operations. Devices, techniques and environmental factors should be built into the structure to permit quick and easy adaptation of enterprise to change in its environment.

6. Principle of Exception. Every manager should take all decisions within the scope of his authority and only matters beyond the scope of his authority should be referred to higher levels of management. In other words, routine decisions should be taken at lower levels and top management should concentrate on matters of exceptional importance.

7. Principle of Continuity. The organisation should be so structured as to have continuity of operations. Arrangements must be made to enable people to gain experience in positions of increasing diversity and responsibility.

8. Principle of Balance. The various parts of an organisation should be kept in balance and none of the functions should be given undue emphasis at the cost of others. In order to create structural balance, it is essential to maintain a balance between centralisation and decentralisation, between broad span of management and long lines of communication, between line and staff. etc. Vertical and horizontal dimensions must be kept in reasonable balance by ensuring that the structure is neither too tall nor too flat.

9. Principle of Unity of Command. Each person should recieve orders from only one superior and be accountable to him. This is necessary to avoid the problems of conflict in instructions, frustration, uncertainty and divided loyalty and to ensure the feeling of personal responsibility for results. This principle promotes coordination but may operate against the principle of specialisation.

10. Principle of Span of Control. No executive should be required to supervise more subordinates than he can effectively manage on account of the limitation of time and ability. There is a limit on the number of subordinates that an executive can effectively supervise. However, the exact number of subordinates will vary from person to person depending upon the nature of the job, and basic factors that influence the frequency and severity of the relationships to be supervised.

11. Principle of Delegation. Authority delegated to an individual manager should be adequate to enable him to accomplish results expected of him. Authority should be delegated to the lowest possible level consistent with necessary control so that coordination and decision-making can take place as close as possible to the point of action.

12. Principle of Absoluteness of Responsibility. The responsibility of the subordinate to his superior is absolute. No superior can escape responsibility for the organisation activities of his subordinates.

13. Principle of Scalar Chain. Authority and responsibility should be in a clear unbroken line from the highest executive to the lowest executive. As far as possible, the chain of command should be short. The more clear the line of authority from the ultimate authority in an enterprise to every subordinate position, the more effective will be decision-making and organisation communication.

14. Principle of Parity of Authority and Responsibility. Authority and responsibility must be co-extensive. The responsibility expected from a position should be commensurate with the authority delegated to that position, and vice versa. In addition, authority and responsibility should be clearly defined for all positions.

Mooney and Reiley has also put some principles for an ideal organisation.

(i) **The Scalar Principle.** This principle states that authority and responsibility should flow in clear and unbroken line from top to bottom of the organisation. When the line authority is clear, it will be easy for organisational members to understand to whom they can delegate, who can delegate to them and to whom they are accountable.

(ii) **The Principle of Unity of Commond.** The unity of command principle states that for any given activity an employee should be made accountable to only one superior.

(iii) **Principle of Functional Definition.** Effective coordination and co-operation demands a clear definition, preferably in writing of authority and responsibility for all decisions and work.

(iv) **Authority Level Principle.** Delegation will prove to be a useless exercise if the superior cannot resist the temptation to make decisions for subordinates.

(v) **Principle of Delegation by Results Expected.** This principle suggests that work and authority should be delegated to the lowest organisational level commensurate with the ability of subordinates to perform.

NEO-CLASSICAL ORGANISATION THEORY

The neo-classical theory has developed as a reaction to rationality and efficiency obsession of the classical theory which failed to recongnise thė significance of the impact of human being on organisation structure. Neo-classical theory has started its development from the findings of famous Hawthorne Experiments. Afterwards many contributions have been added to the field. The essence of neo-classical theory is contained in two points: *(i)* organisational situation should be viewed in social as well as in economic and technical terms; and *(ii)* the social process of group behaviour can be understood in terms of clinical method analogous to the doctor's diagnosis of human organism. The neo-classical theory emphasises on the task of complementing for some of the deficiencies in classical theory. This takes the postulates of classical model and modifies them to suit the needs of human beings in the organisation. Since the theory suggests only modifications in the basic postulates of classical theory, it is referred to as neo-classical theory. The main propositions of neoclassical theory are as follows:

1. The organisation is a social system.
2. The social environment of the job affects people and is also affected by them not by management alone.
3. Informal organisation also exists within the formal organisation and it affects and is affected by the formal organisation.
4. Often there is a conflict between individual and organisational objectives which increases the importance of integration between individuals and organisation.
5. Human being is not totally rational and his behaviour can be predicted in terms of social and psychological factors.
6. Human being has diverse motivational pattern and try to fulfil different types of needs.
7. Communication is necessary as it carries information necessary for organisation functioning and conveys the feelings and sentiments of people work in the organisation.

8. Team work is essential for co-operation among people. This is not achieved automatically but has to be achieved through behavioural approach.

NEO-CLASSICAL THEORY AND ORGANISATIONAL DESIGN

According neo-classical theory, the organisation should be designed in such a way that meets the basic postulates of the theory is discussed above. The basic emphasis of neo-classical theory is on flat structure, decentralisation, and provision of informal organisation. It can be seen that this theory offers modifications over the classical organisation structure. For example, it accepts the concepts of span of control but emphasises on wide span of control of the flat structure rather than narrow span of control resulting into tall structure as envisaged by the classical theory.

1. **Flat Structure.** Neo-classical theory suggests flat structure as against tall sturcture. Neo-classicists feel that tall structure is against the human beings. If suffers from the following problems: communication problem increased differentiation between decision makers and implementers, lack of motivation to people, and being expensive because too many levels are added in the organisation. As against this, flat structure with wide span of control is more suitable for motivating human beings in the organisation; communication chain is shorter and it is free from hierarchical control.
2. **Planning.** According to Fayol planning is the basis and starting point of management activity. It is an effective instrument of control in the hands of management. It provides forethought to management and organisational activities. A good plan of action should provide not only unity and continuity but also flexibility. It should be realistic and in this regard experience very much counts.
3. **Organisation.** From this he means providing for every thing which is needed for its proper functioning like raw materials, tools, personnel, capital etc. According to him

organisation can be both material and human which includes personnel leadership and organisational structure.

Functions of an Organisation. According to him each organisation is required to perform certain functions. In an organisation Manager/Organiser or by whatever name he may be called should ensure that there is no excessive paper control, unnecessary red-tapism and unwanted regulations. Only appropriate and necessary controls should be provided. As said earlier Fayol has divided organisation into two parts namely human and material. He has said that the manager should supervise both and ensure that both are consistent with over all objectives of the organisation, keeping in view its resources and requirements.

The organiser should pay proper attention to unity of command and ensure that the commands are being obeyed. He is in favour of single, competent, energetic guiding authority which should be competent to issue commands and orders. A manager should ensure that individual interest are always subordinated to collective interests of the organisation and all activities going on in the organisation are properly co-ordinated and harmonised so that there are no confusions and disruptions. He has stressed that a good Manager should make full use of his punitive powers against those who indulge in unethical and irregular activities.

4. **Command.** For Fayol it is another element of management. He is of the view that every body in the organisation cannot issue commands. In fact command is an art which is closely linked with personal qualities. A person who has good knowledge of principles of management can issue good commands. One who is authorised or empowered to issue commands should possess certain qualities. He should not get engrossed in details and be well versed in organisation's business and its employees. He should see that the incompetent are eliminated and ensure that his commands aim at unity in the organisation and win loyalty

of personal working in the organisation, not for him but for the organisation. He should set good examples for others and conduct periodically the audit of the organisation.

5. **Control.** One more element of management to which Fayol has drawn attention is control, which he feels is necessary for promptly achieving plan objectives. Controls bring to light errors committed and also the weaknesses of the organisation so that these can be promptly rectified and necessary steps are taken so that the errors do not recur. Controls can prove effective only when those who violate these are punished. In control Fayol has covered checking, auditing and monitoring.

6. **Co-ordination.** In order to facilitate the work of the organisation Fayol has said that all activities in the organisation should be coordinated and harmonised so that all departmental work and activities are carried out without duplication of work and efforts. There is no disharmony and also that over all objectives of the organisation are achieved promptly and economically.

PROBLEMS IN MATRIX STRUCTURE

Matrix structure has many problems in practice because of its too much flexibility. The major problems of matrix structure are as follows and managers should take adequate precautions to overcome these:

1. There is always power struggle in matrix structure. The essence of matrix structure is dual command, and to survive such a form, there needs to be balance of power. However, this balance shifts constantly as people try to maximise their benefits. This results into power struggle among people which may become dysfunctional if top management does not play active role in balancing the power.

2. This structure may not work very well when there is economic crunch. In the case of economic crunch, the

organistion may not be in the same position as there may be many changes in market position, pressure on profit margin, and financial problems. In order to overcome these problems, the organisation may be required to change its strategy which may not correspond to matrix structure. For example, decision process has to be centralised in order to arrive at quick decisions to face adversaries.

3. Matrix structure can develop anarchy if not managed properly. People have to work under multiple command. Besides, there may be informal relations among people. Thus whole concept of flexibility may result into problem because people may not be clear about what they should do; what they are expected to contribute.
4. At the initial level, matrix structure bcomes quite costly because of top heavy management. It does seem to double up management because of dual chain of command. However, this is only initial problem, and in the long run, this can be offset by the benefits accrued form matrix structure.
5. If matrix organisation is not followed properly, there is delay in decision making. The decision-making process is such that many persons are involved in the decision; each person may hold veto power or may not give consent because of power struggle and conflict. In this situation, top management may remain busy in solving internal problems of the organisation and find less time for external affairs.

A persual of the various problems suggests that many of these problems come because of faulty implementation of matrix structure. If it is implemented with proper perspective, many problems will disappear. As it has been pointed out in the beginning that matrix is not merely a structure but it includes systems, culture, and behaviour which must be in accordnace with matrix philosophy.

SPAN OF MANAGEMENT

Span of management represents a numerical limit of subordinates to be supervised and controlled by the manager. This is an important principle of sound organisation. V. A. Graicunas analysed superior-subordinate relationship and developed a mathematical formula based on, the geometric increase in complexities of managing as the number of subordinates increase. This theory of superior-subordinate relationships is based upon theoretical projection by mathematics and not on any impirical observation. He identified three types of superior-subordinate relationship.

(a) **Direct Single Relationships.** These relationships arise from direct and individual contacts of the superior with his subordinates. For instance if a superior has two subordinates there would be two direct single relationships.

(b) **Cross Relationships.** These are mutual relationships among subordinates necessary for working under a common superior. For instance two cross retationships arise between two subordinates such as *(i)* A and B. and *(ii)* B and A. These two relationships are different because in the first case A has a talk with B and in the second case is B with A and both the situations are different.

(c) **Group Relationships.** Group relationships arise between the superior and his subordinates in all the possible combinations. A superior may consult his subordinates with one of them, or with all of them, or with various combinations of them. If a superior has four subordinates. There will be 28 possibilities of group relationships.

Graicunas has given the following formula:

Direct single relationships = n

Cross relationships = n (n-1)

Group relationships = n (2n-1-1)

$$\text{Total relationships} = n\left[\frac{2n-1}{2}+n-1\right]$$

N represents the number of subordinates.

Graicunas theory suffers from certain shortcomings also. Firstly it ignores the improtance of relationships. Secondly it ignores the frequency of relationships. Lastly it fails to give factors which govern the actual span of management. Thus, this theory is not of much help in practical life of managers.

Balue and Cott refer to another formula which provide a means of calculating the span of control actually existing in an organization.

$$S = \sqrt[L]{\lambda 1}$$

Where S = Span of control., L = Number of supervisory levels, N = Number of employees.

According to this formula an organization with 256 employees (N = 256) and four levels in the hierarchy (L = 4) would have an average span of control of 4(S = 4) or

$$S = \sqrt[L]{N}$$

$$= \sqrt[4]{256} = 4$$

This average span must be recognized as only a macro measure or an indicator of the overall organizational character relative to span of control. Extreme care must be exercised in interpreting the average span of control because of details that are easily ignored. Ralph C. Davis has differentiated between the operative and executive spans of control. Supervisors at the operative level supervise more routine types of jobs so that the span may vary from ten to thirty but will likely be between fifteen and twenty; the span of executive control however, will probably be between three and seven. Since the work at higher levels is mostly mental, the supervision must also the mental and thus is more limited.

Some Factors Which Affect Span of Control

(a) Delegation of Authority. An executive who personally takes many decisions is able to supervise fewer people than an executive who provides encouragement and coaching to his subordinate to accept delegated authority.

(b) Availability of Staff. When subordinates get from staff men much of their guidance on methods, schedules, quality standards, and other aspects of their work, they need less contact with their line supervisors. Under such situations, the supervisor can handle more subordinates.

(c) Ability of the Executive. Individuals differ in various qualities like leadership, decision making and communication. An executive who possesses these qualities in greater degree as compared to the others can supervise a larger number of people.

(d) Time Available for Supervision. The span of control should be narrow at the higher levels, because top managers have less time available for supervision. They have to devote the major portion of their time in planning, organising directing and controlling.

(e) Nature of Work. A manager who is confronted with complex problems that often involve many people needs more time to dispose of than an executive who deals with simple and routine problems which involve a few people only. Accordingly, a managing director probably needs to work longer with each of his immediate subordinates than does a first line supervisor who deals with routine problems.

(f) Ability of Subordinates. Fresh entrants to jobs take more of a supervisor's time than well trained persons who have acquired experience in the job. Subordinates who have good judgment, initiative, and sense of obligation needs less help from supervisor than a willing, though non-too-bright, employee.

(g) Repetitiveness of Activities. New and different problems take more time to handle than those that have been faced many times before. Familiar jobs can be accomplished with increasingly less effort. In such cases, span of supervision could be wider.

In short the spari of supervision should be determined for each executive position. As more practical approach is to consider modification in the job and the surrounding. Organisation at the same time that we decide on an optimum span of supervision. Adjustment can be made in several directions as we are dealing with interdependent factors and the important objective is the design a total structure that gives us an appropriate emphasis.

HUMAN RELATIONS THEORY OF ORGANISATION

The Human Relations Theory is discribed as Neo-Classical (New Classical) Theory of Organization. The theory is a modification may an extension of the earlier theories. In the words of Hicks and Gullett, "The basic assumption of neo-classical theory is that psychological and social aspects of the worker as an individual and his work group ought to be emphasised."

Though the theory can be traced from ancient literature yet its development took place in 1920's and 1930's as Harvaid Business School under the leadership of Elton Mayo and his associates conducted research at the Hawthorne Plant of the Western Electric Company. These studies reveal the ideological revolution in organizational theory. The revolution focussed on organization as a social system.

The Hawthorne studies established the informal group as a major explanation of behaviour in organizations. The conceptual horizon of organization was extended to include a large range of sociopsychological variables. Neo-classical approach is discerned in Human Relations books—"Human Relations in Industry" by Gardner and Moorie and "Human Relations in Business" by Davis, to some extent work done in industrial psychology and industrial sociology also is a reflection of new classical point of view.

The Hawthorne experiments conducted between 1924 and 1932 established that social or human relations among the workers played more important part in the determination of productivity than the changes in working conditions. The high morale of the test group workers was deemed responsible for the productivity augmentation. Morale was considered as the consequence of individual, personal, emphatic attention paid to the individual worker and the social structure of work group. Sanctions, even trivial factors *viz.* who sat next to whom, played vital role. The Hawthorne researchers thus came to the conclusion that the workers feeling about himself and his work group was no less important. These experiments reveal that organizations have social and emotional aspects besides economic ones. It was found that productivity of the workers increased where the sentiments of the informal group were in consonance with the objectives of the formal group/organization.

Besides emphasis was laid on the development of the human relations skills which could enable the supervision to effectively bridge the gap between the informal and formal organizations.

Basic Conclusions:

(i) A worker is a social being deriving satisfaction primarily by membership of stable work groups.

(ii) The management should work through small group rather than operate through 'atomized economic automations'.

(iii) Techniques like 'expressive supervision and workers' participation could promote a congenial climate of good human relations resulting unfruitful functioning of work groups.

This approach has been widely accepted both by Public and Private Administration.

ELEMENTS OF THEORY

The writers of this theory have concentrated on three elements *viz.* individual social aspect of work groups and participative management. A brief explanation will not be out of place.

(1) Individual. The theory emphasises that each worker is unique and adapts to the job situation. Certain attitudes develop and also ways of life besides certain skills, technical, social and logical. Each worker has cerain, aspiration and expectations of job situation.

(2) Social aspects of work group. This aspect focusses its attention of the social aspects of man whose main desire is seen in the sense of belongingness, ready acceptance and proper recognition by the Group. In the words of Mayo, "Main social situation in his work group ranked first and the work was incidental" William G. Scott also refers to importance of the informal organization when he remarks,

"....these associations are not specified in the blue print of the formal organization.

(3) **Participative Management.** The increased emphasis on the individual and work groups led to the emergence of participative management. It involves participation of the workers in the decision-making about their work conditions. The workers discuss with supervisors and exercise influence on the decision affecting them. Hawthorne researchers observed, "Before every change of programme the group is consulted.

Chester & Barnard—a contemporary of Mayo—has elaborated his view in, "The functions of the Executive" published in 1938. He disapproves the theory of economic men and proposes the theory of contribution—satisfaction, equilibrium. He was of the view that formal organizations are artifical systems and have grown out of informal organizations the natural systems. The formal organizations sometimes cause the rise of informal organizations which perform three positive functions *viz.* *(i)* They add to communication by providing viable alternatives to formal channels. *(ii)* They maintain the socio-psychological cohesiveness of the organization by creating relationship among individuals that would not otherwise develop. *(iii)* Informal ties and activities allow members to develop feelling of personnel importance and effectiveness.

MODERN THEORY (SYSTEM ANALYSIS) OF ORGANISATION

Modern theory termed as system analysis of organisation emerged in 1950's. It is a unique theory as it takes into considerations all elements both of the whole organization as well as its component parts. It portrays an organization as an adaptive system. For its survival the organization must adapt to changes in the environment. Modern theory considers organization and its environment as interdependent, each dependent on the other for resources.

The theory laying emphasis on synthesis and design makes a provision for small view of organization. Unlike certain theories the Modern Theory (System Analysis) deals integratively with the problems of fully describing and explaining organizational phenomenon. In a way it casts look at the Organization in totality. 'Organization' by March and Simon and 'Modern Organization' Theory by Haire are prominent writings on the subjects.

Hicks and Gullett enumerate characteristics of Modern Theory as dynamic multi-level and multi-dimensional, multimotivated probabilistic multi-disciplinary, descriptive, multi-variable and adaptive.

Nigro and Nigro also point out certain characteristics of all social organizations which are common and are as follows:

CHARACTERISTICS OF ORGANIZATION

(1) Organization, "constantly seek and import resources (inputs) in both human and material form and transform these inputs into products and services using internal, social and technological processes (through points)."

(2) "Organization structure develop around patterned activities that from stable and predictable input throughout and output cycles."

(3) "Overtime structural differentiation and task specialization are common system responses to the search for resources and adaptiveness and as the organization becomes more complex managerial structures for co-ordination and control became more elaborate".

(4) "Feedback in the form of information about environmental responses to organization activities (outputs) is used to keep the system of course with regard to its goals and to evaluate the performance of the organization and its sub-units."

(5) Organizations export their products to the external environment and these outputs usually become the inputs of other organisation.

(6) Organization as system seek equilibrium "or a stable state both internally and in relation to external forces and they achieve equilibrium through a constant process of adaptation to their environment.

Organization as a system banks upon the effective functioning of its part and such systems. Each sub-system discharges a series of needed activities. In any large and complex organization these activities are entrusted to specialized units but they are indispensable to organization and may not necessarily be centralised. The sub-system of an organization are as follows:

(1) **Production or technical sub-systems** are called operation or technical core. These are categorised as the human and mechanical processes. They transform inputs into the primary outputs of the organization.

(2) **Maintenance Sub-System.** They ensure the necessary inputs of human skills of personnel function of all kinds.

(3) **Adaptive Sub-System.** They assist the organization anticipate and respond to changing environmental conditions and demand *e.g.*, Planning units, research and development units.

(4) **Supportive Sub-Systems.** The first tyep of supportive sub-systems procure raw materials and dispose of outputs like purchase-sales etc. The second type specialize in the development of supportive relationship with external actors *e.g.*, search advertising and public relations.

(5) **Managerial Sub-System.** Termed as the administrative structure "co-ordinate and inter-relate the other sub-sytems, resolve conflicts between units, allocates resources and relate external condition to internal garland requirement."

The Modern Thoery goes to the extent of emphasising that organization systems like social systems are construed to be 'cybernetic' their behaviour towards the external environment. That clearly reflects that they are, "self-steering using feedback to guide and control their behaviour". They develop mechanisms to collect, interpret and apply feedback in their decision-making processes in order to acquire the capacity to adapt, correct flows and evaluate performance.

ORGANISATION STRUCTURE

An Organisation Structure referes to the determination of organisation system of an enterprise. Organisation Structure defines the structure of organisation for the enterprise. It determines the programmes are procedures by which the administrative relations of an enterprise and defined and established. No activity of an enterprise can go out of this structure. As the policy of an enterpise determines the limits within which the enterprise has to work. In the same manner, organisation structure determines and defines the shape and size of the enterprise according to which the administrative and organisation decsions have to be taken in the enterprise. Organisation Structure is a frame-work of the activities of the enterprise. It may also be compared with a map of the building to be constructed. Organisation Structure can be defined as, the organisation structure of an organisation deals with its organisational arrangements.

Advantage of An Organisation Structure

Organisation Strcutre has the following advantages in an enterprise:

1. It is Necessary for the Management. Organisation Structure is a necessity for the management of a business and industrial enterprise. In the absence of a clearly defined organisation structure, the management cannot discharge its duties properly because the organisation sturcture determines and defines the relation between all the departments of the enterprise and the rights and duties of all the employees in the enterprise. It also defines the managerial approach of the enterprise.

2. It Reveals the Draw Backs of an Organisation. Organisation Structure is an important document of an enterprise. It determines and defines the activities which can be performed in the enterprise. It also defines mutual relations of various departments and various posts. It also clearly defines the rights and duties of all the employees of the enterprise. It serves as a guideline to explain what should be done in the enterprise. Actual performance of the enterprise is compared with this document. In this way, it reveals the drawbacks of an organisation.

3. It is the Authorised and Latest Document of All the Facts Relation to the Organisation. All the facts recorded in organisation structure are considered to be the authorised and latest available facts regarding organisation of the enterprise. This way, it helps in the settlement of various disputes of the enterprise.

4. Helpful in Delegation. Organisation Structure is helpful in determining the responsibilities of all the employees and defining their duties. It also helps in delegating the proper authority to the employees so that they may discharge their duties easily and efficiently.

5. Helpful in Training. Organisation structure is also helpful in providing the suitable training to the employees of the enterprise. It defines the requirements of all the postages and it also determines the need, nature, and from of training required for the employees.

Disadvantage of Organisation Structure

Organisation Strcutre suffers from the following defects:

1. It is Difficult of Change it. Management is a dynamic science. To make is a real science, it must be practical, No hard and fast line can be drawn in the activities of enterprise. Organisation Structure is the definite determination of activities of enterprise. Therefore, it develops rigidness in the activities of enterprise and it becomes very difficult to make any change in it.

2. It Reveals only the Formal Relations. A very important draw-back of the Organisation Structure is that it is only a formal document. It defines and explains only formal relations among the employees of an enterprise. But in priactice, there are two types of relations among them. Formal, informal and Organisation Structure does not define informal relations.

2. It Creates Conflict. Organisation Structure makes clear difference in the rights and duties of all the employees of the enterprise. It developes the feeling of Boss and sobordinate among them. It also develops the feeling of superior and inferior. It also develops the feeling of senior and junior.

DETERMINANTS OF ORGANISATION STRUCTURE DESIGN

Organisation structure is not a static frame. It undergoes changes with changes in the external environment and internal conditions. While desiging the internal organisation structure, management should consider the following factors:

1. Goals. An organisation is a goal-oriented system. Therefore, its goals play a decisive role in designing its structure. An organisation structure should be designed in such a way that it facilitates the achievement of organisational goals in the most efficient and economical manner. The goals of an organisation determine its tasks and activities. The nature and extent of sub-devision of tasks and their grouping depend on the goal of organisation.

2. Size. Size of organisation is another factor affecting organisational design. As an organisation grows in size, there is a tendency to greater specialisation. The number of sub-units increases and more levels are created in the hierarchy. Impersonal rules and procedures increase formalisation and the organisation becomes more and more structured. Several studies reveal that larger organisations tend to be more specialised, more formalised, more decentralised and more documented.

Certain other studies however, suggest that size has no significance effect an organisation structure. These studies reveal that size has impact on very few organisational variables like vertical differntiation. All aspects of structure cannot to predicted from size.

3. Strategy. Strategy is a contingent plan designed to achieve the objectives. It involves decisions as to what industry the organisation will enter, how will its complete and where. Top managers gernerally formulate strategy after careful analysis of opportunities in the environment and the strengths and weakness in the organisation. Strategy determines the organisation takes and the choice of technology.

Alfred Chandler has clearly established the relationship between the strategy a business adopts and the structure of its Organisation.

Chandler carried out intensive case studies of four of largest American companies. These studies revealed that the companies shifted their organisational design from a simple centralised pattern to a more elaborate divisionalised pattern following changes in population, technological innovations, expending product lines, increase in national income, etc. Thus, changes in corporate strategy lead to changes in organisation structure.

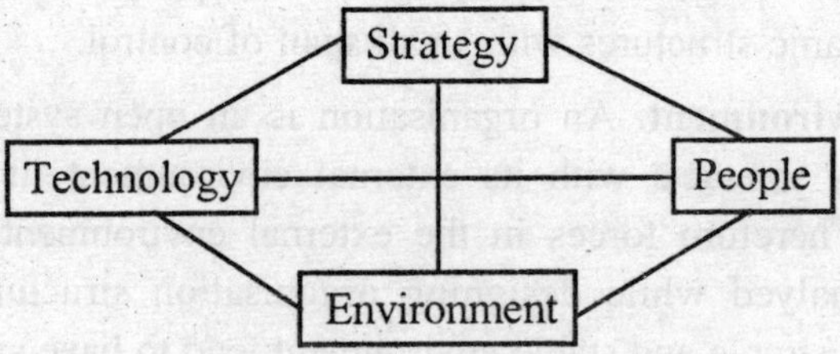

Fig. Determinants of Organisation Design

4. People. Very often, it is taken for granted that people-managers and workers are fit into the structure. But human organisation cannot afford to have machine like designs for long. The organisation structure is a major source of satisfaction for the employees. Therefore, the organisation design should reflect the thinking and way of working of the employees. The philosophy, value system and attitudes of management are important forces affecting organisation structure. For example, Negendhi and Estafen found that two textile mills in India having different philosophy, one seeking long term profit and the other seeking quick proift, had different delegation of authority, span of control and communication pattern. Organisation Structure makes contributions to employees' motivation and performance.

5. Technology. Technology is an important variable in the design of organisation structure. It refers to the way in which work is done, *i.e.*, equipment and technical skills used and the type of work flow in the transformation process. In general, if the technology is routine and simple a less complex structural design is needed. The technology restricts the amount of discretion which can be given to subordinates, hence influencing organisation structure. Several studies by Joan Woodward, Edwar Harvey, William Zwerman, Peter Blau, Charles Perrow and J.D. Thompson have revealed that length of the chain of command, span of management, ratio of managers to non-managers, etc., are correlated with the type of technology employed. After a study of 100 manufacturing firms in Great Britain Woodward found that firms using mass production and assembly line were characterised by mechanistic structures with large span of control. On the other hand, firms employing unit and process technologies adopted organic structures with small span of control.

6. Environment. An organisation is an open system which continuously interacts with its external environment in which it functions. Therefore forces in the external environment must be carefully analyed while designing organisation structure. Firms operating in simple and stable environment tend to have simple and organic structures wherein jobs roles and relationships are not rigidly defined. On the other hand, firm operating in complex (diversity) and dynamic environment are forced to adopt more differentiation and integration in their structures. For example, Burns and Stalker concluded, after a study of 20 industrial firms in the United Kingdom, that successful firms in stable environment were mechanistic in structure while successful firms in dynamic enrionment had more organic or flexible structures. Similarly, Lawrence and Lorsch found that organisational units operating in stable environment were more highly structured than those operating in dynamic environment.

Thus, organisation structure is the result of several operating forces inside and outside the enterprise. These forces are interrelated and interdependent. They suggest that what might be a suitable structure for one organisation may not be suitable for another organisation.

NEED AND SIGNIFICANCE OF ORGANISATION STRCUTRE

Organisation is the foundation upon which the whole structure of management is built. It is the backbone of management. Sound organisation can contribute greatly to the continuity and success of an enterprise in the following ways:

1. **Facilitates Growth and Diversification.** The organisation structure is the framework within which an enterprise grows. Management can anticipate the need for change to facilitate growth and may suitably adjust the organisation structure when the size of business increases.

2. **Facilitates Administration.** A properly designed organisation facilitates both management and operation of the enterprise. It provides proper division of labour, consistent delegation of authority and clear authority relationships. Organisation is the mechanism through which managers direct, coordinate and control the business. If the organisation is ill-designed or it is a make-shift arrangement, the management is rendered difficult and ineffective. If, on the other hand, it is logical and clear-cut, then the first requisite of sound management has been achieved.

3. **Permits Optimum Use of Technology Improvements.** Sound organisation structure provies for optimum use of technical and human resources. The high cost of installation, operation and maintenance of expensive equipment calls for proper organisation. Similarly sound organisation structure helps in optimum use of human efforts through specialisation.

4. **Encourages Use of Human Beings.** Proper organisation provides psychological satisfaction to employees. An Individual contributes his best when he gets satisfaction from his job, his working environment and his relationships. In this way organisation structure facilitates intensive use of human capital. It also creates training and promotional avenues for people.

5. **Stimulates Creativity.** Sound organisation stimulates creative thinking and initiative by providing well-defined areas of work with provision for development of new and improved ways of doing things. it enables managers to turn over routine and respective jobs to supporting positions. A

good organisation enhances capacity of individuals and enables them to take advantage of the accumulated knowledge and experience of preceding generations.

Stating the importance of organisation, the distinguished industrialist of the U.S.A., Andrew Carnegie observed: Take away our factories, take away our trade, our avenues of transportation, our money. Leave us nothing but our organisation, and in four years we shall have re-established ourselves.

Basic Structure and Operating Mechanism

The problem of identifying structure from organisational processes does not mean that there is no difference between the two. There is a basic difference between the two and this distinction is important in understanding the concept and design of organisation structure. The structure of a system is the arrangement of its subsystems and components at a given moment of time. Process is dynamic change in the matter, energy, or information of the system over time. Thus the concepts of structure and process can be viewed as the static and dynamic features and both of these aspects are related rather than opposite. Thus organisation structure can be viewed as established pattern of relationships among the components of the organisation. In large and complex organisations, structure is set forth initially by the design of the major components or subsystems and then by establishing relationships among these subsystems.

Design of basic structure involves such issues as how the work of the organisation will be divided and assigned among various positions, groups, divisions, departments, etc. and how the coordination necessary to accomplish total organisational objectives will be achieved. Besides the formally established organisation structure, people create relationships independent of the formal relationships known as informal relationships or organisation. Thus organisation structure, truly speaking, the totality of both formal and informal relationships. Operating mechanism or organisational process, on the other hand, includes such factors as control procedures, information systems, reward and punishment systems, rules and procedures, and so on. These structural variables, both basic structure and operating mechanism, can be used to identify what is required of organisational members to motivate them to do their assigned part of the organisational objectives, and encourage them to take collective activities.

DIFFERENTIATION AND INTEGRATION IN DESIGNING

Organisation structure refers to the differentiation and integration of activities and authority, role and relationship in the organisation. Thus, there are two considerations in organisation design problem: differentiation and integration. Differentiation is defined as 'the differences in cognitive and emotional orientations among managers in different functional departments, and the differences in formal structure among these departments,' and integration as 'quality of the state of collaboration that are required to achieve unity of effort by the environment." Since various departments are the parts of the whole system, they should not be considered in isolation of others as affecting the economics and efficiencies of work performance. However, since each unit is interacting in a different way with the environment, various units are likely to develcp differentiation to some degree or other, depending upon the specific environment. The extent of organisation differentiation depends upon the certainty or uncertainty of environment and its diversity or homogeneity. Thus designing of one unit may be different from that of other. Applying the concepts of differentiation and integration to organisation design requires various activities in sequence: identification, grouping, and authority relationships among individuals and groups. Thus designing of basic structure involves the following steps:

1. Identification of Activities. In designing the strcuture, managers must identify the various necessary activities that must be performed in order to achieve the organisational objectives. While identifying the various activities, the deductive method is followed which suggests that in order to achieve a particular goal, which steps and functions should be undertaken. It provides a classificatory system that omits nothing and guards against the activities which are unrelated to the goals. The major activities are then classified into a number of sub-activities. While classifying and reclassifying the activities, it should be borne in mind that: *(i)* all the necessary activities are performed; *(ii)* there is no unnecessary duplication in performing various necessary activites; and *(iii)* the various activities are performed in a synchronised or co-ordinated way.

2. Grouping of Activities. Closely related and similar activities are grouped together to form departments, divisions, or sections because co-ordination of numerous activities can best be achieved by grouping them into basic and derivative departments. Grouping may be done on several bases depending upon the situational requirements, Grouped activities in the from of departments, divisions, or sections are assigned to various positions. These positions are occupied by various individuals. The assignment of activities creates responsibility and ensures certainty of work performance, These job assignments are made to different management members who, in turn, distribute the jobs to their subordinates.

3. Delegation of Authority. Since the assignment of the job to an individual creates responsibility on his part, he must have corresponding authority to discharge his obligations. Authority and responsibility are correlated and are taken to be constant companions, because authority without responsibility is a dangerous thing, and responsibility without authority is an empty vessel. Through the process of delegation, authority structure in organisation is created defining who will interact with whom in an official way.

Before proceeding to the first aspect of organisation designing, it is desirable to identify the features and importance of a good organisation structure so that various activities of designing are related with these to make it more effective.

ROLE OF ORGANISATION STRUCTURE

Organisation structure is capable of serving many functions at the same time but can not serve all functions equally well over unlimted time. Structure created for one purpose may not serve other purposes well. Therefore, it is important for managers to determine the outcomes desired from organisation structure, and to match the organisation with changing needs. With multiple needs or roles of organisation structure, a balance will have to be struck and priorities established in the operation of the organisational mechanism. In general, there can be following roles of organisation structure:

(i) Facilitating Management Action. When large number of people work together, some sort of formal structuring is required to place them according to the needs of the organisation. All of them perform various functions which are interdependent and interrelated. As such, there must be plan for systematic completion of the work of each specialised job so that total activities accomplish common objectives. Further these activities should be completed in coordinated way. Organisation structure is the mechanism through which management directs, coordinates, and controls the organisational activities. It is indeed the foundation of management. A properly-designed organisation structure facilitates both management and operation of an organisation. Management actions take place with certainty and continuity only if appropriate functional groups are provided to help managers. The grouping and arrangement of activities directly affect operating results. If the important activities are overlooked or subordinated, the results would be detrimental to the organisation. Need for updated organisation structure can be gauged from the fact that many organisations create separate unity for organisational analysis which looks after the various aspects affected by the organisation structure such as delegation of authority, communication, control, coordination, etc. and tries to find ways for improving them to make suitable for organisational needs.

(ii) Encouraging Efficiency. Organisation structure is the framework within which an organisation functions. In this functioning, efficiency is the major criterion. Therefore, organisational members try to maximise the output of goods or services resulting from a given input of resources, or at least make a respectable showing in that direction. Since chaos or disorganisation works against the ideal of efficiency, there is pressure to develop some measures of systematic, orderly, rational and coordinated effort, and to control waste and loss.

(iv) Stimulating Creativity. A sound organisation stucture based on specialisation stimulates creative thinking by providing well-defined area of work with provision of development of new and improved ways of working. For creativity, it is essential that one is well conversant with the problem on hand. Organisation structure tries to put people at places where they are required. When they work on a job for considerably long time, they are in a position to suggest something new. Many practitioners have contributed to the development of management thinking which shows the results of their creativity which has come because of organisation stucture itself.

(iv) Communication. Organisation structure provides the pathways for communication among organisational members as well between the organisation and its environment. In fact, when we say that organisation structure establishes relationships, we mean that it creates reporting relationships, that is, who will communicate with whom. Similarly, when the organisation interacts with its environment, a communication process is involved. Thus structure serves the purpose of communication. Within organisational boundary, communication is required in horizontal, vertical, and lateral directions, organisation structure, if designed properly, provides lines of communication in all these directions.

(v) Optimum Use of Organisational Resources. Organisational structure tries to make optimum use of organisational resources by ensuring their allocation to points where these are needed. Organisational structure gives higher place to activities which are more important to the achievement of organisational objectives. Thus placing of activities according to their importance provides guidelines for resource allocation. While efficiency in the use of organisational resources is necessary for organisational units is equally important.

(vi) Job Satisfaction. Organisation structure is a source of satisfaction to people. Since organisation provides relatedness among tasks and responsibilities and among people, those who work for an organisation sooner or later come to evaluate the nature of those relationships and of their own relationships to the organisation and to their jobs. Organisation structure provides for each person a place of status which confers a certain standing among his fellows. This works as motivating factor for them. Most of the people spend a large part of their lives at work associated with organisation.

The above roles of organisation structure are important. All these roles can be performed by the structure only when it is properly designed. Further, organisation structure should be viewed as a means towards specific ends. As such, it can be used as a tool, not an end. Like any tool, results depend on the skill with which it is used. Managers need not go out of their way to equip themselves with out-of-date or inadequate organisational tools.

ORGANISATIONAL GOALS

Goal is the main aim or purpose in which organisational resources are directed. It states the directed state of affairs which force an organisation to achieve. In the organisational context the term 'mission', 'objectives' and 'goal' are interchangeably without any attempt to differentiate their meaning. The term mission is a very broad term; it is frequently used in non-business organisations such as social organisations, religious institutions. etc. to describe the major programme demanding strong commitment from members. Objectives and goals are generally used to convey the same meaning.

Charles Perrow felt that organisational goals are the composite of the goals of individual members. This process entails five major factors: *(1)* All individuals enter group membership with a set of needs in their own order of preference. *(2)* Each individual, because of personality, social standing, and numerous other factors, also possesses a certain ability or power to influence others. *(3)* People are selected by the group for membership on the basis of the resources they possess. *(4)* As the membership develops, bargaining takes place among individuals, with those having power displaying greater ability to influence satisfaction of their own needs. *(5)* Eventually, through bargaining, some result or results are selected which provide the highest expected pay off in terms of the compromised needs of group members.

The term 'goal' has acquired a variety of meanings, depending on the perspective of the practitioner. It is sometimes used to legitimize and justify the role of the organization in society or to provide a motive for the organization's activity. In another serlce, goals may be considered as the set of constraints that the organization must satisfy, *i.e.*, profit for the stockholders, satisfaction of employees, meeting government demand for "safe" products, pacifying the environmentalists, and meeting customer requirements.

Etzioni has defined goals as the desired state of affairs which an organisation attempts to realise. They are the endpoints towards which the activities of the enterprise are aimed. They provide direction to various activities.

Objectives depict a future state of affairs which the organisation strives to realise. They set down guidelines for group activity. They constitute a source of legitimacy which justifies the activities of the organisation and indeed its very existence. Moreover, objectives serve as standards for assessing the success of the organisation.

Organisation are social units which pursue specific goals. As a matter of fact, the goals constitute a source of legitimacy which justifies the activities of the organisation and indeed its very existence. Moreover, they serve as standards for assessing the success of the organisation. The goals check the members of the organisation from deviating from the route they have set for themselves. Thus, the goals lay down guidelines for every group activity.

William F. Glueck has suggested that goals serve three purposes: *(1)* they define the organization in its environment and justify its existence to various groups and to society at large; *(2)* they provide for coordination and relate the diverse tasks performed in complex organisations; (3) they establish standards for evaluating the actual performance of individuals and groups.

One of the major problems in the analysis of organizational goals is the distinction between offical goals and actual operational goals. Official goals are often stated in broad, ambiguous terms to justify the activities of the organisation. For example, the official goals of a mental hospital may be to treat mental illness. However, the operational goals are those actually pursed. The mental hospital may provide little in the way of treatment; it may be geared to merely custodial care of patients.

SIGNIFICANCE OF GOALS

An organisation having well-defined goals will not give up long-range development programmes and policies for short-term gains. Planning has no meaning if it is not related to certain objectives. It will be an empty mental exercise if it does not determine what goals are to be accomplished. The goals represent not only the end-point of planning but also the end towards which other managerial activities like organising, directing and controlling are aimed. They provide direction not only to managerial activities but also to other activities. Purchasing, production, marketing and financing are all directed towards the objective of the enterprise. The accomplishment of goals is necessary for the survival of any business enterprise. Well defined objectives in major areas of the business will help in achieving the following benefits:

(1) Stimulates Motivation. Managers should try to fit individual goals into overall organisation was goals and make the job meaningful and worthwile. This will stimulates human motivation.

(2) Basis of Control. Objectives provide the basis of control by clarifying the desired contribution of each job as well as each organisational unit.

(3) Unity of Planning. The managers at various levels make plans of their own. Planning may lose its consistency unless all plans have the same focus of action.

(4) Means of Decentralisation. Menagerial work with appropriate authority and capacity for independent decision is shared by a large number of managers. This may lead to disintegration in place of decentralisation unless there is a common goal. The objectives guide to coordinate and remove conflicts or misunderstanding between various individuals.

The goals of an organization influence its interactions with the environmental suprasystem and other organisations. The efforts to achieve goals affect the ability of the organisation to receive inputs from the environment and thus legitimise its existence. Goals focus the attention of organisational members on actions that are organizationally relevant. They provide the standards for measurement of success. They help determine the technologies required and also set the basis for specialisation of activities, authority pattern, communication and decision networks and other structural relationship. The nature of the goals affects the basic character of the organization.

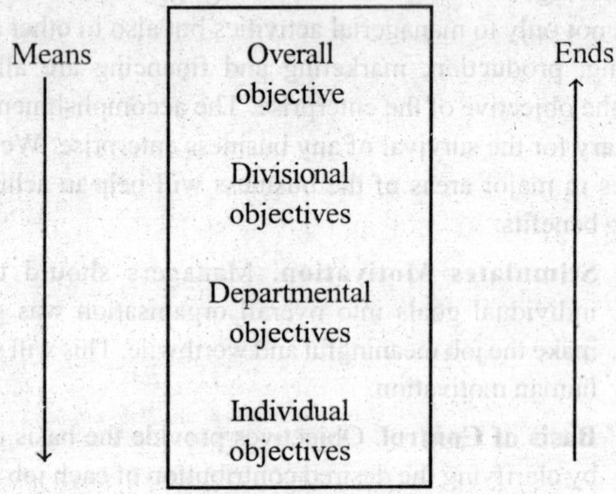

Means-End relationship of organisational goals at intermediate objectives concerned with manufacturing and assembling the major components at the lowest level, the objective of the operative employee consists of performing the detailed work on sub-component parts. This example illustrates that the objective at various levels in a company are integrated and follow a logical sequence as reflected by its organisation chart. Each operation has a specific target which must contribute to the overall objective. In fact, there is the 'end-means' in the company. The objective at the top level provides the basis for setting the objective at the second level which in turn becomes the basis for objective at the third level and so on. In other words, the goal at the fourth level is a means for the third level and so on as shown in Fig.

If an organisation is able to achieve its goals, it is called effective. Organisational effectiveness is based on some extent to an organisation which gives certain resources and means, achieves its objectives without placing undue strain on its members.

R. M. Steers has reviewed seventeen different approaches of assessing OE and found a general absense of agreement among them. The four top ranking evaluation criteria in his study are adaptability-flexibility, productivity, job satisfaction, and profitability. Most surprisingly, 'survival' and 'growth' are least important factors in his study. Steers reached the conclusion that there is a little agreement among analysts concerning what criteria should be used to assess current levels of effectiveness. If the search was to find a single universal criterion of OE then disappointment is understandable.

OE undisputedly defies a single operational definition. There is almost unanimous agreement today that OE requires multiple criteria; that different organizational functions are subject to evaluation employing different characteristics. The essence of the above discussion is that:

1. Effectiveness is not one-dimensional concept that can be precisely measured by a single, clear-cut criterion.
2. Effectiveness is a matter of a label to which an organization has performed according to its capacities, potentials, and general goals.

Perspectives on Effectiveness

There are three different perspectives of effectiveness which are highlighted by David Lawless. *(a)* Individual, *(b)* Group and *(c)* Organisational effectiveness. The relationship among them is:

Individual Effectiveness → Group Effectiveness → Organisational Effectiveness

The perspective of individual effectiveness throws light on the task performance of the members of the organization. This performance is routinely assessed through evaluation, techniques that become the basis for pay rises, promotions and other positive rewards in the organization.

Individuals collectively become a group. Individuals seldom work alone or in isolation from others in an organization. Therefore, it is vital to consider, yet, another perspectives, *i.e.*, group effectiveness.

Organization consists of individuals and groups and therefore OE consists of both individual and group effectiveness. But one point for caution. OE may be more than the sum of individual and group effectiveness. Through synergistic efforts, organizations are able to obtain higher levels of performance than the sum of their parts.

Lawless, however, contends that individual effectiveness does not necessarly cause group effectiveness, nor can it be said that group effectiveness is the sum of individual effectiveness. He further adds that the connecting arrows between each level do not imply a clearcut or specific form of relationships. The relationship, however, among these perspectives vary depending on the type of organization, the task, and the level of technology used in the organization. The fundamental task of management is to identify and establish the causes of these perspectives.

OE is the result of a blend of vast number of variables including technology, environmental constraints, personal competence of the emplyees and the innovative abilities of the managers etc. The causes of individual effectiveness include physical attributes, personality traits, motivation and morale etc. The causes of group effectiveness comprise of leadership, communication and socialization. The causes of organisational effectiveness include the technology, environmental conditions, competence and many other variables.

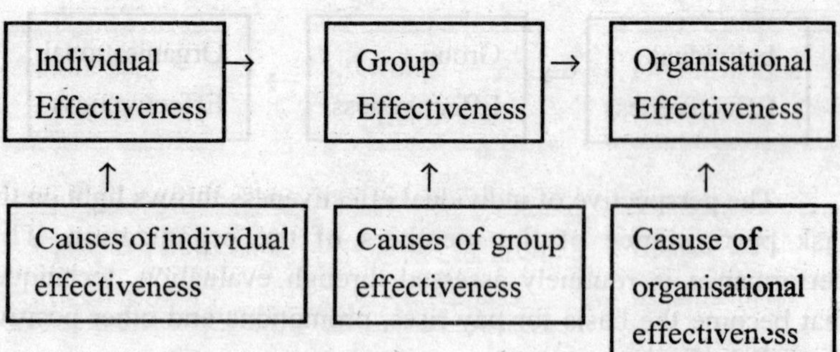

Effectiveness is typically measured in terms of performance, productivity, profit and so forth. Initial attempts by industrial psychologists and sociologists to measure organisational effectiveness were in terms of the attainment of some ultimate criteria. Thorndike identified several of those earlier criteria as productivity, net profit, mission accomplishment, and organisational growth. Campbell employed the following measures to determine organisational success or effectiveness:

(a) Overall performance

(b) Productivity

(c) Employee withdrawal

(d) Rate of return on investment

(e) Employee job satisfaction and motivation

(f) Stability and growth of organisation

(g) Flexibility or adaption

(h) Evaluations by external entities

The major sets of variables that potentially have their influence on effectiveness are as follows:

1. Managerial Policies and Practices. Managerial policies and practices are also related to effectiveness of organisation. These policies and practices include: *(i)* Strategic goal setting; *(ii)* Resource acquisition and utilisation; *(iii)* Performance environment, *(iv)* Leadership and decision-making; and *(v)* Organisation's adaptation and innovation.

Goal setting is a difficult process. If the goal is beyond the capacity of employees working in different departments or for which materials resources are not available, it is bound to meet its own Waterloo.

2. Employee Characteristics. It is employees who may help or inhibit goal achievement of organisation. Thus, it is essential to analyse the factors which are responsible for presenting such a distracting behaviour which stalls organisational effectiveness.

If there is a perceptible difference in individual goals and organisation's goals, it may result in weakening the very fabric of organisational structure. Consequently, efforts should be made to forge integration between personal goals and organisation's objectives. Two situations may arise in this regard: One, an employee may work hard to achieve organisational object which will help attaining personal goal; two, if the individual goal conflicts with organisation's objective, employee effort may be scattered or separated. In other words, the key to success lies with the situation in which both organisation and its members agree to adjust with each other. If the organisation, without compromising with its fundamental programmes and policies, could readjust to accommodate legitimate aspirations of employees, it should do so to achieve effectiveness. In case it is an issue relating to the very existence of the organisation, it will have to take a firm stand to deal with the situation.

3. Environmental Characteristics. Effectiveness *vis-a-vis* environmental characteristics depends on three critical factors: *(i)* the accuracy with which the environmental states are forecast, *(ii)* accurate perception of environmental states, and *(iii)* pragmatism enshrined in organisation system. These are the three sets of factors which determine the appropriateness of organisational response to environmental changes. This requires a proper management information system (MIS) which will monitor such changes in environmental setting that have a bearing on organisation structure. The organisation may have standing arrangements to receive information regarding environmental changes appropriately in time from the economic research division, R and D department, management consultants or legal adviser. These experts will continue to suggest such adjustments in organisational set-up as may be necessary to comply with environmental changes.

The external environments concentrate largely on market, legal and technological milieu which has a direct bearing on factor supply and distribution of goods. The internal environment is deeply influenced by psycho-sociological factors which determine individual responses to organisation's expectations. The effectiveness of organisation will depend on adequate and appropriate response from the personnel in the enterprise to programmes and policies undertaken by the organisation. This will depend on the harmony existing among the members and the uniformity in perception of individuals and the organisation.

4. Organisation Characteristics. Organisational structure exercises a considerable influence on organisational effectiveness. It is generally observed that structure in terms of functional specialisation, size, centralisation of decision-making and even formalisation is likely to increase productivity and efficiency. Even job satisfaction of employees is related to structural dynamics. Equitable division of work and delegation of authority and responsibility and proper direction are likely to generate the feeling of satisfaction among people at work.

Technology and organisational structure are inter-related. The type of technology determines the nature and structure of organisation. For instance, after introduction of capital-intensive technology, the structure designed to suit the labour-intensive technology may become useless. It may require shifting of certain members operating at different levels to either different departments within the same plant or to other plants of the enterprise. Such a changover will require a change in span of control, creating of new and winding up of a few departments and, thus, a new system of relationship and control within the organisation. If the organisation fails to change the structure according to needs of technology, it may never prove to be effective.

APPROACHES TO EFFECTIVENESS

There are four broad approaches of organisational effectiveness namely:

(i) Goal Attainment Approach

(ii) System Approach

(iii) Strategic Constituencies Approach

(iv) Behavioural Approach.

Goal Attainment Approach

In the goals approach, one can compare stated goals and objectives with the actual attainment of those goals and objectives.

This is the traditional and typical view of effectiveness. In practice, there may not be agreement on the goals or the devices to measure goal attainment.

An organization's goal accomplishment is a necessary condition for effective performance. The basic activities in which all organizations must engage help determine what the organizational goals might be, therefore what performance must be, and therefore, effectiveness. These activities can be roughly classified as follows:

1. Acquiring resources
2. Making efficient use of inputs relative to outputs
3. Producing outputs of services or goods
4. Performing technical and administrative tasks rationally
5. Investing in the organization
6. Conforming to codes of behaviour
7. Satisfying the varying interests of different people in groups.

Etizioni defines a goal as "an image of a future state." This definition might include goal statement about a single variable such as profit or the complex satisfying of multiple criteria of the systems theory model. However, formal statements of goal do not necessarily resemble the goal that the organisation is actually working towards. Perrow's distinction between official and operational goals has been accepted by many. Official goals are those that can be formed in annual reports and other such material for public consumption. Operational goals can be discovered by watching what an organization actually does.

It is also useful to try to understand the way in which the goals of organizational members and groups become organizational goals. Hall suggests "the goal of an organization is an abstraction distilled from the desires of members and pressures from the environment and the internal system.

Organiszations are man-made systems designed to accomplish specific goals which can be categorized into three broad classifications of social goals, systems goals, and participant goals. In the classification of social goals, orgnizations are viewed as a part of society and the goal question confronting organizations is "What does the organization contribute to society?" Under system goals, the organization is viewed from the economic perspective and questions of efficiency are posed-that is, how profitable is the organization or what is the return on investment or equality? Participant goals are concerned with the well-being of organizational members and involve worker satisfaction, morale, job involvement, and organizational commitment. However, studying organizational goals from the perspective of social system, and participant goals creates some problems. The three classifications are not mutually exclusive; there is some overlap between the classifications.

James L. Price - A Conceptual Study

Price has reviewed and analysed fifty studies and developed a model comprising of a dependent variable called 'effectiveness' and five intervening independent variables, namely, productivity, morale, confirmity, adaptiveness and institutionalization. Price adhers to a goal-oriented approach and he provides an inventory of propositions outlining the determinants of organizational effectiveness as defined by their level of attainment of goal. In his model there are five systems - economic system, political system. (internal and external) systems), control system, population system, and ecology system (or environmental system). These systems through intervening variables determine effectiveness.

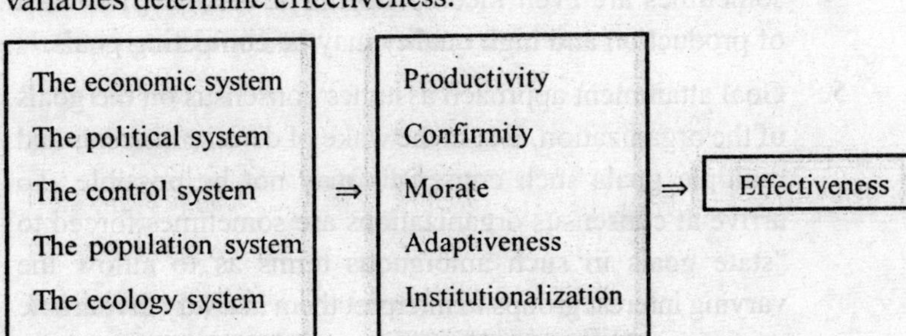

Price provides a comprehensive list of propositions derived from the careful review of the literature on OE.

Some of them are:

(i) Organization which have a high degree of division of labour are more likely to have a high degree of effectiveness.

(ii) Organizations which have high degree of vertical communications are more likely to have a degree of effectiveness.

(iii) Organizations which have a high degree of autonomy are more likely to have high degree of effectiveness.

Problems with the Goal Approach

Goals attainment approach, in spite of its appeal and apparent simplicity, is fraught with many problems. Some of them are:

1. Goal attainment approach is difficult to apply in those organizations that do not produce tangible outputs.
2. Organizations have different types of goals - short-run, long-run, individual, operational and organizational. But the question arises 'whose goals are to be condsidered?' The associated question is 'who measures the goals?' There are no stragiht-forward answers to these questions.
3. The more serious problem is about the measurement and evaluation of performance.
4. The fact that organizations have multiple goals also creates difficulties. The goals compete with each other and sometimes are even incompatible. For instance, low cost of production and high quality may be competing goals.
5. Goal attainment approach assumes consensus on the goals of the organization. But in the wake of diverse interests and multiple goals such consensus may not be possible. To arrive at consensus organizations are sometimes forced to "state goals in such ambiguous terms as to alllow the varying interest groups to interpret them in a way favourable to their self-interests. Various researchers have noted the difficulty of obtaining consensus among managers as to the specific goals of their organizations.

Organisations have multiple goals because of the many different groups of people commonly called stock holders, who have legitimate claims on the organization. These stockholders include investors, managers, and employees of the organization as well as outsiders who are affected by the organization's activities. Outsiders include the general public, customers, unions, suppliers, government, and competitors. Each of these outside groups (stock holders) demand and expect the organization to act in a responsible manner towards the satisfaction of their claims. Investors or stockholders demand appropriate returns on their investment; the general public demands corporate social responsibility in the form of improvement in the quality of life, customers expect quality products and after-sale service; unions seek benefits for members based on their contributions to company success; suppliers excpect dependable buyers; and competitors demand fair competition.

System Approach

Goal attainment approach is biased in the sense that it concentrates only on outputs. But a more comprehensive look at organizational effectiveness calls for judging the ability of organization in acquiring the inputs and in the transformation of inputs into outputs (called the transformation process). This is done through the systems approach.

The systems view aims at such factors as relations with environment to assure continued receipt of inputs and positive acceptance of outputs, flexibility of response of the organization to changing environment, the efficiency with which the transformation takes place in the organizations, the level of employee job satisfaction and the clarity of communication etc. Managers as such have a responsibility to understand the nature of their environment and to set realistic goals that accommodate the environment.

A number of orgnisational theorists and behaviourists have argued for system's effectiveness in terms of its capacity to survive, adapt, maintain itself, and grow regardless of the particular functions it fulfills. However, the clearest statement of effectiveness criteria has come from Bennis. These criteria are:

(i) Adaptability or ability to solve problems and to react with flexibility to change.

(ii) A sense of indentity which represents knowledge or insight on the part of the members about the goals of the organisations and how outsiders perceive them.

(ii) Capacity to test reality which implies ability to search out, accurately perceive, and correctly interpret properties of environment.

(iv) State of integration among the sub-parts of the total organisation such that various parts are not working at cross purposes.

In terms of these criteria, effectiveness cannot be ensured merely by selecting the right type of people and training them for jobs, by keeping them satisfied, or by reducing intergroup competition, etc. Rather the systems conception leads us to a different way of thinking which suggests examination of relationship between organisation and environment.

Edgar Schein suggests that the maintenance of effectiveness is made possible through the adaptive coping cycle. In his words, "the sequence of activities .....process which begin with some change in some part of the internal or external environment and end with more adaptive, dynamic equilibrium for dealing with change". Adaptive coping cycle has the following six stages:

(i) Sensing a change in some part of internal or external environment.

(ii) Importing the relevant information about the change into those parts of the organization that can act upon it.

(iii) Chnaging production process inside the organisation according to the information obtained.

(iv) Stabilizing internal changes while reducing or managing undesired products.

(v) Obtaining of the state of external environment and the degree of intergration of the external environment.

Schein contended that the effectiveness of an organization is either maintained or lost depending on the sensing and use of feedback from the environment.

According to Seashore and Yuchtman's study there are ten effectiveness dimensions in their study of seventy five insurance agencies. These effectiveness dimensions are - business volume, production cost, new member productivity, youthfulness of members, business mix, work force growth, devotion to management, maintenance cost, member productivity, and market penetration. The research scholars postulate that the interdependence between environment and an organization takes the form of an input / output transaction which involves scarce resources. They label their theory as "a systems resource approach to organizational effectiveness". The resources in the environment are limited in supply and any attempt to acquire these resources leads to competition among organizations. They visualize the effectiveness of organizations in terms of the bargaining position that is attained between the competing organizations. According to them, therefore, the key problem in assessment of effectiveness is the identification of competitive dimensions in inter-organizational transactions.

Organisational effectiveness can be assessed by the following steps:

(i) Providing an inclusive taxonomy of resources.

(ii) Identifying different types of resources that are mutually relevant for the organizations under study.

(iii) Determining the relative positions for the compared organizations on the basis of information concerning the amounts and kinds of resources that are available for the organization and its efficiency in using these resources to get further resources.

Problems with the Systems Approach. Though systems approach to effectiveness has a definite edge over the goal-attainment approach in the sense organisations give due respect to the environment to survive, it is not without problems or blackspots.

1. Flexibility of response to environment and such qualitative variables defy appropriate measurement.

2. A second negative point of systems approach is that the focus of systems approach is on means rather than ends.

3. Strategic constituencies approach assumes that an organization faces competing demands from various interest groups both within and outside the organizational environment. Management must net all unimportant and non-competing demands out and select only those critical or strategic constituencies in the environment so as to survive. To see the effectiveness through this approach certain steps should follow:

1. Management should identify all intergral constituencies in the environment on which the survival of organization depends.
2. The relative power of each constituencies should be evaluated by considering the degree of dependence of the organization on them.
3. Management should, then, arrange these constituencies in order of their power and expectations.
4. Identify the expectations those constituencies hold for the organization.
5. Organizational effectiveness then would be assessed in terms of its ability to satisfy these constituencies that are ranked.

The fundamental problem with this strategic constituencies approach is that the task to separate strategic constituencies from the larger environment is not easy. It is difficult because with changing environment these critical areas also change rapidly or change with in on time. What is critical today may not be so tomorrow.

The second negative point is that it is very difficult to assign the weights to these critical constituencies regarding the dependence of organization on them.

Finally, the expectations that the constituencies hold of the organization defy identification and measurement.

Behavioural Approach

It is important to recognize and account for the people who ultimately determine the quantity and quality of orgånization's response to the demands made by the environment.

Behavioural approach to OE emphasizes the role of individual behaviour as it affects organizational success or failure. When employees agree with the objectives of the organization (employer) then it results in perfect integration of the individual and organizational goals. This leads to high degree of organizational effectiveness. It is because when goals converage the individual exerts his effort to the maximum extent. This situation of perfect integration of individual and organizational goals can be aptly labelled as 'myth' as it represents an 'ideal' situation. An ideal situation is one which never touches real. Individual goals vary and differ with organizational goals and the greater the disintegration the lesser will be the effectiveness.

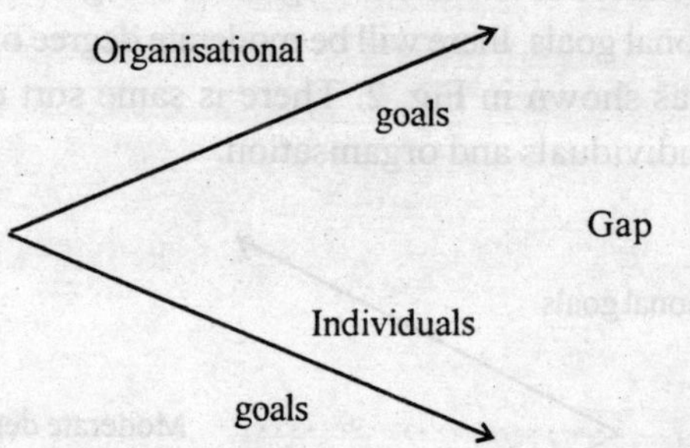

Fig.

When the goals of the organisation and those of the individuals are perfectly integrated, there will be high degree of effectivencess because individuals will cooperate to the maximum for the accomplishment of organisational goals. But this ideal situation is seldom found in practice.

Based on the degree of integration of individual and organisational goals, we shall take three typical cases of organizational effectiveness.

I. When there is low degree of integration of organisational and individual goals, the degree of fusion will be low and effectiveness will also be low as shown in fig. 1. It is the case of an ineffective organisation.

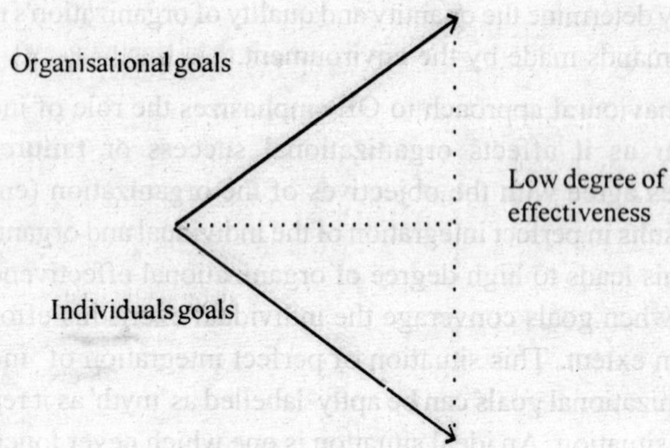

Fig. 1. Low Effectiveness

II. When there is moderate degree of integration of individual and organisational goals, there will be moderate degree of organisational effectiveness as shown in Fig. 2. There is same sort of compromise between the individuals and organisation.

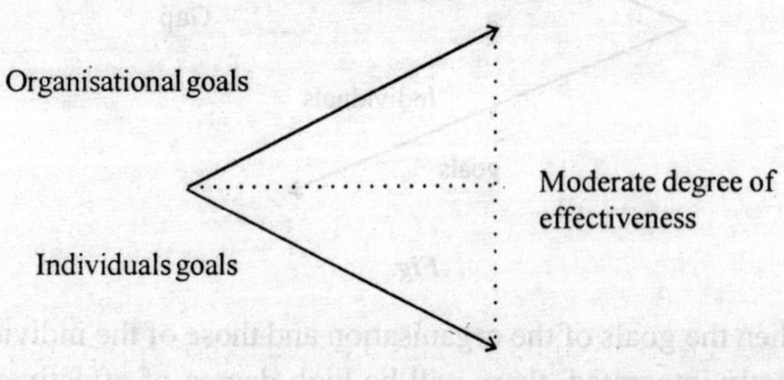

Fig. 2. Moderate Effectiveness

III. When the integration of individual and organisational goals is high, it will result in high degree of organisational effectiveness as depicted in fig. 3. Here the individual goals are identified with the organisational goals. The climate of the organisation is such that either of two things may occur. The individuals in the organisation may either perceive their goals being the same as the goals of the organisation, or see their own goal being satisfied as a direct result of working for the goals of the organisation. Consequently, closer the individual's goals with the organisational goals, the greater will be the organisational effectiveness.

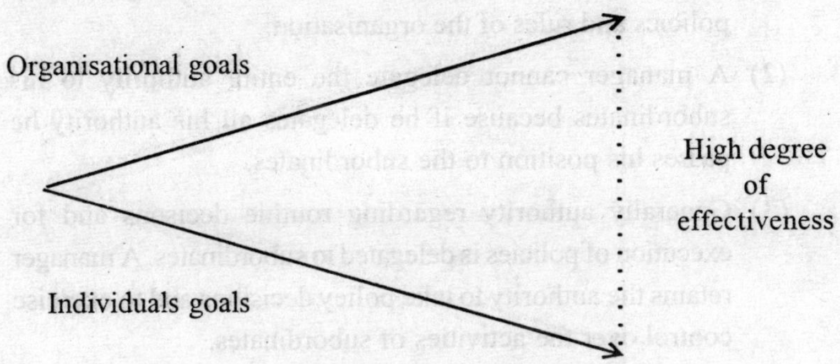

Fig. 3. High Effectiveness

The empirical studies on effectiveness reveal.

1. Different (types of) organisations have different criteria of effectiveness. But (perhaps) productivity is the most single variable in effectiveness literature that is appearing most prominently.

2. A number of different criteria for effectiveness have been revealed by research. External criteria comprises of adaptiveness, bargaining position of resources and the achievement of the organization. Internal criteria include morale, voluntarism, stability and low stress etc.

3. An organisation need not be cent percent effective in all the potential areas but it is enough to optimize effectiveness among technical, social and economic concerns.

DELEGATION OF AUTHORITY

Delegation of authority is the process of manager follows in dividing the work assigned to him so that he performs that part which only he, because of his unique organisational placement, can perform effectively and so that he can get others to help with what remains. In simple words, delegation means assigning work to others and giving them authority to do it. Delegation has the following characteristics:

(1) Delegation takes place when a superior grants some discertion to a subordinate. The subordinate must act within the limits prescribed by the superior. He is not free to use authority arbitrarily but has to use it subject to the policies and rules of the organisation.

(2) A manager cannot delegate the entire authority to his subordinates because if he delegates all his authority he passes his position to the subordinates.

(3) Generally authority regarding routine decisons and for execution of policies is delegated to subordinates. A manager retains the authority to take policy decisions and to exercise control over the activities of subordinates.

(4) Delagation does not mean abdication of responsibility. No manager can escape from his obgligation by delegating authority to subordinates. Therefore, he must provide a means of checking upon the work that is done for him to ensure that it is done as he wishes.

(5) The extent of authority which is delegated depends upon several facors. *e.g.* the ability of the executive to delegate, the ability of the subordinates to accept delegation, the philosophy of management, the confidence of the superior in his subordinates, etc.

(6) Delegation may be specific or general, written or implied, formal or informal. Delegation does not mean avoiding decisions or abandonment of work.

(7) Delegation does not imply reduction in the authority of a manager. A superior retains authority even after delegation. Delegation does not mean a manager loses control and power. He can reduce, enhance or take back the delegated authority.

(8) Delegation is an art because *(a)* it is creative, *(b)* it is practice based, *(c)* it involves use of personal skills, *(d)* it is result-oriented, and *(e)* it is a personalised process.

FACTORS/DETERMINANTS OF DELEGATION OF AUTHORITY

Factors or determinants of delegation of authority can be discussed under the head of delegator, delegrant and organisation factors:

(I) Factors in Delegator (Superior). The qualities of superior managers play an important part in determining the kind of functional and social equilibrium that will be achieved in the superior-subordinate relationships and consequently the delegation of authority. A superior manager is likely to delegate less authority in the following situations :

1. ***Maintenance of Tight Control.*** A manager does not delegate authority because he wants to maintain tight control over the operations assigned to him. He likes to be the busyness and security created by work piled high on his desk. Doing tangible work is a pleasurable activity, whereas spending one's time thinking, planning and other less tangible is a difficult process. The manager may become habituated to the constant contact of subordinate bringing matters to them for approval.

2. ***Love for Authority.*** A superior is unlikely to delegate his authority specially if he is autocrat. Such a manager has intense desire to influence to others, to make his importance felt in the organisation, and to see that his subordinates come frequenty to get their decisions approved. such desires on the part of the manager keep him away from delegation of adequate authority to his subordinates irrespective of their needs.

3. ***Fear of Subordinates.*** A manager may not delegate adequate authority because of fears of subordinates. The fear of a subordinate's growth may be real. It can take two forms. First, the subordinate might show that he can perform the superior's work so well that he becomes entitled to his position, status, title, or prestige. Second, the subordinate's increasing ability might earn him a promotion to some other part of the organisation and the superior may lose the

best subordinate. In this case, the superior may adopt defensive behaviour. He simply fails to delegate the kind of authority that would have had such a result.

4. ***Personality of Superior.*** Personality factors of superior also affect the degree of delegation of authority. For example, an autocrat superior will delegate less authority as compared to a democrat. Similarly, a superior believing in the application of modern management techniques likes to delegate adequately. A superior coming from the rank and file may delegate less. Similarly, a manager who has not been delegated adequate authority in his career is likely to delegate less.

5. ***Fear of Exposure.*** At superior manager, specially a weak one, may not like to delegate simply because adequate delegation may reveal managerial shortcomings being practised. This may happen specially when the superior has poor operating procedures, methods, and practices.

6. ***Attitudes Towards Subordinates.*** Delegation of authority is a particular kind of trust between superior and his subordinates. Therefore, his attitudes towards subordinates, and their attitudes towards him become important in the process of delegation. Negative attitudes work against delegation of authority in several ways. First, if a superior has lack of confidence in his subordinates' capacity, he will not like to delegate them authority. Second, the superior may feel that his subordinates just do not require more authority than they have been delegated. Such feeling may result into inadequate delegation of authority. Third the superior may not have good interpersonal relationships with subordinates which may result into less delegation of authority.

The various factors discussed above either make a superior blind to the need for adequate delegation of authority or he may be aware about the signficance of authority delegation but he may withhold it because he simple does not like to delegate.

(II) Factors in Delegant (Subordinate). The degree of delegation of authority is also determined by the qualities of subordinates. While superior perception about the qualities of subordinates plays an important role in delegation of authority, subordinates themselves affect the degree of delegation of authority. They affect the delegation in several ways. First, some subordinates have more capability to assume more responsibility. Since responsibility and authority go together, competent subordinates may get more authority. Second, the delegation of authority is formal and institutional but its exercise is personal. Thus competent subordinate may assume and exercise more authority than others although working within the context of same set of delegation.

In the following situations, however, subordinates are expected to exercise less authority.

1. When they lack self-confidence;
2. When they lack resources;
3. When they have inadequate positive incentives;
4. When their superior is easily available for decision on their part; and
5. When they fear harsh criticism for unfavourable results.

(III) Organisational Factors. Although personal factors affect the authority delegation to a very great extent, other organisational factors also affect the degree of authority delegation. Individual managers do not have control over these factors but have to work within the context of these factors, so warrant. Various organisational factors such as management philosophy, policy towards centralization or decentralization, etc., determine the delegation of authority at various levels of management.

ADVANTAGES OF DELEGATION

Delegation is an indispensable component of good organisation. It is essential to the existence of a formal organisation. It is one of the 'mainspring of effective management.' According to Koontz and O'Donnell, just as authority is key to the manager's job, delegation of authority is the key to organisation. The primary purpose of delegation is to make organisation possible. It is also claimed that 'effective management is management through delegation' only. These statements stretch the virtues of delegation to a point where we may be forced to believe that without delegation effective action is impossible. In fact, Allen defined delegation as a dynamic process allowing executives to 'get results through others'. That delegation, when used properly, has several important advantages is an indisputable fact as the following list suggests:

1. Superior Related Advantages. The essence of delegation process is empowering another person to act for the manager. There are certain practical reasons for this managerial preference:

(i) To provide for the extension of facilities by the establishment of local centres in different areas.

(ii) To reduce the burden of responsibility carried by him.

(iii) To enable selected activities or services to be more expertly covered and provided

(iv) To provide more time for constructive review, or deliberation in the interests of progress.

Instead of carrying a full briefcase of problems home daily and bury himself in endless routine, the manager, through delegation, would be better off sharing his ever-increasing workload with others and concentrate on important issues. Delegation frees top management from operational responsibilities. It helps the managers to distribute their load of work to others and thus multiply their limited personal capacities.

2. Improves Behavioural Climate. Authority centralization may be highly fascinating to authoritarian leaders. Such leaders believe in making decisions themselves, giving detailed instructions to their subordinates and exercise control from close quarters. Consequently, they overburden themselves to the extent that they never find enough time to concentrate on their own responsibilities of planning, organisation and controlling. The subordinates, in turn, may refuse to obey rules and regulation continuously, their morale will be low and performance may be mediocre. Delegation implies freedom of action sufficient to get the work done. It means freedom to make decisions, to commit mistakes and use one's capacities fully. Without giving the necessary amount of freedom, it may be virtually impossible to rally men and women toward a common purpose. The granting of freedom to act by the superior is evidence of confidence in the subordinate. The subordinate responds by developing a constructive sense of responsibility.

3. Advantages to Organization. At the extreme, if there is no delegation, one person has to do everything and hence, there would be no organisation. But for delegation firms would remain small and an increase in their size would burn up the candle of managerial energies too soon. The primary purpose of delegation, as pointed out earlier, is to make organisation possible. Delegation leads to better decisions, since subordinates closer to the 'firing line' are likely to have a clearer and more complete view of the facts. In addition, effective delegation speeds up decision-making in an organisation. Instead of waiting at the doorsteps of the superior for an audience for a painfully long time, the subordinates can now take decisions independently.

4. Subordinate Related Advantages. Delegation has a 'tonic effect' on the psychology of subordinates. It allows subordinates to grow, enlarge their understanding and develop their capacities. It causes subordinates to accept responsibility and exercise judgment. It raises the subordinates' position in stature and importance. It is delegation of authority that gives subordinates the means with which to act and learn.

PROCESS OF DELEGATION

The process of delegation involves the following steps:

1. Determination of results expected. First of all, a manager has to define the results he wants to obtain from his subordinates for achievement of organisational objectives.

2. Assignment of duties. The manager then assigns specific duties or tasks to each subordinate. He must clearly define the function of each subordinate. While assigning duties and responsibilities, he must ensure that the subordinates understand and accept their duties. Duties should be assigned according to the qualifications, experience and aptitude of the subordinates.

3. Creating accountability for performance. The subordinates to whom authority is delegated must be made answerable for the proper performance of assigned duties and for the exercise of the delegated authority. The extent of accountability depends upon the extent of delegation of authority and responsibility. A person cannot be held answerable for the acts not assigned to him by his superior.

4. Granting of authority. Assignment of duties is meaningless unless adequate authority is given to subrodinates. They cannot discharge their responsibilities wihtout adequate authority. Enough authority must be granted so that subordinates can perform their duties. By granting authority, subordinates are permitted to use resources, to take decisions and to exercise discretion.

An information and control system is established to check and evaluate performance of the subordinates to whom authority is delegated.

Thus, duty, authority and accountability are three fundamental components of delegation. All the three phases of delegation are interdependent.

OBSTACLES TO DELEGATION

Even though delegation is vital for the efficent functioning of an organisation, in practice there are several factors which prevent effective delegation.These problems in delegation may be classified into three categories:

(i) Superior,

(ii) Subordinate, and

(iii) Organisation.

On the Part of Delegator (Non-delegation)

Managers are often reluctant to delegate adequate authority due to tne following reasons:

1. Some managers feel that none can do the job as well as they can do. They think that if they delegate, work will not be done as it

ought to be done. They consider themselves indispensable and do not want to give other people's ideas a chance.

2. Few managers are inclined to accept the risk of wrong decisions which the subordinates might take. Therefore, they do not delegate authority and take all the decisions themselves. They are unwilling to take calculated risk.

3. Some managers may not delegate authority because of their lure for authority. They are autocrats and think that delegation will lead to reduction of their influence in the organisation. They want to make their presence felt and desire that subordinates should come frequently for approval. They like to dominate the whole show.

4. A manager may not delegate authority because he feels that his subordinates are not capable and reliable. He lacks confidence in his subordinates.

5. Effective delegation requires adequate control and a means of knowing the proper use of authority. A manager will hesitate to delegate authority if he has no means to ensure that the authority is being properly used by the subordinates.

6. A manager is not likely to delegate authority when he cannot issue suitable directions to guide the activities of subordinates. Such lack of ability to direct shows that he is unfamiliar with the art of delegation.

7. When a manager is incompetent his work methods and procedures are likely to be faulty. He keeps all the authority to himself for fear of being exposed. He is afraid that if he lets the subordinates make decisions they may outshine him. He is afraid of losing his importance.

On the Part of Subrodinates (Non-acceptance of Delegation)

Subordinates may not like to accept delegation and shoulder responsibility due to the following reasons:

1. A subordinate who is afraid of committing mistakes and does not like to be criticised by the boss is likely to avoid delegation of authority.

2. When the subordinates are already overburdened with duties, they do not like additional responsibilities through delegation.

3. Subrodinates may not come forward to accept delegation of authority when no incentives are available to them.

4.Subrodinates are likely to avoid delegation when adequate information, working facilities and resources are not available for proper discharge of duties.

5. Subordinates may be reluctant to accept delegation when they lack self-confidence.

6. Some subordinates are unwilling to accept authority due to the desire to play safe by depending on the boss for all decisions. They have a love for spoon-feeding.

On the Part of the Organisation

Sometimes superiors want to delegate and subordinates like to accept delegation. But delegation may be hampered due to weaknesses in the organisation structure. Some of these weaknesses are as follows:

1. Splintered authority,
2. Absence of effective control techniques,
3. Environment of internal distrust,
4. Inadequate planning,
5. Lack of Unity of command,
6. Non-availability of competent managers, and
7. Unclear authority relationships.

In any organisation, the degree of delegation depedns upon several factors *e.g.* size of the organisation, decentralised performance, management philosophy, availability of managers, workloads of managers, environmental influence, etc.

MAIN ELEMENTS OF DELEGATION

Delegation is an important part of the organisational process. Main Elements of Delegation are as follows:

1. Granting of Authority. The second essential elements of delegation is the granting of authority because if only the duty is assigned to someone and no authority is given to him for discharging his duty, it will not be possible for him to do so. For the discharge of assigned duty, it is essential that the required powers must also be assigned. Responsibility is incomplete and meaningless without authority is of no use without responsibility.

2. Assigning of Duty. The very first essential element of delegation is the assigning of duty by an executive to his subordinates. In the complicated time of business and industrial development of today, it is not possible for a Chief Manager to do all the activities of enterprise. Therefore, the Chief Manager decides the number of managerial activities and then he decides as to how many activities he can do himself and how many activities he will assign to his subordinates. After taking this decision, he assigns his work to his subordinates so that the pre-determined objectives of the enterprise may be achieved easily and confidently with the help of subordinates.

3. Determination of Accountability. After assigning the duty by an executive to his subordinates and giving them authority for the discharge of this duty, it becomes the duty of Chief Executive to ensure that the subordinates discharge their duty according to the directions issued and if they do not so, the Chief Executive gets the explanation from them for not doing so. He can determine their accountability. Subordinates are always accountable to the senior officers.

NEED FOR DELEGATION

Now-a-days the business activities are so complicated that it is not only difficult but almost impossible for a General Manager to do all the activities of an enterprise. The General Manager may have a little knowledge about all the activities of the enterprise but he can not have thorough knowledge of all the activities of the enterprise. Therefore, he was to delegate some of his works of his subordinates because of the following reasons:

1. Due to Expansion of Business. A business and industrial enterprise has to expand its activities in order to meet the increasing and changing needs of the society. The enterprise has to establish different branches and departments for the expansion. It is not possible for a manager to do all the activities of the enterprise after expansion and, therefore, he has to delegate his duties.

2. Due to Imperfection of Human Being. No person can be perfect in himself. No manager can control all the activities of an enterprise. In addition to it, if a manager wants to do all the activities of the enterprise, he shall not be able to pay due attention to his important works. Therefore, because of this imperfection of human being, delegation becomes necessary.

3. For Developing Managerial Qualities. Management provides an opportunity to the subordinates to take decisions on important subjects and problems of the enterprise by delegating its duties to them. It develops managerial qualities in the managers of middle or junior level which is very beneficial for the growth and development of the enterprise.

4. Due to Specialisation. It is the time of specialisation and it is not possible for a person to specialise all of the activities. It cannot be expected from a manager to be perfect in dealing with all the problems of marketing, production, finance, and personnel departments. Therefore, he has to delegate his work to other.

On the basis of this discussion, we can conclude that "Delegation of Authority is the key to establish just as authority is the key to the manager's job." The organisation of any business enterprise cannot be successful without delegating authorities and responsibilities. There is very important questions regarding delegation whether the responsibilities can be delegated or not? If we deeply consider, we can come to the conclusion that no executive can delegate his responsibilities. He, of course, can take the help of his subordinates in discharging his duties and he can delegate some of his works and some of his authorities to them but the responsibility will not change. The Chief Executive will be responsible as before. If the enterprise suffers any loss, the executive to whom the duty was assigned, will be responsible and accountable to the higher officers. He cannot take excuse that he delegated his authority to his subordinates.

TYPES OR FORMS OF DELEGATION

The Delegation can be divided as follows:

1. Written or Verbal Delegation. When the work is delegated in writing, it is called written delegation on the contrary, when there is nothing in writing and the work is delgated verbally, it is known as verbal delegation. The written delegation is always better than verbal delegation.

2. General or Specific Delegation. Under general delegation, all the activities of an enterprise are delegated to an individual. For an example, the work assigned to the Chief Manager of an enterprise is called delegation. Under specific delegation, an individual is assigned with the duties of a particular type of activities. Such as the duties assigned to Production Manager, Fianance Manager, Marketing Manager, and Personnel Manager is called specific delegation.

3. Formal or Informal Delegation. When the delegation takes place within the definite limits of organisation structure, it is called formal delegation. On the other hand, when the subordinates perform their duties according to their own will and not according to the order of their officers, it is called informal delegation. Generally, the formal delegation takes place in public enterprise while in private enterprises, both types of delegation take place.

4. Administrative, Functional or Technical Delegation. The delegation for the performance administrative work is called administrative delegation. The delegation, made on the basis of activities, is called functional delegation and the delegation of technical activities is called technical delegation.

5. Downward, Upward, or Lateral Delegation. Downward delegation means the delegation from seniors to the juniors, or in other words it is from top to the bottom.; Upward delegation is the delegation from juniors, to the seniors. When the delegation takes place between the officers of equal rank, it is called lateral delegation.

Hindrances or Difficulties in Delegation

The study of above advantages of delegation may have an impression that it is essential for the organisation of an enterprise but it is also subject to certain limitations. Following are the difficulties faced by officers while delegating their authorities.

1. Lack of Confidence. The very first difficulty in the process of delegation is the lack of confidence of officers in their subordinates. They do not feel their subordinates capable and therefore, they hesitate in delegating the authorities to them.

2. Incapability of Subordinates. If the subordinates are not capable of doing the work to be delegated, the officers cannot delegate their authorities and responsibilities to them because it may cause to the misuse of authority by the subordinates.

3. Desire to Administer and Control. A man, by nature, does not want to share his powers and rights. Senior officers like to administer and control the subordinates. They fell that if they delegate their powers to their subordinates, it will adversely affect their rights and because of this reason they do not want to delegate.

4. Unfamiliarity with the Art of Delegation. Delegation of Authorities is essentially an art. It requires theoretical knowledge and practical experience which requires time. Officers, because of the lack of familiarity with the art of delegation, do not dare to delegate their authorities.

5. Other Difficulties. In addition to the above difficulties, there are some other difficulties also being faced by the officers in the process of delegation: *(i)* Incapability of officers in issuing directions to the subordinates; *(ii)* Incapability of officers in maintaining control; *(iii)* Lack of effective control system in the enterprise; *(iv)* Lack of effective communication in the enterprise; *(v)* Lack of willingness among officers to delegate their authorities; *(vi)* Lack of willingness among subordinates to accept challenges; *(vii)* Mutual frictions between officers and subordinates.

Thus, we find that because of the above reasons, the officers hesitate in delegating their authorities to their sobordinates. But all the difficulties discussed above, are created by the officers themselves. None of these difficulties is a real difficulty.

DECENTRALISATION OF AUTHORITY

Business and trade have become international now-a-days. The size of business enterprises has become very large. the nature of business enterprises has been very complexed. In such circumstances, it is not practical and possible too for the top management of an enterprise to look after all the activities of the enterprise. Therefore, centralisation of authority is not a practical form of organisation these days. To overcome the problems of business enterprise and to make it a success. It has become necessary that the top management of the enterprise must pay its attention only on the important problems of the enterprise. Decisions must be taken on every level of management and the subordinates must get full powers and responsibilities. They must be empowered to take the decisions connected to their field to activities and they must be responsible for their fields. This arrangement in an enterprise is known as the decentralisation of authority. Under this arrangement, the authorities are delegated by the top management to the subordinates. The term decentralisation of authority has been defined as under:

Henry Fayol, "Every thing that goes to increase the importance of role of subordinates, is called decentralisation, everything which goes to reduce it, is centralisation."

Koontz & O'Donnell, "Decentralisation of authority is a fundamental phase of delegation to the extent that authority is not delegated, it is centralised."

On the basis of the analytical study of above definition, it can be concluded that the decentralisation is just opposite to centralisation. Under, this, there is no concentration of authority, rather the authority is delegated to subordinates with reference to liability.

PRINCIPLES OF DELEGATION

Delegation of authority is a conscious effort on the part of manager. Therefore, in delegating authority, he should observe certain principles so as to make delegation effective. Unless these principles are observed, delegation may be ineffective, consequently organisation may fail and the managerial process may be seriously impeded. Following are such principles:

1. Delegation by Results Expected. As discussed earlier, delegation should be based on results expected from a position in the organsiation. Since authority is intended to achieve certain outcomes in the organisation, it should be adequate to achieve those outcomes. A manager is expected to perform better if he knows what he has to contribute and he has commensurate authority for that. Delegation by results expected implies that planning exercise has been taken and goals for each position have been set, communicated and properly understood by those who are responsible for achieving these goals. Often managers fail to delegate adequately because either they have very vague idea about the contributions of their subordinates or they just do not bother to determine whether the subordinates have authority to do the things.

2. Clarity of Lines of Authority. Each position in the organisation is linked with others through authority relationships; some directly through line authority, others indirectly. More cleraly these lines of authority are defined, more effective is the delegation of authority. In this respect, classical authors have given two principles which guide the delegation of authority. These principles are scalar chain and unity of command. Scalar chain principle refers to the chain of direct authority relationships from superior to subordinate throughout the organisation. Clearer the line of authority from the top manager to every subordinate position in the organisation, the more effective will be responsible decision making and organisational communication. The other principle, that is, unity of command suggests that a subordinate should be responsibile to a single superior and he should receive instructions from the same superior only.

3. Functional Definition. Closely related with principles of delegation based on results expected is principles of functional definition. In an organisation, the activities are classified and grouped to create departments or units. Each department contributes to organisational objectives. Thus there is a need for co-ordination of objectives and activities of the department in such a way that they contribute maximum to the organisation. This gives rise to the principle of functional definition. The more a department has clear definitions of results expected, activities to be undertaken, authority delegated, and authority and informational relationship with other departments, the more adequately the department can contribute towards accomplishing organisational objectives.

A problem comes when more than one managers can decide the things jointly without referring the matter upward but singly none of them can decide. Such a matter may be related with inter-departmental functioning. A single manager can not make decision because of splintered authority. Splintered authority exists wherever a problem can not be solved or a decision made without pooling the authority delegations of two or more managers. For example, production manager of Plant X can reduce his costs by some procedural changes in plant Y. However, he cannot do this unless he pools his authority with manager of plant Y. Alternatively, he can refer the matter upward and positive thing can happen by the action of common superior. In such a case, it is preferable to consolidate and pool splintered authority rather than referring the matter upward for decision. Splintered authority can not be wholly avoided in making decisions.

4. Level of Authority. Authority level principle suggests that maintenance of intended delegation requires that decisions within the authority competence of individuals be made by them and not be referred upward in the organisation structure. Thus managers should make whatever decisions they can in the light of their delegated authority and only matters that authoirty limitations keep them from deciding should be referred upward.

5. Parity of Authority and Responsibility. A common saying in management is that 'authority and responsibility should always be equal'. It implies that since authority is the discretionary right to cary out assignment and responsibility is the obligation to accomplish them, authority should correspond to the responsibility. Thus responsibility for action can not be greater than implied authority delegated, nor should be less. This parity is not mathematical but, rather, coexistensive, because both relate to the same assignment.

6. Absoluteness of Responsibility. Responsibility is an obligation to get the assigned work done. Since responsibility can not be delegated, a superior can not be achieved of his responsibility for the activities assigned to his subordinates. Similarly, responsibility of subordinates to their superiors for performance is absolute; once they have accepted an assignment and the authority to carry it out, superiors can not escape responsibility for the organisation activities of their subordinates.

MEASURES FOR EFFECTIVE DELEGATION

Effective delegation denotes distribution of authority at various points of the organisation so that managers can take actions according to their responsibility. Responsibility for adequate delegation of authority lies mostly with superiors particularly with top management. Following are some measures which will help in making delegation more effective.

1. Making the Potential Delegator Feel Secure. Typically the non-delegator is a hard worker, fully competent, but he may feel insecure in his job. This is partially the reason why he surrounds himself with less competent people or in any event those who lack the courage to challenge him. He wants to continue as the unchallenged superior and to be looked upon as a necessary man in the organisation team. Therefore, there is a need for creating a feeling for security for him. A number of things can be done for this. First, it should be made very clear that his job and position is secure so long he continues to contribute to the organisation. Second, his contributions for the organisation are not being questioned and attempts are to make him even more effective manager. Third, some apparent status symbols like office and other facilities can be granted to him.

2. Creating Awareness for Need of Delegation. Many managers are not fully aware about the need for adequate delegation of authority. They do not realise that they should do only what their subordinates can not do. In this way, they can multiply themselves and their efforts. This happens specially in the case of those managers who come from operative level and continue to make decisions which their subordinates can do. Through proper education and training, such managers can be convinced about the need for better delegation.

3. Determining Decisions and Tasks to be Delegated. Delegation is adversely affected because there is no clarity about what is to be delegated. A simple and direct means for solving this problem is to list for the delegator all types of decisions and tasks that must be performed and then rate each one in terms of *(i)* their relative importance to the total organisation, and *(ii)* the time required to perform. This information will serve to determine what types of decisions and tasks should be delegated. Usually those decisions and tasks that are relatively less important and more time-consuming should be delegated.

4. Establishing Conducive Organisational Climate. An organisational climate free from fear and frustration goes a long way in determining the success of organisational process including delegation of authority. Organisational climate is essentially psychological and social in character. In conducive organisational climate, managers feel confidence that delegation of authority will be rewarded and penalised. Further delegation of authority should have the support of top level management. It should be reflected in adequate delegation from top level and also in such things as a reasonable and satisfactory compensation, an impartial means for a manager's work, and continuous management development.

5. Choosing the Delegant Wisely. Among unfortunate things that can happen with poor subordinates is that work does not get done. When the results do not appear, the delegator is accountable to his superior in turn. This requires that the delegator must make a careful selection of the person to whom the work is delegated. He must be sure that the man is able to carry the degree of responsibility and effort contemplated in the assignment. Apart from selection, the delegants have to be properly trained and oriented to certain work because many times superiors concerned may not have authority to select their own subordinates.

6. Developing Appropriate Control Techniques. Since a delegator remains responsible even from the tasks he has delegated to his subordinates, he must ensure that his subordinates get the work done. Therefore, proper control and monitoring techniques should be developed to ascertain that delegated authority is being used properly. This does not, however, means that control techniques interfere unnecessarily with the day-to-day functioning of the subordinates. These should be broad based and should focus attention on major deviations from the plans.

7. Tieing Delegation with Planning. A pitfall in delgation is that sometimes it is undertaken without consideration of what is to be achieved by delegation. To delegate without knowing and keeping in mind objectives leads to chaos. Therefore, authority should never be delegated to the managers before the objectives are clear. Authority is utilised to achieve objectives and the extensiveness of the authority should be in keeping the type of activities performed in attaining the objectives. It is better to delegate authority for achieving specific results.

8. Delegating Authority for Whole Job. It is better to give the delegant a chance to participate in a complete undertaking. Broad rather narrow projects serve best imagination and stimulation of ideas. Such assignments serve as an effective means of testing a man's ability to manage and of building his confidence. Frequent delegation on the same subject matter may convey a feeling that the delegator does not want to do the job and wants to get rid of unpleasnt job through delegation. However, through the delegation for whole job, this problems can be overcome.

❐

7

Organisational Behaviour

In every type of organisation such as business, schools, government etc., interaction of people over organisation exists. In an organisation, people join together in some extent of formal structure to achieve an objective and in order to achieve the objective they use some sorts of technology. So there is an interaction of people, technology and structure. All these three elements influence the external social systems and in turn they are also influenced by it. A mix of these four elements is the scope of organisational behaviour.

The people constitute the internal social system of the organisation. They consist of individuals and groups. Groups may be large or small, formal or informal, official or unofficial. They are dynamic. They form, change and disband. Human organisation changes everyday. Today, it is not the same as it was yesterday. It may change further in the coming days. People are living, thinking and feeling being who created the organisation and try to achieve the objectives and goals.

According to Pfiffner and Sherwood, "Organisation is the pattern of ways in which large numbers of people, too many to have intimate face to face contact with all others, and engaged in a complexity of tasks, relate themselves to each other in the conscious, systematic establishment and accomplishment of mutually agreed purposes."

Bakke, however gives a more elaborate definition of organisation. He defines it as "a continuing system of differentiated and co-ordinated human activities utilising, transforming and wedding together a specific set of human, material, capital, and natural resources into a unique problem solving whole engaged in satisfying particular human needs in interaction with other systems of human activities and resources in its environment."

Behaviour is a way of action. It is basically goal oriented. In other words our behaviour is generally motivated by a desire to attain a goal. The specific goal is not always consciously known by the individual. Many times we wonder "why did I do that?" The reason for our action is not always apparent to the conscious mind. The drives that motivate distinctive individual behavioural patterns are to a considerable degree subconscious and therefore not easily susceptible to examination and evaluation.

The basic unit of behaviour is an activity. In fact, all behaviour is a series of activities. As a human being, we always do something: walking, talking, sleeping, etc. and sometimes we do more than one activity at a time. Sometimes, we decide to change from one activity to another. Why do we do so? or why do people engage in one activity and not another? A manager must understand, predict and control the activities of a person at a given moment.

Organisational Behaviour studies the behaviour of people in an organisation. Everybody in the organisation is concerned with improving organisational behaviour. All interact each other and influence behavioural quality of life in the organisation. Managers, however, have greater responsibility because they take decisions concerning all in the organisation. Managers constitute the administrative system and in organisational behaviour, it is their responsibility to integrate the social system with the technical system, just to improve the people-organisation relationship in order to accomplish the human benefits for which it is made.

The administrative view of organisational behaviour contains a number of ideas as follows:

(a) Organisational behaviour focuses mainly on people and technical, economic and structural elements are all related to people.

(b) People are in organisational environment rather than in unorganised social contacts. Thus, it attempts to improve people organisation relations.

(c) The environment is developed in such a way as to motivate the people to work hard to accomplish the organisational goal. Managers motivate the people because only they unlike other factors, can have greater output than the sum of their input through their creativity.

(d) The direction of motivation is towards teamwork, that requires both co-ordination of work and co-operation of people. Co-ordination means effective time and sequence in performing activities while co-operation means the willingness of people to perform the work for attaining the organisational goal.

(e) The organisational behaviour seeks to fulfill both employees needs and organisational objectives. Every employee in the organisation wants to fulfill his needs through organisational activities and the organisation's responsibility is to provide behavioural climate in the organisation so that people can gain need satisfaction and the organisation attains the objective.

There are certain fundamental philosophical concepts on which the development of science depends. Science of accountancy has a fundamental concept 'for every debit, there will be a credit'. In the same way physics has a basic philosophy that elements in nautre are uniform. Organisational Behaviour is also based on same fundamental concepts around which nature of people and nature of organisation revolves. The main philosophical concepts of organisation behaviour are as follows:

(a) **Caused Behaviour (Motivation).** From the study of psychology, we come to know that normal behaviour of a person is caused by certain reasons. These reasons are the outcome of a person's needs of his acts.In the case of needs, people are motivated not by what we think, they ought to have, but by what they themselves want. Wants may be illusory or unrealistic, but they control. Here, management is left with two basic options to motivate the people. It can either show how certain actions can increase their need fulfilment or threaten decreased need fulfilment unless they follow a certain course of action.

Motivation of people is a must in the organisation to push up the work irrespective of the machinery and equipments in use because they cannot be put to use without the man in action. Thus, motivation turns on steam to keep the organisation going.

(b) Individual Differences. People have many things such as grief, excitement, sentiments in common but individually everyone is different from the other in habits, behaviour, brain capabilities, abilities, etc. This fact has also been supported by science. The idea of individual differences comes from psychology. Each person is unique by birth and individual experiences after that make him more different. It is the reason why management treats individual differently. If it were not so, there would be no need of planning of judgement. Some standards could be adopted and minimum judgement would be required thereafter.

Organisational behaviour philosophy begins with the individual differences. A person holds responsibility and enjoy authority and makes important dicisions concerning all but a group of persons cannot do so rather they follow the decision taken by a person.

(c) A Whole Person. Some organisations generally believe that they employ only the brain or skill of person but they are worng in their approach. They employ the whole person. We can make a study of each characteristic separately but in final analysis, they are part of one system making up a whole person. We cannot separate each other. Skill cannot be separated from knowledge or background. Homelife cannot be separated from work-life.

(d) Human Dignity. This concept of human dignity is quite different from the above three concepts about the nature of man. People unlike other factors of production should be treated differently as they are of the higher order in the universe and they should be treated with respect and dignity.

ORGANISATION THEORY *VS.* ORGANISATION BEHAVIOUR

According to S.P. Robbins, "Organisation behaviour is a field of study that investigates the impact that individuals, groups, and structure have on behaviour within organizations, for the purpose of applying such knowledge toward improving an organisation's effectiveness." Organizational behaviour is a distinct area of expertise with a common body of knowledge. It studies three determinants of behaviour in organizations: individuals, groups, and structure. Additionally organisational behaviour is an applied field. It applies the knowledge gained about individuals, groups, and the effect of structure on behaviour towards making organisations work more effectively.

Organisation theory is a discipline which helps in examining organisations thoroughly. It studies how organisations are designed and offer ways by which organizational effectiveness can be increased. But organisation behaviour, on the other hand, is basically concerned with individuals and groups.

Organisation theory differs from organisation behaviour in respect of the following:

1. **Scope of Analysis.** Organisation theory is a macro analysis of the organisation, that is, how the organisation structure is designed to integrate people with organisation. Organisation behaviour, on the other hand, deals with micro aspect of the organisation, that is, individual and group behaviour in the organisation. However, a closer analysis of this difference reveals that it is not meaninful because it is rare that an organisation can be structured and designed without regard to the people and behavioural processes - individual needs, group dynamics, and so on.
2. **Emphasis.** Organisation theory lays emphasis on the sociology of organisation whereas organisation behaviour emphasises applied psychology of organisation.

3. **Nature.** Organisation theory is descriptive and predictive about a particular state of affair in the organisation; organisation behaviour provides ways of influencing human behaviour in certain direction on the basis of such description and prediction. Keith Davis stated that 'from administrative point of view, organisational behaviour seeks to improve the people-organisation relationship in such a way that people are motivated to develop team work that effectively fulfils their needs and achieves organisational objectives'.Thus, organisation behaviour is predictive in nature.
4. **Purpose.** Organisation theory attempts to analyse the design of organisation and explain what is happening in the organisation. Organisation behaviour attempts to explain and predict the behaviour of individuals and groups in organisations.

SIGNIFICANCE OF ORGANISATION BEHAVIOUR

1. Organisational Behaviour Follows the Principles of Human Behaviour. Human beings in the organisation are governed by the same physiological mechanisms both on and off the job. Internal mechanism provide people an extra spurt of the appropriate harmone under times of stress, whether this stress is job or nor-job related. Similarly, people at work are governed by the same psychological principles both inside and outside organisational life. Organizational behaviour is human behaviour in particular setting.

2. Organizational Behaviour is Situational. Psychologists and other behavioural scientists have emphasized for years that individual behaviour is a function of the interaction between personal characteristics of the individual and environmental variables. In order to understand a person's behaviour, the pressures placed upon him in a given situation must be understood. Aggressive behaviours, for example, surfaces when a normally calm individual is forced into constant and close physical proximity with other people.

Pigors and Myers have developed the concept of situational thinking. Their analysis suggests that four situational variables are basic for anyone responsible for getting results accomplished through people.

(a) The human element such as individual differences. This category includes interpersonal relationships and other social aspects of the situation.

(b) The technical factor such as production methods and equipment, management procedures, and specialized skills in any job function.

(c) Organisation-wise policies designed to achieve major organisational objectives.

(d) Space-time dimensions and relationships such as the size and location of a plant, office or work station.

3. Organizational Behaviour Represents a Constant Interaction Between Structure and Process Variables. Structure refers to organisational shapes, and positions. Process refers to what happens, with or without the structure. A retail store may use both formal advertising and public relations functions (structure) to help build its image in the community. However, most of the store's image is formed by word of mouth from satisfied and dissatisfied customers and employees.

Processes emerging within a group or organization are often evident only after they are heading towards completion. It is almost structural requirement in any organization that managers deal with the discontents of their people, yet employees sometimes find other processes for handling them.

4. Organisational Behaviour is Systematic. Systems thinking has become an integral part of modern organisation theory. Organisations are viewed as complex systems consisting of inter-related and inter-locking sub-systems. Changes or alterations in any one part of the system has both known and unknown consequences in other parts of the system. When modifications in the system consequences in response to modifications in the system are called dysfunctions.

General Systems Theory has been utilized in recent years to help understand the complex working of organisations. The great hope of general systems theory is "the creation of a science of organisational universals or a universal science-using the elements and processes common to all systems as a starting point." W.G. Scott and T.R. Mitchell caution, however, that human organisation may not be directly comparable to computer or biological systems, and anologies have to be drawn with caution.

The difference between structure and process represents a vital concept for understanding organizational behaviour. Classical approaches to management neglect interpersonal processes-the human side of organisational life. Erring in the opposite direction (neglecting the influence of structural and technological factors) is a tendency on the part of some social psychologists.

MODELS OF ORGANISATIONAL BEHAVIOUR

Organisations differ in the quality of organisational behaviour that they develop. These differences are substantially caused by different models of organisational behaviour being followed by management in each organisation. The model that a manager holds usually begins with certain assumptions about people and leads to certain interpretations of events. Underlying theory, therefore, is an unconscious but powerful guide to managerial behaviour. Managers tend to act as they think. Eventually this means that the underlying model that prevails in an organisation's management (especially in the firm's chief executive officer) extends throughout that firm.

Since the dawn of industrial revolution, four models of organisational behaviour have been followed by managers of different organisations at different times. These are autocratic, custodial, supportive and collegial as shown below.

1. Autocratic Model. As the name suggests, this model depends on power of the boss. Those who are in command must have the power to demand. In an autocratic environment, the managerial orientation is official authority. This authority is delegated by right of command over the people to whom it applies. Management believes that it knows what is best and the employee's obligation is to follow orders. It assumes that employees have to be directed, presuaded, and pushed into performance, and this is management's task. Management does the thinking; the employees obey the orders. This conventional view of management leads to tight control of employees at work.

Under autocratic model, the employee orientation is obedience to the boss, not respect for a manager. The psychological result for employees is dependence on their boss, whose power to hire, fire and "perspire" them is almost absolute. The boss pays minimum wages because minimum performance is given by the employees. They are willing to give minimum performance-though-sometimes reluctantly-because they must satisfy subsistence needs for themselves and their families. Some employees give higher performance because of internal achievement drives because they personally like their boss, because the boss is "a natural-born leader", or because of some other factor; but most of them give only minimum performance.

2. Custodial Model. Workers being managed under the autocratic model often feel insecurity and frustration. They may even show aggression towards their boss and their families and neighbours. That is why progressive managers felt that there must be some way to develop better employee relationships so that insecurity and frustration could be dispelled. The custodial model was used by such managers. It depends on economic resources. If an organization does not have the wealth to provide pensions and pay other benefits, it cannot follow a custodial approach. The resulting managerial orientation is towards money to pay wages and benefits. Since employee's physical needs are already reasonable met, the employer looks to security needs as a motivating force. The custodial approach leads to employee dependence on the organisation rather than on the boss. The employees are satisfied and happy but they are not strongly motivated, so they may give only passive cooperation. The result tends to be that they do not produce much more vigorously than under the autocratic approach.

3. Supportive Model. The supportive model had its origin in the "principle of supportive relationships". As stated by Rensis Likert,

"The leadership and other processes of the organisation must be such as to ensure a maximum probability that in all interactions and all relationships with the organisation each member will, in the light of his background, values, and expectations, view the experience as supportive and one which builds and maintains his sense of personal worth and importance.

The supportive model depends on leadership instead of power or money. Through leadership, management provides a climate to help employees grow and accomplish in the interests of the organization the things of which they are capable. The leader assumes that the workers will take responsibility, develop a drive to contribute, and improve themselves if management will give them a chance. Management's orientation, is to support the employee's job performance, rather than simply supporting employee benefit payments as in the custodial approach.

4. Collegial Model. The term "collegial" relates to a body of persons having a common purpose. It is a team concept. The collegial model is basically an extension of the supportive model. It is very useful in research laboratories and similar work environment. The collegial model depends on management's building a feeling of partnership with employees. The result is that employees feel useful. They feel that managers are contributing also, so it is easy to accept and respect their roles in the organisation. Managers are seen as joint contributors rather than as bosses.

The managerial orientation under collegial model is teamwork. The employees feel an oligation to uphold quality standards for the better image of their company. The employees are self disciplined. In this kind of environment, employees normally feel some degree of fulfillment, worthwhile contribution, and self-actualization, even though the amount may be modest in same situations.

MANAGEMENT AND ORGANISATIONAL BEHAVIOUR

Organisational Behaviour studies the behaviour of people in an organisation. Everybody in the organisation is concerned with improving organisational behaviour. All interact each other and influence behavioural quality of life of the organisation. Managers, however, have greater responsibility because they take decisions concerning all in the organisation. Managers constitute the administrative system and in organisational behaviour it is their responsibility to integrate the social system with the technical system, just to improve the people-organisation relationship in order to accomplish the human benefits for which it is made. 'From the administrative point of view organisation behaviour seeks to improve the people organisation relationship in such a way that people are motivated to develop teamwork that effectively fulfills their needs and achieves organisational objectives.' (Keith Davis).

The administive view of organisational behaviour contains a number of ideas as follows:

(i) Organisational behaviour focuses mainly on people and technical, economic and structural elements are all related to people.

(ii) People are in organisational environment rather than in unorganised social contacts. Thus, it attempts to improve people's organisation relations.

(iii) The environment is developed in such a way as to motivate the people to work hard to accomplish the organisation goal. Managers motivate the people because only they unlike other factors, can have greater output than the sum of their input through their creativity.

(iv) The direction of motivation is towards team work, that requires both co-ordination of work and co-operation of people. Co-ordination means effective time and sequence in performing activities while co-operation means the willingness of people to perform the work for attaining the organisational goal.

(v) The organisational behaviour seeks to fulfill both employees needs and organisational objectives. Every employee in the organisation want to fulfil his needs through organisational activities and the organisation's responsibility is to provide behavioural climate in the organisation so that people can gain need satisfaction and the organisation attains the objective. Thus both—people and the organisation—are benefitted in this manner.

(vi) Both employees and the organisation gain effectively by getting higher benefits with minimum costs. Organisational behaviour attempts to reduce the wasteful activities through economic and psychological means and thus increasing the effectiveness of the people and the organisation.

ELEMENTS OF AN ORGANISATIONAL BEHAVIOUR

The main elements of organisational behaviour system are:

(a) Social environment

(b) Attitudes and situation

(c) Philosophy and goals

(d) System of controls

(e) Formal and informal organisations

(a) Social Environment. Each organisation comes into contact with other institution and is affected by them. These are its social environment.

(b) Attitudes and Situations. The system of controls is an organisation influence with the attitudes of workers and with situational factor to yield a motivation for a designated person at a given time. If any of the three - control, attitude and situation differs, the motivation will also be different. There is a contingency relationship between the three. Each one attracts the other. For example, suppose, control is tightened or situation is changed, and other two factors remain constant motivation will naturally be different and produce different results.Thus motivation is determined by the interaction of controis, attitudes and situation. All operate in equilibrium within the social system.

Thus, effective organisational behaviour system results in productive motivation. Such kind of motivation should get an above average performance out of average people. Problems in the organisation are reduced to a minimum because it develops problem solvers out of problem makers. It establishes two way relationship i,e., manager and workers jointly influence each other and both are benefitted. Power rests with people rather than power over them.

(c) Philosophy and Goals. The climate of an organisation drives originally from the philosophy and goals of those who join together to create it. A person joins the organisation with his psychological, social, and economic wants which we express in both individual and group ways. These different interests - individual and group - come together in a working social system.

The philosophy of organisational behaviour is drived from both fact and value premises. Fact premises represent the view of how people or things in common behave, *i.e.*, it is a universally recognised fact. It is a well known fact that gravity of earth will pull everything down on the earth and therefore., no body will dare jump from a multi-storied buliding otherwise he will be no more. Value premises, on the otherhand, represent the view of desirability of certain goals. A person who is miserable, unhappy from his life may jump from the upper top of the multistoried building with an intention to die. He also knew the fact premises of gravity but his value premises had changed.

The goal of an organisation is to produce goals and services and to provide them to the society. To produce is no aim in itself. The main and improtant aim of an organisation is to satisfy the comsumers' needs. Production is done by workers and is supplemented by the resources of another group called shareholders or owners and in the midst of another group called public. Every group - workers, shareholders and public - has its own tastes and distastes and it is the responsibility of the organisation to develop the tastes and minimise the distastes of each group. It should work for the maximum satisfaction of each group combined with the satisfaction of consumer.

(d) System of Controls. All organisations influence their members by means of a control system that reflects the intermingling of formal organisation, informal organisation and social environment. The intermingling, becomes possible through communication and group processes.

(e) Formal and Informal Organisation. The philosophy and goals of people are implemented by leadership (manager) working through formal and informal organisation. Formal organisations interpret the philosophy and goals of the organisation and implement them in a rigid manner. The main premises of formal organisation are planning, policies, organisation structure and procedure. Though planning is done, policies are framed and organisation structure and procedure are fixed by the management yet all these are implemented by the workers at lowest level and therefore, should be in easy language. Planning, policies, structure and procedures should be communicated to all concerned so that they can prepare themselves and develop their abilities to work accordingly. The main aim of organisation policy is not to bring uniformity in action but it guides people in taking decisions

Modern human behaviour policies prefer to emphasise points what a person is to do and what he is not to do so that he may became a duty-conscious employee.

APPROACHES TO ORGANISATIONAL BEHAVIOUR

Organisational Behaviour has four basic approaches. These are:

1. Contingency Approcah. Under traditional management, manager was the person who organised, delegated and divided the work. Management applied the principles for getting things done universally regardless of the type of organisation and situation involved. This concept of universality was supported by its followers even in the field of organisational behaviour. Though occassional exceptions might be admitted, yet the ideas were more or less universal.

But the position has changed now. Behavioural researches have proved that there are some concepts that are useful in all circumstances otherwise different organisatonal environments require different behavioural relationship for proper effectiveness because behavioural situations are much more compilcated now-a-days. This approach was called Contingency Approach to organisational behaviour. This approach suggests that there is no one best way to tackle the human problem. Each situation must be analysed carefully before taking any action and at the same time discouraging universal concept about people. This approach helps to use in the most appropriate manner all the current knowledge about organisation. It is sometimes called Situational Approach because appropriate action depends upon the situational variables.

2. Inter-Disciplinary Approach. Organisational behaviour is an integration of all other social sciences and disciplines, that help in understanding the behaviour of people at work in the organisation. Organisational behaviour is neither psychology, nor sociology, nor organisation theory, rather it is integration of all along with other disciplines. Each one or a mix is applied wherever appropriate while dealing with people at work. Man is studied as a whole therefore, all disciplines concerning men are integrated. But it does not mean that they cannot study the men and their activities from different angles independently but they are integrated in a workable relationship in the behavioural world. The field of organisation behaviour is much like that of medicine which integrate physical, biological and social science into a workable practice.

Various social sciences like psychology, sociology, organisation theories, economics etc. have contributed a lot in understanding the human relations. Human needs, motivation, conselling and individuals differences are some of the important areas of contribution by psychologists. Role theory, informal organisations, status and group dynamics are sociological development in organisational behaviours.

3. Systems Approach - As discussed earlier, organisations are social systems. There are so many variables in the system which influence each other. The whole or a large part of the whole may be affected by action of or against one person. So, a manager or supervisor must consider the situation behind the scene before taking any action because such an action may affect the whole system. Effects may be positive or negative, so a cost-benefit-analysis should be made taking into consideration the organisation as a whole system because it may influence organisation elsewhere.

4. Human Resources or Supportive Approach - The human resources approach is developmental. It is concerned with the growth and development of people towards higher level of competency, creativity and fulfilment as people are the central theme in the organization. This approach can be very easily understood by comparing it with the traditional management approach where manager decided to do something and then got it done through people according to his directives and under his strict control and supervision without taking workers into confidence just to satisfy his whims. The human resources approach, on the other hand is developmental and facilitative. It helps people grow and facilitate them in developing self-control, responsibilities and other abilities in them so as to create a climate where all can contribute to the organisation to the limits of their improved abilities. It will result in operative effectiveness.

This approach is also called supportive approach because in this approach manager's role changes. He does not control the employees to get the work done, rather support them to grow to their full abilities. supportive managers provide a good organisational climate in which people can grow and be productive.

These four behavioural approaches facilitate the understanding of organisational behaviour.

□

8

Organisational Conflict

TYPES AND BASIS OF CONFLICT

On the whole conflicts present a gloomy picture of the organisation but it is not so. Traditionalists were of view that management should develop the structure not to let the conflicts arise. Non-classicists emphasised that management should avoid conflict and provides job satisfaction on the job through power-equalisation techniques. Modernists are of the opinion that they are inevitable to appear and the management should try to understand the people and try to direct them towards maintaining a better understading rather than to eliminate them because they are bound to appear in the organisation. We can envisage conflicts in three types or basis in an organisation:

1. Conflicts at the Individual Level

Conflcits at individual level in an organisation may be viewed in two ways—intra-individual and inter-individual.

(i) **Intra-individual Conflicts.** It is a situation where an individual is in a problem of decision making within himself.

(ii) **Inter-individual Conflicts.** When two individuals are in confrontation with each other, it may be said an inter-individual conflict. Inter-individual conflict may be between two individuals of the same group. In that case, it may be called 'intra-group conflict'. If conflct is between two members of the different groups and it may simply be regarded as inter-individual conflict but if it is blown up, it may develop as inter-group conflict.

Cases of Conflicts at Individual level. There are a number of causes why individual conflicts arise within an organisation. We may summarise them as follows:

(i) The one of main reasons of conflicts at individual level is mismatching of individual needs with organisational rewards. A man joins the institution with a number of psychological needs which he expects to be satisfied and in turn works to achieve organiation goal. He also brings certain beliefs, values and perception to the organisation. As he starts working, he elaborates beyond his formal behaviour and funds himself unable to translate his ideas into reality because his initial needs constantly change on the one hand, and he is bound to work under certain rules and regulations. Therefore, conflict arises with the clash of individual and organisational goals.

(ii) The second cause of conflict may be the situation of widespread uncertainty and scarcity of acceptable alternatives which is caused by the complexity of problem and lack of fast experience in handling such problems. The less the complexity of decision situation and the greater the amount of past experience with a decision situation the less probable the intra-individual organisational conflict is. For example, a policy of frequent transfer from one department to another will cause uncertainty in the minds of people because they cannot accumulate experience.

(iii) Conflict may also develop if there exists a disparity between aspiration levels and achievement that causes individual dissatisfaction. The greater the disparity, the higher is the probability of individual conflict. The best solution of such disparity lies in providing better environment in the organisation otherwise the gap between aspirations and achievements will continue to develop and if there is considerable time lag in the adjustment, the conflict with *insify*. The disparity between these two varible develops especially in times of low organisational performance or where organisational performance and aspirations both rise, any check on the fulfilment of aspirations will cause conflict.

If the disparity between aspiration level and achievements exist persistenly for a long time, it develops frustratively aggeressive behaviour or the individual concerned will make an attempt to overcome an obstacle. Studies show that the relationship between frustration and aggression is not inveriable. Sometimes due to persistent frustrain, the individual adjusts his sights and reconciles with situation.

(iv) Sometimes intra-individual conflict is an outcome of inter-individual conflcit. Many a time, the organisation puts two individuals in a conflicting situation. For example, if the organisation has reward system depending upon individual performance but performance is not an independent factor, it is rather interdependent. Such situations open up the flood gates of inter-individual and intra-dividual conflict.

2. Conflicts at Group Level

Conflicts at the group (formal and informal) level may also intra-group conflicts and inter-group conflicts:

(i) Intra-group Conflicts. When conflict develops between two individual members of the same group, it is intra-group conflict. Sometimes intra-group conflicts develop due to the following reasons:

(a) The group faces novel problem,

(b) New values are imported form the social environment, or

(c) A person's extra-group role given birth to intra-group conflict.

(ii) Inter-group Conflicts. When two members of different groups come into conflict, it may be an inter-individual conflict-groups are not involved in the conflict but when inter-individual conflict between members of two groups involve there assumes the proportion of an inter-group conflict. Sometimes intra-group conflict divides the members of the group into two small groups then the intra-group conflict is also transformed into inter-group conflict.

Sources or Causes of Group Conflicts

The source of inter-group conflict lies in:

(a) Need for joint decision making; and

(b) The differentiation of goals or of perception or of both.

Both the above conditions must be satisfied for an inter-group conflict. If there is a need of joint decision making and all people agree on the proposal, there would be no conflict. Similarly, there is differentiations of goals or perception or both but on decision of all persons are not necessary even then, there is conflict. But in real organisational situations, both conditions exist till numerous inter-group conflicts arise.

(a) The need for decision making arises because of the following:

(i) There are limited resources with every organisation which have to be shared with all groups. Moreover, technologically considerations create inter-dependence and therefore, activities are to be scheduled. Need for sharing of limited resources and schedule of activities make groups so inter-dependent that no one group can take decisions independently.

(ii) There may be need for joint decision making to determine the appropriate area for joint decision making such as authority and power relationship. Who will enjoy how much authority and what functions should be performed by whom. This decision making does not create any problem if the attitude of all the groups is cooperative. The problem arises only when groups and subgroups internalise their subunit goals regardless of overall organisational goals. These groups in such circumstances become competitive rather than complementary.

(iii) Lack of availability of resources in plenty posseses serious problem. Mutual dependence on limited resources is, in fact an organisation life and that sets people in competition for acquisition of means. This problem may arise intra or inter group posing high tension. This type of competition is disruptive of group cohesiveness. Resources may be financial or personnel or materials etc.

(iv) The need for joint decision making increases with the increase in the organisational level as things are coordinated at higher levels. The phenomenon is greatly found in interdependent departments. The interdependence is most important to the head of all departments rather than to heads of various departments. So they claim and counter claim and the conflict develops. Sometimes conflict may develop between head of all departments (superior) on heads of the various departments (subordinates).

(b) The differentiation of goals or perceptions or both occurs because of the following:

(i) **Individuals Backgrounds Such as Family, Education, Culture, Experience, etc.** Differ and so their values, beliefs and norms also differ which they bring to the organisation. Their own goals and professional ethics may have considerable effects upon them. The organisation attempts to obtain a homogenous set of people through recruitment procedures.

(ii) **Often Individuals and Groups are Set in Competition for Positions or Resources Which are Sacrce.** The situation worsens of the rewarding system is linked to a very vague criterion, capable of different interpretation for different rewarding authorities. If resources are further reduced, this will generate tensions among people and groups. Moreover, reward distribution in organisation is also dependent upon he bargaining strength of the members of the group, no consistent with one's merits. Organisational environment also influences the reward system. As the reward remains undefined and ill-defined hence inconsistencies and ambiguities creep into the system which in turn causes goal differentiation.

(iii) **A Person may be Member of Different Informal Groups and those Groups may have Different Goals.** At times, not only the goals of some groups of which he is member may conflict but also the roles he plays in different groups may conflict.

(iv) **The division of Labour and Task Specialisation Creates Groups Which Internalise Their Subunit Goals Reagrdless of Overall Organisational Goals.** Which themselves are generally highly non-operational, imperfectly rationalised, ambiguous or vague. The obvious case is that of line and staff personnel. The former has to implement what latter proposes. The goals of the two kidns of personnel come into conflict.

(v) **Differentiation of Goals in an Organisation Increases.** As the interactions of people are reduced because by interaction, they develop cohesiveness.

Thus we have seen that conflicts at group level may be intra-group and inter-group conflicts. March and Simon have illustrated that inter-group conflicts arise mostly between interconnected departments. They closes the connections the greater will be the felt need for joint decision making and less the differential of goals the less the differentiation of perceptions. The actual degree of conflict depends upon the strength of the indivdiual effects the interaction among them.

3. Conflicts at the Organisation Level

Conflicts at organisation level may also be of two types: *(i)* intra-organisational and *(ii)* interorganisational. Interaorganisational conflicts comprise of all intra-individual, interdividual, intra-group and inter-group conflicts because they all are the parts of the same organisation. They may assume organisation wide proportions and turn into hierarchical conflicts functional conflicts professional versus functional conflicts, management versus shop floor conflicts or union versus union conflicts. What we have discussed above, is all about intraorganisational conflicts.

The interorganisational conflicts are assumed between two organisations or between a business organisation and the government.

TRADITIONAL AND MODERN APPROACHES TO CONFLICT

The early approach to conflict asumed that all conflict was bad. Conflict was viewed negatively, and it was used synonymously with such terms as violence, destruction, and irrationality to reinforce its negative conotation. Conflict, by definition, was harmful and was to be avoided.

The traditional view was consistent with the attitudes that prevailed about group behaviour in the 1930s and 1940s. Conflict was seen as a dysfunctional outcome resulting from poor communication, a lack of openness and trust between people, and the failure of managers to be responsive to the needs and aspirations of their employees.

The view that all conflict is bad certainly offers a simple approach to looking at the behaviour of people who create conflict. Since all conflict is to be avoided, we need merely direct our attention to the causes of conflict and correct these malfuntionings in order to improve group and organisational performance. Although research studies now provide strong evidence to dispute that this approach to conflict reduction results in high group performance, many of us still evaluate conflict situations utilizing this outmoded standard, so, too, do many boards of directors.

The board of Sunbeam-Oster followed the traditional approach when they fired the company's chairman, Paul Kazarian, in 1993. Three years earlier, Kazarian took over the company when it was in bankruptcy. He sold off losing businesses, restructured the remaining application operation, and turned a $40 million loss in 1990 into a $47 million profit in 1991. A few days before he was fired, the company reported a 40 per cent jump in quarterly profits. But Kazarian's "crime" was that he rubbed a lot of people in the company the wrong way. He aggresively confronted managers, and suppliers. People complained that his style was abrasive. Kazarian, however, defended his actions as necessary: "You don't change a company in bankruptcy without making a few waves. I wasn't there to be a polite manager. I was there to create value for stockholders."

The Human Relations View/Modern View

The human relations position argued that conflict was a natural occurance in all groups and organizations. Since conflict was inevitable, the human relations school advocated acceptance of conflict. Proponents rationalised its existence: It cannot be eliminated, and there are even times when conflict may benefit a group's performance. The human relations view dominated conflict theory from the late 1940s through the mid-1970s.

The Interactionist View

While the human relations approach accepted conflict, the interactionist appraoch encourages conflict on the grounds that a harmonious, peaceful, tranquil, and cooperative group is prone to becoming static, apthetic, and nonresponsive to needs for change and innovation. The major contribution of the interactionist approach, therefore, is encouraging group leaders to maintain an ongoing minimum level of conflict. enough to keep the group viable, self-critical, and creative.

Whether a conflict is good or bad depends on the type of conflict. Specifically, it's necessary to differentiate between functional and dysfunctional conflicts.

FUNCTIONAL AND DYSFUNCTIONAL ASPECTS OF CONFLICT

A basic question that arises is whether conflict has only dysfunctional aspect or it generates functional utility to the organisation under some conditions. This question becomes important because for long, conflict has been held as villain for the organisational functioning, but at the same time, behavioural scientists have been trying to use conflict in constructive way. It suggests that under some situations, conflict can generate positive response in the organisation. Thus a conflict may have both positive and negative aspects. For example, Boulding has recognised that some optimum level and associated personal stress and tension are necessary for progress and productivity, but he portrays conflict primarily as a potential and social costs. These views suggest that under some circumstances conflict may be functional but in other cases, it is dysfunctional. Let us analyse both these aspects.

Functional Aspect of Conflict

Most experts today view conflict as a potentially useful aspect of organisation. It is claimed that an organisation void of constructive conflict is an organisation void of excitement, diversity and viability. Conflict prevents stagnation; stimulates interest and curiosity. Thus a minimum level of conflict is necessary because it helps organisation in the following ways:

1. **Stimulant for Change.** Conflict provides stimulus for change in the systems which are not conducive to the organisation. The existence of conflict means that there is something wrong with the systems of working. Thus it spotlights problems that demand attention, forces clarification of their nature and sources, and channels organisational efforts towards finding better solution of the problems. This way, conflict can focus the areas where changes should be brought.
2. **Creativity and Innovation.** Normally a conflict of certain degree arouses creativity and innovation. In an atmosphere of open confrontation, people tend to put forward more imaginative solutions to problems. A climate of challenge compels people to think through their own ideas before airing them out. Thus a conflict can help people to test their capacities to learn and develop.

3. **Avoidance of Tension.** Conflict can be used as source of avoiding tension and frustration. People can express their tension and frustration by means of conflict. This helps in releasing tension and bring people back to normal situation.
4. **Group Cohesion.** Generally, a group shows more cohesion when it faces threat from external sources in the form of inter-group conflict. Group cohesiveness is a situation in which all members of the group work together for a common goal, on where every one is ready to take responsibility for group cause. If group cohesion is high, interaction among members is high and the amount of agreement in group opinion is high.

DYSFUNCTIONAL ASPECT OF CONFLICT

While the positive aspects of conflict are few and limited, negative aspects are many and serious. Conflict to the extent of healthy competition may produce better results but beyond that it may be destructive. For example, conflict between management and workers has led the closure of many organisations or has turned them into loss-making units. Similarly conflict between line and staff or interdepartmental conflict creates a lot of problems in the organisation. In general conflict may create following problems:

1. **Stress of Tension.** While group cohesion provides satisfaction, conflict creates tension and stress. It exacts its toll on the physical and mental health of parties to the conflict. Intense conflict generates feelings of anxiety, guilt, frustration and hostility. A win-lose situation is created in the organisation in which winners try to injure the feelings of defeated.
2. **Diversion of Energy.** The most important dysfunctional aspect of conflict is that it leads to diversion of energy from constructive activities to destructve activities. People try to focus more on their personal goals rather than organisational goals. They spend more time on designing tactics for winning in conflictful situation rather than pursuing organisation goals. Long term goals of the

organisation begin to suffer as short-term problems become more important. In extreme cases, even sabotage and illegal activities may take place.

3. **Disequilibrium in Organisaton.** Conflict affects equilibrium of the organisation and produces disequilibrium. Every individual contributes something to the organisation and gets inducement in return. An organisation is said to be in equilibrium when contribution matches inducement for all or most individuals. When there is conflict, this equilibirum is affected adversely because the individuals' contributions do not match their inducement as they are using some of their energies in conflictful behaviour. This creates problems to the organisation and ultimately to the individuals because an organisation can not exist in this disequilibrium for long, and therefore, there is no question of engaging individuals in it. However, if organisation continues to exist, it will try to bring equilibrium either by getting rid of such individuals whose contributions do not match their contributions, or by modifying them to increase their contributions. The similar process will also take place when contributions exceed inducements.

Thus it can be seen that conflict will ultimately result into destructive activities. Therefore, it is necessary that management takes adequate steps either to eliminate the emergence of unnecessary conflict or if generated, to turn it into constructive one. This requires understanding of conflict and its management. Though conflict may arise at various levels and in various forms, its intensity is felt in terms of individual and group level. Thus conflict can be analysed at individual level—goal conflict, role conflict, and interpersonal—and intergroup level.

CONSEQUENCES OF CONFLICT

The following are some of positive consequences of conflict:

1. Cohesion and Satisfaction. Inter-group conflict and competition drives groups closer together. Under conditions of mild inter-groups conflict, group membership can be very satisfying to members. The whole purpose and internal unity of athletic groups, for example, would disappear if there were no conflict. In the face of a common enemy, group members close ranks and put aside former disagreements. For example, petty conflicts between cricket team members are generally put aside before the big game.

2. Major Stimulant for Change. Conflict spotlights the problems that demand attention, forces clarification of their nature and channels organizational efforts toward finding better solutions. It initiates a search for ways to polish and refine objective, methods and activities.

3. Group Think is Avoided. Without strong vocal disagreement, group think could overpower a highly cohesive group, preventing it from making rational decisions based on fact. Conflict also counteracts the lethargy that often overtakes organization.

4. A Minimum Level of Conflict is Optimal. Conflict is necessary to the organizational life. It is necessary for the internal stability of organisations. It also helps individuals in reducing accumulated ill-feeling and tensions between them.

5. Conflict Fosters Creativity and Innovation. It prevents stagnation, it stimulates interest and curiosity. In an atmosphere of open confrontation people tend to put forward more imaginative solutions to problems. A climate of challenge compels individuals to think through their own ideas before airing them out. Conflict can help individuals to test their capacities to learn and develop. A scholar who exposes his theories and research to the scrutiny of his colleagues may be stimulated to a deeper analysis when he is confronted with conflicting data and theoretical analysis by a colleague.

Negative Consequences of Conflict are as under:

1. Instability and Chaos. Under intense conflicts collaboration across individuals, groups and departments decreases or vanishes. Tensions will continue to mount up and each new conflict will split organization subunits further apart leading to communication break downs. In the heat of such an internecine warfare, the disputants squander awayenergy and resources that could be devoted to better use.

2. Diversion of Energy. One of the most dreadful consequences of conflict is the diversion of the group's time and effort toward winning the conflict rather than toward achieving organizational goals. Parties focus on their own narrow interests and tend to put their own aims above those of the organization. Long term goals begin to suffer as short term problems become more important; too much energy is drained off in trying to put out the 'fires'. In extreme cases, sabotage, secrecy and even illegal activities occur.

3. Conflict Creates Stress in People. Conflict exacts its toll on the physical and mental health of the combatants. Intense conflicts generate feelings of anxiety, guilt, frustration and hostility. Winners try to injure the feelings of the defeated. Losers feel defeated and demeaned. The distance between people increases. A climate of mistrust and suspicion develops. Discussion replaces cohesion. Losers indulge in non-cooperation and pay scant attention to the needs and interests of other group members.

LEVELS OF CONFLICT IN ORGANISATION

March and Simon have classified the conflict as: *(i)* Individual conflict, *(ii)* Group level conflict, and *(iii)* Organisational conflict.

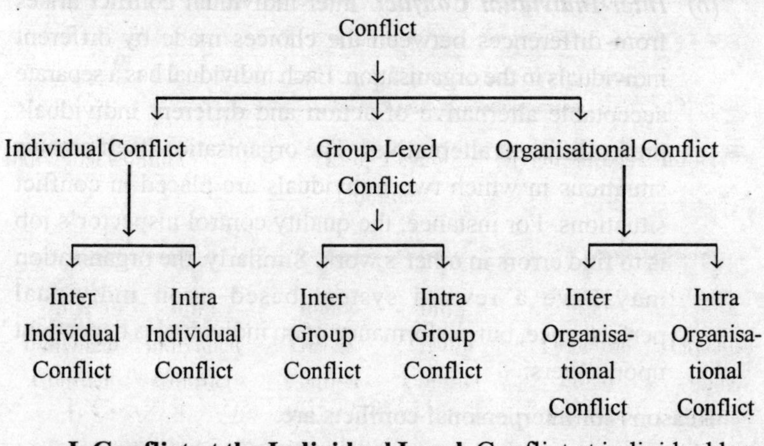

I. Conflict at the Individual Level. Conflict at individual level in an organisation may be viewed in two ways—Intra individual conflict and Inter individual conflict:

(a) ***Intra Individual Conflict.*** Intra personal conflict is internal to the person and is probably the most difficult type of conflict to analyse. To begin with, all of us have needs. These needs form the basis for our behaviour at work, at home, at play and in every activity we pursue. Everything we do is directed at satisfying some need. Organizations are basically formed for the purpose of meeting humanistic and economic needs of individuals. However, the nature of formal organization is such that it tends to create innumerable problems for individuals working therein. The goals of organizational life are in direct conflict with the individuals goals of workers causing them to be frustrated, alienated and threatend. In the words of Davis "organizations are systems of medieval torture which suppress and subjugate their victim—the individual. Most of the people working in organizations are like inert instruments, mere appendages in the production process. There is little chance to be creative. As organizations grow, they tend to be less responsive to the needs of individuals. In addition to loss of freedom the individual is stripped off his identity also.

(b) ***Inter-Individual Conflict.*** Inter-individual conflict arises from differences between the choices made by different individuals in the organisation. Each individual has a separate acceptable alternative of action and different individuals prefer different alternatives. The organisation itself creates situations in which two individuals are placed in conflict situations. For instance, the quality control inspector's job is to find errors in other's work. Similarly, the organisation may have a reward system based upon individual performance, but performance of an individual is dependent upon others.

Reasons for interpersonal conflicts are:

1. **Clashes of Values and Interests.** Conflict that so commonly develops between engineering and manufacturing personnel shows how differences in values might underlie

conflict. Members of the engineering department might place a premium on quality, sophisticated design and durability while members of the manufacturing department might value simplicity and low manufacturing costs.

2. **Power and Status Differences.** Interpersonal conflicts arise from unequal distribution of power and status. As pointed out by Abraham Zalenznik, "Organizations are political structures." They operate by distributing authority and setting a stage for the exercise of power. Similarly status inconsistencies lead to conflict.

3. **Scarce Resources.** Interpersonal conflict is almost automatic anytime there is scarcity. Conflicts over scarce resources are exceedingly common in organizations. Where the scarcity is absolute (the recource level cannot be enhanced) it is very difficult to manage interpersonal conflicts. For example if three qualified individuals vie for superior positions in the organization and there is only one such position, interpersonal conflict may develop to an unmanageable level.

4. **Personality Differences.** Some people have difficulty in getting along with each other. This is purely a psychological problem and it has nothing to do with their job requirements or formal interactions.

5. **Perceptions.** Varied backgrounds, experiences, education and training result in individuals developing different perceptions of similar realities; the result being an increase in the likelihood of interpersonal conflict. The belief that somebody else is out to away our share of resources may create ill-feelings between us and that person. An individual who perceives conflict is likely (between managers and subordinates) to act in a manner conveying conflict intentions. Vertical conflicts develops usually because superiors try to control subordinates and subordinates tend to resist.

II. Group Level Conflict. Conflicts at group (formal and informal) level may also be intra group conflicts and inter group conflicts.

(A) Intra-Group Conflict

A group consists of two or more persons who are in interaction with each other, have a well defined structure of role and status relations and have a system of values and norms of behaviour for the smooth working of the group. Intra-group conflict arises when differences over an issue crop up between the members of the group. Intra-group conflict may arise in three ways:

(a) when the group faces a novel problem,

(b) when a person's extra-group role comes into conflict with his intra-group role.

(c) when new values are imported from the social environment into the group, or

Individuals are generally members of different groups for different purposes. Inter-individual conflicts may gradually lead to an intra-group conflict. It is also possible that in case of an intra-group conflict of serious nature, members of the group may be divided into two groups and, thus, the intra-group conflict may be transformed into their inter-group conflict.

(B) Inter-Group Conflict

The inter-group conflict arises when: *(a)* there is the existence of a positive felt need for joint decision-making; *(b)* there is differentiation of goals *i.e.* different persons have different views regarding goals; and *(c)* there is difference in perceptions of reality. These conditions are prerequisites of inter-group conflict to arise because there would be no decision problem in the absence of any one of these conditions. Even if there is a need for joint decision-making, there would be no difficulty in decision-making if all the people have common views about goals and think alike.

III. Organisational Conflict. Conflict at organisation level may also be of two types *(a)* intra-organisational and *(b)* Inter-organisational conflict.

(a) Intra-organisational Conflict. Mainly three kinds of internal strain can be identified.

(i) *Horizontal Conflict.* It refers conflict between employees or departments at the same hierarchical level in an organisation. The source of conflict between departments consists of pressures toward suboptimization. Each department may suboptimize by independently trying to achieve its own departmental goals.

(ii) *Vertical Hierarchical Conflict.* Vertical conflict separates people in various levels of the occupational ladders in organization. It refers to any conflict between levels in an organization. It occurs usually in superior-subordinate relations. C.G. Smith identified three reasons for vertical conflict, *(1)* inadequate communication between levels, *(2)* Conflict arises essentially from differences of interests between position holders occupying different status in the organizational hierarchy, and *(3)* a distinct lack of shared perceptions and attitudes among members in various levels. Vertical conflicts arise because superiors attempt to control subordinates and subordinates tend to resist forcing the superior to increase the dosage of impersonal rules to exact obedience and gain control.

(iii) *Line and Staff Conflict.* Controversy and conflict are inherent in the concept of line and staff. It is not an easy task to divide and distribute expertise, authority and roles in equitable quantities between the line generalists and staff specialists. The concept authorizes the splitting of various functions into two categories: hierarchical and non-hierarchical, that is, creation of low status and high status persons. The splitting of functions into hierarchical and non-hicrarchical levels and the creation of low status and high status positions creates a discrepancy between expected and actual authority leading to resentment and frustration to all the parties involved. Line managers look upon staff specialists as 'unnecessary impediments in the otherwise simple and efficient administration of production operations". There is no chance of a conflict if the people do not feel need of joint decision making even though there are different views about goals and / or different perceptions.

Conflicts often arise in the organisation because every group wants a higher share of the organisational resources and does not want to understand the problems and limitations of other groups. Competition among the various groups or departments may lead to high tensions or certain occasions.

(b) ***Inter-organisational Conflict.*** The phenomena in inter-organisational conflict are much the same as those arising within an organisation. The bases of inter-organisational conflicts are essentially the same as the base of intergroup conflict. Most commonly cited reasons for interorganizational conflicts like incompatible objectives, conflicts over status, prestige and money are present in interorganizational conflict also. As pointed out by March and Simon, "many of the phenomena of intergroup conflict within the organization are almost indistinguishable for the phenomena that we might consider under interorganizational conflict.

PURPOSES OF CONFLICT

Conflict with outside organizations serves four purposes by:

1. Promoting closer bonds of unity among individuals within the organization. "Organizations frequently organize themselves against something, and, in the absence of a perception of conflict their reason for existence is weakened or disappears; and they suffer from internal disorganization or even dissolution".
2. Making organizational members aware of the strategy and tactics of the antagonist.

3. Building new life into organizational objectives and values. A conflict usually simplifies the purposes of an organization, simply because the objective of winning or surviving the conflict comes to dominate over all others. A situation of conflict heightens the larger purpose of the organization and so augments the internal rewards that come from a feeling of participation in these larger purposes.

4. Acts as an agency of social control.

POSITIVE ASPECTS OF CONFLICT (ADVANTAGES)

Traditional management theory considers conflict as harmful and recommends its suppression. But this view no longer holds good. Conflicts can never be wiped off completely. Moreover, a conflict is not altogether bad. It has creative elements as well. Therefore, the emphasis should be on harnessing it for improvement rather than fighting considering it harmful. The conflicting parties should approach the conflict in terms of problem solving rather than in terms of 'win-lose'. The win-lose tendency generates hostilities, rules out constructive solutions, and the parties think in terms of sectional gains and concessions rather than mutual benefits.

Modern writers consider conflict as something which is inevitable. They feel that a minimum level of conflict is necessary for the good health of the organisation. Conflict is also integral to the process of change. If we look at conflict from this point of view, we will come across the following functions of conflicts:

(i) Conflict provides an opportunity for releasing tension which otherwise would remain suppressed.

(ii) Conflict compels the individuals or group think again and again before adopting a course of action.

(iii) The thinking process followed by the conflict may lead to innovations in policies, procedures and behaviours.

(iv) Conflict is a test of capacities of the individuals and groups. It provides challenge to them. If they are able to meet the challenge successfully, they will feel satisfied and highly motivated.

(v) When a group is faced with a conflict, its members display creativity in identifying various alternatives. In the absence of a conflict, they might not have been so much creative.

(vi) Conflict brings about group cohesiveness among the members of the group as every member cooperates to meet the pressure of conflict problem.

(vii) When a conflict arises, it may help identifying the weaknesses in the system.

That conflict is socially useful and is supported by the majority of conflict theorists. It has been found that the closer the group, the more intense the conflict. Groups or relationships that originate in caring give rise to a host of socially functional forces, and conflict is often an essential medium in forming those forces. Conflict mobilizes energies, develops identity, clarifies options, can secure social commitments, and contributes to innovativeness. But conflict is not always constructive; indeed, there is evidence that levels of conflict regularly exceed the desirable. According to Katz and Kahn, "For any system certain kinds and levels of conflict will be optimal for certain criteria... Our opinion is that most organisations show levels of conflict considerably above the optimum.

NEGATIVE ASPECTS OF CONFLICT (DISADVANTAGE)

The negative potentials of conflict are quite obvious. Just as internal conflict within an individual can destroy his ability to function, similarly internal conflict within an organisation may result in some sort of block in decision-making. In complex organisations, the results may range from insurrection and schism to the creeping paralysis of deadlock and disinterest. For those who want to destroy an organisation or its effectiveness, there is probably no more effective method than the promotion of internal conflict. The destructive possibilities of inter-organisational conflict are even more apparent. It may result in unnecessary competition and may put the existence of a small organisation in danger.

The undesirable consequences of conflcits at various levels in the organisation are listed below:

(i) In case of intra-individual and inter-individual conflicts particularly, some dynamic personnel may leave the organisation if they fail in the resolution of conflicts in their favour.

(ii) Conflict may create high tension among the individuals and groups and a stage may come where it is beyond the capacity of the management to resolve the conflict.

(iii) Conflict may create a climate of suspicion and distrust among the people in the organisation. It may create discord in place of cooperation.

(iv) Conflict may be a source of dissatisfaction to the losing party.

(v) Conflict may destract the attention of the organisational members from the organisational goals. They may waste their time and energy in the perpetuation of conflict rather than resolving it.

(vi) Conflicts may weaken the organisation as a whole if the management is not able to handle them properly. If the management tries to suppress conflicts, they may acquire gigantic proportions in the later stages. And if the management does not interfere in the earlier stages, unnecessary troubles might be invited at the later stages.

Conflict are not always bad. Whether a conflict is desirable or not, depends upon what purpose is served by it. For instance, conflicts may provide an opportunity for releasing tension which otherwise would remain suppressed. Conflicts also provide opportunity for review of existing conditions and making better alternatives acceptable to the parties concerned. Though a conflict may threaten the emotional well-being of individuals, it may also be a positive factor in personal development. It may generate a challenging spirit and make the management pool resources to accelerate the pace of progress overcoming the speed breakers. Conflicts and problems are the price of progress. Conflict, therefore, are not necessarily discouraging, but the attitude towards them can be.

How can a Conflict be Resolved in an Organisation

Since the conflicts in organisations may have serious consequences, so the question is how to approach to the resolution of conflict. R. Blake has suggested three alternative approaches to the problem of dealing with conflict:

1. "Conflict is Inevitable; Agreement is Possible". On this view, one may decide to fight it out. This would result in a win-lose power struggle such a struggle may appear beneficial to the winner immediately following the struggle, but the main issues of conflicts can hardly be solved this way. Alternatively, the parties may depend on third party judgement or on fate. But still the main issues are likely to remain unresolved.

2. "Conflict may be Inevitable, but Agreement is not Possible". On this assumption, the parties may decide to withdraw from interaction or become indifferent to the problems they face. This approach may also provide temporary satisfaction and benefits to some, but may not lead to any meaningful resolution of conflict.

3. "Although Conflict may Arise in Various Situations, Agreement is Possible". This is regarded as the most positive approach to deal with conflicts. Here both parties would recognise that there is a need for solving the problem that has arisen. On this premise, the parties may begin interacting with each other. The problem may first be identified and then ways and means devised to solve it. A typical example of this method is collective bargaining. By negotiating and frank bargaining, it may be possible for the parties to arrive at solutions which are less temporary and more widely acceptable to all then other solutions. Moreover, negotiations provide opproutunities to groups and persons to understand each other's strengths and weaknesses, abilities and constraints.

Schmidt and Tannenbaum have suggested four approaches which may be used by a manager at different times to deal with the conflicts. These are: *(1)* avoidance, *(2)* repression *(3)* sharpening into conflict, and *(4)* transformation into problem solving.

(1) Avoidance of Differences. A manager can avoid the occurrence of many differences among his subordinates. For example, he can place people ingroups whose experiences are similar, who have had similar training and who come from a similar level of society. Because of something in common, these people tend to see things in the same manner, to have common interest and objectives, to approach problems in much the same way. The behaviour of such groups is more predictable and it is easy for the manager to avoid conflicts. Another way of avoiding differences is the controlling of interpersonal contacts of the people.

The important question arises here is whether the conflicts should be suppressed in the beginning or not. Most of the people view conflict something very bad and so according to them it should always be avoided. This approach may work well in certain situations only. The manager who uses this approach continuously runs the risk of reducing the total creativity of his staff. In an atmosphere where differences are avoided, no new idea will come into surface and the old ideas are likely to go unexamined.

(2) Repression of Differences. The manager using this approach keeps the differences under cover. He is aware that certain differences exist among members of his group, but would not allow the open expression of these differences. He may do this by continually emphasising loyalty, cooperation, team work and other similar values in the groups. He will try to ensure that potentially conflicting persons come together only under circumstances which are highly controlled. Another way of developing an atmosphere of repression is by rewarding agreement and cooperation and by punishing those who disrupt the harmony of the group.

This approach is useful when the latent differences are not relevant to the organisation's task. Individuals may differ on many things like religion, politics, castes and so on, and there may be no need to reach agreement on some of these differences in order to work together effectively on the job. It may also be appropriate to repress conflicts when adequate time is not available to resolve the potential differences among the individuals involved. Many a times, hidden agenda come forward in the meeting. People discuss a subject and the ways they discuss it and the positions they take with respect to it will determine the nature of differences. When strong feelings are involved in unexpressed differences, the blocking of these feelings may create frustration and hostility among the members of the group.

(3) Mediation or Transformation of Conflicts into Problem-solving. The persons involved in the conflict can bring to bear on the problem a greater variety of insights. If the differences are seen as enrichening, the individuals involved are likely to come up with a better solution because many problems can be seen clearly only if the individuals who see different aspects can come together and pool their information. When it comes to choosing the course of action for a given problem, differences among the individuals in the organisation can help to increase the range and variety of alternatives suggested.

The transformation of conflict into problem solving situation may also help to deal with some of the feelings which often accompany disagreement, frustration, resentment and hostility. The manager using this approach may help to channel the energy generated by feelings into creative rather than into destructive activities. For this, he should clarify the nature of the conflict and give recognition to the feelings of individuals involved.

(4) Confrontation or Sharpening Differences into Conflicts. When a manager is aware that differences exist among the members of the group, he may try to create an arena in which conflicting parties may fight it out. He will, however, ensure that persons understand the issue over which they differ and the procedures by which they can discuss their differences and the kinds of roles which each person is expected to perform during the struggle. The value of this approach lies in the fact that individuals realise the costs of conflict and resolve that this will not happen again.

However, a conflict may prove very costly. It destroys the energy of the people involved in it. It may also happen that this approach may give rise to more conflicts which are not good for the health of the organisation. Therefore, the manager following this approach should take effective steps to keep the conflict within organisational bounds.

Thomas and Kilmann have suggested five approaches to conflict management which are appropriate under different situations. These are: *(i)* Competing, *(ii)* Collaborating, *(iii)* Compromising, *(iv)* Avoiding, and (v) Accommodating. These are discussed below:

(i) Competing. It is a power oriented approach of resolving tensions. Competition is useful when the resources are limited and the system has to be pruned. For instance, during the periods of budget cuts, the departments having less competitive strength are the worst sufferers.

Also, in times of emergencies, where quick decisive action has to be taken and there is no time to seek collaborative, compromising, or accommodating solutions, the competing mode is useful. Here, one uses power and makes unilateral decisions taking the "win-lose" approach. Likewise, when one has to take unpopular decisions such as enforcing discipline, unpopular rules, cost cutting and so on, unilateral power-based strategies to put an end to conflicts are appropriate.

(ii) Compromising. Compromising is taking an intermediate position by both the parties. Each party tries to find some expedient, mutually acceptable solution which partially satisfies both parties, though neither is full satisfied. A compromising stance addresses the issue without avoiding it, but does not explore the alternatives in a way that would be completely satisfying to both parties as in the case of collaboration. Compromising involves "splitting the differences", exchanging conscessions, and seeking a quick middle-ground solution.

Compromising is a useful mode when the goals pursued are important, but not so important that it is worth potential disruptions by taking very assertive or unyielding positions. For instance, the production and maintenance departments might both want 60 hours of overtime to be sanctioned to each, but when only a total of 80 hours are made available to both, each might agree to use 40 hours. Each has compromised by giving up some, but not all. They have split the difference. Compromising is also a good conflict resolution mode when two parties with equal power are strongly committed to mutually exclusive goal such as in labour-management bargaining situations.

Compromise is an expedient mode to settle complex issues in the shortrun till a more thorough and permanent solution to the problem can be found. It can also be used as a backup mode when both collaboration and competition fail to work effectively in resolving conflicts.

(iii) Collaborating. Collaborating involves an attempt to work with the other party to find solutions that would be satisfying to both parties. Here, the underlying concerns both parties are explored in depth, the disagreements examined in detail, and resolutions arrived at by combining the insights of both the parties. A creative solution usually emerges because of the joint efforts of both the parties who are keen on gaining from the situation without hurting the other. Collaboration is a very useful mode when finding integrated solution is necessary and in the interest of both the parties.

(iv) Avoiding. This approach is used when the individual is both unassertive and uncooperative-that is, the party has a very low concern for his own and his opponent's needs. While avoiding, the individual might diplomatically sidestep a conflictful issue, postpone addressing it till later, or totally withdraw physically and / or psychologically from a threatening situation.

Avoiding can be very functional when the issue involved in the conflict is of passing importance, or when more pressing issues are to be handled by the individual within a limited time frame. Avoiding can also be the only alternative when one's power is very low and there is no chance of satisfying one's own concerns. For instance, if the personality of the head of the department is such that whenever a clerk enters his cabin, he just yells at the individual, the clerk will simply avoid going to the department head's cabin when he is inside. There is no way that the personality of the individual can be changed by the clerical staff who are low on the hierarchical ladder. Avoidance is also tactical when the potential damage of confronting the situation out weighs the benefits of resolution.

(v) **Accommodating.** Accommodating might take the form of selfness generosity, or obeying another's orders rather unwillingly, or giving in to another person's point of view. In all these cases, the individual neglects his own concern to satisfy the concerns of the other party. There is an element of self-sacrifice in this mode. Accommodating is useful in situations where the individual realizes that he is wrong. By yielding to the other's point of view, the individual indicates to the other that he is reasonable. Also when an issue is much more important to the other person than to the individual, by accommodating, the person maintains good will and a cooperative relationship, and also builds social credits. Think of the situation where two employees want to leave the office early on a particular day-one because her child is sick, and the other because she wants to pay a casual visit to her cousin-but only one can go early.

❐

9

Organisational Communication

The term 'communication' is derived from the Latin word 'communis' which means 'common'. This stands for the sharing of ideas in common. Communication of ideas establishes a common ground for understanding. Management is concerned with getting things done through others, a task that invariably requires that manager must communicate with other people. In fact every thing a manager does involves communication. For instance, to take a decision, a manager needs information. The information has to be communicated to the manager. Once a decision is made, again communication takes place, as the decision has to reach the concerned parties. Communication thus, is the artery of an ogranization through which the decisions and instructions of the management flow down to the lower rungs.

Communication may be defined as follows:

1. Communication is, fundamental and vital to all managerial actions, is the process of imparting ideas and making oneself understod by others.

2. Communication is the sum of all the things one person does when he wants to create understanding in the mind of another. It is a bridge of meaning. It involves a systematic and continuous process of telling, listening and understanding.

3. Communication may be broadly defined as the process of meaningful interaction among human beings. More specifically, it is the process by which meanings are perceived and understandings are reached among human beings.

4. Communication may be formally defined as any process whereby decisional premises are transmitted from one member of an organisation to another.
5. Communication is the broad field of human interchange of facts and opinions and not the technologies of telephone, telegraph, radio, and the like.

Communication is defined as the inter-personal and inter-organizational interchange of integral information. By communication, we mean the flow of material, information, perception, and understanding between various parts and members of an organization.... all the methods, means, and media of communication (communication technology), all the channels networks, and system of communication (organization structure), all the person-to-persons interchange (interpersonal communication). It includes all aspects of communication—up, down, lateral; speaking, writing, listening, reading, methods, media channels, networks flow; interpersonal, intra organizational, and inter-organizational.

Essential Elements of Communication

After a deep and analytical study of above definitions, it can be concluded that there are four Essential Elements of Communication. These are as follows:

1. **Communication.** There must be a message. The message may be in form of writing or verbal. It may be in the form of message, order or request.
2. **Receiver.** There must be a receiver of message. Generally the receiver is a subordinate. However, the receiver of message may be the senior officer also.
3. **Sender.** There must be a sender of meassage.
4. **Feed-back.** Feed-back of message is necessary for the communication. Communication is a circular process. Every communication leads to some reactions or feed-back which in turn generates future communication.

IMPORTANCE OF COMMUNICATION

Communication is the foundation of all group activity. It is the element which sets the enterprise in motion and provides life to the dead structure. Communcation is essential not only in business but in all types of organisations. In fact, it is difficult to imagine any kind of inter-personal activity without communication. "It is no exaggeration to say that communication is the means by which organisation activity is unified. It is the means by which behaviour is modified, change is effected and goals are achieved." To be specific, sound communication offers the following benefits:

1. Implementation of Plans. Plans and decisions must be effiectively conveyed to those who can translate them into action. Effective communication is the *sin qua non* for quick and successful implementation of the management decisions. Managers issue specific orders and instructions through communication. They inform employees about the goals, policies and procedures of the organisation as well as about rationale of the job. Communication is the artery through which decisions and instructions flow downward. In order to get maximum results from people, correct and detailed instructions must be given at the right time. Similarly, the difficulties experienced by workers should be conveyed to the managers so that they can amend or issue new instructions. Without a rich flow of communication from his boss, the subordinate cannot judge which direction he should be going and how well he is doing.

2. Planning and Decision-making. Communication provides to managers the information and ideas necessary for sound planning. The widest possible participations in planning is a preconditions for getting the task done. This can be effectively secured only through the media of communication. Communication enables a manager to diagnose the problem and to gather information for making sound decisions.

3. Training and Development. Communication is vital or the orientation and training of both workers and executives. In modern industry training and development of personnel is an ongoing process. The degree of learning depends not only on the contents of the training programme but on how effectively the knowledge and skills are transmitted. Communication is knowledge and without knowledge employees remain ignorant.

4. Motivation and Morale. Managers use communication to secure acceptance of their ideas and orders. They can improve the job satisfaction of employees by providing feedback information on their performance. Sound communication facilitates delegation and decentralisation. Communication plays a vital role in building up high morale in the organisation. As an influence process communication is an essential part of guidance, motivation and leadership functions of management.

5. Public Relations. A business enterprise comes into contact with several social groups, *e.g.*, customers, investors, trade unions, government and the local community. It must maintain cordial relations with these groups in order to develop a favourable image. It must continously strive to convince the public that its actions are in the interest of society. Otherwise the reality becomes whatever customers, employees and government officials want to believe.

6. Human Relations. In order to secure maximum productivity with the minimum cost, there must be perfect co-operation and trust among management and labour. Sound communication enables workers to express their grievances which reduces tension and industrial unrest. Most of the conflicts in industry arise due to misunderstood motives and ignorance of facts. Proper communications help to minimise friction and to maximise mutual understanding and co-operation. Management can sell its ideas and reduce resistance to change through effective communication. Communication inspires change which is the moving symbol of living organisations.

COMMUNICATION PROCESS

Communication has been defined as a process. The process is a concept of changing rather than static existence. Events and relationships are seen as dynamic, continuous and flexible, and as such, must be considered as a whole, a dynamic, interaction both affecting and being affected by many variables. Thus, various elements might be involved in this process in whose case there may not be unanimity amongst various authors and thinkers. A communication process may involve various elements as shown in Fig. 1

Sender—Ideas—Encoding—Channel—Receiver—Decoding

↑ ↓

Feedback

Fig. 1. The Communication Process

Thus, the above figure shows the following elements in this process:

1. Sender. The person who intends to make contact with the objective of passing information, ideas to other persons is known as sender.

2. Ideas. This is the subject-matter of communication. This might be opinion, attitude, feelings, views, suggestions, orders, etc.

3. Encoding. Since the subject-matter of communication is abstract and intangible, its transmission requires the use of certain symbols such as words, actions, pictures, etc. Conversion of the subject-matter into these symbols is the process of encoding.

4. Channel. These symbols are transmitted through certain channels, *e.g.*, radio, telephone, air, etc., depending upon the situation of the two parties, *viz.*, sender and receiver.

5. Receiver. Receiver is the person to whom message is meant for.

6. Decoding. Receiver converts the symbols received from the sender to give him the meaning of the message.

7. Feedback. Feedback is necessary to ensure that the receiver has received the message and understands it in the same sense as sender wants. Further, it also acts as an energising factor, thereby changing the course of action in the communication.

COMMUNICATION NETWORK

In an organisation, there are a number of channels or paths connecting various positions for purposes of communication. The sum-total of these channels is referred to as 'communication network'. This is made up of two types of channels which are inter-related and inter-dependent, *viz.*, formal and informal. The existence of these channels is necessary for organisational communication to take place. Further, these channels also determine to a very significant extent the smoothness, rapidity, and correctness with which the messages flow in an organisation. Thus, if the channel is too narrow considering the volume of messages flowing through it, messages may get delayed or blocked. If the channel is too long or circutious, again the same thing may happen.

1. Formal Channel. The formal channel, as the very name implies, is the deliberately created, officially prescribed path for flow of communication between the various positions in the organisation. It is a deliberate attempt to regulate the flow of organisational communication so as to make it orderly and thereby to ensure that information flows smoothly, accurately and timely to the points to which it is required. Further, it is also intended to prescribe for filtering of the information to various points to ensure that information does not flow unnecessarily thereby causing the problem of overload.

This officially prescribed communication network may again be designed on the basis of single or multiple channels. A single channel communication network prescribes only one path of communication for any particular position and all communications in that position would have necessarily to flow through that path only. Ordinarily, this path is the line of authority linking a position to its line superior. This is what is commonly referred to as 'through proper channel', *i.e.* through the line of superior-subordinate authority relationships and its implication is that all communications to and from a position should flow through the line superior or subordinate only.

The channel of communication under this system is, no doubt, narrow, but ordinarily, it does allow for flow of essential information. Besides, it is easy to maintain, orderly in nature, supports the authority of the superiors and provides for closeness of contact thereby reducing channels of miscommunication.

It has certain basic limitations, such as, bottlenecks in the flow, enhanching organisational distance, greater possibilities of transmission errors, screening at various filtering points. etc. One way of overcoming these limitations is to provide a number of communication channel linking one position with various other positions, *i.e.*, the system of multiple channels.

2. Informal Channel or Grapevine. The informal channel of communication, also known as 'grapevine', is the result not of any official action, but of the operation of social forces at work-place. The term grapevine arose during the days of U.S. Civil War. At that time, intelligence telephone lines were strung loosely from tree to tree in the manner of a grapevine, and the message thereon was often distorted; hence any rumour was said to be from the grapevine. Today the term applies to all informal communication. While formal communication exists to meet the utilitarian needs of the organisation, informal communication is the method by which people carry on social, non-programmed activities within the formal boundaries of the system. It, thus, exists outside the official network, though continuously interacting with it.

Many authors on this subject opine that the communication through informal channel generally performs a positive service to the organisation. It operates with much greater speed. Moreover, there might be certain subject-matters of communication which do not require their transmission through the formal channel. This channel also satisfies the communication needs of the various persons in the organisation, more particularly those persons who freely mix up with others and rely upon informal relationships. Informal communication is thus a need-fulfilment device generated when it is found that the existing formal communication is inadequate or insufficient. The requirement of speedier communication creates conditions for informal communication which is supplemental to the formal one. Chester Barnard opines that 'communication function of the executives includes the maintenance of informal executive organisation as an essential means of communication. The functions of informal executive organisation are the communication of intangible facts, suggestions, suspicions that cannot pass through formal channels without raising issue calling for decisions without dissipating dignity and objective authority. In a research study by L.M. Prasad, it was found that between 50 and 100 per cent subordinates communicating unfavourable work performance, problems relating to work, unfavourable reactions to various organisational practices, used to communicate through informal channel.

Informal communication, on the other hand, has certain basic limitations. It is less orderly and less static also. Sometimes, messages communicated through the informal channel are so erratic that any action based on these may lead to a difficult situation in the organisation. In this case, the irresponsibility of the persons communicating through the informal channel is the most important factor. Since origin and direction of the flow of information is hard to pinpoint, it is difficult to assign responsibility for false information or morale lowering rumours. Moreover, as each person conveying the message may add, subtract or change the original message according to his motive, informal communication problems multiply.

The informal communication is a part and parcel of the organisational process. The only thing management can do in this respect is to take suitable action to minimise the adverse effect of this channel. Management must be aware, through the understanding of the informal communication, the utility and the positive contributions to the operation of the organisation that the informal communication can make. As such, proper analysis of informal communication and a suitable clarification in this respect will be helpful in making its use towards organisational efficiency.

Types of Grapevine Informal Communication

Four types of informal communication channel have been identified single strand, gossip, probability and cluster as shown in Fig. 2.

In single strand network, the individual communicates with other individuals through intervening persons. In the gossip network, the individual communicates non-selectively. In probability network, the individual communicates randomly with other individuals according to the law of probability. In the cluster network, the individual communicates with only those individuals whom he trusts. Out of these informal network, the cluster is most popular.

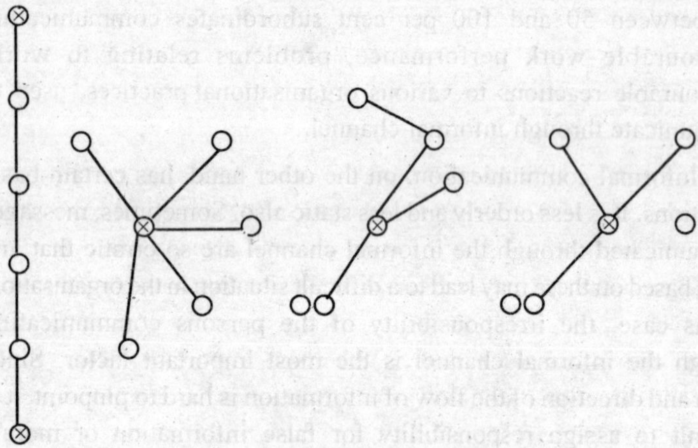

Fig. 2 Informal Communication Network

Rumour. The word rumour is sometimes used as a synonym for the whole informal communication, but there is a difference between the two. Rumour is grapevine information which is communicated without any standard of evidence being present. It is the injudicious and untrue part of the grapevine. Since, in most cases, it is incorrect information, it is presumed to be the most undesirable feature of grapevine. Rumour is a product of interest and ambiguity in a situation. Since perception of interest and ambiguity differs among individuals, rumour tends to change from person to person. Depending upon the interest, each person subtracts or adds something to the original message through the process of elaboration and assimilation.

Communication Media. The subject-matter of communication, *i.e.*, messages, ideas, suggestions, etc., being abstract and intangible, their transmission and receipt require use of certain symbols, which become the media of communication. These symbols may be *(i)* words either oral or written; *(ii)* pictures including graphs and diagrams; and *(iii)* actions or gestures including facial expressions. Each of the media may be either used exclusively, that is, to the complete exclusion of others, or, as is very commonly the case, two or more of these may be used to supplement each other. For example, in face-to-face communication, diagrams and charts may be used to clarify what one is taking about. Of these, oral and written method of communication are the most important.

Oral Communication. In oral communication, both the parties to the process, *i.e.*, sender and receiver, exchange their ideas through oral words either in face-to-face communication or through any mechanical or electrical device, such as telephone etc.

Oral communication is very helpful in face-to-fact two-way communication where persons can exchange their feelings, fully and clarity regarding any doubt or ambiguity may be sought. It has, as such, very high degree of potentiality for speedy and complete interchange of information. Possibility of gestural communication being used along with oral one increases the effectiveness of this type of communication since actions speak louder than words. Important points may be emphasised through actions. Rank and file employees as well as supervisors and even managers often prefer oral communication. They enjoy the opportunity to ask questions and to participate.

Oral communication suffers from the disadvantages of absence of any permanent record of communication. Sometimes, it becomes time consuming specially in meetings and conferences when after various deliberations, nothing concrete comes out. Sometimes, oral communication is not taken seriously by the receiver and basic objective of communication in this case is not achieved.

Written Communication. Communication in writing - written words, graphs, diagrams, pictures, etc. may take the form of letter, circulars, notes, manuals, etc.

Written communication possesses the capacity of being stored for future reference. The communication efforts may be minimised by simultaneous communication to various points such as through circulars, etc. It also enables the communication to take place between distantly placed parties without much cost. Written communication is more orderly and binding on subordinates and superiors to take suitable actions in the organisation.

Written communication, however, suffers from major drawbacks. It is very time-consuming both in terms of preparing the message and in terms of understanding the message. There is a greater chance of communication being misunderstood. Sometimes it is more costly in comparison to oral communication.

ORAL AND WRITTEN COMMUNICATION : A COMPARISON

Each of the different media of communication has its strengths and weaknesses which determine its uses and suitability for communication in any particular context. Thus, in some cases, oral communication might be useful while in others, written communication may be necessary, as both of these have their own relative merits and demerits, as discussed above. As such, one cannot depend upon a particular medium of communication and both of these media are complementary to each other. That is why, in practice, both these media are used. Oral communication, however, is more useful where the subject-matter is complex and a final decision requires deliberations from the persons concerned. Moreover, in day-to-day business and in routine types of activities, oral communication may be relied upon.

FORMS OF COMMUNICATION

The oral and written communication may take a number of shape or forms depending upon the situation. The following list presents some possible and commonly used ones in communication in different directions:

1. Horizontal Communication

Oral	*Written*
1. Lectures, conferences, meetings	1. Letters, memos, reports
2. Telephone and other devices	2. House organ
3. Social and cultural affairs	3. Handbooks and manuals
4. Grapevine, rumours	4. Annual reports
	5. Union publications.

2. Downward Communication

Oral	Written
1. Personal instructions	1. Orders and instructions
2. Lectures, conferences and meetings	2. Letters, memos, circulars
3. Interviews, counselling	3. Bulletin and notice boards
4. Social and cultural affairs	4. Posters
5. Grapevine; rumours	5. Hand books and manuals
	6. Annual reports
	7. House organs
	8. Union publications

3. Upward Communication

Oral	Written
1. Face-to-face conversation	1. Reports
2. Interveiws	2. Personal letters
3. Meetings and conferences	3. Grievances
4. Social and cultural affairs	4. Suggestions system
5. Grapevine, rumours	5. Complaints system
6. Union channels	6. Attitude and moral surveys
7. Telephone and other devices	7. Union publications

Of these, it is not necessary that all of these would be used in a particular organisation, but it will be determined by the organisational needs, its size and resources, management attitude towards these forms, etc.

DIRECTION OF COMMUNICATION

Communication, as defined earlier, requires two parties, the sender and the receiver, their juxtaposition *vis-a-vis* each other determining in the organisation context, the particular dimension of the communication flow. Thus, the communication flow within the organisation may be inter-scalar when two parties are at the different managerial levels or inter-scalar when they are at the same hierarchical level-this is also known as horizontal communication. The inter-scalar communication may again be classified as downward, when the message flows from the higher to lower level, or upward when it is the other way round.

1. Horizontal Communication. It is the flow of information between persons of the same hierarchical level. Formal organisation provides for horizontal communication by means of right of persons at any level to consult or work with others at the same level. Communication among peers, in addition to providing task coordination, also furnishes emotional and social support to the individual. Horizontal communication is impeded in the organisation that overstresses functional departmentalisation. The creation of functional departments of units creates problems, of coordination and communication between members of such units. Some companies develop committee structure near the top level of the organisation to assist the chief executive in achieving coordination and better horizontal communication in terms of control function in the organisations.

2. Downward Communication. Downward communication within the organisation flows from a superior either in the same line of command or in the different one. It stands out as a great force for controlling, influencing and initiating activities of organisation members. Communication in this category includes *(1)* orders and instructions about job, *(2)* directions about understanding of job and its relationships with other jobs, *(3)* organisational policies and procedures, *(4)* feedback of subordinates' performance, *(5)* reprimands, criticisms, etc., and *(6)* questions inviting upward communication. In the organisation, people at lower levels have a high degree of fear and respect towards such communication which leads to high degree of acceptance of such communication. Coordination, distoration and resistance are three important problems that characterise the downward communication process.

3. Upward Communication. Upward communication flows from a subordinate position to a superior position. It includes information about *(1)* subordinates' work performance, *(2)* problems relating to work, *(3)* performance appraisal of their subordinates, *(4)* feedback of understanding of orders, instructions, etc., *(5)* clarifications of orders, etc., *(6)* opinion, attitude, feeling, etc., *(7)* procedures, methods, practices followed in doing the work, *(8)* criticisms, *(9)* new ideas and suggestions, and *(10)* personal and family problems. Upward communication is more susceptible to various obstructions and bottlenecks discussed later on, because of its special nature. Managers, often times, fail to realise that upward communication cannot be taken for granted, as is the case with downward communication. This is so because, unlike downward communication, upward communication is devoid of any support of managerial hierarchy. On the contrary, it has to flow in a direction directly opposite to the flow of official authority, from the dependent subordinates to the superiors on whom they (subordinates) are directly or indirectly dependent for the satisfaction of their needs.

PROCESS OR MACHINERY OF EFFECTIVE COMMUNICATION

For communication, at least two persons—a sender and a receiver—are required irrespective of the mode of communication. The sender (may be called a source) conceives the idea, puts it in such terms that can be coveyed, decides the mode of communication,

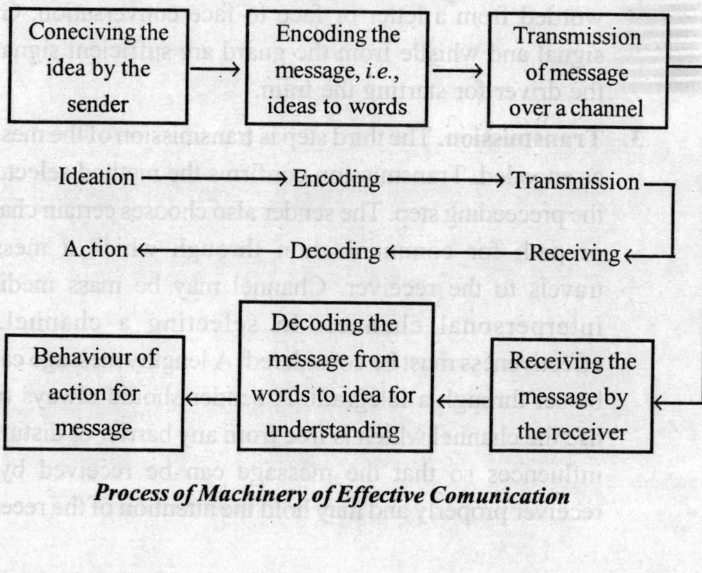

Process of Machinery of Effective Comunication

conveys it, the receiver receives it, tries to understand and finally takes an action according to the information or direction received from the source. This whole Process or Machinery of effective communication may be depicted as follows:

Thus the entire sequence of communication requires at least above six steps, *i.e.*, Ideation, Encoding, Transmission, Receiving, Decoding and Action. We should discuss these steps hereunder:

1. **Ideation.** It is a preliminary step in communication where sender creates an idea to communicate. In other words he thinks what message should be send. This is the content of communication and a basis of message. He must have something to say before he can say. This step is very crucial because other steps are actionless without any message.
2. **Encoding.** Under this step, sender organises their ideas into a series of symbols that he feels, they will communicate the mesage to the inended receiver. It includes selection of methods of communication as well as receiver. The wordings may be different in different messages to be sent through different methods. A telegram may be differently worded from a letter or face to face conversation. Green signal and whistle from the guard are sufficient signals to the driver for starting the train.
3. **Transmission.** The third step is transmission of the message as encoded. Transmission confirms the method selected in the preceeding step. The sender also chooses certain channel or path for communication through which a message travels to the receiver. Channel may be mass media or interpersonal channel. In selecting a channel, its effectiveness must be considered. A lengthy message cannot be set through a telegram. A sender should always try to use the channel which is free from any barrier or disturbing influences so that the message can be received by the receiver properly and may hold the attention of the receiver.

4. **Decoding.** Decoding means tanslation of symbols encoded by the sender into ideal understanding. Understanding the message by the receiver is the key to the deconding process. If the receiver does not understand the message or misunderstands it or pretends to misunderstand it whereas he has understood it correctly, the communication is ineffective. This happens because perceptions of two people are quite different.

   Understanding is with the receiver. A communicator can only make sure that he has communicated the message and it reaches the receiver and understanding the message is only a choice of receiver whether to understanding it or not. Decoding in this way is tanslation of words or symbols received into idea.

5. **Receiving the Message.** The fourth step is receiving the message by the receiver who pays the necessary attention in receiving the message. Any neglect on the part of receiver may make the communication ineffective or it means the message its lost. In case of oral message, a receiver has to be good listener. But listening alone is not sufficient, he should be willing to understand also.

6. **Action.** It is response by the receiver of the communication received from the sender. He may like to ignore the message or to store the information received or to perform the task assigned by the sender or something else.

Rule of Five in Communication. In the above process of communication, out of six steps, first three are to be taken by the sender and last three by the receiver. There are two more steps which are generally desired by the sender from the receiver in a organisational situation but both these steps are not essential to a completed communication. These steps are 'Acceptance' and 'Feedback'. Sender wants that his message must be accepted by the receiver so that cooperation and motivation may improve and the sender may come to know that the receiver has understood his message correctly. Similarly, sender wants feedback. It means that receiver generates a message to the sender in response to sender's original message. This may help the sender, evaluate the effectiveness of his message so that sender can modify his subsequent messages. Although these two additional steps of the receiver are not essential for completing a communication, but these are essential in generating an effective long-run working relationship.

When all the expectations of the receiver in communication process are considered, they are sometimes called the Rule of Five in communication, *i.e.*, *(i)* receiving, *(ii)* understanding, *(iii)* acceptance, *(iv)* action, and *(v)* feedback. If these five steps are complete from the receiver's side, the communication is effective and successful.

ELEMENTS OF COMMUNICATION

The process of Communiation consists of the following elements:

(i) Communicator. The person who conveys the message known as communicator or sender. By initiating the message, the communicator attempts to achieve understanding and change in the behaviour of the receiver.

(ii) Message. It is the subject-matter of any communication. It must exist in the mind of the comunicator if commmunication is to take place.

(iii) Communication Symbol. The sender of information organises his idea into a series of symbols (words, signs, etc.) which he feels, will communicate to the intended receiver or receivers. Communication may also take place through physical gestures.

(iv) Communication Channel. The communicator has to choose the channel for sending the information. Communication channel is the media through which the message passes. It may be either formal or informal.

(v) Receiver. The person who receives the massgae is called receiver. The communication process is incomplete without the existence of receiver of the message. It is the receiver who receives and tries to understand the message.

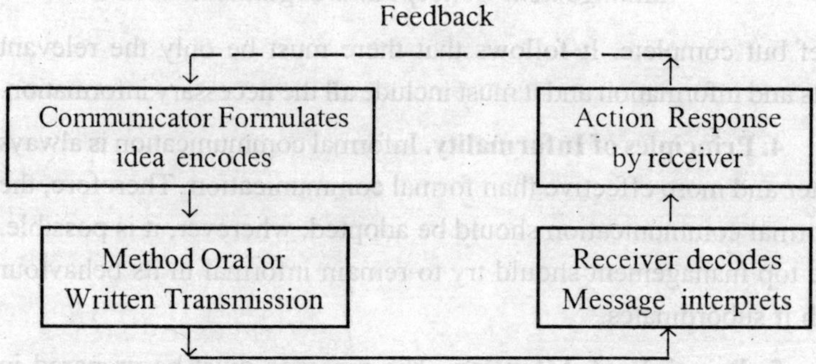

Transmission Through Formal or Informal Channel

PRINCIPLES OF COMMUNICATION

Effective communication is essential for effective management. The success of an enterprise depends to some extent on the effectiveness of its communication system. The co-operation of the workers in the achievement of objectives of enterprise and the co-ordination between management and workers can be expected only if there is an effective system of communication in the enterprise. Therefore the system of communication must be based on some certain principles. Important Principles of Communication are as under:

1. Consistency. The principle of consistency must also be followed. It means that there must be consistency in all the messages communicated. The messages should not be contrary to each other. The messages should also be consistent with the plans, policies, programmes and objectives of the enterprise.

2. Principle of Time. Information should be communicated at the proper time. If message is communicated after its due time, it will be of no use, and similarly, a message communicated before its due time may also be fruitless. Therefore, the message must be communicated at the proper time.

3. Clarity, Briefness and Completeness. The very first principle of effective communication is that it must be clear. The meassage must be communicated in simple, easy and commonly accepted language. The message must be meaningful. It must be brief but complete. It follows that there must be only the relevant facts and information and it must include all the necessary information.

4. Principles of Informality. Informal communication is always better and more effective than formal communication. Therefore, the informal communication should be adopted, wherever, it is possible. The top management should try to remain informal in its behaviour with it subordinates.

5. Principle of Attention. The message must be prepared in the manner that the receiver may pay his full attention to the message. The receivers should be motivated to pay their full attention to the message and to follow it.

6. Principles of Politeness. The message of communication must be polite. The language must be very polite and humble so that the receiver of message may accept the message and implement it easily. Hard language may and should also be used if the need arises to do so.

7. Principle of Continuity. A very important principle of effective communication is that it must be a continuous process and not a function. There must be continuous communication between the top management and the subordinates.

8. Principle of Co-ordination. Communication is only a means and not an end in itself. It is means to achieve the predetermined objectives of the enterprise. It is a means to get the co-ordination of all the subordinates and to see that all the activities are performed satisfactorily. Therefore, the system of communication must be based on co-ordination of authorities of different departments and different employees of the enterprise. It should be such that it may help in achieving a spirit of co-operation among all the employees of organisation.

9. Principle of Proper System of Communication. This principle states that a proper system of communication **must** be adopted to make it very easy and effective too. Selection of a particular method of communication system depends upon many factors as the sender of message, receiver of message, nature of the message, need of the message etc.

10. Communication Path. Communication path is the channel through which a message is communicated from one person to another. This must be simple. Following factors are included in the communication path—*(1)* Preparation of message, *(2)* Communication of message to the right person at the right time, *(3)* To check the facts, *(4)* To decide about use of facts, and to collect the information and to prepare the documents.

MEASUREMENT OF THE SUCCESS OF COMMUNICATION

The communication system is considered to be successful only when the receiver of message acts according to instruction of the message as the sender of message intended to communicate and then he follows and implements it. Following are the measuring methods which may help in the measurement of the success of communication.

1. To Ask Questions. The first method of the measurement of success of communication is to ask some questions from the persons to whom the messages were communicated. Some are the questions which may help in measuring success of communication. These questions may be as follows:

(1) Whether the message has left wanted effect on receiver?

(2) Whether the receiver has accepted the message?

(3) Whether the receiver has understood the message?

(4) Whether the receiver has implemented the message?

(5) Whether the receiver has accepted and implemented the message willingly ?

If the answers of receiver of message to these questions are positive, it may be assumed that the communication has proved success.

2. Reports. Another method of measuring the success of communication may be to prepare the reports on success of communication. These reports may be periodical and may be used by lower levels to report the various facts to the higher levels. The facts dealt in these reports may be the productivity; absenteeism, accidents etc. These reports may also be helpful in measuring success of communiation.

3. Study of the Reaction of Receivers. The other method of the measurement of the success of communication is to study the reaction of receivers of message; them it may be assumed that the communication has succeeded.

4. Surveys. The last method of measuring the success of communication is to hold survey about it. Under this method, a questionnaire consisting of different questions asked in different manners relating to the effectiveness of message of communication is sent to the receivers of message. They are requested to fill it up and to send it back. On the basis of answers of receivers of message, the effectiveness of communication is measured.

BARRIERS OF COMMUNICATION

The various inadequacies that can be identified through communication evaluation are required to be analysed in terms of various factors—obstructions and barriers—that impede flow of communication. There might be a number of such barriers impeding the flow of communication in the organisation. These may be classified as *(1)* external *(2)* organisational, and *(3)* personal factors. However, such as classification does not suggest that these are mutually exclusive. Rather, such a classification is helpful in understanding the nature of communication barriers.

I. EXTERNAL BARRIERS

Barriers to communication may be either external to the parties involved or they might be internal to them. External barriers may affect communication in any context, whether organisational or otherwise. Such external barriers may be in the following forms:

1. Semantic Barriers. There are obstructions caused in the process of receiving or understanding of the message during the process of encoding and decoding ideas and words. These barriers arise from the linguistic capacity of the parties involved. Words are the principal communication instrument but a common difficulty with the words is that each word has several meanings. For example, in English language, the word round has seventy five meanings. The Oxford Dictionary records an average of twenty-eight separate meanings for each of the 500 most-used words in the English language. Similar is the position in other languages. Thus, words sometimes fail to convey real meaning. Moreover, they work as barriers in communication in the following manner:

(i) ***Faulty Translations.*** Every manager receives various types of communications from superiors, peers, subordinates and he must translate information destined for subordinates, peers and superiors into language suitable to each. Hence the message has to be put into words appropriate to the framework in which the receiver operates, or it must be accompanied by an interpretation which will be understood by the receiver. This needs a high level of linguistic capacity. Approximate understanding of words and the consequent faulty translations lead to impaired efficiency and heavy costs.

(ii) ***Badly Expressed Message.*** Lack of clarity and precision in a message makes it badly expressed. Poorly chosen and empty words and phrase, careless omission, lack of coherence, bad organisation of ideas, awakward sentence structure, inadequate vocabulary, platitudes, numbering repetition jargon, failure to clarify implication are some common faults found in this case.

(iii) ***Specialist's Language.*** It is often found that technical personnel and special groups tend to develop a special, peculiar and technical language of their own. This increases their isolation from others and builds a communication barrier. Whatever be the intention of this special language, it hinders their communication with persons not in their speciality, because of the receiver's ignorance of that type of language.

(iv) ***Unclarified Assumptions.*** There are certain uncommunicated assumptions which underlie practically all messages. Though a message appears to be specific, its underlying assumptions may not be clear to the receiver.

2. Emotional or Psychological Barriers. Emotional or psychological factors are prime barriers in inter-personal communication. The meaning ascribed to a message depends upon the emotional or psychological status of both the parties involved. In a communication, apart from the message, there is a meta-message, that is, what one gets out of a message when decoding. Meta-message is the most pungent thing in a sweetword language. In getting a meta-message, the emotions of the receiver play a vital role and he may not be at a wavelength as that of the communicator. Keith Davis opines that these "exist in the people's minds or because of their actions, such as being hard to contract or difficult to understand. These barriers to communication are just as effective as an actual physical wall. Often these human barriers are more like filter paper than a brick wall. They let through some communications, but hold back others, thereby making communication inadequate... This 'half-way' communication gets "half way" results.

The following are some emotional barriers:

(i) ***Loss by Transmission and Poor Retention.*** When communication passes through various levels in the organisation, successive transmissions of the same message are decreasingly accurate. It is said that in case of oral communications about 30% of the information is lost in each transmission. Even in case of written communication, loss of meaning might occur as far as the appended interpretation, if any, is concerned. Poor retention of the information is again a malady. It is shown that employees retain about 50% of information only, whereas supervisors retain about 60% of it.

(ii) ***Inattention.*** The preoccupied mind of a receiver and the resultant non-listening is out of the major chronic psychological barriers. It is a common phenomenon that

people simply fail to react to bulletins, notices, minutes and reports.

(iii) ***Premature Evaluation.*** Rogers and Roethlisberger in 1952 first pointed out this barrier. Premature evaluation is the tendency of prematurely evaluating communications, rather than to keep an uncompromised position during the interchange. Such evaluation stops the transfer of information and budgets in the sender a sense of futility. This barrier can be reminded by "empathy", non-evaluative listening, where the communication is listened to in a non-committal and unprejudiced way, so that sagacious dicision and action can follow.

(iv) ***Undue Reliance on the Written Word.*** Written word is no substitute for sound face-to-face relationships and that employees cannot be persuaded to accept companies' viewpoint and policies through, "slick", easy to read, well-illustrated publications, unless there is a fair degree of mutual trust and confidence between the organisation and its employees. Further, a written communication might fail to explain the purpose of order, procedure or directive. Chester Barnard has laid down that a communication must appeal to the receiver as consonant with the organisation's purpose and with his own personal interest. Written communication often tells what is to be done, but not why it should be done, and it lacks the persuasive quality. Moreover, a written communication can be above the level of readership, and failure to ascertain the response to communication is also there.

(v) ***Distrust of Communicator.*** It arises out of ill-considered judgments or illogical decisions or frequent countermanding of the original communication by the communicator. Repeated experience of this kind gradually conditions the receiver to delay action or act unenthusiastically, hence making the communication unsuccessful, though apparently it is complete.

(vi) ***Failure to Communicate.*** It is quite an accepted fact that managers often fail to transmit the needed messages. This might be because of laziness on the part of the communicator, or assuming that "everybody knows," or procrastination or "hogging" information or deliberately to embarrass.

II. ORGANISATIONAL BARRIERS

An organisation being a deliberate creation for the attainment of certain specified objectives, day-to-day happenings within it require being regulated in such a manner that they contribute to attain these objectives in the most efficient manner. This is usually attempted through a variety of official measures such as designing the organisational arrangement for performance of various activities, prescribing of various policies, rules, regulations and procedures, laying down of norms of behaviour, instituting a reward-and-punishment system, etc. All the inner processes, including communication in different directions, are markedly affected by these prescriptions. As such major organisational barriers may be as follows:

(i) ***Organisational Rules and Regulations.*** Organisational rules and regulations affect the flow of communication by prescribing the subject-matter to be communicated and also the channel through which these are to be communicated. The rules may restrict the flow of certain messages and may leave many important ones. On the other hand, communication through proper channel in a specified way prescribed by these rules delays it and works against the willingness of persons to convey the message. This barrier is strongly operative in Indian public sector enterprises where observance of rules and regulations is more rigid.

(ii) ***Organisational Policy.*** The general organisational policy regarding communication acts as an overall guideline to every one in the organisation regarding how he is nromally expected to behave in this matter. The policy might be in

the form of explicit declaration in writing, or as is very commonly the case, it has to be interpreted from the behaviour of organisation members, particularly people at the top. If this policy is not supportive to the flow of communication in different directions, communication flow would not be smooth and adequate.

(iii) ***Status Relationships.*** The placing of people in superior-subordinate capacity in the formal organisation structure also blocks the flow of communication and more particularly in upward direction. Greater the difference between hierarchical positions in terms of their status, greater would be the possibility of communication breakdown.

(iv) ***Organisational Facilities.*** Organisational facilities provided for smooth, adequate, clear, and timely flow of communication may take a number of forms. Some of these have been mentioned earlier in the communication media such as meetings, conferences, complaint box, suggestion box, open door system, social and cultural gathering, etc. If these are not properly emphasised generally people fail to make effective communication.

(v) ***Complexity in Organisation Structure.*** In an organisation where there are a number of managerial levels, communication gets delayed, chances of communication getting distorted are more and the number of filtering points are more. This is more true in case of upward communication, because people generally do not like to pass up the adverse criticism either of themselves or of their superiors.

III. PERSONAL BARRIERS

While the organisational factors discussed above are, no doubt, important influences operating on communication, a host of actors internal to the two parties—sender and receiver—to this process also exert important influences on its operation, as communication is basically an inter-personal process. Here, for the sake of convenience in the analysis, these barriers have been analysed separately and these are relevant in the case of downward and upward communication.

Barriers of Superiors. The role of superiors in communication is very vital. Because of their hierarchial relationships with subordinates, they act as barriers in a number of ways which are discussed below:

(i) ***Fear of Challenge Authority.*** A person in the organisation always tries to get a higher position and prestige to satisfy his needs. As such, managers in general try to withhold the information coming down the line or going up as frequent passing of information may disclose their weakness.

(ii) ***Attitude of Superiors.*** The attitudes of superiors towards communication in general or in any particular direction affect the flow of messages in different directions. For example, if this attitude is unfavourable, there is a greater possibility that messages would not flow adequately from and/or to superiors.

(iii) ***Insistence on Proper Channel.*** One of the basic features of superiors' exercising of the authority is that they wish to remain in communication links and they do not like any type of by passing in communication. Communication through bypassing may, sometimes, be necessary but superiors treat this as thwarting of their authority and blocks the flow of communication.

(iv) ***Lack of Confidence in Subordinates.*** Superiors generally perceive, correct or otherwise, that their subordinates are less competent and capable, they are not able to advise superiors or they may not have some information coming downwards.

(v) ***Ignoring Communication.*** Sometimes superiors consciously and deliberately ignore the communication from their subordinates to maintain their importance. This works against the willingness of subordinates to communicate.

(vi) ***Lack of Awareness.*** Sometimes, superiors may lack the awareness about the significance and usefulness of communication in different directions in general or of particular subject-matter. In such a case, communication flow is blocked.

(vii) ***Lack of Time.*** Superiors feel, whether correct or otherwise, that they are overburdened with the work and they have little time to talk to their subordinates.

BARRIERS OF SUBORDINATES

Vertical communication in either direction can take place only when subordinates also actively participate in this process. There are various factors in the subordinates that adversely affect such active participation on their part. Some factors which have been traced in the case of superiors are also applicable here such as attitude, time availability, awareness about the significance, etc. Two factors are more important in the case of subordinates and these are responsible for blocking communication in upward direction.

(i) **Lack of Proper Incentive.** Lack of motivation to communicate also refrains subordinates to communicate upwards. The reward and punishment system of the organisation is more responsible for this. Thus, if a novel suggestion by a subordinate does not evoke any attention from the organisation, he would not convey it.

(ii) **Unwillingness to Communicate.** Sometimes, subordinates do not communicate upwards certain information because they are not willing to do so. Thus, if a subordinate feels that he is likely to be adversely affected by a particular piece of information to his superior, he would not be willing to supply it. Information going up is utilised for control purposes and subordinates would not be willing to give any information to their superiors about any unfavourable happening and if its application is necessary they would modify the information in such a way so as to protect their own interest.

OVERCOMING BARRIERS

To make commnication effective, managers must attempt to remove the barriers. Thought there are no prescribed techniques or ways of overcoming barriers. Following ways helps in overcoming barriers communication.

1. **Feedback.** One easy way of overcoming barriers to communication is to have a feedback. The manager immediately after communicating a message can ask to receiver 'did you follow what I said?' then the receiver's response is feedback. Feedback need not always be verbal. Actions speak, many a time, louder than word. For example, a lecturer when lecturing a lesson can watch the eyes of students for non-verbal cues' to see whether they are really understanding the lesson.
2. **Regulate the Flow of Information.** The principle of management by exception is advocated to alleviate the overload of managers so that they can concentrate on the messages of high priority. Another sound approach could be that incoming communication may be condensed or edited. Yet, another logical approach is to arrange the messages in order to merit, what and when the actions are to be taken. Such prioritizing reduces the likelihood that a critical communique will get overlooked or just ignored.
3. **Listen Carefully.** Communication problems arise because of poor listenting. Listening is different from hearing. Hearing is passive where as listening is active and intellectual process. Many of us are poor listeners. While listening, one should stop talking, should be patient, hold his temper, ask questions, remove distractions, should immensely concentrate on what speaker is saying. Good listening removes communication barriers.
4. **Simplifying Language.** Language is perhaps the biggest barrier to communication. Effective communication is achieved when a message is both received and understood.

As far as possible managers should try to avoid complicated jargon and use simple language that a subordinate understands. More essentially a manager should speak the subordinate's language.

5. **Watch Non-verbal Cues.** In the case of oral communication the sender should observe the actions of receiver and find whether they go along with the understanding. It is because many a time actions speak louder than words. A manager is therefore to watch non-verbal cues carefully. In organizations grapevine cannot be totally eliminated. A manager should make best use of grapevine. He should be careful when dealing with grapevine because it can carry damaging rumours that adversely affect the effectiveness of communication. It is better for the manager to make use of formal channels of communication to lessen this potentially destructive force.

6. **Constrained Emotions.** Many time emotions severely cloud and distort transference of meaning. When either the subordinate or the manager is mentally upset over an issue they are quite likely to misconstrue the message. The plausible solution is to defer from further communication until he has regained composure and coolness.

How to communicate effectively? This is the question being encountered by many managers, non-managers. The following are some of important points which one can adopt in improving the communication skills.

1. Listen attentively; find areas of common interest listen for main ideas.
2. Attend to behavioural cues as well as language or diction.
3. Plan ahead; be prepared; avoid important situations if possible; and keep the message brief.
4. Avoid steriotyping and the assignment of individuals or ideas to right categories.

5. Distiguish between the desire to know and the need to know.
6. Distiguish among facts, references, and conclusions.
7. Avoid attributing motives to others.
8. Say enough, but leave some things unsaid.
9. Don't shun all conflicts, but avoid the unnecessary conflicts.
10. Withhold value judgements about context or delivery, until strategically appropriate.

❐

10

Organisational Change and Development

Organisational change calls for a change in the individual behaviour of the employees. Organisations survive, grow, decline or die depending on the changing behaviour of the employees. Any organisational change whether introduced through a new structural design or new technology or new training programme basically attempts to make employees change their behaviour. It is because unless the behavioural patterns of the members change the change will have a little impact on the effectiveness of organizations. But behavioural changes are the most difficult and marathon exercises. They are not expected to be brought about overnight rather they devour more time. Lewin's model provides a useful vehicle for understanding change process in the organisation.

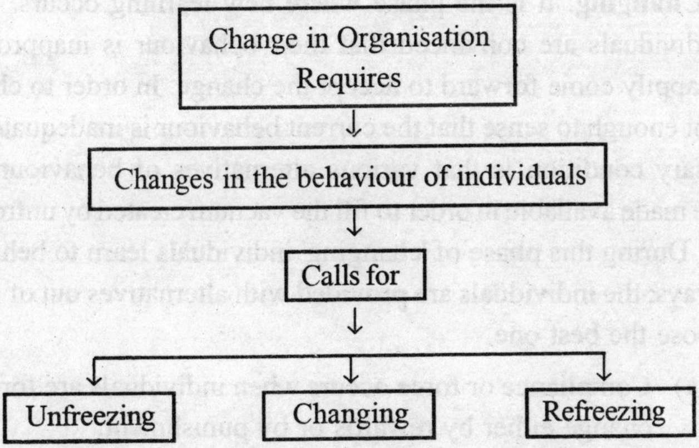

Unfreezing. It refers to making individual aware that the present behaviour is inappropriate, irrelevant, inadequate and hence unsuitables to the changing demands of the present situation. Edger Schien outlines the following elements which are vitally necessary during this unfreezing phase.

1. The physical removal of the individuals being changed from their accustomed routines, sources of information and social relationships.
2. The undermining and destruction of social support.
3. Demeaning and humiliating experience to help individuals being changed to see their old attitudes or behaviour as unworthy and think to be motivated to change.
4. The consistent liking of reward with willingness to change and of punishment with unwilligness to change.

Unfreezing is, thus, the breaking down of the existing mores, old taboos and traditions—the primitive way of doing things, so that the people are ready to accept new alternatives. It involves, discarding the orthodox and conventional methods and introducing a new dynamic behaviour that is most appropriate to the situation.

The essence of this unfreezing phase is that the individual is made to realize that his beliefs, feelings and behaviour are no longer appropriate or relevant to the current situation in the organization.

Changing. It is the phase where new learning occurs. When the individuals are convinced that their behaviour is inappropriate they happily come forward to accept the change. In order to change, it is not enough to sense that the current behaviour is inadequate. The necessary condition is that various alternatives of behaviour must also be made available in order to fill the vacuum created by unfreezing phase. During this phase of 'changing' individuals learn to behave in new ways; the individuals are provided with alternatives out of which to choose the best one.

(a) Compliance or force occurs when individuals are forced to change either by rewards or by punishment.

(b) Internalization occurs when individuals are forced to encounter a situation that calls for new behaviour.

(c) Identification occurs when individuals recognize one among various models provided in the environment that is most suitable to their personality.

Refreezing. During this phase individuals internalize the new beliefs, feelings and behaviour learned in the 'changing' phase. That is to say a person accepts the new behaviour as a permanent part of his behaviour repertoire. He has to practice and experiment with the new method of behaviour and see that it effectively blends with his other behavioural attitudes. It is very important for the manager concerned with the introducing change to visualize that the new behaviour is not extinguished soon.

STEPS INVOLVED IN ORGANISATIONAL CHANGE

Some changes are of such a nature that affects the whole organisation and has several consequential effects. For example, a promotion at higher level affects several hierarchical levels below. If the job of an individual is being changed, it will change his role set, also his self-concept which is in part a product of his culture, his reference groups and also his education and training. All these, he will bring in line with the formal task to display a cooperative behaviour. If the formal task role and the self-concept differ and cannot be in congruent there will be adaptive response either to leave the organisation or to make an attempt to change formal task role or to change the self-concept. In this way, any action has a chain reaction and causes a series of other changes, depending, naturally, upon the extent of its strength. Such changes that have a wide impact in the organisation, are organisational changes.

Any change in the organisation affects the people in terms of skills status social relationship or otherwise but organisational change is just like a major surgical operation. If if remains unsuccessful, it may endanger the very existence of the organisation, and if successful, it may give a new life to the organisation. Therefore, there is a need of careful planning. Allen lists the following steps in this regard:

(i) development of clear objectives;

(ii) analysis of existing organisation;

(iii) preparation of an ideal plan;

(iv) trying out the plan;

(v) preparation of phase plan;

(vi) establishment of uniform nomenclature; and

To be on a safe side, it should be undertaken only when it is felt necessary and only with the proper planning for that we must try to understand what we have and what we would like to have. Such organisational changes should not be very frequent and we should have a time prospective and project into the future.

In implementing organisational change, it affects people throughout the organisation, so there may be many upsets and set backs. Status system titles and appellations may seriously be disturbed and designations should be immediately awarded as soon as the change is complete. Some people may be given training to re-equip them for handling new jobs. As change often evokes resistance, step should be taken to overcome them.

INDIVIDUAL FACTORS FOR RESISTANCE TO CHANGE

There are many factors responsible to resistance to change at the individual level. Degree of force or resistance depends on how people feel about the change. This feeling may be based on actual factors or may be governed by emotional factors. Thus in actual operation, many factors generate resistance to change.

1. Problem of Adjustment. Perhaps most important factors for resistance to change is the problem of adjustment. Each individual tries to maintain a sort of equilibrium, both at formal level as well as at informal level. When change comes, it requires people to make adjustment so as to cope with the new situation. People seek *status quo* because once they establish equilibrium, they may not like that it is disturbed. *Status quo* gives them more satisfaction because the existing equilibrium has been arrived at by eliminating those forces which give people discomforts. When change is introduced, this equilibrium does not remain as satisfactory as it was before the change. The change may present various difficulties because people have to engage themselves gain in the process of forming a new equilibrium.

2. Economic Reasons. People resist change if they feel that it is likely to affect them unfavourably so far as their economic needs are concerned. The greater the amount of loss perceived, greater is the degree of resistance. People may perceive serveral types of economic losses because of change, major of them being as follows:

(i) Fear of technological unemployment;

(ii) Fear to reduced work hours and consequently reduced monetary benefits;

(iii) Fear of demotion and consequently reduced pay;

(iv) Fear of speed-up and reduced incentive wages; etc.

It can be seen that many of the above factors are quite real and not merely imaginary. For example, automation may replace many workers and they will be put out of employment if no alternative employement is provided by the organisation, or the organisation is not able to increase its volume of operation so as to absorb all workers. This is the reason why automation is resisted by workes, and they are guaranteed alternative jobs.

3. Obsolescence of Skills. Change may result into obsolescence of skills specially when altogether a new method of working is adopted. With the adoption of new method of working, old techniques become useless and consequently old skills become obsolete. Therefore, when people sense that new method of working poses a threat of replacing them or in some way affecting them adversely, they will resist it. It is not necessary that with the adoption of new method, people with old skills will be replaced, there may be other consequences also like reduction in authority of the position which they have been holding, attaching less importance to the jobs they have been performing, and so on. For example, with the introduction of computers, the jobs of accountants may be changed completely, and unless they adopt themselves to the new situation, their utility will be redcued and their job will become less important to the organisation. Thus either accountants change themselves which is not an easy task, or try to stall the move of putting computers. Thus fear of obsolescence of skills may be reason for resisting change.

4. Emotional Factors. There are many emotional factors which also generate resistance to change. As indicated earlier, people may not analyse the likely impact of change in an objective manner but they may be governed by their feeling emotions, attitudes, etc. thus many factors will produce resistance to change like fears of unknown, ego defensiveness, group norms and social displacement.

(i) ***Fear of Unknown.*** People fail to evaluate the impact of change because it is future-oriented. Therefore, some amount of uncertainty is always there. It is a tendency to discount future impact because of two reasons. First, people may derive benefits or otherwise in future while they have to pay the cost at the present. Naturally they will discount the future. The unknown poses a constant threat to people. Therefore, the fear of unknown makes people uncomfortable, and the impact of change, is unknown.

(ii) ***Ego Defensiveness.*** Sometimes people resists change because it is ego deflating. Ego defensive people always resist such a change. Every one has some ego which he tries to maintain. Ego is the state of a person's way of behaving, thinking and feeling. Any attack on these, actual or perceived by the person, will be resisted. For example, a force is unlikely to accept a change suggested by a worker because he may feel that his ego has been hurt.

(iii) ***Group Norms.*** People also resist change because the group to which they belong resists it. Though each person interprets change individuals, often he expresses it through the group. He follows the group norms. The degree and extent of group pressure on individual to resist the change will depend on two factors. First, how loyal an individual is towards the group. If he is loyal to the group, he will resist the change even though it may be beneficial to him. Second, how the group perceives it as a separate class than

change agent. Higher is the difference between two, higher will be the degree of resistance and its impact on individuals.

(iv) ***Social Displacement.*** Introduction of change often results into social displacement of people like breaking of informal groups and relationships. When the friendship with fellow-members is interrupted, there is a possibility for the employees to experience psychological let down. Therefore, they dislike new adjustment, breaking up of present social relationships, reduced social satisfaction, and feeling of outside interference in the form of change.

Many emotional problems relating to change are difficult to overcome because these are based on non-logical considerations rather than the rational considerations. People's perception of the likely impact of change is affected considerably by their personal factors and group factors to which they belong rather than technical aspect of change.

ORGANISATIONAL FACTORS FOR RESISTANCE TO CHANGE

Beside individuals, the organisation also may resist the change. Some of the organisations are so designed that they resist innovation and change. For example, organisations that perform a narrowly prescribed assortment of functions oppose change. They create strong defence against change. This is the reason why many organisations fail to change over the period of time, though this phenomenon may be disatrous to them. Major organisational factors for resistance to change are as follows:

1. **Threat to Power and Influence.** A change is likely to be incorporated successfully if it has the blessing and support of top management. When people, at the top level, consider change as a potential threat to their position and influence, they resist it. A change is likely to produce new power equilibrium with more emphasis on knowledge and new skills. This new equilibrium may reduce the amount of power and influence of people at the top which may not be liked by them. Therefore, they may resist any such change.

2. **Organisation Structure.** Some forms of organisation structures are more resistant to change, for example, bureaucratic structure. A bureaucratic structure where lines of communication are clearly spelled out, jobs are precisely defined, works against change. Since all these are prescribed rigidily, there is very little scope of making changes. Moreover, the flow of information from top to bottom level is stressed. Therefore, there is every possibility that any information initiating or necessitating change may be screened out at the higher level itself because change does not suit to the present organisation structure.
3. **Resource Constraints.** Many organisations resist change because of resources constraints. It is to be noted that all organisaions have limited resources because resources are limited by their basic nature. However, some organisations may feel resource constraints more than others. In such a case, the organisations may not like to incorporate change because it involves some additional cost at least in the beginning.
4. **Sunk Cost.** Organisations may also resist change because they have invested in fixed assets and other resources. These costs cannot be recovered unless the assets and resources are put to productive use. When change is incorporated, many of these resources become useless. This may be true for assets as well as for persons also. For example, earlier it has been seen that change may result into obsolescence of skills. However, an organisation will have to bear the costs because it can not dispense of these people. Similarly, assets can not be replaced because of change in technology.

OVERCOMING RESISTANCE TO CHANGE

The basic problem in managing and introducing change sucessfully is to overcome resistance to change, whether rational or otherwise. Unless resistance to change is eliminated properly, the change may not be as beneficial to the organisation as intended. On the contrary, change may become dysfunctional if it has been forced without properly handling the problem of change. Thus the use of formal authority in bringing change in the organisation may not be desirable in most of the cases. But management should adopt techniques and actions through which people accept change willingly rather than forced to accept change. In order to overcome resistance to change, efforts can be made at the level of individual as well as at the level of group. Though efforts at both these levels may be complementary and sometimes even overlapping, people react differently at individual level and a group level. Therefore, efforts are required at both these levels.

EFFORTS AT INDIVIDUAL LEVEL

A Change may affect some people in one way, others in another way, while some others may not be affected at all. Therefore, resistance may come from people as individuals and not as group, and efforts can be made to overcome resistance at individual level. For example, creation of a new unit or merger of two units into one because of change in organisation structure may affect some people favourably, others unfavourably while large majority may not be affected at all. In such a case, resistance may be at the individual level. In situations where individual resistance takes the form of group resistance, it can be tackled at the level of individual because he is the starting point. Following efforts are useful to deal with resistance to change at individual level:

1. Education and Communication. One of the most easy techniques to overcome resistance to change is to educate people, train them to adopt change, counsel them, and communicate them the various aspects of change. Management can change the basic values and attitudes of people by training and psychological counselling. People can be educated to become familiar with change, its process, and working. They must be taught new skills, helped to develop new relationships and attitudes. Since this is a long process, it can be successful if it is taken on countinuous basis. Similarly role of communication in overcoming change is very important. Often many types of resistance come because of misunderstanding. For example,

Pestonjee has observed that resistance to change is likely to take place when *(i)* change is not made clear to the individual who is going to be influenced by the change; *(ii)* different people see different meanings in change and strong forces deterring them from making the change; *(iii)* change is made on personal ground rather than impersonal requirements or sanctions; and *(iv)* change ignores the already established institutions in the group. Thus it can be seen that resistance to change can be overcome through proper communication. In this context, managers can obtain better result when they explain the people about *(i)* what the change is, *(ii)* when it is to be introduced, *(iii)* how it will be implemented, (iv) why the change is needed, *(v)* what is the objective of the change, and *(vi)* how the change will be beneficial to all. This will help people to visualise the need and logic of change; they will appreciate it in much better way and will accept it easily.

2. Participation and Involvement. Participation and involvement can be used in overcoming resistance to change either on regular basis or for a particular change programme. Here the basic strategy of the change agent is to involve resistors in some aspect of design and implementation of change so that they do not block the change. Participation and involvement are the processes to bring people who are likely to resist the change to understand it through continuous dialogue. This is not one-time action but it should be continuous over the period of time. It implies explanation and then discussion of the proposed change. It includes finding out from the people how they interpret the change and what they think about it. The fundamental idea in this process is to encourage the people to say what they feel about the various aspects of the changes. As this process goes, the level of resistance to change tends to decrease, understanding of change increases and personal involvement in the change increases.

3. Commitment. Commitment is a step further to participation and involvement. It is an agreement between change agent and change resistors to take active part in the actual mechanics of the change. If there is strong resistance by few members of the organisation, commitment to take part in the change programme can be obtained in private from each member. Later on, it can be obtained in public so that members may feel committed to the programme, and at no level, they will sabotage it. Commitment to chaneg is a dynamic process meaning thereby that it changes over the period of time depending on the factors.

4. Leadership. Leadership is a process of getting consent of people and support willingly. Since a manager can not always use his formal authority to get support for the change, he should rely on his personal skills and qualities to impress people for the change. He can create a climate where people not only accept change but they are willing to propose changes. A manager with strong leadership qualities can use personal reasons for change without arousing any resistance.

MANAGEMENT OF CHANGE

Management of organisational change is a complex process. Organisations change does not occur instantaneously. Instead, it involves formidable exercises on the part of management. It requires considerable planning. Since there may be many negative aspects of change, it should be undertaken in planned way. Therefore, organisational change is referred to as planned change. Process of planned change can be broken down into sub-processes. A model of this process is described in Fig. and consists of six sub-processes linked in a logical sequence. A manager can consider each of them, either implicitly or explicity, to undertake a change programme. However, the prospects for initiating change are enhanced when the manager explicitly goes through each successive step.

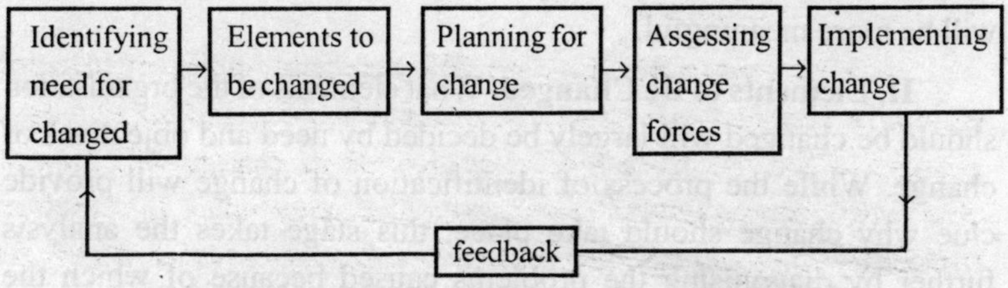

Model for Management of Planned Change.

I. Identifying Need for Change. The first basic step in planned change is to identify when change in the organisation is required because change for the sake of change may produce much stronger resistance while useful and necessary changes may get support form people. Though there are various external forces necessiting change in an organisation, it is better if the organisation analyses how change in external forces affect it. If a change in external forces does not affect the organisation, there is no need for change. Thus the most information for identifying need for change comes from the organisation's feedback and control data. Indeed, the process of change can be viewed as a part of control function, specially the corrective-action requirement. Some of the features of the organisation may indicate the need for change like cost of production, declining profit, employee turnover, role conflict, need for expansion and growth, etc. Such indicators may force management to analyse what actions can be undertaken to overcome these.

Identification of need for change depends on gap analysis, that is, the gap between desired state of affairs and actual state of affairs; the difference between what the organisation is achieving and what it should achieve. However, this gap analysis should be seen on progressive basis because desired state of affairs is not a fixed concept. The organisation may go on changing its objectives over the period of time. Moreover, gap analysis can be made on the basis of likely gap because any change in any factor affects the operation of the organisation. For example, if there is entry of new competitor in the market, this may not affect the organisation immediately but may affect at a later stage. Thus gap may exist subsequently. Here the past records of the organisation may not be sufficient but projected data will be more meaningful.

II. Elements to Be Changed. What elements of the organisation should be changed will largely be decided by need and objectives of change. While the process of identification of change will provide clue why change should take place, this stage takes the analysis further by diagonising the problems caused because of which the change is necessary. For example, declining profit may require change but does not specify what are to be changed. Therefore, it is necessary to diagnose the factors which are responsible for declining profit. Usually change is required in three major elements of the organisation: organisation structure, technology, and people. The nature and extent of change in these elements will depend on the type of problem being faced by the organisation. Structural changes may include job design, job definitions, basis of departmentation, span of control, organisational policies and procedure, coordination mechansim, power structure, flow of tasks, etc. Technological changes include changes in plan and equipment, techniques for doing work, production methods, engineering processes, etc. When technology changes, the organisation has to change in some form or the other. Changes in people include changes in their behaviour, interaction pattern, informal grouping, skills, attitudes, etc. Some changes may affect the organisation on all these dimensions while others may affect only limited aspect. For example, a change in technology from manhandling to automation may require change in people but at the same time change in organisation structure also.

III. Planning for Change. At this stage, managers should plan about how the change can be brought in the light of the above two sub-processes. Planning for change includes who will bring the change, when to bring change, and how to bring change. The first question who will bring change relates to the persons who will work as change agent. Though every manager is change agent as he brings occasional changes in his area of operation, major changes require that some persons are specified for the purpose. The second question when to bring change is related with time dimension of change. While deciding time element of change, many factors have to be considered, such as nature of forces which are likely to resist the change and the time taken to bring them to accept change, time taken in training and development of people to make them more suitable for the change situation, time required to make resources available for the change, etc. How to bring change requires drawing up of procedure, that is, chronological ordering of various events of the change. Normally, change expanding over a period of long time requires continuous process of putting change effort at one aspect, measuring its impact and correcting dysfunctional aspects resulting from change, putting change in another aspect, etc. This process goes on over the period of them.

IV. Assessing Change Forces. Before executing the plan for change, it is necessary to assess forces which affect change in either way. The planned change is not automatic, rather there are many forces in individuals, groups, or even organisation which may either accept the change or resist it, though in most of the cases, there may be resistance. Therefore, unless the major forces resisting change agree to change, it may not be possible for the management to implement the change successfully.

Various forces affecting the change work on the principle of 'force field'. a concept given by Kurt Lewin. In a group process, there are some forces favouring to maintian an equilibrium while some may oppose the equilibrium at a particular point. Equilibrium is reached when the sum of the driving forces equals the some of restraining force as shown in Fig.

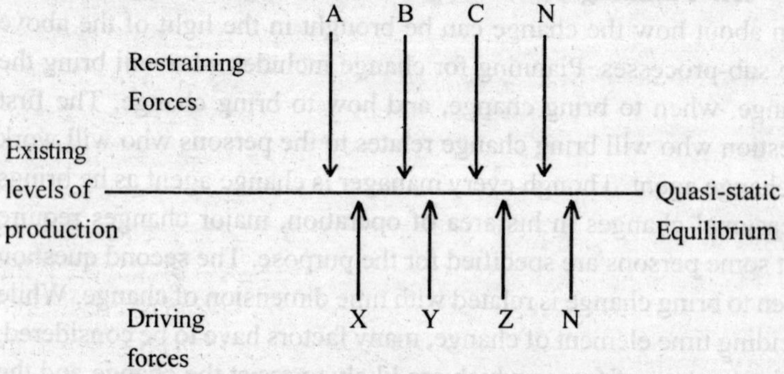

Lewin's Force Field

The above figure shows that existing level of activities, which is a quasi-static equilibrium is reached when restraining forces and driving forces are equal. This equilibrium is quasi-static because it may continue for some time, and if there is any change, new equilibrium is achieved. Thus when any change is introduced, the balance of driving and restraining forces changes making forces to behave differently depending on the nature of the change. There may be three types of situations when both driving and restraining forces are operating. Management can take one of the following actions:

(i) If the driving forces far outweigh the restraining forces, management can push driving forces and overpower restraining and change can be implemented.

(ii) If the driving forces and the restraining forces are equal, management can push up the driving forces and at the same time, can covert or immobilise the restraining forces to implement the change.

(iii) If the restraining forces are stronger than the driving forces, management can drop the change programme if it is not possible to change these forces. In alternative case, it can attempt to change these forces by postponing the change programme to be undertaken at more opportunate time.

V. Implementation of Change. If the driving forces are stronger than the restraining forces or these can be converted favrouably, management can implement the change programme. The implementation of change programme requires the application of various technqiues and interventions suitable for the change programme. For example, a change programme may require change in people which can be brought through appropriate training. Similarly, many organisation development interventions can also be used to get effective result. Changes in various aspects of the organisation, as necessary can be introduced.

VI. Feedback and Follow-up Actions. Management of change requires feedback and follow-up actions to ensure that change programme is progressing in right direction without producing any dysfunctional effect. Since a change programme is likely to solve problems and produce other problems, though of minor magnitude, it is desirable that management has constant watch as the change programme progresses. Problems created by the change should be tackled imediately so that it gives better results to the organisation.

Feedback received from the initial attempt of change programme may be used to modify the subsequent programme. Normally the impact of the change programme is measured in terms of its objectives. Therefore, objectives of the change should be defined operationally so that measurement is easier.

REASONS FOR ORGANISATIONAL CHANGE

Change is a natural process in human life, and since people constitute an organisation, it can not remain isolated from the effort of changes. Normally, in any organisation, change is required because of pressure of two kinds of forces: external and internal. An ogranisation which is capable of integrating both these forces is better equipped to achieve its objectives. However, this intergration itself is a dynamic process. Integration achieved at a particular point of time becomes irrelevant when there is any change in external and internal forces. Thus a new level of integration is required. Let us see how various external and internal forces put pressure on an ogranisation to change:

1. External Forces. Every organisation exists in some context, that is external environment, on simply referred to as environment; no organisation is an island in itself. There are various constituents of environment. These constituents are governments, customers, suppliers, creditors, shareholders, and society as a whole. Changes occur in these forces, and in turn, they put pressure on the organisation to change. For example, if because of some reasons, government increases the excise duty on the product being produced by the organisation, it is forced to incorporate it in its production cost and ultimately resulting into either increase in its price or to sustain loss. This is a very simple example to change. Normally, changes are more complex because these are affected by so many forces in the environment. Thus changes in social, political, economic, technological, and legal environment force the organisation to incorporate changes. Such changes may be in one or more areas of major functions, production processes, product to the produced, labour-management relations, organisation structure and processes, etc.

2. Internal Forces. Besides external forces, changes may be required because of internal forces also. Though there may be many sources and reason why a change is required because of internal forces, three factors are more common: deficiency in the present organisation, change in personnel and avoidance of inertia development.

(i) ***Deficiency in the Present Organisation.*** Changes are necessary when the present organisation—structure, processes, and systems—is not capable of achieving organisational objectives. Many dysfunctional behaviours occur because of deficiency in the organisation. In order to control those behaviour, some sort of changes have to be brought. Such changes would be directed mostly to overcome deficiency of the present organisation.

(ii) ***Changes in Managerial Personnel.*** Changes in managerial personnel occur because of their retirement, removal, transfer, or even promotion. When new personnel come at the place of old ones, they do not simply replace the old but they bring new ideas, thinking and values not necessarily shared by old managers. Moreover, changes take place in informal relationships also. The result is that the organisation has to bring necessary changes to accommodate all these.

(iii) ***Avoidance of Inertia Development.*** It is a better strategy to bring changes in the organisation to avoid inertia development. When people work constantly in a rigid environment, they become resistant to change. When the organisation wants to bring change, it faces lot of problems. Therefore, many organisations take up the work of personnel development, a kind of change in personnel, on regular basis. This helps to get better equipped personnel but at the same time, it ensures that the organisation remains dynamic and any change can be brought easily.

Because of these factors, several types of changes are possible in the organisation. These can be grouped into two: those relating to work and those relating to organisation. Changes in work may be in the form of change in technology, change in work process, enlargement of work volume, etc. Changes in organisation may be in the form of changes in organisational structure, organisational process, organisational systems, organisational objectives and policies, managerial personnel, etc.

OBJECTIVES OF PLANNED CHANGE

The planned change is needed to meet the overall objectives of the organisation. Since, there may be changes in the forces—both internal and external—affecting organisational functioning, the organisation has to make suitable change to meet its objectives. Thus, objectives for such change may be twofold: *(i)* modification of the organisation's mode of adaptation to changes, values, and other behavioural construct of poeple in the organisation.

1. Individual Adapation. The first objectives of planned change is to achieve individual adaptation. The organisation cannot reach to the objective of its environment adaptation unless some basic internal adaptation is achieved. These internal factors may be individual, organisation structure, technology and task. Individuals are the first in this context. For organisation effectiveness, people have to change themselves so that they can cope with the requirement of changed circumstances. Such changes may be required in their attitudes, communication system, way of behaving, leadership and work styles, and other relevant organisational behaviour. Such changes must be made according to the need for the new situation.

2. Environmental Adaptation. Organisation is basically adaptive-coping system. It has to work in environment which is marked by dynamic characteristics. Every organisation has a tendency to maintain balance and equilibirum. Because of changes in the environment, the organisational equilibirum is affected. If the changes are minor and come within the purview of existing programmes, the organisation will accommodate them automatically. However, if the change cannot be adapted to the existing framework, the organisational equilibrium will be imbalanced and organisational effectiveness is adversely affected. In this case, the organisation requires some innovation. This innovation is in the form of various changes which the organisation has to incorporate.

3. Structural Adaptation. Organisation structure is the pattern of relationship among various position holders. Structural adaptation involves changing the internal structure of the organisation. This change may be in the whole set of relationships, work assignment, and authority structure. Change in organisation structure is required because old relationship and interactions no longer remain valid and useful in the changed circumstances.

4. Task Adaptation. Technological changes may bring many types of changes in organisational task. Task focuses on the job performed by the individuals in the organisation. Since there may be many new types of jobs, the existing job techniques may not be suitable. Moreover, there may be new job load because of job enlargement. In such a case, a new equilibrium has to be found out which matches people with jobs. In this matching process, there may be several problems which must be encountered by planned change.

5. Technology Adaptation. The impact of recent technological development has forced the organisation to take into account the role of technology in oganisational success. In order to cope with the changed environment which may include technological factor as well, the organisation has to incorporate new technology. Thus, this technological adaptation forces directly the organisation to change its task.

It can be observed that a change will bring disequilibrium in the organisation. In order to achieve new equilibrium, the organisation has to modify many aspects of the organisation. All these aspects are inter-related. This is what the systems approach of organisation theory suggests. Thus a systems approach to organisation change has to be followed. For example, if an organisation is not able to face competition in the market because of its old technique of production is to change itself according to the needs of the hour. In this process, the organisation will acquire suitable technology. When this technology is put into operation, it may change the job content completely; old jobs being replaced by new jobs. This change requires change in people because they may not be able to work with new machine. Such change may be brought either by recruiting new employees or training them for new jobs. The second alternative may be preferable because there may be environmental constraints on replacing old employees. Since, the job structure is changed, the internal relationships may not be suitable. Thus, all these factors are inter-related and simultaneous changes have to be made in all these aspects. This is the basic objectives of planned change in the organisation. Such interaction may be presented as follows:

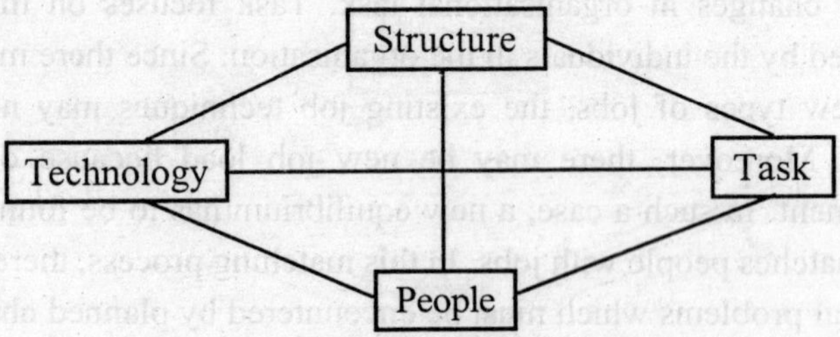

Factors in Organisational Change

ORGANISATIONAL DEVELOPMENT

Organisational development is a discipline directed towards using behavioural science knowledge to assist organisations adjust more rapidly to change. There are two important factors which have caused the use of organisational development as a technique of planned change. First, training for change does not work properly only through reward structure on the job unless there is a proper change in the environment of the organisation in which people work. Second, in a dynamic environment, the change is extremely rapid. Organisational development helps a lot to free up communication tightness by increasing the amount, trust and candour of communication. It seeks to build problem-solving capability of communiaction by improving group dynamics and problem of confrontation. The important objectives of organisational development are:

1. To increase the level of trust and mutual emotional support among all organisational members.
2. To increase the incidence of confrontation of organizational problems both within groups and among groups in contrast to 'sweeping problems under the rug'.
3. To create an environment in which authority of assigned role is augmented by authority based on knowledge and skill.
4. To increase the level of enthusiasm and personal satisfaction in the organization.
5. To find synergistic solutions to problems with greater frequency.
6. To increase the openness of communications, laterally, vertically.
7. To increase the level of self and group responsibility in planning and implementation.

OD change efforts place a premium on humanistic values and goals consistent with these values. In fact OD is a way of looking at the whole human side of organizational life. The emphasis of OD on human dimensions of organisation is reflected in the following cardinal list of humanistic values:

1. Providing opportunities for people to function as human beings rather than as resources in the production process.
2. Providing opportunities for each organization member, as well as for the organization itself, to develop to his full potential.
3. Seeking to increase the effectiveness of the organization in terms of all of its goals.
4. Providing opportunities for people in organizations to influence the way in which they relate to work, the organization, and the environment.

5. Attempting to create an environment in which it is possible to find exciting and challenging work.

6. Treating each human being as a person with a complex set of needs, all of which are important in his work and in his life.

Thus, OD develops a view of people in organization that is radically different from the traditional approaches about organizations. Tannenbaum and Davis have identified a new set of values, though not completely accepted, that OD tries to bring about ultimately. Organisational development is based on certain assumptions:

(i) Highest productivity can be achieved when the individual goals are integrated with organisational goals.

(ii) Growth of individuals is facilitated by relationships which are open, supportive and trusting.

(iii) Cooperation is more effective than conflict. In healthy organisation efforts are made at all levels to treat conflict as a problem subject to problem solving methods.

(iv) The work habits are a response to work environment rather than personality traits. Efforts to change work habits should be directed towards changing how the person is treated than towards attempting to change the person.

(v) Free expression of feeling is an important ingredient for commitment to work.

TECHNIQUES OF ORGANISATIONAL DEVELOPMENT

Intervening in the system refers to all the planned programme activities during the course of an organisational development programme. Organisational development interventions are set of structured activities in which selected groups are engaged with a task. It constitutes the action thrust of organisation development, team development, laboratory training, managerial grid and intergroup team building. The intervention should take place at all three levels, namely, individual, group and organisation.

Here we can classify the organisational development into three categories:

(1) Behavioural Techniques. These techniques include:

(a) Sensitivity training

(b) Role playing

(c) Management by objectives

(d) Grid organisational development

(2) Non-behavioural Techniques. These include:

(a) Change in organisation structure

(b) Work design

(c) Job enrichment

(3) Miscelloneous Techniques. These include:

(a) Survey feed-back

(b) Process consultation

(c) Team building

SENSITIVITY OR T-GROUP TRAINING

One of the popular techniques in OD is sensitivity training. It is a method of changing behaviour through unstructured group interaction. Sensitivity training is sought to help individuals toward better relations with others. The primary focus is on reducing interpersonal friction.

In sensitivity training the actual technique employed is T-group (T stands for training). It is a small group of ten to twelve people assisted by a professional behavioural scientist who acts as a catalyst and trainee for the group. There is no specified agenda. He merely creates the opportunity for group members to express their ideas and feelings freely. Since the trainer has no leadership role to play, the group must work but its own methods of proceeding. A leaderless and agendum free group session is on. They can discuss anything they like. Individuals are allowed to focus on behaviour rather than on duties.

Essential Elements of Sensitivity Training

The following are certain essential elements of sensitivity training:

(i) The primary objective to sensitivity training is to break through the barrier of intellectualization and verbalization to facilitate the participants experiencing his own behaviour and effect. It says "open your eyes. Look at yourself. See how you look to others".

(ii) An attempt should also be made to develop a very permissive atmosphere so that members may feel themselves free to discuss even if they feel that comments are impolite, selfish and ridiculous.

(iii) It is on experienced based methodology aimed at changing behaviour through unstructured group interaction.

(iv) There should be some frustration so that deep examination of self may be possible, so criticism of one another results in frustration.

(v) Sensitivity training emphasize the process rather than the content of the training and focuses upon emotional rather than conceptual training.

(vi) It is necessary that the group should be small so that participation may be effective.

After having a research on T-group there reveals some positive and negative aspects. On positive side it is found that:

1. Communications are improved a lot and the leadership skills have been reported well.
2. It promotes an opportunity to gain insights into personal blind spots, and people become aware of the norms of the group, role flexibility and a sense of belonging to the group.
3. Participants are reported to have become more open and self understanding.
4. Sensitivity training can apparently result in more supportive behaviour, more considerate managers and more sensitive people.

Problems in Sensitivity Training

In sensitivity training some problems may be faced by the members of the group. Such as:

(i) A member of the group may be irritated because his ideas are regularly ignored by the group. It may be because of his defensive nature and lack of initiative.

(ii) Someone's superior attitude is uncovered as being defensiveness about his weaknesses.

(iii) Another member who takes initiative may become authoritarian and fails because he faces group resentment.

With a view to overcome the problems, the trainer tries to keep himself detached, keeps some stability and creates learning situations and off and on introduces ideas.

Criticism of Sensitivity Training

It is a very controversial laboratory training method because it is a frustrating and challenging type of training that has developed from the specialists in group dynamics and non-directive counselling. The criticisms are generally made on the following grounds:

* Another major limitation with T-group training is that it may result in psychological damage to some employees who do not take well to criticism. T-group experience can be a continuing source of frustration and anxiety. The anxiety and pressure the participants undergo can have an adverse effect on their mental health. House contends people become unsettled and uncomfortable about their opinion and comments made on them by others. The adverse effects will be much more on unprepared or insecure participants. Many participants reports that they are tense, angry, frustrated and disenchanted. In fact, individuals vary in their capacity to face themselves. And therefore some participants call the T-group a blood bath and a psychological nudist colony in which people are stripped bare to their attitudes. An other reason for psychological damage is that some people feel humiliated if

their behaviour is criticised and they might react in such a fashion that the whole session becomes frustrating and upsetting.

* T-group training lays heavy concentration on individuals alone. Its utility to the total organization is limited. Since T-group training is essentially concerned with the 'here and now of the group' its relevance to actual organizational problems is a matter of debate. T-groups have been criticised on the basis of being 'too effective' in the sense that they have a tremendous influence on those involved in them. After having subjected to the training the participants usually become more sensitive to others.
* Sensitivity training raises the question of invasion of privacy if employee is required to attend and express his emotions unwillingly. Here is a line between voluntary choice and coercive pressure. And if the training is meant for promoting the employees to a special status in an organisation, the people who lack it are naturally be passed by other persons who are properly underwent training then, they are being coerced to submit to what they perceive is an invasion of privacy.
* Under sensitivity training, trainers sometimes act as manipulative social engineers. They impose autocratically democratic value on stripped bare groups and try to indoctrinate them with the dogmatism of group action. Trainees point to the implicit assumption of consumers that is often imposed and not agreed upon. In a group where members understand each other but they may still disagree, is implicity considered a failure. But still they agree to support the group process inspite of the fact that they really disagree.

Despite all these limitations it is still widely used because:

1. Some trainers boldly reject medical definition of psychological injury rather, they view psychological de-

compensation as vital step in the process of personal growth. This leads to the advocacy of 'psychotic experience as a desideratum of personal growth'.

2. The advantages of training outweigh their drawbacks.
3. Group members disband after the training and in the absence of a systematic follow up of the participant members, casualties are unlikely to come to the surface.
4. When highly trained people are used as trainees T-group training will not have many limitations. The failure of T-group training may be due to personal limitations of the participating members. For instance, Argyris contends that "out of as many as 10,000 cases there had been only four individuals who had psychotic episodes and who became seriously ill, and all these people had previous psychiatric histories.

Some necessary conditions are needed for the success of T-group training.

(i) Careful selection of the T-group leader.

(ii) Careful selction of participants so that the members do not have the symptoms of emotional instability.

(iii) Careful study of performance requirements.

(iv) Continued research to determine the participants' characteristics and conditions required for using T-group training.

(v) Provision of reserve precautionary procedures to be instituted in the event of the failure programme. These precautions may include alternative methods for coping with the desired changes and the provisions for safety and well being of the participating members.

TEAM BUILDING CYCLE

Team building is an attempt to assist the work group in learning how to identify, diagnose and solve its own problems. Team building programme deals with new problems on an on-going basis. It is an effective technique by which members of an organisation group diagnose how they work together and plan changes that will improve their effectiveness.

Team building attempts to improve effectiveness of work groups by allowing the group members to concentrate on:

(i) Setting goals or priorities for organizational groups.

(ii) Analysing or allocating the way the work is performed.

(iii) Examining the way the group is working.

(iv) Examining the relationships among the people doing the work.

Thus the fundamental aim of team buildings is to help the group members in examining their own behaviours and developing action plans that foster task accomplishment.

Necessary Conditions for the Success of Team Building Programme

Before attempting to undertake the team building exercise the management has to ensure that:

(i) Basic interdependence among the members of the group exist (when task interdependencies do not exist, then team building is an inappropriate intervention).

(ii) The group members understand the stated goals clearly.

(iii) The group members unanimously agree with the objectives.

(iv) The group is capable of taking corrective action on the problems identified or at least will be able to tackle some reasonable percentage of them.

SURVEY FEEDBACK

As its title suggests, the method used by the consultant is to survey the situation and feedback it to the group. The feedback information is then discussed and worked on by the team members. Who gradually learn to take over from the consultant the process of surveying what they are doing and feeding it back to themselves as an essential aid to their long term development as a team.

Organisational development interventions survey feedback has much appeal and application. The intervention, which enjoys a widespread use now a days, include a package of four steps:

(i) Develop an Action Plan. Survey feedback programme will be rendered incomplete and meaningless if it does not contain the provision of developing an action plan to deal with the problems. The management should develop an action plan that is both straightforward and workable. In this stage, participants are asked about their recommendations, about how to resolve the problems that are uncovered in the survey.

(ii) Follow-up. Without continuous feedback and correction of the programme this intervention (for that matter any intervention) will be short-lived. It will be at the most an interesting experience. Normally, several months after the survey is conducted a check should be made to determine whether the actions plans are implemented or not.

(iii) Feedback of the Information. Reporting the information and the key findings to employees is another crucial step in survey feedback. The survey feedback results are fed directly to the participants rather than to the top management. The information that is fed must be clear and accurate. Further, survey-generated results must be presented in a non- threatening and constructive manner to the employees. Usually, the data are fed back in group-discussion and problem-solving sessions and the OD expert conducting the survey feedback programme summarizes the findings in a clear-cut manner and elicits employees reactions to them. But in the recent years, emphasis was placed upon sending written summaries of the results of the participants. This way this approach is devoid of emotional involvement of organizational members, making it more productive as OD technique.

(iv) Collection of Data. All the information are gathered through comprehensive questionnaire. The self-report questionnaire can be tailored to specific organization and designed to answer highly specific questions, or it can consist of standard pattern that is useful in many organizational settings. The items contained in the questionnaire focus on such key organizational issues as employee satisfaction quality and styles of leadership and various facets of organizational climate like decision-making and coordination.

Necessary Conditions for the Success of the Survey Feedback Approach

For survey feedback to be successful management should ensure that:

(i) The questionnaire it employs must be valid and reliable.

(ii) Employees must be willing to report their views and reactions honestly.

(iii) The OD consultant conducting the programme must be skilled at interpreting the survey data.

(iv) Top management must be willing to use the information it gathers.

(v) Organizational members trust each other (It is because distrust leads to response bias).

(vi) Participants do not feel deceived, manipulated or misrepresented.

(vii) The sessions are conducted in a factual, task-oriented environment.

(viii) Each group has enough discretion to consider and act upon its findings and analysis.

GRID TRAINING

One of the most publicized techniques of OD is the Grid organisation development. Grid training is based on the Managerial Grid developed by Robert Blake and Jane S. Mouton: It is a comprehensive step-by-step approach and represents a breakthrough in organization development. Whereas sensitivity training is used as a tool for OD, Grid training approach offers a complete plan for OD.

Grid identifies a range of management behaviours based on various ways in which task-oriented and people-oriented styles can interact with each other. Instead of decolonizing the two dimensions of leadership - concern for production and concern for people, Blake and Mouton contend that managers should be concerned with both people and production oriented in order to achieve effective performance results.

The specific objectives of a grid organization development programme are to:

(i) study the organization as an interacting system and apply techniques of analysis in diagnosing its problems;

(ii) evaluate the styles of leadership and techniques of participation most likely to produce high-quality results.

(iii) understand the importance and rationale of systematic change in contrast to change by evolution and revolution;

ROLE PLAYING

Role playing may be described as a technique of creating a life situation, usually are involving conflict between people and then having persons in a group play the parts or roles of specific personalities. In industry, it is used primarily as a technique for modifying attitudes and interpersonal skills. It is spontaneous acting of a realistic situation under classroom conditions. The trainees play their roles more or less on the principles already taught to them. Other trainees of the group are observers and critics. The purpose of role playing is to aid trainees to understand certain business problems and to enable observers to evaluate reaction to them. Role playing is generally used for human relations and sales training.

Role playing brings the following merits:

(i) Persons may observe as many different approaches to a problem in a few hours under role playing method as they would in years of normal experience, because different persons play different roles in a different way resulting in different solutions of one problem. Thus they come to know the merits and demerits of each approach taken by each person or group.

(ii) At times, trainees play the roles without having any knowledge of approaches to solve the problem. It attempts to understand the behaviour of persons in different situation because they try to solve the problem according to their skill.

(iii) They can develop imagination by observing others' roles and with a certain amount of imagination, they can project themselves into roles other than their own. It is just like a dramatic part.

(iv) Daily role playing adds to the experience of the persons. They become experienced in the art of role playing.

(v) It broadens the experience of the person by trying different approaches in realistic situations while in actual situations only one approach is available. He can now apply the best suited approach to the problem in actual situations out of those experienced by him under role playing method.

Alongwith these merits, role playing has certain weaknesses, which partly offset its utility:

(a) Some trainees may place more emphasis on show off and acting than on the problem involved.

(b) Some individuals become too involved in acting and loose sight of the purpose of the exercise.

(c) It is time consuming and expensive because it requires experienced instructor without him effective directions can not take place.

GAMING

The gaming is the another laboratory method of organisation development. Gaming is a group exercise in sequential decisions making under simulated organisational conditions. Trainees are divided in small groups and these groups are in competition with each other. Groups make decisions within a system model provided to them beforehand and it is partly known to them. Decisions, then are processed through computers according to the model, which serve as a feedback to subsequent decisions. Usually but not always, less time is provided to cover large span of time, *i.e.*, a quarter year for marketing may be covered in an hour.

Games and simulations excercises were originally developed for business and military training such as in areas of inventory control, maketing action and air defence and, were, later used for development organisation behaviour because participants were working in teams in various types of environments. Under these conditions, game shows how the leadership is evolved, what kinds of communication are effective, the disastrous market results of internal group conflict, human factors influencing decisions and the effect of success upon group cohesion.

Advantages. The method shows the following plus points:

(i) As because time is short, the people gain much experience with different practices in a short time.

(ii) The learning process can be cut short through feedback and discussion with the instructor or trainer when the decision is taken by each group.

(iii) This system of training is most suitable for administrative problems and it has a better balance in rational and emotional issues.

Disadvantages. The method claims the following disadvantages:

(i) Games tend to stress on participants because participants have pressure of less time and of competition. Members become so involved that they let their guard down react to stress in their normal pattern.

(ii) It may be possible that there is such deep involvement that the participants take it for real and is not receptive to feedback.

ORGANISATIONAL DEVELOPMENT

Organisational development is a strategy which is planned and implemented from top with a view to bring about planned organisational change for the purpose of increasing organisational effectiveness. It is basically a long-range programme, not a oneshot deal, attempting to change the behavioural attitudes and performance of the total organisation. It is not a one-time training and development programme but is on going and cycling process. It is a complex educational strategy which aims to bring about a better fit between the human beings who work in and expect things from organizations and the busy, unrelenting environment with its insistence on adapting to changing times.

According to Keith Devis. "Organisational development is an intervention strategy that uses group processes to focus on the whole culture of an organisation in order to bring about planned change. It seeks to change beliefs, attitudes, values, structures, and practices - in fact, the entire culture of the organisation - so that the organisation can better adapt to technology and line with the fast pace of change." Thus organisational development is just like a training to the employees to mould themselves in a planned way so that the necessary changes may be introduced in the organisation without much resistances of workers and it is possible only through the change in the whole culture, *i.e.*, beliefs, attitudes, values, structures, and practices of the organisation.

Organisational development's origin is dependent upon following causes:

(1) There is a desire for more experimental learning processes in employee training. It means that the people learn during training period by human problems they face on the job. As soon as they experience the problems relating to human behaviour, they discuss and analyse them with their superiors or colleagues and learn something from this experience. This type of behavioural approach is much better than the traditional approaches of lectures and discussions. It is training on the job about human behaviour and the person concerned learns from experience on the job.

(2) The second cause of organisational development is the fact that reward structure on the job did not adequately reinforce training, hence training momentum in the transition from a classroom to a work situation is excessively lost. The environment in the organisation does not support the training and therefore many well designed training and development programmes failed. So, it is better to change the entire organisation so that it will support the training that is provided.

(3) The third cause is the fast speed of change itself. It needs organisation to be much effective so that it may survive and prosper. The organisational development attempts to develop the culture of the whole organisation so that it may respond to change more uniformly and capably. It develops free communication among workers. It improves the problem solving ability by improving group dynamics or force.

CHARACTERISTICS OF ORGANISATIONAL DEVELOPMENT

Organisational development implies on the following characteristics:

1. System Oriented. Organisational development is system oriented. It is concerned with the interactions of various parts of the organisation which affect each other. It is based on open, adaptive systems concept. It recognises that organization strucutre and managerial performance are mutually interdependent.

2. Goal Setting and Planning. Organisational development is concerned with the entire organisation, the change agent defines the goals of group and will see to it that together they all work to achieve them.

3. Use of Change Agent. The another characteristic of the organisational development is that it uses change agent or consultants and not the experts to guide and affect the change. Thus change-agents or consultants are process consultants and not experts consultants and their role is to guide groups towards more effective group processes rather than playing the role of experts and telling them what to do.

4. Problem solving. Organisational development is concerned with the problem solving, It seeks to solve the problems through practical experiences gained on the work and not merely through theoretical discussion as in a class room. These problems mainly occur at the time when working on the job hence the problems are real and interesting to them. Thus, it develops an attitude of problem solving among workers on the jobs.

5. Normative Re-educative Strategy. OD is based on the principle that "norms form the basis for behaviour and change is a re-educative process of replacing old by new ones". For instance, some OD programmes signify major departures from bureaucratic structure of an organization and call for changes in managerial leadership styles. OD is based on well-established principles regarding the individual and group behaviours in the organisation and hence it is relatively easy for the OD practitioners to launch and diffuse the required changes by educating them.

6. Contingency Oriented. Organisational development is situational and contingency oriented. As because people learn to develop their behavioural concepts through experience, they can suggest various ways to solve a particular problem and to adapt any of them most suited in the present situation, considering all contingencies. Conversely, the traditional training programme suggests only one best way.

7. Dynamic Process. Organisational development consists the effort to guide and direct change as well as to cope with or adapt to impose change. It recognises the fact that the goals of organisation change and new behaviour patterns through experience. People develop behavioural concepts through experience and no expert guidance is needed for this purpose.

8. Experimental Learning. Organisational development provides experimental learning to help the participants to learn new behaviour patterns through experience. They can discuss and analyze their own immediate experience and learn from it. People develop behavioural concepts through experiences and no expert guidance is needed for this purpose.

9. Long-range Effort. OD is not designed to solve short term, temporary or isolated problems. It is a long term approach meant to elevate the organization to a higher level of functioning by improving the performance and satisfaction of organization members. OD programmes generally cover a period of three to five years.

10. Research Based. Most of the OD interventions are research-based. Change agents do not just introspect the employees and introduce changes, rather, they conduct surveys, collect data, evaluate and then take decisions. OD programmes are generally conducted by a special task force and involve the utilization of outside behavioural consultant's faculties.

11. Feedback. Organisational development supports feedback to participants so that they may be able to collect the solid original data on which decision are based. For this purpose participants may be divided into several groups according to the functions. Each such group takes its own decision on the subject referred to it, and then, the decision is forwarded to the other group for feedback. Each group comes to know the impression of other groups about it and then groups meet together to thrash out any misunderstanding developed among them.

12. Group Processes. Organisational development uses the group processes rather than individual process. It makes sincere efforts to improve the group performance. There are group discussion, intergroup conflicts, confrontation and team building. Sensible efforts are made to develop and improve interpersonal relations, open communication channels, build trust and encourage responsiveness to others.

13. Humanistic Values. Organisational development programmes are often based on humanistic values. The values are positive beliefs about the potential and desire for growth among employees. To be effective and self renewing an organisation needs employees who want to increase their skills and contributions.

PRE-REQUISITES FOR EFFECTIVE USE OF ORGANISATIONAL DEVELOPMENT

Successful organizational development tends to be a total system effort. It is not a programme with a temporary quality; it is rather aimed at developing the organization's internal resources for effective change. To increase the probability of success of the OD programme the following conditions must be fulfilled:

1. Support for OD Programme should Begin with Top Management. OD is a system-wide concept requiring at least psychological involvement of all the parts of system in the organization. Of all the support for the programme is essential and this support should begin with the top management. In certain cases the programme dies just because of lack of support of top management. To overcome such failures OD programmes are designed using a vertical slice of the organization where all the members in the chain of command are exposed to the development process. For the success of the programme the support of individual members is also essential.

2. Enough Time Must be Allowed so that the Effects of an OD Programme are Realized. Things in organization are not expected to change drastically over a brief period of time. Managers who introduce intervention to change will be invariably disappointed if they expect quick results of OD programmes. It is because OD aims at changing the conditioned behaviour of members which is rather difficult and time-consuming affair. Conditioned behaviour does not change quickly and instantaneously and it takes a considerable span of time.

3. Use the Apporpriate Intervention. For the success of OD programme use of appropriate intervention is essential. If the intervention is inappropriate it will have undesirable consequences. Depending on the target group the organization must use the intervention. For instance, if the focus is on individuals then sensitivity training or Grid Phase I or any other type is called for. On the other hand, if the focus is on teams and groups, then survey feedback, or process consultation or family T-group training is called for. Further, if the target group is the intergroup relationships then Grid phase III or survey are used.

4. Organisation must Communicate the Objectives of Programme Clearly. The objectives of the programme must be made crystal-clear to all the participants and organizational members before the programme is launched. If the organization cannot communicate the objectives effectively then it is quite likely that the programme may be doomed to fail. Further, organization must recognize that a problem exists and must desire moving toward a solution to the problem. Some organizations, even when they do not confront problem, take chances by introducing changes that may prove to be costly later. Oragnizations should 'see and hit' the target; rather than 'hit and then see' if any target is there. Quite often organizations become aware of the new programme and have a feeling that it would be good to try to implement it even if no specific problem exists at that time.

5. The Role of Outside Consultant Must be Understood. A consultant is an OD practitioner, often labelled as "interventionist", "change agent" or "process consultant". The OD consultant in his technical bag contains the necessary behavioural knowledge, technical problem-solving abilities and clinical skills. He also processes the personality and interpersonal competence to use himself as an instrument of change. But his role in the organization must be properly understood to ensure the success of OD programme. Organizations should not rely frequently on the consultants, if so, it becomes a lucrative practice. If the outside consultant diagnoses the problem and prescribes the solution himself then the organization is not better off to solve the problems in future. It will have to resort to consultant once again if any problem arises in future.

CRITICISM

OD, just like any new programme, suffers from the lack of research, lack of documentation, and far more heat than light. But it is a source of inspiration to those who feel the need for human-based approach to organizational change. But OD programmes have been subject to criticism by managers and researchers. People are of the view that the diagnostic interventions are stirring up discontent in the organizations. Of all, the most frequently observed criticisms are the following:

1. OD is Criticised because of the Paucity of Research About Its Effectiveness. It is difficult to evaluate OD as it is still in its infancy. Further, it is difficult to measure number, nature and magnitude of confounding variables. OD operates under substantial handicap, *i.e.*,the diffficulty of defining its process and results in measurable and verifiable terms. For instance, how does one define "openness and trust" and "organizational climate"? Researchers criticise OD because not enough solid research evidence supports its widespread application.

2. OD Makes the Dichotomy Between the 'Task' and 'Attitude' Apparent. Another major shortcoming of OD is the apparent dichotomy between 'the task technique' and the 'attitude' only adherents. The former is sophisticated cost cutting method of scientific management school whereas the later is concerned primarily with developing positive and open interpersonal attitudes—which are difficult to measure.

3. OD Makes People Unfit for the Real Organizational World. After attending OD workshops, many participants convert to such values as openness, trust and sharing of power etc., that are educated by OD practitioners. By exhibiting these features the members are often punished rather than rewarded in the organization. Andrew DuBrin contends that "open people have a difficult time competing with highly political and sometimes devious organization members.

4. Resistance to Change is a Chronic Problem to Attain the Goals of OD. The deep-seated resistance to change represents a serious obstacle to OD. According to Burrack and Smith "resistance at the top and firmly embedded at the middle of management." They observe that antiplanning attitudes, collective bargaining to preserve outmoded jobs and technology and favour of technologial changes more than social changes are the factors that contribute to such resistance. Eventhough an intervention results in some short-range changes, the force of resistance soon take place overthrowing whatever progress has been made through OD. It is often noticed that the firm returns to its traditional ways of doing things after the OD programme is over.

PROBLEMS IN ORGANISATIONAL DEVELOPMENT

Organisational development, however, has invited sharp criticism to increase organisational viability and effectiveness because many OD programmes have failed. Much of the enthusiasm created at the beginning of OD programmes vanished over the period of time. In early 60s, OD became quite successful with many professional consultants offering high services and programmes to various organisations. By 70s, however, substantial disenchantment with OD became evident because of many controversial OD techniques like sensitivity training, confrontation techniques, etc. Research studies have also failed to conclude significant contributions of OD in All organisations, particularly in bottom-line ones. Therefore, OD can be taken as panacea for curing all organisational problems. In general, OD is criticised on the following lines:

1. There is discrepancy between ideal real situations. OD tries to achieve ideal without taking into account real.
2. OD makes people unfit for the real organisational world because no organisation can adopt open concept.
3. Resistance to change is a natural phenomenon and OD puts undue pressure to change. Hence it fails even as a long-term strategy.
4. OD fails to motivate people with low level to achievement needs. if an organisation is ladden with these people, it is useless to try OD.
5. OD programmes are often quite costly, and only large organisations can afford this luxury without any guarantee of positive outcome.

It can be seen that many of these criticisms are based on reality and experience. People realised its dysfunctional aspects only when many OD efforts failed. However, it may be emphasised that OD programmes are likely to fail when these are not undertaken properly.

In fact, there have been cases of wrong implementation of OD programmes and hence failure. For example, events has identified three factors which have been responsible for the failure of OD programmes: *(i)* failure of the management consultant group to correctly tailor the programme to actual needs of the organisation; *(ii)* failure to correctly model appropriate personnel behaviour in the programme; and *(iii)* failure to increase employee motivation through participation and development of personal growth and self-esteem. Thus it can be visualised that OD itself may not be dysfunctional but application may be. Therefore, in order to make best use of OD efforts, some specific efforts are required. Some of these efforts are as follows:

1. There should be genuine support of OD programme from top management.
2. Organisation must formulate the objectives of OD programme very clearly and specifically.
3. Enough time should be allowed so that the effects of OD programme are realised.
4. Only fully competent OD consultant should be pressed for the service and he should develop understanding with internal change agents.
5. There should be proper use of OD interventions. These should be based on the specific needs of the organisation.

PROCESS OF ORGANISATIONAL DEVELOPMENT

OD can be taken as a process of changing people, structure and other related aspects of an organisation. Thus it consists of many sub-processes or steps. However, people do not agree about the various steps involved in OD process. While some experts mention about three steps—diagnosis, intervention, and evaluation, General Motors of United States of America has identified eight steps in its OD programmes. These are awareness, acceptance, readiness and commitment to work, diagnosis and search, application, measurement of improvement, institutionalisation and self-renewal. Abad Ahmed, an Indian OD expert has identified six steps in OD. These are motivation for change, data collection and problem identification and diagnosis, strategy for change, intervening in the system, reinforcement and follow-up, and monitoring and evaluation. The difference in various steps as described by various authors and experts is due to the defining scope of a particular step. Moreover, since OD is an interactive process a process in which interrelated events more over time towards some goals—many of the events overlap, and in actual practice, a clear-cut demarcation between various events becomes difficult. Further, many experts include awareness of the problem requiring the application of OD in the process of OD while many do not see as its part. For the sake of discussion, various steps in OD process can be described as problem identification and diagnosis, planning for change, intervention in the system and evaluation and feedback.

Organisational development is a continuous process. It takes at least one year to have a start and may continue for indefinite time. It is a complicated process and hence needs top management support. It involves the following steps:

1. Collection of Data. Data gathering is perhaps the most important activity in the process of OD. Personal interviews, personal observations and questionnaires are the most common ways through which the data is collected. Different types of problems require different data and as such the question of "which method" to use depends upon the nature of problem the organization encounters.

2. Planning and Implementation. After diagnosing the problem, the OD expert turns his attention to the planning of change and implementing it. OD interventions come into picture here. Intervention is considered to be the action phase in OD process. Intervention is a set of planned, programmed activities and techniques by which organizations and their clients collaborate in an OD programme. According to French and Bell, "interventions consist of the long range evolving applications of OD techniques targeted for changing individuals, groups, or the total organizations".

The range and number of available interventions is not small but extensive. The particular intervention to be used depends on the target group in the organization. One intervention differs from another in terms of the intensity or depth with which it penetrates into the working of the organisation. An effective OD programme does not consider all interventions, but selects the appropriate one that suits the requirements. But sometimes more than one intervention is used in the programme.

3. Action Planning and Problem Solving. Data are used by the group to suggest specific recommendations for change. They discuss the problems, faced by the organisation and sketch specific plans including who is responsible for problems and what action should be taken and at what time.

4. Initial Consultation. The first step in the organisational development process is to approach the organisational development consultant to determine the type of O.D. programme to be developed. The consultant may be a professional consultant from outside or he may be internal service personnel expert in organisation development programmes. At the point, the consultant may have consultations with person from various levels in the organisations in order to gain the knowledge of imports. For this purpose, he may interview such persons or he may adopt any other way to be acquainted with the necessary information.

5. Team Building. During the whole process, group meetings are convened to discuss the programme and the consultant in the whole process encourage the groups to examine how they work together as a group or as a team. The consultant helps them see the value of open communication and trust them. These are essential pre-requisties for improved group functioning. Consultant also encourage team building through organising meetings with managers and their immediate subordinates so that they can improve the functioning of the work group with the guidance of consultant.

6. Appraisal and Follow up. The consultant further helps the organisation in making an appraisal of the programme and find out the deficiencies if any. He can develop additional programmes in areas where the original programme is felt ineffective and results are poor and that requires improvement.

7. Interventions in the System. After the techniques for OD programme and time sequence are determined, OD consultant attempts to change the organisation and its people. It is long-term affairs and hence a gradual process. For example, most of the OD programmes begin with training to people in the light of the proposed organisational change.

8. Problem Identification and Diagnosis. The real process of OD begins when the target organisation engages a consultant, and the consultant tries to identify the problems requiring the application of OD. Management may identify the organisational problems in terms of certain end-result variables like declining profitability, employee turnover, lower productivity, etc. However, any significant attempt cannot be made unless one knows the reasons for such end-result variables. Therefore, the task of OD consultant is to identify various problems and reasons because of which the organisation is not able to achieve its objectives. For this purpose, the consultant may collect relevant data from the organisation. At this state, the role of OD consultant is just like a medical practitioner who diagnoses the disease of a patient based on symptoms and various diagnostic tests.

9. Planning for Change. When the real problems of the organisation are identified, OD consultant plans the various courses of action in the light of these problems. Since there are many techniques involved in OD programme, attempts are made to transform diagnosis of the problems into a proper action plan involving the overall goals for OD, determination of the approach suitable for attaining these goals, and sequence for implementing the approach. Major consideration is given to the techniques and methods used to arrive at desirable organisation system, its subsystems and their interrelationship. Planning aspect is important because further steps of OD depend on it. Moreover, planning should not be taken on a fixed basis because many changes have to be incorporated once OD programme is implemented and its feedback is received.

10. Evaluation and Feedback. Evaluation and feedback is the final step in OD process. This step relates to the evaluation of the results of OD programme so that suitable actions may be taken to encounter any problem or to modify further programmes. Careful monitoring and evaluation of OD programmes provide feedback regarding what is going on. When any discrepancy appears between what is intended and what is happening, the change agent goes back almost to the first step, that is problem identification and diagnosis, though in this case work involved may be slightly different. In the very beginning of problem identification and diagnosis; emphasis is more on data collection and its analysis; at this stage, emphasis may be more on analysis of OD programme techniques themselves. Moreover, feedback can also be used as an energising factor which will indicate what further action is necessary. Most common techniques for getting feedback are critique sessions, systematic appraisal of change efforts, and analysis of pretraining and post-training behavioural patterns based on actual operation.

Thus, the above social process and the steps discussed are not the same with every type of organisation. They may differ from organisation to organisation depending upon the culture of the society in which it is being applied. For example, where trade unions have political bent, the workers are on the board of directors. There is also more industry government interaction. In such climate, organisational development is more concerned with power and political implications of the action plans.

❐

11

Decision Making

Decision making is a kind of commitment, a resolution to do or not to do, an act to adopt or to reject an attitude. Decision making is a part of everyday life. Whether you are at a board meeting or in the play ground, you are almost constantly making decisions, sometimes working on several at the same time. There may be major or minor but some of these might have proved to be effective decisions, viz, appropriate, timely and acceptable. Same of your decisions might have been wrong, but you knew that there was something worse than a few wrong decisions and that was indecision. It could probably be shown that if the manager of a telephone company ordered ten telephone poles removed and an underground system installed using different locations, The carrying out that order could involve 10 thousand decisions made by 100 workers located at 15 points. The decision to move the poles would probably also require some consideration of the social, legal, economic and physical facts of the environment.

In the decision process the attitudes are always involved because attitudes often develop unconsciously, they are hard to see part of the decision-making process until decisions are actually made. For example, many men in the business world today resist the idea that women should bold managerial or executive positions. Social and legal pressures currently being brought to bear on such resistance have had something to do with changes in business attitude and organisational policy. If attitudes continue to change, we can except to see many more women in top managerial positions in near future.

While taking decision's we should keep the six fundamentals *i.e.* ACTION.

A - Analyze the problem and gather data

B - Consider the alternative solution

C - Take action; select a solution

O - On going evaluation of the solution.

N - Need for change; consider the need for modification of the original decision.

Analyse the Problem. Problem cab be defined as obstacles that prevent the achievement of goals or purposes. Often, the surface problem is only a symptom of a more important problem. For example having a fever is a symptom of something more serious - perhaps a cold, the flu, or even pnenmonia. Similarly, in a company with rapid employee turnover, The turnover itself is not the real problem; it is a symptom of more serious trouble. The question that-needs to be asked is; why is there so much employee turnover? Attempting to cure a symptom usually does not cure the cause. An asprin may bring down the fever, but it will not cure the illness. Similarly, a retirement programme may enconrage some employees to stay on the job, but it will not cure their desire to leave. It is also necessary to delve deeply into a situation to locate the real problem and define it. For example, a supervisor may believe that he or she is confronted with a problem of conflicting personalities in the department. After checking into the situation, the supervisor may find that the problem is not one of personalties at all; rather, the work functions and specific responsibilities of each employee have been outlined clearly. Once the problem is defined, it must be analyzed in order to be solved. Collecting information for use in analysis is sometimes recommended as the first step in good decision making, but untill the problem has been identified and defined, you will not know what to look for. What somtimes happens is that the problem has to be redefined and reanalyzed as more information is found, because the new information casts so much light on the nature of the original problem that its original boundaries are no longer accurate. First of all look to find out the problem not the solution.

Consider the Alternative Solution. During decision making there is need to learn to think about all possible alternatives. Even when one of the available alternatives is desirable, it is better to have choices than to be left with no choice at all. Doing nothing is also a decision, it can be worthwhile or it can be fatal. The auto industry's failure: *(1)* to make design changes, *(2)* to reduce production during an economic slow down and *(3)* to reduce the number of plants are examples of doing nothing. Brainstorming is one of the best known methods for developing alternatives to problems. The free wheeling, receptive atmosphere of a brain-storming session often produces workable solutions.

When more than one person is involved in making decision, it is often a challenge to arrive at a solution with a minimum of conflict. For example, suppose that the sales personnel of a cosmetics firm insists on a particular kind of packaging for a new product because of its eye-catching appeal. The production department; however, is firmly opposed to this packaging on the grounds of expense and difficulty of manufacture. Both groups are right, at least within their respective areas of concern. Solution to this kind of conflict. are usually plentiful as soon as the parties involved agree to explore alternative choices together.

Take Action-a Solution. After the alternative solutions have been developed, the probable desirable and undesirable conseqences of each should be tested mentally. The selection must be the best solution from the point of view of time and energy as well as money. The decision makers selection will probably be based on a combination of factors, such as experience, intuition, advice, experimentation and computer forecasts. Many decisions are based on experimentation. When experimentation is not too costly, it is worth following. Even on a small scale, experimentation is almost always justified by good results. Moving employees around according to specific skills, changing work schedule or changing the location of desks in a department to see if production rises or falls are examples of small scale experimentation, which can sometimes yield surprising results. When experimentation is not possible the decision maker must select an alternative based on the most objective forcasting possible - the premise of strategic analysis, for example that decisions are different because the initial objectives, assumptions and expectations are defferent.

Implement a Solution. When a plan has been accepted, it must be put into action carefully and watched closely to ensure that it works.

General Foods Corporation provided a good example of planning for implementation when it decided to close down four plants in four states and combine operations in one new, larger plant in yet another state. About 2000 employees were notified of the move by letter a year before the move was scheduled to take place. A few months later, a policy statement on transfer and termination was calculated to all employees, indicating the company's intention to transfer those employees who wish to move. Transferred employees were given job preference over newly hired people. General Foods assisted those who did not wish to transfer in finding other employment.

Ongoing Evaluation. All ramifications of a chosen solution can not be seen readily until the plan is put into action. Even as the solution is being tried, you and your subordinates will see ways in which to improve the implementation plan. On going evalution is a necessity in developing a plan and the key word in this stage is "feed back". You will need to solicit feed back or advice, openly from employees working on the project as well as from your peers and your superiors.

Need for Change. After the solution has been tried, it must consider the need for modifying the original decision. New information, experience and new ideas will help to shape the project into a better plan. However, after the plan has been tried and improved, the final analysis may be that the decision was a poor one. We must be ready for that possibility, profit from the mistake and move on to another solution.

As much time can be spent in refining our decision as we spend in analyzing the problem and collection the data. Whether it involves a professional goal or new methods of routing manufactured goods, a decision can have a long-lasting effect on us. The time spent on the refinement of the decision is often well worth it. Remember when you have a big decision to make, think of ACTION, analyze the problem, consider alternatives, Take action, implement the soultion, make the on going cvaluation, and make necessary changes.

SHORT-AND LONG-RANGE DECISIONS

Short-Range Decisions. Short-range decisions are usually routine decisions what involve little risk or uncertainty. Many industries and business organisations try to create work environments in which as many decision-making functions as possible are standardized for greater production efficiency. The assembly line is the classic example of decisions made into a set of routine behaviours. (See Figure)

Perhaps you who are supervisors are more concerned with short-range decisions and the effectiveness of those decisions. There is one basic precept that will make you a better manager. Learn to persuade others to do willingly what you want them to do. Here are eight principles of persuasion for short-range decisions.

1. Make it clear where you stand and why you take that positon.
2. Use emotions to persuade, as emotional appeals are more effective than facts, particularly in the short run. An emotional catalyst helps to leaven the facts.
3. Take your time. Even intelligent people have trouble with new ideas.
4. Repeat your message in as many different ways as possible.

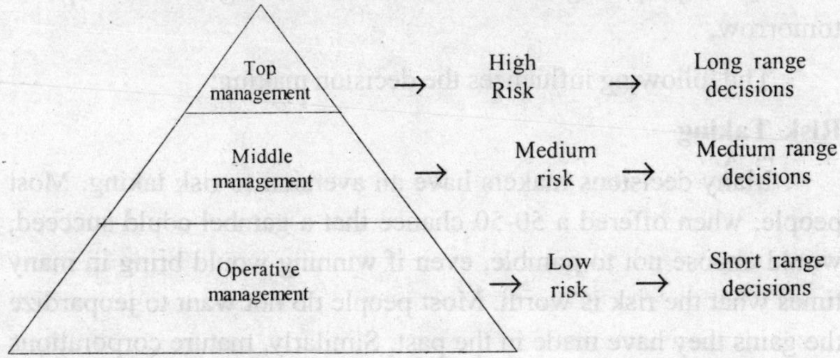

5. Expect resistance.
6. Strive for positive personal involvement. Seek allies.
7. Show that the desired action is possible.
8. State your motives frankly, as self-interest is normal.

Long-Range Decisions

Long-range decision making requires a process different from that for making routine decisions. Long-range decisions require planning and planning always involves the future. Whenever you plan for the future, you automatically encounter a certain amount of risk and uncertainty. In a short-range decision, the outcome can be seen readily. The outcome of a long-range decisions is not as easy to see but it does involve predictability. In drawing up a life insurance policy for example, both the customer and the insurance broker are involved in predicting the long-range usefulness of the policy. The customer may predict a need for the policy; however, the broker may predict that the customer won't need it.

Peter Drucker says that it is easier to define long-range decision making by what it is not than by what it is. First, it is not forecasting people neither predict nor control the future. Long-range decisions do not deal with future decisions, but rather with the probable results of present decisions. The long-range planner does not ask, "What should we do tomorrow?" Instead he or she asks, "What do we do today to be ready for an uncertain tomorrow?" For example, organizations engaged in training programmes for minorities and for women are preparing for the desirable working relationships of tomorrow.

The following influences the decision making:

Risk Taking

Many decisions makers have an aversion to risk taking. Most people, when offered a 50-50 chance that a gambel could succeed, would choose not to gamble, even if winning would bring in many times what the risk is worth. Most people do not want to jeopardize the gains they have made in the past. Similarly, mature corporations are not in business of gamble their corporate existences on a 50 percent chance of high returns.

Most risk-taking decisions, however, involve only a small fraction of total corporate resources. And the opportunities for this type of risk occur dozens of times every year. Taking several 50 percent chances every month to risk a small precentage of total resources for a tenfold return would appear to be very good business practice indeed and should pay off handsomely in the long run. Yet businesses, like people, want to make the least risky choices. They are in the habit of taking monetary risks with relatively small amounts of capital; but whether the risk is low or high, decision makers often act as if their fate, of their company's, hangs in the balance. Many decisions that should be made are often suppressed because of the fear of failure or of losing everything.

Attitudes Toward Success and Failure. Fear of failure can stalemate the decision-making process. Worry about the unknown results of a decision can be paralyzing. As long as no decision is made, no judgement can be reached as to whether the decision is a good one or not. By not making decisions, peoples lose the opportunity to learn either from their failures or their successes. Only by making decisions can one learn how to make successful decisions.

Personal Biases. When making decisions it is impossible to appeal to neutral principles to determine the rationality of competing systems. In the name of one kind of logic another kind of logic is rejected. Each system of thought, be it religious, political, economic, scientific, or poetic, has its own rationale.

Systems of reason are influenced by habits, reflexes, prejudices, appetities, and emotions. All logic is biased by personal feelings and affinities. Sometimes these feelings are appropriate to the stituation; somtimes they are not. When making decisions, it helps to know your personal biases. Often the price that has to be paid in making a decision is the sacrifice of a particular set of biases. In many instances, it is only in this way that one be aware of the various alternatives.

Experience. Knowledge gained by experience is a helpful guide to decision making and its importance should not be underestimated. The greater the number of successful decisions, the greater the confidence one has with dealing with more decisions. On the other hand, it is dangerous to follow experience blindly. It is too easy for the person with many years of experience to fail to listen to innovative ideas from others. Personal biases, based on experience, can insulate the individual from anything new.

Intuition. Intuition and hunches also help to determine decisions. Hunches are based on information or experience recorded in the subconscious. The predisposition to make a certain decision comes to the conscious mind, but without articulated reasons, Often, intuition can provide the essential direction for solving a problem in a certain way, while the justification comes later. Decisions based on intuition gain much more credibility when they are also supported by logic and experience. Unfortunately, it is often difficult to tell the difference between intuition and bias.

As Max Gunther points out in The Luck Factor, "The fats on which the hunch is based are stored and processed on some level of awareness just below the conscious level. This is why the hunch comes with that peculiar feeling of almost-but-not-quite knowing." Further he warns against disregarding those "odd little hunches that are trying to tell you what you don't want to hear." Most executives will not admit to being clairvoyant, but they may see ways to solve business problems that defy computer logic, and the bottom line profit can be spectacular.

Seeking Advice. It is one thing to be aware that at times you will be the only one who can make a decision. It is quite another to seek opinions about what action should be taken. Listening openly to what other people have to say can greatly enlarge the potential of making a good decision. Other people can also act as sounding boards by providing a chance to hear one's ideas. The person who makes a practice of not consulting others takes greater risks in making decisions because he or she is isolated from feedback.

ROLE OF DECISION MAKING

Decision making lies deeply embedded in the management process and is the only vehicle for carrying managerial workload. Decision making permeates through all managerial functions and covers every area of the enterprise. Decision making is the sole way in which managers can discharge their functions of managing. Management, as a specialized activity, can be carried on only in the form of decisions. The task of decision making is the distinguishing mark that identifies a person as the manager of any undertaking. Management and decision making are bound up inseparably, and they go hand in hand.

Whatever a manager does he can do it by taking some decision from a number of alternative courses of action. Whether a manager orders or advises, plans or organizes, approves or disapproves a work hires or fires an employee, he is engrossed in the process of decision making. An uninformed manager who manages his job traditionally may not be aware that he is making decision constantly. But a little reflection will reveal that he cannot move even a step in his managerial work without decisions. In other words, the management process consists of a bundle of decisions in all areas and for all activities of the enterprise. All matters relating to planning, organization, direction and control are settled by managers through decisions which are executed into practice by operators of the enterprise.

Deciding and Planning. Deciding is no doubt a form of planning.Like planning, deciding affects in most cases a future course of action and involves choosing among alternatives. For that matter, deciding and planning have cognate meanings. Planning as a whole with its component parts like objectives, policies and procedures is the outcome of decision making. Further more, as planning is necessary for other managerial functions of organizing, directing and controlling, decision making too has pervasive influence on all managerial functions. Because of this situation, decision making is regarded by many writers as a part of the planning process. But many and varied operating orders and instructions are given by the middle and supervisory managers for getting the work accomplished through people. Such ordering and instructing involve decision making within the framework of planning.

Classification of Decisions

Decisions are broadly divided into two categories; the first includes the typical, routine or unimportant decision and the second is made up of important, vital or strategic decisions. Routine decisions involve no extra- ordinary judgement, analysis and authority, since they are to traverse along more or less fixed avenues. Ends of the enterprise are clearly established and the definite means to secure the ends are also given. Within the given means and ends, routine decisions demand a power of selection of the shortest path, as the connecting link between means and ends, on the part of managers. On the other hand, strategic decisions aims at determining or changing the means and ends of the enterprise. They require a thorough study, analysis and reflective thinking on the part of managers. Strategic decisions are usually taken by top managers, while routine decisions are made mostly by lower-level managers.

Decisions are also classified from other approaches with a view to revealing their routine or strategic nautre. First, from the standpoint of futurity of the decision, decisions may be deemed either as routine or as strategic ones. For more distant future the risk and uncertainty involved in decisions increase proportionately. Decisions of this nature are to be carefully thought through and analysed before they are made effective, since they commit the enterprise to enter into speculation about the uncertain future and introduce important changes in its affairs. But the risk element is reduced in decisions requiring the solution of current problems or problems of the near future and such decisions are taken within defined jurisdiction. Where the degree of risk and uncertainty is high, decisions are reserved for top-level managers; otherwise they are pushed down to the lower level of management.

Secondly, according to the frequency or rarity of some decisions, they may be looked upon as routine or strategic decisions. The routine decisions are often repeated so as to reduce their uncertainty and risk to a minimum, and they are usually taken against a familiar background. Particularly, when such decisions are taken within the framework of established policies and procedures, they become so routine in character that such decisions can be taken by managers of the lower level. But in the case of rare decisions not covered by established policies and procedures, the mamagers are required to probe the matters to the bottom to find out any hidden difficulty, to utilize any untapped resource, or to unlock any revealing situation. The rare decisions, in most cases, require a searching analysis on the part of top managers.

Thirdly, from the approach of their impact, decisions may affect on department, several departments or the enterprise as a whole. Decisions to be made effective, must be supported by necessary authority. A departmental manager cannot take a decision affecting other departments, areas or functions of the enterprise. It is a truism to state that managers must decide matters falling within their jurisdictions. Enterprise decisions are taken at the highest level, inter-departmental decisions are made by the superior manager in collaboration with managers of the affected departments, and departmental decisions by managers of their respective departments. This order of arrangement is followed in the case of routine decisions. But strategic decisions, wherever they may arise, cannot be made in this fashion. Even a departmental decisions may be raised to the status of strategic one because of the elements of either rarity or futurity of decisions.

Fourthly, some decisions require judgement of non-economic factors like ethical values, moral conduct or human behaviour in the enterprise. The presence of these quality considerations in decision making calls for a judicial function that can only be discharged by managers of the higher level. To ensure unbiased decisions on these qualitative and intangible problems, decisions of this nature are pushed up to the top of the organization. Many questions of human relations are not decided by the personnel department head, but they are taken up by superior managers. Human problems that are fully covered by established policies and procedures are, however, decided at a lower level.

Finally, decisions can also be classified into programmed and unprogrammed decisions. Programmed decisions are standing decisions in repetitive situations, and they include objectives, policies, procedures, standards and rules. Unprogrammed decisions are special-purpose decisions that require creativity and a greater amount of judgment and they include programmes, budgets and strategies. Programmed decisions can be easily delegated to lower levels of the organization. But unprogrammed decisions require the attention of superiors.

APPROACHES OF DECISION MAKING

The following are the ways by which the decision has been taken:

Individual Decisions. First, there are the small businesses, of which Chester Barnard believes there are more than most people think. The owner-manager may have difficulty delegating decision-making power to subordinates because of a belief that power and prestige are lost when authority is delegated. Actuality, more work can be gained by delegation and more experience can be gained by the subordinate. The supervisor who believes in delegation spends less time checking up on employees and thus has time for more important work. Ideally, the employees get a chance to develop themselves by correcting their own errors. A climate of confidence results when the employees are allowed to check up on themselves, without the boss looking over their shoulders.

Decisions by a Powerful Few. In decisions made by the few, or in oligarchic decision making, major decisions are made by a small group of at least three but no more than seven. In addition to participating in joint decisions, each person usually has an area in which he or she has the final say, such as in sales or production matters. Oligarchic control can create delay, or even bring action to a standstill if there is a deadlock and on one has the final power to decide. In one large corporation, three executives with equal power were deadlocked over several important labor matters.

Decisions by Group. Many firms use consultative decision making to bring those employees with technical bacgrounds and know-how to the conference table. The technical staff is more likely to participate in making decisions when specific skills are involved than in those areas requiring long-range planning. Group decision making can be an exceedingly complex affair, but two facts hold true. First, majority decisions usually represent something less than total group commitment. Few groups operate with total group consensus. Second, the more abstract the matter being considered, the greater the chances of agreement. Put another way, the more concreate the matter, the less the chances for full agreement. For example, at one company, contract negotiations came to a halt over a clause about hiring "part time employees." The term needed definition. One proposed revision was, "A part time employee is one who works less than forty hours a week, on irregular schedules, and is not subject to the benefits of regular employees." Another was, "A part time employee is anyone who works less than forty hours a week." Clearly, the second definition covered many more people than did the first, and offered a wider range of interpretation. The company wanted the broad definition so that it could choose who would be entitled to regular benefits. The UNICEF wanted the narrow definition so that it could then claim all employees as dues payers. An agreement was reached only by structuring a definition more abstract than either party wanted, "Part time employees are all those employees who are not regular employees." While this more abstract definition did not not solve any concrete problems, it did allow negotiations to continue.

Making decisions in groups can have several advantages over individual decision making. But once you have chosen to use a group, several matters must be considered. There are at least five decision-making procedures-the ordinary group procedure and brainstorming, the statistical method, the Delphi technique, and the Norminal Group Technique.

Ordinary Group Procedure. This procedure entails calling a group together, presenting the problem, and asking for comments. The meeting is open ended, with free-flowing discussion and few controls, but the chairperson controls the speakers so that everyone does not talk at once. Robert's Rules of Order is used when necessary. Finally, the consensus is stated by the leader once one is reached.

Brainstorming. This procedure deals with the development of many alternatives to problems and not with the evaluation or selection of one of the ideas. Brainstorming sessions are designed to generate ideas to solve specific problems. The key to brainstorming is that it is devoted solely to creative thinking. All criticisms and discussions of suggested ideas are deferred until a later time. Brainstorming is only one step in the problem-solving process - a way of finding ideas that might be applicable to the solution of a problem.

Brainstorning can be done individually, but sessions seem to work best with about five to seven participants. Tests have demonstrated that free associations of ideas are from 65 to 93 percent more numerous when working in a group than when working alone. The problem should be as specific as possible, even if it means breaking the problem down into parts. The backgrounds of people in the group, and their acquaintance with details of the problem, do not seem to matter.

Intitial sessions may be as short as five minutes, later ones as long as an hour or more. Because ideas usually come so fast that many are lost, be sure to keep a record of all ideas, no matter how inane or impractical they seem. A tape recoder is a valuable tool for maintaining a record of the meeting because the leader should never stop the spontaneous actions of the group to write down the information. The chairperson enforces the "no criticism" rule by using a bell to signify an infraction of the rule. Keep the meeting in a light, humorous spirit. The leader can repeat phrases and add to them to stimulate action and motivation. Once all the ideas are accumulated, it is time for judgment. The information can be reviewed, and the panel can evaluate the material with hopes that a couple of excellent ideas are available out of more than twenty or thirty that were generated. The appraisal session can even come a day or two after the brainstorming session rather than immediately following it.

METHODS AND TECHNIQUES

Statistical Method. This method uses the ideas of a group of individuals, but does not ask these people to interact with one another in a group setting. The method is limited to quantitative problems. First, several people make individual estimates of the best answer to a problem. The estimates are then collected, and one of a variety of aggregation procedures is used to determine the final solution.

The mean or average of the responses is one procedure often used. For example, if a group decides to continue the project, it might want to project the amount of subsequent expenditures. In problems of this type, the average estimate is often quite accurate because overestimates and underestimates tend to concel each other out.

If people make quick, thoughtful estimates, statistical aggregation incures little cost and can be particularly effective. No social pressure can influence the choice. However, no group is ever formed, so the social rewards associated with communal activity are also lost.

Delphi Technique. Members of the Rand Corporation, under Norman Dalkey, developed the Delphi technique, which extends the statistical method to include feedback and reestimates. The group does not need to meet face to face. Individuals can be sampled from almost anywhere in the world. The Delphi technique is used frequently to gather ideas and direction from experts within a particular field. In the Delphi procedure, the chairperson acts as the administrator of an estimate-feedback chain. The first of several questionnaires is constructed to state the problem as clearly as possible and is sent to the Delhi panel. Because the group never meets, there is no easy way to clear up any misunderstandings; thus, the problem statement must be particularly clear. Potential solutions are returned to the chair person, who summarizes the solutions suggested and feeds them back to the panel in a second questionnaire. Preferences are again solicited in a third questionnaire-feedback report. By such a process, the best solution is decided on by the panel of experts.

Because both the Delphi techniques and the statistical method do not require individuals to meet together to make decisions, they avoid social pressure but lose the advantages of togetherness. Thus the economics of the situation tend to dictate the numbers of members of the Delphi panel, with seven as the minimum. Another problem with the Delphi technique is time. Having to wait for everyone's response before sending out another questionnaire makes the Delphi process very slow. However, some people feel strongly that group meetings are a waste of time; with the Delphi technique they can still contribute their skills to group problem solving. Also, when it is impossible to convene a particular set of individuals, the Delphi technique works well.

Nominal Group Technique. The Nominal Group Technique (NGT) is the most recently developed procedure. By combining some of the characteristics of the other techniques, NGT is characterized as a moderately structured decision process with the interpersonal characteristics of face-to-face groups.

NGT passes through several stages. After the problem is stated clearly, group members sit together quietly and individually generate as many alternatives as they can. After about fifteen minutes, ideas are presented in round-robin fashion. Each indivudual presents a single idea, taking turns, until all the group's ideas have been presented. The leader records them in full view at the front of the room. As in group brainstorming, individuals are encouraged to hitchhike on others' ideas. This process seperates the ideas from the individual who has suggested them. Although each of the ideas is not strictly anonymous, as in the Delphi technique, the round-robin recording process may reduce some social pressure.

After everone is clear about the entire set of suggestions, a voting or rating process is used to reach a group decision. Each group member might vote for the five alternatives that he or she feels are best, rank-ordering them from 1 to 5. Alternatively each of the ideas can be rated on a 10-point scale, from good (1) to bad (10). Votes or ratings are written on private ballots. The chairperson tabulates the votes and announces them to the group. In most cases, the first ballot identifies a small set of possible solutions. If the vote should reveal a clear-cut winner, the group is finished. Also, this procedure provides backup alternatives should the initially chosen solution fail to produce a desired outcome.

TYPES OF MANAGERIAL DECISIONS

There are many types of decisions which you would be required to make as a manager. Three most widely recognised classifications are:

1. Person and Organisation Decisions
2. Basic and Routine Decisions
3. Programmmed and Non-programmed Decisions.

The first classification of Personal and Organisational decisions was suggested by Chester Barnard, nearly fifty years ago in his classic book: "The Functions of the Executive". In his opinion, the basic difference between the two decisions is that "personal decisions cannot ordinarily be delegated to others, whereas organisational decisions can often if not always be delegated" (Barnard, 1937). Thus, the manager makes organisational decisions that attempts to achieve organisational goals and personal decisions that attempt to achieve personal goals. Note that personal decisions can affect the organisation, as in the case of a senior manager deciding to resign. However, if you analyse a decision you may find that the distinctions between personal and organisational decisions are a matter of degree. You are, to some extent, personally involved in any organisational decision that you make and you need to resolve the conflicts that might arise between organisational and personal goals.

Another common way of classifying types of decisions is according to whether they are basic or routine. Basic decisions are those which are unique, one-time decisions involving long-range commitments of relative permanence or duration, or those involving large investments. Examples of basic decisions in a business firm include plant location, organisation structure, wage negotiations, product line etc. In other words, most top management policy decisions can be considered as basic decisions. Routine decisions are at the opposite extreme from basic decisions. They are the everyday, highly repetitive, management decisions which by themselves have little impact on the everall organisation. However, taken together, routine decisions play a tremendously important role in the success of an organisation. Examples of routine decisions are an accountant's decisions on a new entry, a production-supervisor's decision on what territory to cover. Obviously, a large proportion (most experts estimate about 90 percent) of the decision made in an organisation are of the routine variety. However, the exact proportion of basic to routine types depends on the level of the organisation at which the decisions are made. For example, a first-line supervisor makes practically all the routine decisions whereas the chairperson of the board makes very few routine decisions but many basic decisions.

Simon distinguishes between Programmed (routine, repetitive) decisions and Non-programmed (unique, one-shot) decisions. While programmed decisions are typically handled through structured or bureaucratic techniques (standard operating procedures), non-programmed decisions must be made by managers using available information and their own judgement. As is often the case with managers, however, decisions are made under the pressure of time.

An important principle of organisation design that relates to managerial decision making is Gresham's Law of Planning. This law states that there is a general tendency for programmed activities to overshadow non-programmed activities. Hence, if you have a series of decisions to make, those that are more routine and repetitive will tend to be made before the ones that are unique and require considerable thought. This happens presumably because you attempt to clear your desk so that you can get down to the really serious decisions. Unfortunately, the desks very often never get cleared.'

After going through the three types of classification of managerial decisions, you could see that there is no single and satisfactory way of classifying decision situations. Moreover, the foregoing classifications have ingnored two important problem-related dimensions: *(1)* How complex is the problem in terms of number of factors associated with it; and *(2)* how much certainty can be placed with the outcome of a decision. Based on these two dimensions, four kinds of decision modes can be identified: Mechanistic, Analytical, Judgemental, and Adaptive.

1. **Mechanistic Decisions.** A mechanistic decision is one that is routine and repetitive in nature. It usually occurs in a situation involving a limited number of decision variables where the outcomes of each alternative are known. For example, the manager of a bicycle shop may know from experience when and how many bicycles are to be ordered; or the decision may have been reached already, so the delivery is made routinely. Most mechanistic decision problems are solved by habitual responses, standard operating procedures, or clerical routines. In order to further simplify these mechanistic decisions, managers often develop charts, lists, matrices, decision trees, etc.
2. **Analytical Decisions.** An analytical decision involves a problem with a large number of decision variables, where the outcomes of each decision alternative can be computed. Many complex production and engineering problems are like this. They may be complex, but solutions can be found. Management science and operations research provide a variety of computational techniques that can be used to find optimal solutions. These techniques include linear programming, network analysis, inventory reorder model, queuing theory, statistical analysis, and so forth.
3. **Judgemental Decisions.** A judgemental decision involves a problem with a limited number of decision variables, but the outcomes of decision alternatives are unknown. Many marketing, investment, and resource allocation problems come under this category. For example, the marketing manager may have several alternative ways of promoting a product but he or she may not be sure of their outcomes. Good judgement is needed to increase the possibility of desired outcomes and minimise the possibility of undesired outcomes.

4. **Adaptive Decisions.** An adaptive decisions involve a problem with a large number of decision variables, where outcomes are not predictable. Because of the complexity and uncertainty of such problems, decision makers are not able to agree on their nature or on decision strategies. Such ill-structured problems usually require the contributions of many people with diverse technical backgrounds. In such a case, decision and implementation strategies have to be frequently modified to accommodate new developments in technology and the environment.

DECISIONS MAKING AND AUTHORITY

The need of correlationship between authority and responsibility becomes crystal clear from the decision making process. The responsibility of a manager can only be discharged through decision making. In all areas and at all levels, managers act through decisions. But without the grant of requisite authority, managers can neither take decisions nor make them effective. They must have sufficient authority to make all necessary decisions within their respective jurisdictions. To deny authority to managers for decision making amounts to retarding their performance and pulling down their efficiency.

The principle of decision making requires that the task of decision making should always be pushed down as far as practicable. Top managers should be relieved of the burden of taking too many unimportant decisions. There are two advantages of this practice. On the one hand, decisions are taken by operating managers who are close to the field of work and who have a thorough knowledge of local problems and situations. As a result, decisions are likely to become more realistic in character. On the other, top managers can concentrate on important problems in order to give meditative thought and effective judgement over the issues for comming to a decision. Unless they are free from making routine decisions, top managers cannot make creative thinking and take decisions concerning innovations, the vital contributory to the progress of any enterprise.

However, there are important limitations to the shifting of responsibility. Future decisions, rare decisions, qualitative decisions as well as enterprise decisions cannot be shifted down to the lower level of management. Strategic factors involving the degree of change or risk are to be taken into consideration, and they alone will determine how far down the decision can be made.

Limits of Individual Authority on Decision Making

As decision making has a number of steps—making the diagnosis, analysing the problem, developing alternatives and selecting the best course of action it is hardly possible for a manager to make decisions through his singular effort and thinking only. Activities of a business interlock with one another and require joint consideration for the solution of most business problems. For ensuring this joint consideration, the facts, ideas, suggestions or opinions are collected from different persons before making any decision. To facilitate sound decisions on the part of managers, some phases of the decision- making process are assigned to others working in separate and distinct roles. Single-handed decision making is very uncommon rather than the customary practice.

Even when subordinate managers make any routine decision, their authority is greatly circumscribed by existing standing plans and prevailing informal traditions of the enterprise. Such plans and customs provides limits, guides and assumptions for decision making. It is these standing plans and customary practices that develop a consistent pattern of executive behaviour, and at the same time, allow individual managers to take independent decisions of their own. Apart from authority constraints, there are other constraints on decision making, *e.g.*, biological, physical, technological and economic constraints.

INDIVIDUAL AND GROUP DECISIONS

Decisions are reached by individual managers as well as by several managers acting in a group. Alternatively, group decisions are taken by superior managers in collaboration with their subordinates. Routine decisions are mostly taken by individual managers who can thereby avoid delay, hesitation and deadlocks associated with group decisions. One-man decisions are the familiar practice in all small businesses, and to some extent, this system prevails in large businesses also. In some cases, however, individual managers do not like to share the power of decision-making with others for the fear of losing their status and prestige in the enterprise. But important and strategic decisions which introduce any change in the organization cannot be made effective without the active support of affected people. Inter-departmental decisions must be taken by the group as a matter of necessity. For putting the decisions into effect, the group participations in decision making has acquired special importance with a view to winning employee acceptance.

Even when decisions are made by the group, participation in the first two stages of decision making becomes unnecessary. Making diagnosis of the problem and its analysis can be done by individual managers, and group participation here leads to the procrastination and delay in decision making. But developing alternative solutions and the picking up of the best solution can be more effectively done through group participation which improves the quality of decisions by securing benefits of different ideas, suggestions and experiences. There are, however, some serious limitations of group decisions.

DECISION MAKING AND OPERATIONS RESEARCH

In recent years, the scope of intuitive judgment in decision making is gradually being curtailed and a greater emphasis has been put on quantitative approach involving the use of mathematics and statistics. This quantitative approach to decision making is referred to as operations research. Operations research has proved itself to be an invaluable technique of decision making, particularly with regard to planning and controlling functions of management. Operations research found its first application during World War II in the analysis of military problems in Great Britain. Operations research utilizes the applied mathematical and statistical methods to find out some basic pattern of relationships among a number of variable factors in any operating situation. Basically, it applies the probability and sampling theories for mathematical analysis and synthesis of a problem through the establishment of significant relationship.

The various factors of a problem are reduced into quantitative terms for mathematical measurement and analysis. Effects of those choosen factors or situations are also estimated by assignment of quantitative values. From the quantifying values, models are constructed in terms of mathematical equations. With the help of these equations, possibilities of all alternatives are clearly revealed. To apply operations research of the analysis of business problems, the entire enterprise is looked upon as a group of related activities with common objectives. Otherwise, the quantitative technique may give misleading results from what is known as "sub-optimization". The development of electronic computers has facilitated the growth of operations research for finding out the best course of action along with its probabilities and potentialities.

Application of Operations Research

The quantitative analysis of business problems is made through a number of techniques and tools, such as linear programming, probability theory, sampling theory, queuing theory or waiting line theory, simulation, dynamic programming (*e.g.*, the Programme Evaluation and Review Technique of PERT), operational gaming (*e.g.*, the business game), input-output analysis, search theory and formal game theory. Of the different tools and techniques of operations research, the first five are of proven value and the last five have limited or little application in their present state of development. Lindsay, Franklin A. in his book New Techniques for Management Dicision Making, holds the view that probability theory, simulation and operational gaming will have a major impact on management in the near future. Varied business problems that have been subjected to quantitative analysis by operations research include production scheduling, control of production runs in oil refineries, purchasing policies, capital budgeting, freight and transportation costs, assignment of salesmen to market areas, pricing, selection of advertising media and location of plant, store or warehouse. The American Management Association in its Report No. 20 in 1958, Operations Research Reconsidered, has indicated the results of a survey of the industrial application of operations research, and it is found in the Report that areas like production, long-range planning, sales and marketing and inventory have seen the greatest application of operations research.

Limitations of Operations Research. There are a number of limitations of operations research which may be stated as follows:

1. In the quantitative analysis of operations research, certain assumptions and estimates are made for assigning quantitative values to factors involved. If such estimates are wrong, but result would be equally misleading.
2. Many management problems do not lead themselves to quantitatives measurement and analysis. Intangible factors of any problem concerning human behaviour cannot be quantified accurately and all the patterns of relationships among the factors may not be covered. Accordingly, the outward appearance of scientific accuracy through the use of numbers and equations becomes unealistic.
3. The quantitative methods of operations research are in many cases costly, elaborate and sophisticated in nature. Although complex problems are fit for analysis by tools of operations research, relatively simple problems have no economic justification for this type of quantitative analysis.
4. A knowledge of some concepts of mathematics and statistics is prerequisite for the adoption of quantitative analysis by managers. According to the present trainning and experience of most managers, the actual use of these tools may be confined to a few cases.
5. Operations research is not a substitute for the entire process of decision making and it does not relieve managers of their task of decision making. In one phase of decision making, *viz.*, selection of best solution through the evaluation of alternatives, operations research comes into the picture. Managers have to prepare the groundwork for the introduction of operations research through several steps in decision making *viz.*, diagnosis of probelm, analysis of problem and development of alternatives; and even after

the selection of best solution by operations research, managers have to put the decision into effect and to institute a system of follow-up.

DECISION MAKING AND MANGEMENT INFORMATION SYSTEMS

The "Systems" approach to the information flow throughout the enterprise has been of valuable assistance to rational decision making. To reduce the scope of subective judgment in decision making and to increase the supply of facts to managers for their decisions, the information system has added a new dimension to the decision-making process and has been recognized as a new concept to top-management function. It is an all- inclusive system for providing management with better information for effective decision making. It is partly a by-product of computer technology which dictates centralization of data handling and information development for the benefit of the entire organization. Under the computer technology, functions of data manipulation, calculation and data storage (or, as they are collectively called "data processing") can be performed accurately with a terrific speed and at a comparatively lower cost. Primary data or items of raw information are mainly created in certain areas of the business production, purchasing, sales and personnel. These primary data in varying combinations are fed into the computer centre as input for being processed into various kinds of information as output. Because of the systems approach, the whole organization is looked upon as one entity with interrelated parts which are provided with desired information from a commom centre through the processing of primary data in various ways.

In the past, data manipulation through manual operation used to take place separately in different functional areas of the busniess. As a result, a number of defects crept into office work and clerical operations, viz, duplication of effort, multiplicity of reports, lack of requisite information, inaccuarate and untimely information and utter inefficiency in office work. All these defects have been eliminated by the integration of data handling and information development activities under one agency of data processing. Activities concerning not only data processing, but office systems, operations research and others as well have been organized as a top-level job under the "management services" manager. The development of this information system is expected to improve the process of decision making by permitting managers to base their decisions on greater information, to enlarge their visions for developing alternatives, to make a thorough and speedy analysis of problems and to comprehend in a better way the impact of their decisions on the enterprise and its objectives.

DECISION MAKING PROCESS

When a manager makes a decision, it is in effect the organisation's response to a problem. As such, decisions should be thought of as means rather than ends. Every decision is the outcome of a dynamic process which is influenced by multiple forces. This process is presented in Fig. However, this process should not be interpreted to mean that decision making is a fixed procedure. A process is basically a dynamic concept rather than static. Events and relationships are dynamic, continuous and flexible and must be considered as a whole in which many forces interact; a force affecting others and being affected by others. Therefore, the decision-

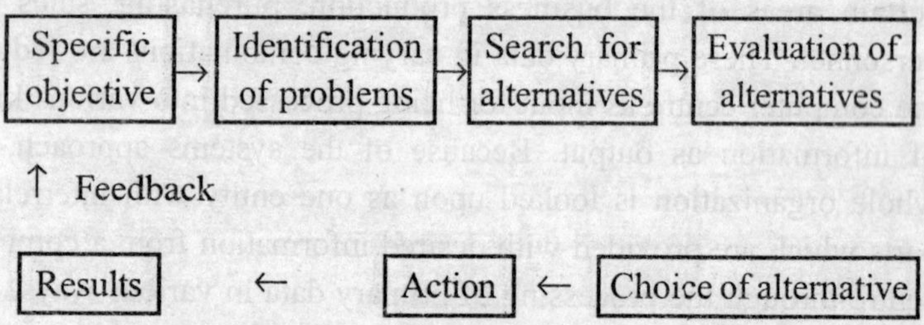

Fig. Decision Making Process

making process as presented in Fig. should be seen as sequential process rather than a series of steps to enable decision maker to examine each element in the progression that leads to a decision. Moreover, the process reveals that it is more applicable to non-programmed decisions than to programmed ones. Problems that occur infrequently, are unstructured, and are characterised by a great deal of uncertainty regarding their outcome, require the manager to utilise the entire process. For frequently occurring, structured problems, it is not necessary to consider the entire process. If a policy is established or a specific rule or procedure developed to handle such problems, it will not be necessary to develop and evaluate various alternatives each time the problem arises.

1. Specific Objective. The need for decision making arises in order to achieve certain specific objective. Every action of human being is goal directed. This is true for decision making also which is an action. Therefore, The starting point in any analysis of decision making involves the determination of whether a decision need to be made. Infact, setting of specific objective itself is an outcome of an earlier decision. However, since the objective setting is an outcome of earlier decision, this may not be considered truly as the first step of decision process but provides framework for the decision.

2. Problem Identification. Since a particular decision is made in the context of certain given objectives, identification of problem is the real beginning of decision-making process. A problem is a felt need, a question thrown forward for solution. It is the gap between present and desired state of affairs on the subject-matter of decision. It is just like the diagnosis of patient by the doctor. When a doctor makes a diagnosis he has a normal, healthy person and he also has a fairly clear concept of what a healthy person is. With this model as the desired result, he looks for disparities in the patient's actual state of health or factors which indicate that his future health will fall short of normal. In the case of management decision, however, a manager cannot rely on a commonly accepted norm such as healthy person. The objectives, if set precisely and specifically on the subject-matter of decision, will provide clue in identifying the problem and its possible solution. Further in management, a problem exists whenever one faces a question whose answer involves doubt and uncertainty. If there is no solution to the problem, it cannot be treated as problem from decision point of view, though the consequences of not solving this problem may be terrible.

(i) ***Diagnosis.*** The term diagnosis has come from Medical Science where it is used as the process of identifying a disease from its sign and symptoms. A symptom is a condition or set of conditions that indicates the existence of a problem. For example, a patient has certain symptoms on the basis of which his disease can be identified. Symptoms occupy an essential place in the problem-solving process for they signal the existence of problem and guide the search for the underlying problem. For example, if an organisation has high turnover of its employees, it indicates that something is wrong with the organisation. The symptom of high turnover may provide the clue to the real problem and managers can overcome the problem by taking appropriate action (decision making involves in taking action). Often managers fail to diagnose the problem correctly and sometimes they treat symptom as problem. Therefore, they should do this exercise very carefully.

(ii) ***Analysis.*** While the diagnosis of problem gives the understanding of what should be done in terms of decision making, analysis of problem takes it a step further. The analysis of the problem requires to find out who would make decision, what information would be needed, and from where the information is available. This analysis may provide managers with revealing circumstances that help them to gain an insight into the problem. the whole approach of analysis of problem should, however, be based around critical factors like the availability of information for making decision, criticality of decision, and the time available for making decision. For example, information may be available from external and internal sources and some of the information may not be available at all. Similarly the criticality of decision will determine the level at which the decision can be made.

3. Search for Alternatives. A thorough diagnosis defines both a specific problem and the situation in which the problem exists.

With this definition in mind, a decision maker seeks possible solutions. A problem can be solved in several ways, however, all the ways, cannot be equally satisfying. Further, if there is only one way of solving a problem, no question of decision arises. Therefore, the decision maker must try to find out the various alternatives available in order to get the most satisfactory result of a decision. Identification of various alternatives not only serves the purpose of selecting the most satisfactory one, but it also avoids bottlenecks in operation as alternatives are available if a particular decision goes wrong. However, it should be borne in mind that it may not be possible to consider all alternatives either because some of the alternatives cannot be considered for selection because of obvious limitation of the decision maker or information about all alternatives may not be available. Therefore, while generating alternatives, the concept of limiting factor should be applied. A limiting factor is one which stands in the way of accomplishing a desired objective. If these factors are identified, managers will confine their search for alternatives to those which will overcome the limiting factors.

A decision maker can use several sources for identifying alternatives: his own past experience, practices followed by other, and using creative techniques. Past experience, applied in most cases of decision making, takes into account the actions taken by the decision maker in the past with obvious differences between the former challenges and the present one. The successful action of the past may become an alternative for the future. This is a very simple approach but has obvious limitations because there may be so much changes in the decision context that old action becomes totally irrelevant.

4. Evaluation of Alternatives. After the various alternatives are identified, the next step is to evaluate them and select the one that will meet the choice criteria. However, all alternatives available for decision making will not be taken for detailed evaluation because of the obvious limitations of managers in evaluating all alternatives. The energy of managers is limited and psychologically most of them prefer to work on plans that have good prospect of being carried out.

In narrowing down the number of alternatives, two approaches can be followed: constraint on alternatives and grouping of alternatives of similar nature. The decision maker develops a list of limits that must be met by a satisfactory solution. He may treat these limits as constraints, that is, he may check proposed alternatives against limits, and if an alternative does not meet them, he can discard it. In the second approach, various alternatives can be grouped into classes on some specific citeria important to decision making. A representative alternative from one group may be selected for future analysis. Then having found the group that shows up the best, decision maker can concentrate on alternatives within this group. This method is very helpful in decision making regarding the location of plant, warehouse, etc.

Having narrowed down the alternatives which require serious consideration, the decision maker will go for evaluating how each alternative may contribute towards the objectives supposed to be achieved by implementing the decision. Evaluation of various alternatives dissects an alternative into various tangible and intangible factors. Tangible factors are those which can be quantified because they are quite obvious like the cost per unit, investment required, output to be received, etc. Such factors can be measured easily, though their happening may not be measured with certainty; for example, demand projection at a given price in a particular alternative.

5. Choice of Alternative. The evaluation of various alternatives presents a clear picture as to how each one of them contributes to the objectives under question. A comparison is made among the likely outcomes of various alternatives and the best one is chosen. Choice aspect of decision making is related to deciding the most acceptable alternative which fits with the organisational objectives. It may be seen that the chosen alternative should be acceptable in the light of the organisational objectives. Thus it is not necessary that the chosen alternative is the best one. This concept is based on the satisfying approach rather than the maximising approach of decision making. In choosing an alternative, the decision maker can go through three approaches; experience, experimentation, and research and analysis.

(i) ***Experience.*** Managers can choose an alternative based on their past experience if they have solved similar problem earlier. Reliance on past experience plays a larger part than it deserves in decision making. Managers rely more on experience than alternative methods of choice. Past experience has some benefits but it has certain limitation that it blocks making correct choice specially when the environmental factors are more flexible.

(ii) ***Experimentation.*** Experimentation which is generally used in scientific enquiry involves that a particular alternative is put in practice, result is observed, and the alternative giving the best result is selected. For example, many organisations go for test marketing of their products before the products are really introduced in the market. During the test marketing, the actions can be taken to change product features which are not acceptable. Experimentation as a method for choice of an alternative can be used on a limited scale because of cost and time factor.

(iii) ***Research and Analysis.*** Research and analysis is the most certain method of selecting an alternative, specially when major decision are involved. This approach entails solving a problem first by comprehending it. This involves a search for relationships between the more critical variables, constraints, and planning premises that bear the objectives sought. In the second stage, the alternative is broken into various components. Their individual impact on objective is evaluated and the impact of all factors of an alternative is combined to find out the total impact of the particular alternative. The one having the most positive impact is chosen. Since this requires making lot of calculations, often the help of computer is taken. In fact, various computer-based models have been developed to make the choice of an alternative easier.

Though various approaches are available for choosing an alternative, the decision maker's personal values and aspirations affect what alternative will be chosen. In fact, in one way, the decision making is the translation of one's values and aspirations into action. Thus the rational process of decision making is considerably affected by the personal factors. Further managers should take into account the uncertainty of outcome of a decision. Therefore, they should be ready with alternative action if one fails. In order to do this, managers should often be ready with contingency plans.

6. Action. Once the alternative is selected, it is put into action. Truly speaking, the actual process of decision making ends with the choice of an alternative through which the objectives can be achieved. However, decision making, being a continuous and on-going process, must ensure that the objectives have been achieved by the chosen alternative. Unless this is done, managers will never know what way their choice has contributed. Therefore, the implementation of decision may be seen as an integral aspect of decision.

Implementation of a decision requires the communication to subordinates, getting acceptance of subordinates over the matter involved in the decision, and getting their support for putting the decision into action. The decision should be effected at appropriate time and in proper way to make the action more effective. The effectiveness of action is important because it is only effective action through which organisational objectives can be achieved, and right decisions help in effective action.

7. Results. When the decision is put into action, it brings certain results. These results must correspond with objectives, the starting point of decision process, if good decision has been made and implemented properly. Thus results provide indication whether decision making and its implementation is proper. Therefore, managers should take up a follow-up action in the light of feedback received from the results. If there is any deviation between objectives and results, this should be analysed and factors responsible for this deviation should be located. The feedback may also help in reviewing the decision when conditions change which may require changes in decision. Therefore, a successful manager is one who keeps a close look at the objectives and results of the decision and modifies his decision according to the changes in the circumstances.

Effective Decision

The decision-making process goes through the various stages and the basic objectives of all these stages are to solve problem through the decision. The solution of the problem depends on how effectively the decision is made and implemented. Thus an effective decision is one which is action-oriented, goal-directed, and provides efficiency in implementation. These three aspects of effective decision can be presented below:

1. ***Goal Direction.*** Organisations are goal-directed units and, therefore, any organisational process, including decision making should be goal-directed to enable the organisation to meet its objectives. Naturally, the values of a decision and the associated action is related to the dispatch with which the goal is achieved. While the value of a decision is dependent on the attainment of a given goal or set of goals, such attainment is a function of both the accuracy of the decision and its implementation. In evaluating a decision, then, a distinction should be made between the effects of goal attainment brought about by better decision and those attainments arising out of execution.
2. ***Action Orientation.*** Decisions are action-oriented and are directed towards relevant and controllable aspects of the environment. Decisions are totally pragmatic in nature and their value is dependent on the success of the actions that follow. Decisions may be treated as an intervening variable which may ultimately lead to the end-result variables. From this point of view, decisions should ultimately find their utility in implementation. Therefore, the decision to be effective, must specify the various actions which are to be taken to achieve the objective necessitating decision making.
3. ***Efficiency in Implementation.*** An effective decision should provide the way in which it can be implemented. Therefore,

decision making should take into account all the possible factors not only in terms of external context but also in internal context so that a decision can be implemented properly. Often the results are obtained by proper implementation of proper decision. Therefore, a brilliant decision may fail if it is not suitable for implementation by the organisation. From this point of view, three characteristics of an effective decision have been identified: *(i)* the viability of the decision; *(ii)* the degree of congruency between prediction and the reality or viability of the solution as it occurs; and *(iii)* the enthusiasm and skill with which the proposal is pursued the attractiveness of the venture.

Making Effective Decision

Any decision can be made effective if decision-making process is followed properly. However, to make decision affective, managers should take care of certain variables effecting their decision making and its implementation. The attempt should be to make a realistic decision rather than attempt at an ideal decision. This can be done if following factors are taken into consideration.

1. ***Application of Limiting Factor.*** Managers can do better if they apply the principle of limiting factor principle. In choosing from among alternatives, the more a manager recognises and solves for those factors which are limiting and critical to the attainment of desired objectives, the more clearly and accurately he can select the most desirable alternative. In order to identify the limiting factors, the manager should take a complete analysis of external environment and strengths and weaknesses of the organisation. The analysis will bring out what the organisation can do and cannot do. Therefore, the manager can refrain from taking such a decision which cannot be implemented by the organisation. However, the concept of limiting factor is not static. Therefore, limiting factor may vary from one decision situation to another, or for the same decision situation over the period of time. For example,

in the past, if availability of the funds was a limiting factor in a decision situation of acquiring a plant; in today's context, delivery of plant may become a limiting factor. Such a factor can be identified by complete analysis of decision situation.

2. ***Categorical Interpretation.*** At the very outset it may be emphasised that logical decision can be made if the real problem is interpreted and identified with indepth study and observation. Often what happens that managers do not analyse the problem carefully and they take symptoms as the problems. Moreover, they have a tendency to assume certain things without adequate basis and analysis. For example, many of the costs are assumed, sales are taken for granted, or a particular behaviour is always anticipated. These make the problem identification much difficult and the real problem necessitating decision making does not get adequate consideration. Therefore, in order to avoid such a situation, it is desirable that problem should be defined properly. It is often suggested that a problem is half solved if it is identified properly.

3. ***Adequate Information.*** Information is the life blood of an organisation because all decisions are based on this. More is the quantity of reliable information, higher is the validity of decision. Therefore, every aspect of decision should be backed by sound and adequate proofs. If the facts underlying a problem are collected and care is taken to analyse the situation as well as the problem in the light of collected information the basic spade work in making a decision is complete. However, there is a limit for collecting information because of time and cost factors. Therefore, manager must decide the extent to which he will go for further information. Generally the manager should not go for additional information whose marginal contribution to decision making is lesser than its cost of collection. Beyond this, the manager should use his experience and common

sense. However, problems come when the experience and common sense are used disproportionately. Managers often rely too much on their experience and common sense and they commit blunders. In the absence of adequate information, it is better to defer a major decision rather than making wrong decision because the cost of deferring decision will be lesser than making wrong decision.

4. ***Considering Others Views.*** While making decision, it is desirable that all alternatives are considered before arriving at a decision. Equally desirable is the fact that while making decision, others' views should also be considered adequately. Often what happens is that a decision is affected by preferences and values. Moreover, interpretation of many qualitative facts in an alternative is subject to personal judgement. Therefore, if various views on the same point are taken into consideration and given adequate weight, they will contribute to the quality of decision. Sometimes many views may seem to be impractical but they may turn to be highly practical if time relevance is not ignored. The basic idea of taking others' views is not that the manager will act accordingly but he must take into account the other alternatives as suggested by others. It is very old saying that 'listen to every body but do according to your judgment.'

The observance of the above principles should not be taken to mean that chance element in decision making can be avoided altogether. The fact is otherwise. Since a decision's impact is for future, the chance factor cannot be eliminated altogether. It can be considerably reduced if the above principles are followed. They will provide sound basis for decision making.

❐

12

Formal and Informal Organisations

Formal organisation is a system of conscious coordinated activities or forces of two or more persons towards a given objective. Chester Barnard found that the essence of formal organisation is consious of common objectives and asserted that formal organisation comes into existence when persons are able to communicate with one another, and are willing to act in cooperation and share an objective. This is a very broad definition of the term 'formal organisation', because it refers to any kind of group action with a common objective. Hower and Lorsch have defined formal organisation as "*(i)* the pattern of formal relationships and duties-the organisation chart+ job descriptions and position guides; and *(ii)* formal rules, policies, work procedures and similar devices adopted by the management to guide employee behaviour in certain ways, within the structure of formal relationships."

Formal organisation refers to the structure of well defined jobs, each bearing a definite measure of authority, responsibility and accountability. The structure is deliberately designed to enable the organisational members to work together for the achievement of common objectives. The formal organisation lays down the patterns of relationships, and rules and regulations to which the individual must adjust. It tells every organisation member to do certain things in a specified order, to obey orders from designated individuals, and so on. Coordination and communication also proceed according to the prescribed pattern.

Formal organisation is built around four key pillars; namely, *(i)* division of labour, *(ii)* scalar and functional process, *(iii)* structure, and *(iv)* span of control. Division of labour and specialisation is the basic principle of formal organisation. The whole work is divided into a number of small operations and each operation is performed by a different person so that there is maximum specialisation. The scalar and functional processes imply the growth of the organisation both vertically and horizontally. The structure of the organisation refers to the overall arrangement in the organisation which ensures proper balance between different parts of the organisation and secures the execution of all operations and the achievement of organisational objective. The span of control refers to the number of subordinates directly reporting and accountable to one's superior.

INFORMAL ORGANISATION

The informal organisation refers to people in group associations at work, but these associations are not specified in the blueprint of the formal organisation. The informal organisation means natural groupings of people in the work situation. Whenever people work together, they envolve informal groups bound together by common, social, technological, work or goal interests. Such groups constitute an informal organisation. Informal organisation represents relationships between individuals in the organisation based on interest, personal attitudes, emotional, prejudices, likes, dislike, physical location, similarity of work etc. these relation are not developed according to the procedures and rules and regulations laid down in the formal organisation structure.

Informal organisation comes into existence because of the limitations of the formal organistaion. It represents natural grouping of people in work situations. The birth of small informal groups in an organisation is a natural phenomenon. The informal groups may overlap also because an individual may be a member of more than one informal groups. Management cannot eliminate the informal groups because it does not create them. In many cases, informal groups come into being to support and suppliment the formal organisation.

RELATIONSHIP BETWEEN FORMAL AND INFORMAL ORGANISATIONS

Managers must recognise the existence of informal groups in organisations if they are to effectively accomplish their tasks. The formal and informal relationships may be studied separately but ultimately they must be integrated into a total organisation package for more complete view of organisational behaviour. George Homans suggested such a model where both the formal and informal relationship can be studied in an integrated fashion. The model is essentially based on three concepts: activities, interations and sentiments. Activities are concerned with what a person actually does. Interactions are the interpersonal contacts and relationships that one has with others. Sentiments reflect the emotional reactions of the organisation participants to various organisational issue as shown in figure below.

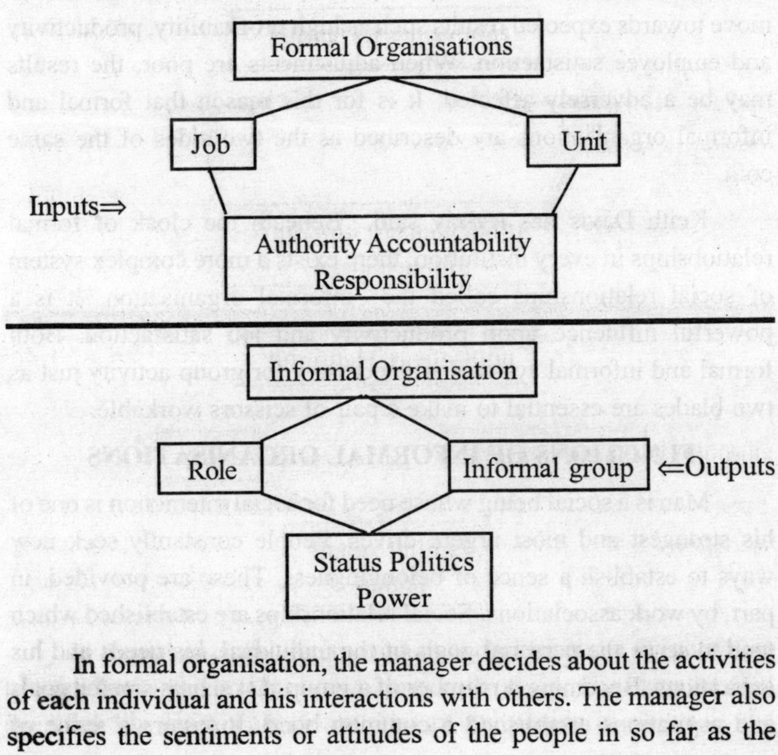

In formal organisation, the manager decides about the activities of each individual and his interactions with others. The manager also specifies the sentiments or attitudes of the people in so far as the

willingness to work is concerned. The authority, responsibility and accountability of each individual are thus defined in a formal organisation. However, while performing their tasks, employees develop activities, interactions and sentiments other than those required by the management.

The informal relationships are unlimited and varied in nature. Activities, interactions and sentiments affect the status and power an employee may enjoy and the polities he may play in the organisation. The status, power and politics are the foundations of informal organisation even though these are not exact substitutes to authotity, responsibility and accountability.

Both formal and informal organisations are integrally related. The final structure is determined by the inputs such as management policies and plans, needs of personnel economic and social environment, etc. When the relationships are sound, the organisation move towards expected results such as high profitability, productivity and employee satistaction. When adjustments are poor, the results may be a adversely affected. It is for this reason that formal and informal organisations are described as the two sides of the same coin.

Keith Davis has rightly said, "Beneath the cloak of formal relatiobships in every institution, there exists a more complex system of social relationships called the informal organisation. It is a powerful influence upon productivity and job satisfaction. Both formal and informal systems are necessary for group activity just as two blades are essential to make a pair of scissors workable.

FUNCTIONS OF INFORMAL ORGANISATIONS

Man is a social being whose need for social interaction is one of his strongest and most urgent drives. People constantly seek new ways to establish a sence of belongingness. These are provided, in part, by work associations. Social relationships are established which tend to serve the personal goals of the individual, his needs and his aspirations. Becoming a member of a group that shares similar goals and aspirations established a common bond. It fosters a sense of identity with a peer group, whose influence over him may become stronger than that exercised by management.

Formal organisation are job-oriented in terms of functions and authority; informal organisations are people-oriented in terms of personal and group goals. The informal organisation never appears on an organisational chart, and it is seldom included in the overall planning of a company's operation. It is not established by authority or decree, but it develops as people associated with one another. A manager can create a formal organisation and abolish it. He cannot create an informal organisation or abolish it. It evolves within the formal, structured organisation. As long as people need social intercourse, informal groups will exist.

In every organisation, informal groups arise to perform certain vital functions. According to Keith Davis, these functions are as follows:

(1) To provide social satisfaction to the members of the group which they otherwise fail to achieve through the working of the formal organisation. Informal organisation is established to fulfil needs of the members to build their social image, status and achieve social recognition.

(2) To perpetuate cultural values of the group which are dear to the members. This function is necesary to keep the organisation united and preserve its integrity.

(3) To have better communication which is otherwise not possible in the 'formal' organisation. It operates to satisfy needs, urges and requirements of members of a group to avoid long and difficult channels of communication of a formal organisation. Informal organisation provides 'short cuts' and 'easy ways' to fulfill information function for the benefit of the informal group.

(4) To create device to facilitate social control. Through this function of social control, the behaviour of the members of the organisation is controlled internally and externally. The

member of an informal organisation conforms to the accepted pattern within the prescribed 'norms' and regulated conduct acceptable to majority of the members.

Chester I. Barnard has liked three importnat functions of an informal organisation:

(1) As a means of communication, establishing in norms of conduct between superior and subordinates;

(2) "Maintenance" of cohesiveness in formal organisations by regulating the willingness to serve and the stability of objective authority;

(3) The maintenance of the feeling of personal integrity, of self-respect, of independent choice.

NATURE OF INFORMAL ORGANISATION

Informal organisation arises from social interaction. Hawthorne experiments that informal organisations are an integral part of the total work situation. Informal organisations are the network of personal and social relations which arises as the people come in contact with each other and are not the result of formal authority. Power in informal organisations is attached to person and not to the position and it is given by the members of the group irrespective of the position in formal structure. It is quite unstable since it relates to the sentimetns of the people of the group. Managers. generally are the leaders in the formal organisation and they like to abolish the informal groups. But they cannot do so because they know that they have not established them so they cannot abolish. The we find that the characateristics of informal organisation are as follows:

(i) It arises from social interaction of members in the group. The members of the group do not care for the formal channels of communication and communicate a man with each other.

(ii) The main purpose of its formation is to meet the personal needs of the groups and acts as an agency of social control.

(iii) It arises spontaneously and naturally. Involvement of members consciously or unconsciously given birth to such groups. A person may become its members at any time he likes.

(iv) Informal organisation is a part of total organisation. It is quite impossible to find a completely formal or completely informal organisation.

(v) Informal organisation is based on informal authority that is linked with the person and not with the position. Any member of the group may be designated as its leader because of his age, seniority, job knowledge, information, personality etc.

(vi) It develops from customs, contacts and habits of social group.

(vii) It tends to remain smaller, less-permanent and less stable.

(viii) Management of the organisation generally regards these organisations because of their valuable impact an productivity and job satisfaction. So formal managers should study the informal relationship among its members before dealing with them.

ADVANTAGES OF INFORMAL ORGANISATIONS

The major benefits from the organisational organisations are :

(i) It is a social structure formed to meet personal needs of the members of the group. Such needs cannot be met by formal structure.

(ii) Informal organisation is an useful channel of communication. It is developed by the members of the group. They remain in close contact to each other and know what is going to happen before the formal communication reaches them.

(iii) Informal organisations are to lightes the work load or the management. When management is sure that informal organisations are with them, they feel tell completed to have a check on the workers frequently.

(iv) Informal organisations may fill in the gaps in a manager's of informal group may help in correcting the defective plans by making their valuable suggestions and improve them in implementation also.

(v) Social conventions and group norms are given due recognition. It develops cooperations among the members of the group.

(vi) In the presence of informal organisations managers act carefully in making plans, policies and actions. Managers are aware that they are sufficent check on their powers of authority. They also know that if they measure their powers a be fitting reply may be given by the workers.

(vii) Informal organisations are safety valves for employes frustrations and other emotional problems. The frustration and other problems may not occure because they are discussed with others in the group of friendly manner.

(viii) Informal organisations are complimentary to formal organisation.

(ix) It has a powerful influence on the productivity and job satisfaction.

DEMERITS OF INFORMAL ORGANISATION

While these are distinct advantages for informal organisation, there are disadvantages too such as:

(i) It may restrict output. The informal group may set its own work pace and agree on a level of putput which does not permit one member to outperform another. The group may establish goals that are at variance with those announced by the management.

(ii) It may create dissatisfaction. If a group does not accept a worker, he may find his work more distasteful than he would otherwise. His dissatisfaction may cause excessive absenteeism, or he may require a transfer, or perhaps quit the job completely.

(iii) It may enforce severes self-regulation. The informal organisation tends to discipline its members through social pressures, social ostracism, or in extreme cases, through physical threat or harm. Failure to comply with group standards of acceptable work output could lead to attempts by the group to bring the dissident member into line. The group can make life miserable for the non-conformist. Subtle attempts may be made to upset his work routine or to prevent his functioning effectively. Social ostracism or exclusion from the group privileges is a severe penalty for a person who must have group acceptance and approval to satisfy his strong need for social interaction.

(iv) It develops additional confromity. Wholehearted association with an informal organisation demands that a person accepts another kind of conformity to avoid conformity and routine, he gravitates towards an informal group but find this acceptance has its price. He is expected to conform to the codes and standards of the informal group and to identify with its interests and goals. Under these conditions, a person exchanges one type of conformity for another.

DISTINCTION BETWEEN FORMAL AND INFOMAL ORGANISATIONS

Simon differentiates between a formal and informal organisation on the basis of allocation of zones of activity, establishment of authority relationships, procedures and lines of communication. He said that, "for the most part, these relationship can be described rather abstractly". Both these constitute a "total" organisation because a formal scheme of organisation always differs from an actually operating one, *i.e.*, many interpersonal relationships are exhibited which are nowhere available in the formal scheme and, secondly, the 'actual' interpersonal relationships may be contradictory to the formal relationships. Simon thus concluded that informal organisation refers to "interpersonal relations in the organisation that affect decisions within it but either are omitted from the formal scheme or are not consistent with that scheme. It would probably be fair to say that no formal organisation will operate effectively without an accompanying informal organisation". Informal organisation is spontaneous, automatic, and inevitable extension of a formal organisation although it is not officially prescribed.

Some of the management thinkers consider the formal-informal controversy as unnessessary. To them the formal-informal dichotomy is only useful as a "conceptual too". Its "face validity often induces to a false and elusive security, in reality behaviours cannot be governed on the assumption that such absolute categories exist. Nevertheless, this distinction has become so ingrained in popular parlance in the professional literature that it is impossible to avoid its use.

In acutal organisational situations, formal and informal activities, sentiments and interactions get so mixed up that it is difficult to segregate them. People behave as 'whole' human beings and not in compartmentalised fashion. There is no sense in trying to understand the structure and process of a formal organisation without closely looking into the 'underworld' and the 'sub-culture' organisation is more than a human social counterpart of the formal organisation. It is a sort of countervailing power of the rigidity, dehumanisation and the opperssiveness characteristic of the formal organisation. The informal organisation provides to the individual in the organisation a stronger social forum than the formal organisation to discover his identity, to shape his value, to satisfy his needs, to ventilate his feelings, to find solace and comfort and to realise his potential.

It is true that informal organisation is so transitory, lacking stabilised structure and concrete network of relationships that its existence is subject to tremendous changes, *i.e.*, informal organisational structure and pattern of behaviour is so in such a "flux" that any substantial distinction becomes often ridiculous. Despite all this, informal structures do exist along with formal one, constantly changing their form and behaviour pattern. The professed goals sometimes are difficult to achieve because group goals run counter to ideals of the organisation. Selznick says, "in that conflict the confessed goals will tend to go down in defeat, usually through the process of being extensively ignored" by the operation of goals constituting the goals of various goups.

FORMAL ORGANISATION VS. INFORMAL ORGANISATION FORMAL ORGANISATION

Formal Organisation	*Informal Organisation*
1	*2*
1. It is a planned structure based upon work to be done and to which the people must adjust by means of authority, duties and accountability.	Informal organisation is an outcome of automatic growth and development of human and social relations unofficial in character, emergent of social and personal needs.
2. A Formal organisation has a hierachy of jobs, authority, relationships and rules for compliance and codes for punishment in case of deviations from rules.	Informal organisation has a leadership strucrture, rules, standards, norms, way of rewarding complianc but all neither neither prescribed nor followed by any mandatory procedures for execution.
3. The channels of communication are well defined. The basic emphasis is on downward communnic·tion. Formal communication follows the route of scaler chain. Individuals are required to behave in a prescribed manner in their work situation. Inter-action and behaviour are structured in an objectively rational manner. Behavioural violations are dealt with according to the due processes of organisational law and order.	Communication follows the pattern of a grapevine and is multi-directional. The flow of information may be in any direction and cut across the formal channels. Interactions are less inhibited. Behaviour is more natural and is socialised. It is a product of: *(a)* the attitudes and values which individuals individuals bring with them into the organisation, *(b)* the required behavi-ours normal in the formal organisation, and *(c)* the informal group culture to which the individuals are attached.

Contd.

1	2
4. There is emphasis on work speciali-sation through utilisation of indivi-dual's talent, and abilities friendships racial origins.	People are indluenced in their coope-rative efforts by recognition of desires, cliques, sentiments and social customs.
5. The motivating force in a formal organisation is economic incentive in the form of promotion, increment, etc.	The motivating force is fulfilment of social an dpersonal needs.
6. Individuals belong to one work group only and are to work under one sup-erior. Hence their area of opeartion is circumscribed.	Individuals can be members of more than one work group according to their choice. An individual can be a leader in one group and a follower in another. He can be a leader for particular matters and a follower in others. there is no rigidity about group membership.

MANAGEMENTS RESPONSE TOWARDS INFORMAL ORGANISATIONS

Management cannot wish away the existence of informal organisation since it does not create it. The only option felt with management is to identfy its existence, its leadership, its goals, its cultural organisation aids management in the realisation of its organisational goals. In this context, it is very important for management to identify the leadership of the informal organisation and to try to achieve its cooperation for the realisation of organisational goals.

Most often informal groups tend to be small. Each has its leader, who was not elected or appointed but earned this status because of age, seniority on the dominant personality, special capability, physcial strength, or some other characteristics. But in a larger informal group, there may be more than one leader whom the group will follow under given circumstances. An individual with more formal education than the others may be looked up in matters that require formal communication. He may be asked to speak for the group in dealings with management, union, or other informal groups. Another member, possessing more job experience and technical expertise may be consulted when guidance is needed in solving some problems connected with the job.

Knowing and understanding the leadership of the groups with whom he deals can be extremely useful to a manager. Favourable relationships with the leaders and seek their advice on technical matters or human relations problems and training them to become competent workers in their formal job assignment. Open two-way communication can be encouraged on a continuing basis for mutual benefit. A manager must be careful not be reduce the status of the leader in the eyes on his constituents, and especically carefull not to reduce the status of the leader in the eyes of his constituents, and especially careful not to show any favouritism to any of his constituents.

Informal communication, though may have certain ill consequences, can also be used by an enlightened manager to plug the loopholes of the formal communication system. Informal Communication is very fast and ensures that informal communication does not pruduce rumours and if a rumour spreads, it should not be allowed to damage the functioning of the organisation. In short, management can use every aspect of informal organisation to achieve the organisatinal objectives

GRAPEVINE PATTERN

The grapevine information may be oral or written or by observation. Which cannot be communicated offically that can easily be communicated through this system. Information received through this media may be hundred percent correct or entirely wrong. It may leak through authority travels rapidly and number of persons recieve it. The management has to keep pace with it. Informal communication system or grapevine is made up on all channels of communication that fall outside the officially designated channels that are spelled out in rules, regulations, and manuals of the organisation. Where formal channels are silent on the subject important to members of the organisation informal net work becomes strong. Grapevine cannot be sbolished, rubbed out, hidden under a bucket, chapped down, tied up or stopped. If anybody tires to abolish or stop it or suppress it, it will emerge out at some other place and if we out off one of its sources, it will move to another one. Thus, its abolition is not possible. It is a human birth right, because whenever people congregate into groups, the grapevine is sure to develop whatever be the method or source. It is the expression of the natural motivation to communicate the information. It is the exercise of freedom to speech, it is natural and normal by activity. It is quite uninterested in social interaction or in knowing or telling that what is happening around him. It means that he is malady used in th society otherwise he cannot keep himself unknown about what is happening with other members. It is a job characteristic of a person that has an important influence on that person's role on the grapevine. So, certain employees are more active on the grapevine and spread or help communicate the information, not because of his personality but because of his close proximity of a person who possesses the news. Of course, it is a personality characteristic also. Some people by nature are reserved and keep everything confidential while some others are more prone to disclose the information they have.

Following are the features of grapevine

(i) Grapevine is influential either positively or negatively but nothing can be said certain whether its net effect is positive or negative because its effects may vary among different work groups and organisation.

(ii) It cannot be done away with irrespective of its positive or negative effects so management must adjust to it. The management, therefore, should know who its leader is, how it operates and what information it carries. Managers should listen to its leader and study their emotions.

(iii) It has a tremendous capacity to carry information good or bad to the organisation or to the people.

(iv) It moves fastly. Being flexible and personal, it spreads information faster than most formal comminication system.

(v) It has unusual ability to penetrate even the highlest company security because of its capacity to cut across. It is a source of much more information than management wants to release.

Information spread like a cluster chain on grapevine rather than a long chain because each link in the chain tends to inform not only one person but several persons at a time. What it implies is that in the initial stages, an individual transmits information to a number of individuals say three or four. These three or four persons or any one or two of them will pass on the information to others usually more than one person and in this way, all become known to the information in no time. As the information becomes known to more and more person and becomes stale it dies out because those who receive it to not repeat it, *i.e.* the number of persons being informed by an individual goes on declining.

If we accept the idea of cluster chain, we can conclude that only a few are active communicator in the group on the grapevine for any particular bit of information and others are simply receiver of information and do not spread it.The acative communicator are called bais on individuals.

The grapevine is more a product of the situation than it is of person and if proper situation and motivation are given, any individual may become an active communicator on the grapevine. Keith Davis has suggested three situations for becoming an active communicator:

(i) When there is excitement and insecurity about job.

(ii) When our friends and associates are involved in the situation.

(iii) When it is news and not a state information because research shows that the greatest spread of information takes place immediately after it becomes known.

IMPORTANCE OF GRAPEVINE

Grapevine is bound to exist in an organisation. Management has to accommodate itself with the following benefits:

(i) The Grapevine may also serve as advance warning signals for management of an emerging crisis or intended action by workmen. Thus they gain by the information they received from the informal groups. They can think over the problem and its ways out well in advance in order to tackle the problem efficiently.

(ii) It is a good means to know the reaction of people on contempleted policies and actions. Sometimes management takes the advantage of situation by feeding the message on grapevine and to get the reaction of people about the policies or decision before they implemented. They take decision or amendments according to the reaction to whether it is possitive or negative.

(iii) Grapevine provides managers much feedback about employees and their work experience thus increasing their understanding about their work-force and work situations. They can plan their actions or take decisions supportive to the employees.

(iv) Managers can seek support of the employees through grapevine. It helps interpret management to the workers so that they may be more supportive. It especially helps translate managements formal order into employees language and in this way making up for the failure of the management in comunication.

(v) Whenever a message is to be used very quickly managers may get it processed on grapevine which may spread it like a jungle-fire.

(vi) The groups and persons may be persuaded not to insist certain demands and they may be told informally about the consequences of steps, proposed to be taken by the management

(vii) It is useful for Trade Unions. They use grapevine as an important channel of communication for spreading exciting news and provoking members for violent activities. Grapevine which is an important channel of communication sometimes it provides some disadvantages to the workers and management also which are as follows:

(i) The one important feature of the grapevine is its fact speed. Due to this characteristic, sometimes, information are misheard or misinter-preted which help in spreading rumours and because the management is unable to stop undesirable rumours due to its fast speed, it may lead to confrontation.

(ii) The leakage of some important confidential message may prove fatal to the organisation or to the position holder. Leakage of policy matters or action against an employee may be examples of such types

Rumours

Grapevine which is a source of information under which all informations passed that may be wrong or may be correct also. The part of information which is not true spreads among the members of the group of management and it becomes a rumour due to lack of standards of advice. Rumour is the most undesirable feature of the grapevine. It is the part of grapevine information which is commiunicated without having secure standards of evidence being present and which is incorrect, unverified or enters. If people do not have any interest in the subject or there is no ambiguity in the situation, *i.e.*, all facts are clear, then no person has any cause to rumour where people have interest- positive or negative- in the subject matter it causes rumour only when these exists an ambiguity for which verification is not possible. It means both interest and ambiguity are must to begin or to maintain a rumour.

Since rumour is subjected to interest and ambiguity perceived by each person, it changes as it passes from person to person keeping the main theme intact, but not the details. It is subject to filtering and reduced to only a few rememberable words while passing it to no others. It is given shape by the communicator according to his interests. Sometimes people elaborate details by adding new details serving their interests.

The rumours which are incorrect and may by harmful for the organisation, may endanger the life of people of the area. The following steps may be taken to control this devastating epidemic:

1. Realising facts may be the next step to stop or weaken rumour so that truth may prevail over the rumour. Serious rumours should be attacked immediately without any further delay otherwise people will distort the further happenings to confirm to the rumour.
2. Usually a face to face supply of facts is the most effective step because it helps removing ambiguity in each individual's mind by giving proper answer to that ambiguity. The facts should be supplied directly without first mentioning the rumour. The communication of facts is more effective if it comes from a source which is supposed to have true facts. Dependable informal leader may be contacted. Facts may be shared with him as soon as possible and he will help management stop the rumour.
3. The very first step in dealing with rumour is to understand and anaylse the causes before it starts. Getting at causes is wise use of the preventive approach instead of a tardy curative approach. When people feel reasonably secure, understand thing that matter to them and feel on the team, there are few rumours because there is very little ambiguity in the situation. But when people are maladjusted or wrongly informal about their environment, they are likely to become rumour-mongers. So, prevention is better than a cure.
4. If, still rumour do start, management should analyse the situation and if it seems harmless, then it should not waste organisation time in combating it because it will soon die out automatically. But, if it is really serious enough to damage effectiveness or reputation, the management should try to stop it.
5. Unions may also be asked to help the management in combating rumour. Although union does not control the

grapevine, yet it has influence over the group. Labour management conflicts may increase the intensity of the problem. Any reduction in conflict may reduce rumours. If union steward cooperation is gained, it will help management combating rumour provided the steward is strong informal leader.

6. Regardless of the importance of rumour, it should be listened to carefully. Though it is based on untrue information yet it carries the feelings of the individuals and the group. The management, in this way come to know where ambiguities are and what the interests of employees are. So that he may understand the reason of its origination. It helps management in settling the disputes amicably.

Thus, the above steps may certainly help the management in combating or controlling the rumours.

INFORMAL GROUP

As discussed earlier, groups can be divided on the basis of their formalisation, and there can be either formal or informal groups. There is a general tendency to call informal group as informal organisation because the term organisation is used to denote whole of the organisation as well as its parts also and groups are part of the organisation. Informal organisation emerges within the context of formal organisation to overcome its limitations. The actual organisation structure is the result of the formal and informal organisational relationships. What is given in the formal chart denotes formal organisation but it merely shows the lines of interactions which should be maintained but not necessarily maintained. In practice, these lines are modified by the impact of informal relationships, commonly known as informal organisation.

The informal organisation can be viwed as a shadow organisation. It refers to people in group or association at work place but these association is not specified in the blueprint of the formal organisation. It arises naturally, spontaneously from the interaction of people. Thus informal organisation refers to unofficial relationships that inevitably occur between individuals and groups within the formal organisation.

REASONS FOR INFORMAL ORGANISATION

Informal organisation is inevitable along with formal organisation and to obtain a total picture of an organisation structure in its true form, one must consider informal organisation also. The basic reason behind the emergence of informal organisation is the inadequacy of formal organisation structure to meet the needs of both members and organisation. Either it does not provide the most convenient way of interactions or it may produce some psychological pressure on the member of the organisation. Thus members ty to find out alternative way of interactions. Particularly in the following circumstances, people try to establish informal organisation.

1. Psychological Fatigue of Routine Tasks. Due to increasing level of specialisation, people concentrate on single task or a few simple tasks. Simple and routine type of tasks have undesirable influence on the people. They become bored by their tasks and may feel psychological fatigue. They are unable to relate the meaning of their tasks to the whole organisation. Greater the degree of specialisation, greater is the concentration of fragmented tasks, and grater is the degree of boredom. This boredom is far from ideal condition. Therefore, people try to overcome this boredom through interactions which may provide them stimulus which is possible through informal organisation. Through informal interactions, they are able to release the tension created on the job. Informal organisation, thus, has the capability to fill up the psychological vacum created by dull, boring, and monotonous jobs.

2. Desire to Socialise with Others. It is a natural tendency that people like to socialise in the organisation in order to satisfy their social and ego needs. Normally, such needs are not satisfied by the formal organisation but such needs are quite important for people. Informal organisation provides

them opportunity to interact with people of their liking based on so many factors like personality factors, caste, religion, place common interests other than organisational relationships, etc. Similarly on any one or more of these aspects provides satisfaction to people through interaction which they can not get through formal interaction. This is the natural way of need satisfaction and, therefore, becomes important reasons for the emergence of informal organisation. For example, Davis observes that "along with men's technical imperative, there is also a social imperative to work together. Man is social being. He wants to belong, to associate with others rather to work in isolated loneliness. Out of this basic drive of man, the informal organisation arises.

3. Hierarchical Control and Communication. Modern large organisation are characterised by hierarchy with formal chain of control and communication. There exists a superior-subordinate relationship with a natural tendency of exercise of control by superors while subordinates may not like control. When a subordinate is not able to thwart such hierarchial control, he tries to find out an association where he does not face similar type of control, he tries to find out an association where he does not face similar type of control. Thus, he joins informal group. Moreover, formal organisational process, particularly communication, may be quite lengthy and time consuming while people may like to work through a shorter way. Thus they develop their own way of interaction.

4. Various Functions of Informal Organisation. Besides the above reasons, informal organisation contributes in several ways to the interests of its members. These may be in the areas of *(i)* protecting their interest, *(ii)* working as regulatory device, *(iii)* protection of cultural values of members, *(iv)* validation of their beliefs, *(v)* outlet for

overcoming frustraction, and *(vi)* exploitation and development of leadership potential. Similarly, informal organisation also works for the interest of formal organisation in several ways like *(i)* filling gaps in managerial abilities, *(ii)* restrain on manager's area of operation, *(iii)* medium of communication, and *(iv)* source of information. It can be observed here that though an informal organisation may contribute to formal organisation, but its basic objective is to contribute to the members' interest.

Woking of Informal Organisation

As against formal organisation where organisational process-role, status, authority relationships, decision making, communication, etc. are prescribed, there is no such prescription in informal organisation. these processes do take place in informal organisation too but without any definite set of structure. These informal processes interact with formal processes and affect them but at the same time are affected by the latter. In particular, three informal processes are quite important which affect the functioning of formal organisation. These are authority structure, leadership, and communication. Let us see how these work is informal organisation.

1. Authority Structure. Informal organisation emerges because of personal and social relationships and not because of formal relationships. Therefore, there is no question of authority through delegation from up. Authority in informal organisation is personal and not positional. Infact, informal organisation works on the basis of mutual understanding and acceptance of others. Therefore, authority arises because people accept someone's ability to control the informal organisation. From positional point of view, every member has equal right. It is possible that someone may hold some personal power in the informal organisation with his official authority, however, such power can not be more than what other members of the informal organisation enjoy. Therefore, the influence process in the informal organisation is personalised and a person may exercise influence to mould the behaviour of members based on his capacity to satisfy the needs of members. Because members feel satisfaction through a particular person, they may agree to be influenced by the person. For example, Davis has observed that "power in informal organisation is earned or given permissively by group members, rather than delegated; therefore, it does not follow official chain of command. It is more likely to come from peers than from superiors in the informal hierarchy."

2. Leadership. Leadership is the ability to persuade others to seek defined objectives enthusiastically. It is the human factor which binds a group together and motivates it towards goals. While in the case of a formal organisation, superior assumes the role of a leader, in informal organisation, there is no formal leader. The leadership role may come from any one in the informal organisation. Let us see the role of an informal leadership and the type of person likely to assume the role of leadership. A leader performs vital functions that contribute to the group's ability to survive in its environment. These functions are as follows: *(i)* A leader initiates action in the group; *(ii)* he facilitates consesus; and he provides a link between the group and outside world such as managers, other groups, etc. Normally any one performing these functions may become leader of the group. The person who emerges as leader is perceived by others in the group as being the best abke to satisfy the group's needs.

The position of an informal leader changes when he is appointed as superior of the group. This happens because of two reasons. First, with his appointment as superior, he gets formal authority which was not available to him as informal leader. This authority enables him toincrease or decrease the satisfaction of his subordinates second, he has obligation not only to satisfy his subordinates but also to achieve the organisation objectives. Thus there may be conflicting roles to be performed by him–meeting of organisational objectives and satisfaction of members' needs. Therefore, unless he maintain a proper balance between these two roles, he is likely to fail as a formal leader. There have been instances where good informal leaders have been ineffective as formal leaders because of their inability to balance the conflicting roles.

3. Communication. Informal organisation develops its own media and channels of communication. Communication is mostly oral and many carry the information which can not be obtained through the formal channel. Informal organisation is a need fulfilment device generated from within and also from without when it is found that the existing formal communication channel is inadequate to supply the required information or information at right time. The requirement of speedier communication generates the need for informal channel which is supplemented to the formal one. Informal communication network is called grapevine which may take several shapes in terms of communicative relationships.

DIFFICULTIES DUE TO INFORMAL ORGANISATION

The working of informal organisation produces both functional and dysfunctional effects. As discussed earlier, various functions of informal organisation serves the needs of its members as well as of formal organisation. However, an informal organisation may present several dysfunctional effects specially if it is not handled properly. Many managers look at informal organisation as devil within the formal organisation because it creates lot of problems in managing. The major problems that emerge because of the operation of informal organisation may be in the following directions.

1. **Generation of Rumour.** Rumour is a specific proposition for belief, passed from person to person usually by words of month, without securing the standards of accuracy in the communication. Rumour deals with temporary events in a way that implies that whatever is said is true through there is not much authentic information to support it. Rumour is spread through informal organisation. The basis for the circulation of rumour is ambiguous circumstances and relieving of emotional tensions felt by people because of ambiguity. If there is no official communication on any aspect of important happening in the organisation, it will be communicated through rumour which may be far from truth. This creates problems for both management and

employees. It may be destructive in the sense that it affects morale of people adversely as every one goes on adding information from his own side most suitable to him.

2. **Resistance to Change.** Informal organisation produces resistance to change in the organisation. Every group promotes certain values and norms which are considered to be desirable for it. In course of time, members guard these values and norms resulting in a perpetuation of the status quo. Any intended change by the management facing alteration of commonly shared values and norms is vehmently resisted. Though people perceive the outcome of a change programme individually, specially, if the outcome is precise and definite, often they show their reaction in group. Since informal organisation is bound by values and norms, there will be considerable amount of resistance to change. For example, if members perceive that a layoff is imminent, though in actual it is not necessary, because of rationalisation of work, they will resist it. Since the resistance comes in the form of group, it becomes quite effective. The need for modern organisations to bring continuous changes is high.

3. **Role Conflict.** An individual perceives role conflict when he has to fulfilconflicting requirements of two or more roles. It may be observed that a person may perform several roles at the same time. Due to informal organisation, a person has to perform two roles, one relates to his official position and another relates to satisfaction of members of his group. These two roles and often conflicting, that is, performance of one role may be at the cost of the other. Since people have tendency to associate with informal groups, such role conflict may come in the way of performance of official duties. Higher the degree of role conflict, higher is the dysfunctional impact on organisational functioning. Thus, generation of two many

informal organisations may be determental to the organisation.

4. **Conformity.** Informal organisation exerts strong pressures for conformity. Conformity almost carries negative connotation in formal organisation because it involves behaviour which conforms to officially prescribed one. In the case of informal organisation, conformity means to act according to the general standards of informal organisation. This can make group members reluctant to act independently, creatively, or assertively, for the fear of losing group approval and membership. Pressure for conformity may result into restricted output as found by Hawthorne Experiments. Sometimes, informal leaders manipulate the group towards undesirable needs or their own selfish ends. Therefore, there is considerable chance that members of the group may use the resources of the organisation not for it own benefits but for the benefits of others.

5. **Social Costs.** Informal organisation is costly from social point of view also. No doubt, it is quite effective device to overcome frustration and other malfunctioning of an individual, it may result into wastage of time and resources. When informal groups are engaged in gossiping, joke telling, or idle conversation that satisfy some of the membes' social needs, they incur social costs. More time wasted in such things, more is the operating costs for the organisation because all these things take place within the stipulated office time.

❐

13

Organisation Culture

Every organisation has a culture. It has its own cultural norms that constitute the expected, supported, and accepted ways of behaving. These norms are mostly unwritten and tell employees the way things really are. These influence everyone's perceptions of the business from the Chief Executive to the lowest worker. All oraganisation members contribute to norms by accepting and supporting them. But management's behaviour has a special impact because of its strong modelling influence. Senior management can make a mark on their companies by understanding, building and managing culture.

An organisation culture consists of two basic components *(i)* the primary values of the organisation, or 'what we believe in' or values and beliefs, and *(ii)* its pervasive managemnet style: "What role and behaviours are expected if we are to be successful" and how we do things around us. These two components of culture significantly affect the degree to which desired results from the employees are obtained. Values, which are an element of culture, are important component in the action scheme of individuals and indicate the direction in which organisation are likely to move in the future. Values have significant impact on individual behaviour. Values determine what the employee considers he should do.

It will be appropriate to know here the importance of understanding culture. A strong culture is a powerful lever for guiding behaviour. It helps employees to do their jobs better, expecially in two ways.

(i) An effective culture is a system of informal rules that spell out how employees are to behave most of the time.

Employees know what is to be done and its impact on productivity is amazing.

(ii) An effective culture enables people to feel better about what they do, so they are more likely to work harder. It removes a lot of uncertainty.

In brief the culture provides a sense of common direction and guidelines for day-to-day behaviours. It enables the companies to succeed because their employees can identify, embrace and act on the values of the organisation. Employees know what their company stands for and what standards are to be upheld, and therefore, their decisions in line with these. They also feel as if they are an important part of the organisation. All these have a motivating effect. This is an advantage of having shared values.

DEVELOPING ORGANISATION CULTURE

A framework for developing an effective organisation culture can be as under:

(i) **Formulating Statement of Organisational Philosophy.** The starting point in cultural development involves assessing and formulating a statement of organisational philosophy and communicating it to empolyees. Most basically, philosophy statements clarify the organisation's values in various areas such as relationships to customers; growth, strategies mission, social reponsibility and, most important managerial style. For this purpose an innovative approach to analysing managerial behaviour (on specific roles is called for) and then constructing an effective culture.

(ii) **Sharing Values.** It is universally agreed that values should be shared by all empolyees. What bring values to life is their extensive sharing leading to awareness of the values and why they are important.

(iii) **Adhering Faithfully to the Values.** Simply communicating Corporate Philosophy to all employees is only the beginning for creation of a strong, congruent culture. The real thing to be seen is that the desired culture is reflected by pervasive roles, behaviours, and activities that support the organisation philosophy and values. Any inconsistency will undermine the strength of the culture.

(iv) **Managerial Modelling Behaviour.** As empolyees behaviour is trongly influenced by managerial behaviour, the process of cultural change has to start with senior management. All the managers can be made aware of the behavioural and role expectations required of them by the desired culture.

BENEFITS OF ORGANISATION CULTURE

Some of the benefits of an effective culture are discussed below:

(i) Culture has the pontential of giving meaning and purpose to an employee's organisation life, over and above just doing one's job for his salary. It provides the significant meanings and guiding concepts an organisation imbues in its members for example, high quality standards, a focus on productivity improvement and innovation, meeting customer delivery requirements, a belief that problem solving and team work are important, participative style in decision making, and a belief that people are important resources to be managed. Thus it provides greater commitment to the organisation's objectives.

(ii) Culture provides more than the 'social glue' that holds the organisation together. It also provides the lubrication that allows the organisation's gears to mesh in high speed. It increases employee effort, pride and loyalty.

(iii) Effective culture reduces employee turnover.

(iv) It enables more effective problem solving at all organisation levels.

(v) Effective culture provides the ability to grow rapidly through directing more effort toward implementing plans, programmes, and objectives and less effort toward fighting fires, plugging holes, constantly resolving conflicts about how thing should be done, and so forth.

(vi) It provides the employees a way of life in the company and not to merely took for jobs.

(vii) It is important for organisation's continuity.

(viii) It enables managers to understand how culture works if they want to accomplish what they should do. Managers give extraordinary attention to whatever matters are stressed in the value system and this in turn tends to produce good results.

Risks and Pitfalls of Strong Culture

The power of organisation values is that people care for them, which is a great strength. But power of values can be problem too. As Peters and Waterman state, less effective and poorly performing companies often have strong cultures too, but dysfunctional ones. Some of the risks involved are: *(a)* risk of obsolescence, *(b)* risk of resistence to change, *(c)* risk of inconsistency (managerial behaviour contradicting to professed values).

To summarise the aim of this chapter is to understand, first the meaning of the organisation culture because a distinguishing characteristic of highly successful organisations is a strong, well developed culture. It consists of values and beliefs of the organisation and managerial style expected if we are to be successful. Second aspect is to know the benefits of culture. Organisation values provide a sense of common direction and guidelines for day-to-day behaviour of employees. It has great motivating effect for improved performance. Effective culture enables achieving of objectives and implementation of programmes rapidly. Then we discussed the risks of having strong culture particularly if it is dysfunctional one. Some of the risks are obsolescence, resistence to change and inconsistency in implementing professed values. At the end we have presented a framework for developing organisation culture. This consists of *(i)* formulating a statement of organisation philosophy, *(ii)* sharing with all employees, *(iii)* adhering faithfully to the values, and *(iv)* managerial modelling influence.

In the second part of this series, we will discuss experiences of some of the organisations in shaping and developing organisation culture. Attempt will be made to describe the process and conceptual framework they are following in exploring and analysing the existing managerial styles and developing desired culture.

ELEMENTS OF ORGANISATION CULTURE

Every organisation has a culture. It has its own cultural norms that constitute the expected, supported, and accepted ways of behaving. These norms are mostly unwritten and tell employees the way things really are. These influence everyone's perceptions of the business from the Chief Executive to the lowest worker. All organisation members contribute to norms by accepting and supporting them. But management's behaviour has a special impact because of its strong modelling influence. Senior management can make on their companies by understanding, building and managing culture.

It consists of values and beliefs of the organisation and managerial style expected. Second aspect brought out was the benefits of culture. Organisation values provide a sense of common direction and guidelines for day to day behaviour of employees. It has great motivating effect for improved performance. Effective culture enables achieving of objectives and implementation of programmes rapidly. It is important for continuity of the organisation effectivencess. Then we discussed the risks of having strong culture particularly if it is dysfunctional one. Some of the risks are - obsolescence, resistence to change and inconsistency in implementing professed values. As a concluding part we had presented a framework for developing organisation culture. This consists of *(i)* formulating a statement or organisation philosophy, *(ii)* sharing with all employees, *(iii)* adhering faithfull to the values, and *(iv)* managerial modelling influence.

In this chapter an attempt has been made to bring out things. First is to delineate on the elements of culture, and their significance. In the latter part some important aspect of organisation culture are discussed.

Some of the elements of culture are - values, heroes, rites and rituals, cultural network and business environment.

(i) Values are the Core of the Culture. Values are the basis of any culture. Values are something that have worth or carry importance to individuals. Values help shape human behaviours. They provide a sense of common direction and guidelines for day to day behaviour. Culture also includes wide range of beliefs. Both values and belief's provide guidelines for employees to follow in their work. Putting of both these into action, brings about success. An example of this is "Productivity through people" was a slogan adopted in 1980 by the Bhopal Unit of Bharat Heavy Electricals Limited during its Organisational Development effort. Values and beliefs of an organisation also indicate what matters are to be attended carefully. These play an important role in communicating to outside world, what to expect of a company. An example of this is "24-hour parts service anywhere in the world" - an extraordinary commitment to customer needs adopted by Caterpillar, USA.

(ii) Another Element of Culture is "Heroes". If values are the soul of the culture, heroes personify these values. Heroes are great motivators. They reinfroce the basic values by various ways such as, providing role - models for employees to follow; symbolising the company to the outside world; preserving what makes the company special; setting a standard of performance; building a workforce that identifies personal achievement with the success of the firm; create institutions. Heroes have a vision, are experimenters and have unshakable character and style. They can be counted on when things get tough and rough.

(iii) Yet Another Element of Culture is the Rites and Rituals. If corporate culture and values are to thrive (and not die) these must be ritualised and celebrated. These rites and rituals have a very powerful influence on "the way we do things around here". Heroes of corporate culture give a lot of attention to the orchastration of all rituals of work life. These may be performed in the company in form of play exercises, jokes, teasings etc.), rituals (dramatisation of the company's basic cultural values); and ceremonies (display culture so that it is remembered). These rituals may be of different types such as social rituals, work rituals, management rituals, recognition rituals etc.

(iv) **Finally, Cultural Network is an Important Element for Communication Within the Organisation.** This network consists of story-tellers, priests, whispers and gossips. It ties all parts of the company irrespective of position or titles. The network is important because it not only transmits information, but it also transmits the significance of the information for the employees. This network can reinforce the basic values of an organisation and also sets a new climate for change.

IMPORTANT ASPECTS OF ORGANISATION CULTURE

Culture embraces the values and norms that actually influence the behavioural processes. In a way, they are the unwritten rules. They are perhaps more influential than the writtten ones, because they are internalised and affect behaviour. There are several aspects to the culture of an organisation.

(i) Work standards.
(ii) Initiative
(iii) Trust
(iv) Support
(v) Innovation
(vi) Differences.

(i) **Work Standards.** The coercive power of discipline is declining. Monetary incentive have a limit. They tend to encourage calculative bargaining. Norms built up over time influence productivity. Does the average individual perceive and accept the norm around him to be the pursuit of excellence, in terms of quality, quantity, cost and timeliness? Or does he learn to check himself because of the restrictive norm in the culture?

(ii) Initiative. The individual has potential. The structure may attempt delegation. But its success depends on the behaviour of the delegatee as well as that of the delegator. Does the delegatee get informal value message than when he sees a problem or opportunity, he is expected to be self-starter? If the norm is to await instruction, it is a big handicap for excellence.

(iii) Trust. The larger an institution the more difficult it is to engender interpersonal and intergroup trust. At the same time, it is more necessary. A norm of openness would help interaction, communication and cooperation. A culture of testing indicates hidden agenda and suspicion.

(iv) Support. The essence of strategy is that an institution with limited resources, but a sound strategy can succeed in competition with a larger institution without a viable strategy. One of the requirements is that individual and groups support each other by sharing facilities, people, data, etc. The opposite norm of hoarding will reduce the potential for excellence.

(v) Innovation. One of the key components of the managerial role is innovation. There is need and scope for innovation in almost every sphere of an institution. But successful innovation depends on a cultural norm of experimentation. The norm implies that any promising idea may be tried out on a small-scale. If it works, it can be replicated on a larger scale. The opposite norm of resistance implies a pervasive hostility or apathy to new ideas.

(vi) Difference. Ends and means are always source of differences. But it is out of differing view points that creative problems-solving can take place. The condition for that is that there should be a norm of confronting and resolving such differences. Attempts to circumvent by manipulating authority or denying differences indicate an avoidance norm. The creative potential of differences for organisational excellence will be stifled.

To sum up, it may be mentioned that an organisation which falls towards the right side of the spectrum on the dimension of culture - has good pospects of moving towards excellence. All the elements of culture discussed above contribute towards building culture.

The Significance of Corporate Cultures

Mcuh has been written about organisational cultures in recent years. It is suggested that every organisation has a culture or a patterned set of activities that reflects the organisation's underlying values. Cultures don't occur randomly. They occur because leaders spend time on and reward some behaviours and practices more than others. These practices become the foundation of the organisation's culture. For example, in one organisation few top Directors spend time wandering around, informally meeting with and talking to employees. Such leadership behaviour set the cultural tone of caring about the listening to people. Similarly, Chairman in an organisation spent a great deal of time with customers. His practice led to a Company culture of commitment to customers. Leaders can shape cultures by carefully monitoring where and how they spend their time and by encouraging and rewarding employees to behave in certain ways.

Culture plays two central roles in organisations. First, it provides organisational members with a way of understanding and making sense of events and symbols. Thus, when employees are confronted with certain complex problems, they "know" how to approach them the "right" way. Like the Eskimos who have a vocabulary that differentiates the five types of show, organisations create vocabularies to describe how things are done in the organisation. At IBM, it is very clear to all insiders how to form a task force and to solve problems since task forces and problem solving are a way of life in IBM's culture.

Second, culture provides meaning. It embodies a set of values which helps justify why certain behaviours are encouraged at the exclusion of other behaviours. Companies with strong cultures have been able to commit people to the organisation and have them identify very personally and closely with the crganisation's success.

Dynamics of Organisational Change

Firstly, Organisations do not change unless there is trigger which indicates change is needed. This trigger can be as extreme as is our company's impending bankruptcy or as moderate as an abstract future-oriented fear that an organisation may lose its competitiveness. For example, General Electric's trigger for change is a view that by 1990 the company will not be world competitive unless major changes occur to productivity, innovation, and marketing.

A Change Releases Mixed Feelings.

Secondly, a felt need for change releases a mix of forces, both a positive impetus for change as well as a strong negative individual and organisational resistance. These forces of resistance are generated in each of three inter-related systems-technical, political and cultural—which must be managed in the process of Organisational transitions. Individual and organisational resistance to change in these three systems must be overcome if an organisation is to be revitalized.

Managing technical systems refers to managing the coordination of technology, capital, information and people in order to produce products of service desired and used in the external market-place. Managing political systems refers to managing the allocation of organisational rewards such as money, status, power and career opportunities and to exercising power so employees and departments perceive, equity and justice. Managing cultural systems refers to managing the set of shared values and norms which guides the behaviour of members of the organisation.

The technical, political, and cultural resistances are most evident during early stages of an organisational transformation. At GM the early 1980s were marked by tremendous uncertainty concerning many techical issues such as marketing strategy. production strategy, organisation design factory automation, and development of international management. Politically, many powerful coalitions were threatend. The UAW was forced to make wage concessions and accept staffing reduction. The white collar workers saw their benefits being cut and witnessed manjor layoffs within the managerial ranks. Culturrally, the once dominant managerial style no longer fit the environmental pressures for change: the "CM way" has no longer the right way.

TRANSFORMING ORGANISATION CULTURE

Quick-fix Method

Overcoming resistance to change reuires transformational leadership, not defensive, transactional managers who are in search of the one minute quick-fix. The transformational leader needs to avoid the trap of simple, quick-fix solutions to major organisational problems. Today many versions of this quick-fix mentality abound: the book, One Minute Manager, has become a best seller in companies in need of basic transformation. Likewise, in Search of Excellence has become a cook book for change. In fact a number of Chief Executives have taken the eight characteristics of the "excellent" companies and are trying to blindly impose them on their organisation without first examining their appropriateness. For example, many faltering organisations try to copy such company practices as Hewlett-Packard's (HP) statement of comany values. Because they read the HP has a clearly articulated statement of company values - the HP equivalent of the ten commandments - they want to create their list of ten commandments. The scenario which has been carried out in many major U.S. firms in the past year goes something like this: the CEO wants to develop the company value statement, so organises an off-site meeting in order to spend a couple of days developing the company XYZ corporate value statement. The session is usually quite enlightening - managers become quite thoughtful, and soul-searching take place. At the end of the session, the group is able to list the XYZ company's "ten commandments". The Chief executive is delighted that they are now well on the way to a major cultural change. He brings the ten commandments back to the corporation and calls in the staff to begin the communication programme so that all company employees can learn the new cultural values. This ends the transformational process.

The problem with the ten commandments quick-fix is that the chief executives tend to overlook the lesson Moses learned serveral thousond years ago - namely, getting the ten commandments written down and communicated is the easy part; getting them implemented is the challenge. How many thousands of years has it been since Moses received the ten commandments, and yet today there still seems to be an implementation challenge. Transformational leadership is different from defensive, transactional leadership.

TRANSFORMATIONAL LEADERSHIP STYLE

There are three identifiable programmes of activity associated with transformational leadership:

1. **Creation of Vision.** The transformational leader must provide the organisation with a vision of a desired future state. While this task may be shared with other key members of the organisation, the vision remain the core responsibility of the transformational leader. The leader needs to integrate analytic, creative, intuitive thinking. Each leader must create a vision which gives direction to the organisation while being congruent with the leader's and the organisation's philosophy and style.

   For example, in the early 1980s at G.M. after several years of committee work and staff analysis, a vision of the future was drafted which included a mission statement and eight objectives for the company. This statement was the first articulation of a strategic vision for General Motors since Alfred Sloan's leadership. This new vision was developed consistently with the leadership philosophy and style of Roger Smith. Many people were involved in carefull assessing opportunities and constraints for General Motors. Meticulous staff work continued in committee discussions to evoke agreement and commitment to the mission statement. Though this process a vision was created which paved the way for the next phases of the transformation at G.M.

G.M. ended up with a new vision because of transformational leader proactively shaping a new organisation mission and vision. The long term challenge to organisational revitalisation is not "how" the visions are created but the extent to which the visions correctly respond to environmental pressures and transitions within the organisation.

2. **Mobilisation of Commitment.** Here, the organisation or at least a critical mass of it accepts the new mission and vision and makes it happen. At General Moters, Roger Smith took his top 900 executives on a five day retreat to share and discuss the vision. The event lasted five days not because it takes that long to share a one-paragraph mission statement and eight objectives, but because the process of evolving commitment and mobilising support requires a great deal of dialogue and exchange. It should not be noted that mobilization of commitment must go well beyond five days retreats; nevertheless, it is in this phase that transformational leaders get deeper understanding of their followers. Leaders who guide organisations through revitalization are distinct from previous leaders and gamesmen who spearheaded managers to be winners in the growth days of the 1960s and early 1970s.

   After transformational leaders create a vision and mobilize commitment they must determine how to institutionalise the new mission and vision.

3. **Institutionalisation of Change.** Organisations will not be revitalized unless new patterns of behaviour within the organisation are adopted. Transformational leaders need to transmit their vision into reality their mission into action, their philosophy into practice. New realities, action, and practices must be shared throughout the organisation. Alterations in communication, decision-making, and problem-solving systems are tools through which transitions are shared so that visions become a reality. At a deeper level, institutionalization of change requires shaping and reinforcement of a new culture that fits with the revitalized organisation. The human resource systems of selection, development, appraisal and reward are major levers for institutionalising change.

The Three-Phase Process

1. **Endings.** All individual transitions start with endings. Endings must be accepted, understood before transitions can begin. Employees who refuse to accept the fact that traditional behaviours have ended will be enable to adopt new behaviours. The first task is to disengage, which often accompanies a physical transaction. For example when trasferring from one job to another, individuals must learn to accept the new physical setting and disengage from the opposition. When transferred employees continually return to visit former colleagues, this is a sign that they have inadequately disengaged. The second task is to disidentify. Individual self-indentity is often tied to a job position in such a way that when a plant manager is transferred to corporate staff to work in the marketing department, he must disidentify with the plant and its people and with the self-esteem felt as a plant manager. At a deeper personal level, individual transanctions require disenchantment. Disenchantment entails recognising that the enchantment or positive feeling associate with past situations will not be possible to replicate in the future.

To help individuals cope with endings, transformational leaders need to replace past glories with future opportunities. However, leaders must also acknowledge individual resistances and senses of loss in a transitional period while encouraging employees to face and accept failures as learning opportunities.

2. **Neutral Zone.** The key to individuals being able to fully change may be in the second phase which is the neutral zone. This phase can be interpreted as a seemingly unproductive "time out" when individuals feel disconnected from people and things of the past and emotionally with the present. In reality, this phase is a time of reorientation where individuals complete endings and begin new patterns of behaviour.

However, running across the neutral zone too hurriedly does not allow the ending to occur nor the new beginning to properly start. A death and rebirth process is necessary so that organisational members can work through the disintegration and reintegration. To prass through the neutral zone requires taking the time and thought to gain perspective on both the endings - what went wrong, why it needs to be changed, and what must be overcome in both attitude and behavioural change - and the new beginning - what the new priorities are, why they are needed, and what new attitudes and behaviours will be required. It is in this phase that the most skilful transformational leadership is called upon.

A timid, bureaucratic leader who often reels in the gcod old days will not provide the needed support to help individuals cross through the neutral zone. On the other hand, the militaristic dictatorial leader who tries to force a "new beginning" and does not allow people to work through their own feelings and emotions may also fail to bring about change.

3. **New Beginnings.** After individuals accept ending by working through neutral zones, they are able to work with new enthusiasm and commitment. New beginnings are characterised by employees learning from the past rather than revealing in it, looking for new scripts rather than acting out old ones and being positive and excited about current and future work opportunities rather than dwelling on past successes or failures.

To conclude for transformation of our organisations a new brand of leadership is necessary. Instead of managers who continue to move organisations along historical tracks, the new leader must transform the organisations and head them down new tracks. What is required of this kind of leader is an ability to help the organisation develop a vision of what it can be to mobilize the organisation to accept and work toward achieving the new vision, and to institutionalise the changes that must last over time.

We call these new leaders transformational leaders, for they must create some thing new out of somthing old; out of an old vision, they must develop and communicate a new vision and get others not only to see the vision but also to commit themselves to it . Where transactional managers make only minor adjustments in the organisation's missions, structure, and human resource management, transformational leaders not only make major changes in these three areas but they also evoke fundamental changes in the basic political and cultural system of the organisation. The revamping of the political and cutural systems in what most distinguishes the transformational leader from the transactional one.

ORGANISATIONAL CLIMATE

According to Joe Ketly, "Climate may be thought of as the perception of the characteristics of an organisation." Organisational climate conveys the impressions people have of the organisational internal environment within which they work. It may also be viewed as the degree to which organisational rules are enforced by the administrative component. It may refer to the extent to which persons are treated as "human beings" rather than as "cogs" in a machine.

Organisational climate is the summary perception which people have about an organisation. It is a global expression of what the organisation is. Organisational climate is the manifestation of the attitudes of organisational members toward the organisation itself. An organisation tends to attract and keep people who fit its climate, so that its patterns are perpetuated at least to some extent.

Organisation climate is a relatively enduring quality of the internal environment that is experienced by its members, influences their behaviour, and can be described in terms of the values of a particular set of characteristics of the organisation.

Forehand and Gilmer have defined organisational climate as "a set of characteristics that describe an organisation and that: *(i)* distinguish one organisation from another, *(ii)* are relatively enduring over a period of time, and *(iii)* influence the behaviour-of people in the organisation."

It is often felt that any one individual may influence the organisational climate to some degree, but the tracing of the effects of individual behaviour on the climate would be quite complex and beyond the scope of this chapter. However, it may be possible to have "as many climates as there are people in the organisation." When considered collectively, the actions of the individuals become more meaningful for viewing the total impact upon the climate and determining the stability of the work environment. It should be noted that the climate is to be viewed from a total system perspective. While there may be differences in climates within subsystem (departments), these will be integrated to a certain extent to denote overall organisational climate.

CHARACTERISTICS OF ORGANISATIONAL CLIMATE

1. **Distinct Identity.** It reflects how an organisation is different from other organisations. It gives a distinct identity to the organisation.

2. **Enduring Quality.** It is built up over a period of time. It represents a relatively enduring quality of the internal environment that is experienced by the organisational members.
3. **General Perception.** Organisation climate is a general expression of what the organisation is. It represents the summary perception which people have about an organisation.
4. **Qualitative Concept.** It is an abstract and intangible concept. It is difficult to explain the components of organisational climate in quantifiable units.
5. **Multi-dimensional Concept.** There are several dimensions of the concept of organisational climate such as individual autonomy, authority structure, leadership style, pattern of communication, degree of conflicts and cooperation, etc.

Dimensions of Organisational Climate

It is very difficult to measure organisational climate because it is a multidimensional concept. The important components that collectively represent the climate of an organisation are as discussed below:

(a) ***Members' Orientation.*** The dominant orientation of an organisation is the main concern of its members, and this is an important determinant of climate. If the dominant orientation or concern is to adhere to established rules and regulations, the climate will be characterised by control; on the other hand, if the orientation is to produce excellence, the climate will be characterised by achievement.

(b) ***Degree of Control.*** The control systems may be either rigid or flexible. If the control is rigidly followed, there will be impersonal or bureaucratic atmosphere in the organisation. The scope for self-regulation will be the minimum.

(c) ***Type of Structure.*** It clarifies who is to direct whom and who is responsible to whom. It serves as the basis of interpersonal relations between superiors and subordinates. If the authority is centralised at the top level, the scope for participation in decision-making by the subordinates will be low. Where authority is delegated to the subordinates, there will be an atmosphere of participative decision-making.

(d) ***Risk Taking.*** How members respond to risks and whose help is sought in situations involving risk are important in any organisation. If individuals feel free to try out new ideas without any fear, they will not hesitate taking risks. Such an atmosphere will be conducive to innovative ideas.

(e) ***Interpersonal Relationships.*** An organisation's interpersonal-relations are reflected in the ways informal groups are formed, and operate to satisfy the social needs of members. If informal relations supplement the formal procedures, the organisation will be benefited. But if some powerful groups develop who acquire power in the organisation, they may displace the goals of the organisation. Conflicts in the organisation might also be common.

(f) ***Individual Freedom.*** If the individuals are given sufficient freedom or autonomy to work and exercise authority, there will be efficiency in operations. Self-control will lighten the burden of the higher level executives.

(g) ***Communication.*** Communication is concerned with the flow of information: its direction (top-down, bottom-up, horizontal), its dispersement (selectively or to everyone concerned), its mode (formal or informal), and its type (instructions or feedback). For instance, if organisational communication is based much on top-down formal mode, the subordinates will not be able to express themselves. They may feel frustrated as management does not entertain their ideas, suggestions and reactions.

(h) ***Conflict Management.*** Differences among people and groups in organisations are not uncommon. If they are managed effectively, there will be an atmosphere of cooperation in the organisation. If they are suppressed or not handled properly, people will be unhappy and there will be an atmosphere of distrust and non-cooperation.

(i) ***Degree of Trust.*** The degree of trust or lack of trust among various members and groups in the organisation affects the climate. If there is mutual trust between different individuals, groups and also between management and workers, there will be peace in the organisation. The members will cooperate with one another for the attainment of organisational objectives.

(j) ***Reward System.*** The system of rewards and punishments is an important component of organisational climate. When the rewards are based on merit and productivity, there will be an atmosphere of competition among employees for higher performance. They will put more and more hard work to develop themselves and earn higher rewards such as increments and promotions. But if the rewards are based on the pleasure of the boss, there will be baisness in the distribution of rewards. The meritorious employees will get discouraged.

(k) ***Management Orientation (Style).*** The dominant style of managers and supervisors may be task-oriented or relations-oriented. If the task-orientation is predominant, the leadership style will be autocratic. The employees will have to increase their productivity or face punishment.Their morale will be low in the long-run.

The oganisational climate will be considerate and supportive if the managers are relations-oriented while dealing with the workers. The needs and aspirations of the workers will be given due importance. This will produce team spirit in the organisation.

Significance of Organisational Climate

The study of the climate of an organisation is necessary for an insight into important dimensions such as communication, cooperation, creativity, employee satisfaction, morale, etc. All these factors determine the effectiveness of the organisation. An organisation is likely to be more effective if there is two-way communication and employees are cooperative and have better perception of the organisation Such employees have higher job satisfaction and feel committed to the organisation. Their productivity will also be higher.

The role of climate in employees satisfaction and organisational effectiveness can be shown with a hypothetical model that specifies the relationship between the major sets of variables. Alongwith structure, technology, external environment and managerial policies and practices exert important influences on climate. The emerging climate represents the arena in which is influenced by managerial policies, organisation structure and technology and external environment. When climate is conducive to the needs of individuals, we would expect goal directed behaviour to be high. The ultimate behaviour or outcomes are determined by the interaction of individual needs and perceived organisational environment. The feedback regarding resulting level of performance contributes not only to the climate of the particular work environment, but also to possible changes in managerial policies and practices.Thus, climate has an important influence on performance and satisfaction of the employees. If the climate is favourable, there would be greater organisational effectiveness.

The factors indicated in the figure represent major determinants of climate in an organisation and as such represent important areas of management concern. If employees' performance and job satisfaction are to be improved, the management must modify these factors so that the employees view climate as favourable to them.

❑

